After Lean Production

After Lean Production

Evolving Employment Practices in the World Auto Industry

Edited by

Thomas A. Kochan
Russell D. Lansbury
John Paul MacDuffie

ILR Press—an Imprint of
Cornell University Press
Ithaca and London

First published 1997 by Cornell University Press.
First printing, Cornell Paperbacks, 1997.

Printed in the United States of America

Cornell University Press strives to utilize environmentally responsible suppliers and materials to the fullest extent possible in the publishing of its books. Such materials include vegetable-based, low-VOC inks and acid-free papers that are also either recycled, totally chlorine-free, or partly composed of nonwood fibers.

Library of Congress Cataloging-in-Publication Data

After lean production : evolving employment practices in the world auto industry / Thomas A. Kochan, Russell D. Lansbury, John Paul MacDuffie, editors.
    p. cm.
  Includes index.
  ISBN 0-8014-3382-7 (cloth : alk. paper). — ISBN 0-8014-8413-8 (pbk. : alk. paper)
  1. Automobile industry workers—Employment. I. Kochan, Thomas A. II. Lansbury, Russell D. III. MacDuffie, John Paul.
  HD8039.A8A235 1997
  331.12'9292—dc21   97-14355

CLOTH PRINTING
10 9 8 7 6 5 4 3 2 1

PAPERBACK PRINTING
10 9 8 7 6 5 4 3 2 1

Contents

Tables and Figures

Acknowledgments

In 1990, a group of researchers from eleven countries came together at the Organization for Economic Cooperation and Development (OECD) in Paris to discuss how to interpret the changes occurring in employment relations within and across their respective countries. Out of this meeting emerged an international network that first studied changes across countries at the national level and then encouraged the formation of sectoral studies, one of which focused on the auto industry. The International Motor Vehicle Program at the Massachusetts Institute of Technology (MIT) provided financial support and a venue for the participants to meet early in the project to organize this effort. Initial drafts of their research reports were discussed at the tenth World Congress of the Industrial Relations Association in Washington, D.C., in 1995. Supplemental funding for the project was also provided by the Alfred P. Sloan Foundation and the MIT Industrial Performance Center. We appreciate the help all these organizations provided in building the research network and bringing us together over the years.

Throughout the project Susan C. Wright has served as coordinator, manager, editor, and liaison for everyone involved. We have grown accustomed to Susan's quiet professionalism. We speak for all involved in this and the many other efforts Susan coordinates for us at MIT and in the industrial relations profession in saying a simple but genuine "Thank you" for another job well done. We also want to thank the other key member of our office team, Karen Boyajian, for keeping the operation working and for pitching in to help with this project in a cheerful and ever-efficient fashion.

Fran Benson at Cornell University was an enthusiastic supporter of this project since we first brought it to her attention. It is always a pleasure to work with Fran and her colleagues and we appreciate the extra effort they put in to get this volume out in a timely fashion. Erica Fox, the unfortunate copy editor assigned this project, had to make sense of arcane acronyms and partial bibliographic references from multiple countries and in multiple languages. She has done a remarkable job. We hope this project hasn't convinced her to change professions.

Finally, thanks to the hundreds of men and women involved in the auto industry who provided access and the data required for this study. This is their story—one of constant pressure to adapt to the changes we report here. We hope this book helps them make sense of their world.

T. A. K.

R. D. L.

J. P. MacD.

After Lean Production

PART **I**

An International Perspective on the Auto Industry

1 Introduction

Thomas A. Kochan, Russell D. Lansbury,
and John Paul MacDuffie

For more than two decades, participants in the automobile industry worldwide have been struggling to adjust to increasing international competition, changing consumer tastes, and new approaches to organizing production and associated employment practices. Although the most visible drivers of these changes have been the Japanese producers and their successful increase in market share, in fact the process is more dynamic than is normally recognized and is influenced by multiple players from many countries. In the 1960s, for example, the U.S. producers were the "kings of the road," dominating their own vast domestic market and building capacity and market share in the other large market of the time, Europe. The Germans demonstrated their engineering prowess by capturing first the reputation for building the best-engineered upscale cars available and then, with Volkswagen, capturing the hearts (if not the market share) of the small-car segment of the market with their seemingly ever-present and everlasting Beetle.

Without doubt, however, it was the Japanese who dominated the car industry in the 1970s and 1980s. They not only captured increased market share in North America and established a foothold in Europe, Australia, and parts of Asia, but they set the terms of the debate over how to produce automobiles efficiently and with high quality. Indeed, the success of the Japanese, or more specifically the Toyota production system (see Mondon 1983; Cusumano 1985; Shimada and MacDuffie 1987), was elevated to the level of folklore when the authors of the book *The Machine That Changed the World* (Womack, Jones, and Roos 1990), based on research conducted in the International Motor Vehicle Program (IMVP) at MIT, coined and popularized the term "lean production."

3

The authors of *The Machine That Changed the World* made a bold prediction. They argued that lean production was "a better way of making things which the whole world should adopt as quickly as possible" (225). In their view, lean production was the *one best way* to organize the production of automobiles. Companies seeking to compete successfully in any part of the world would need to learn how to adopt lean production techniques. Those that did not would fall by the wayside in an increasingly competitive world market.

Nevertheless, lean production continues to have its critics and its skeptics. The critics view it as essentially an old-fashioned "speed up" production system dressed up as a new idea: a modern version of Frederick Taylor's methods of controlling the workforce and maximizing managerial control (and profits) on the backs of workers. The skeptics doubt that lean production will sweep across the world as predicted. They emphasize the importance of local conditions and changing industry practices and reject theories that suggest there is indeed one best way or single set of best practices for performing work of any kind, including the assembly of automobiles.

At the core of these debates lie employment practices: the way work is organized, how workers and managers interact, the way worker representatives respond to lean production strategies (the auto industry being among the most unionized in the world), and the nature of the adaptation and innovation process itself.[1] What seems to bind together most of the critics and skeptics of lean production is the view that employment practices are shaped not in a deterministic fashion by methods of production, or by some singular technological or economic imperative, but by a multiplicity of factors. Thus, the skeptics and critics expect the world of auto production to be more diverse and varied in the future than the lean production advocates and theorists predict.

Is the future likely to be dominated either by a single trajectory or by a random scatter plot of diverse practices? Alternatively, is there a discernible systematic pattern that varies and is changing in predictable ways? Are new paradigms emerging out of the adaptation and innovation process observable around the world? Does learning transfer smoothly across plant, company, and national boundaries? These are some of the broad analytical questions motivating this project.

Is anything more at stake here than another academic debate? Clearly there is. The automobile industry is viewed as strategically important in nearly every country that now produces cars, as well as in several newly

---

[1]The term *employment relations* is used to encompass elements usually included in both industrial relations and human resource management, although at times in this book the latter is addressed separately.

industrializing countries, including Malaysia, China, India, South Africa, Thailand, and Brazil, that hope to use automobile manufacturing to move up the value-added development curve. South Korea is an example of a country in which success as an automobile producer in the world market has signaled its arrival as an economic power of international significance. Autos also represent a source of well-paid jobs for blue-collar, white-collar, technical, and managerial employees. In most countries where autos are produced, wages for those employed in this industry are above the overall national median earnings level.

For both these reasons, the lean production debate is partly about the outcomes against which the performance of a strategically important industry should be judged. Is "leanness"—that is, producing high-quality products with minimum labor and capital—the best or only relevant performance measure? Most observers of the auto industry would think not—particularly scholars from the industrial relations field who urge the use of a performance model that recognizes the multiplicity of interests or stakeholders with legitimate claims on the industry. These would include not only shareholders but workers, customers, suppliers, and environmentalists, as well as those responsible for macroeconomic policy. We will focus directly on only two of the stakeholders in this project—shareholders/employers and the workforce—and indirectly on the overall economy or society.

Finally, in many countries, particularly the United States, the auto industry has served as a bellwether of innovation in employment conditions for the industrial relations system and economy as a whole. It was Henry Ford who introduced the "five dollar a day" wage in 1916; it was the United Automobile Workers (UAW) and the Big Three—General Motors, Ford, and Chrysler— that led the way in collective bargaining from the late 1940s through the 1970s with innovations such as long-term contracts with cost-of-living escalator clauses in the 1940s, supplemental unemployment benefit funds and other forms of layoff adjustment insurance in the 1950s, and neutrality agreements governing union recognition in new plants in the 1960s. During the 1970s, the first national agreement to experiment with quality of work life improvement strategies was signed in the auto industry, while in the 1980s and 1990s, a wide variety of workplace, collective bargaining, and strategic-level innovations in labor-management relations were attempted and ultimately institutionalized.

Similar examples could be cited from other countries. In Italy, Fiat's tumultuous labor relations history, from the "hot autumn" of 1968 to the historic strike and large-scale restructuring of the 1980s, was mirrored by similar if less visible shifts in Italian industrial relations over this time period (Locke 1995). In Sweden, Volvo became the most prominent experimenter when it introduced alternatives to assembly-line production systems at Kalmar and Uddevalla (Berggren 1992; Sandberg 1995), which coincided with union-initiated policies on industrial democracy, supported by legislative changes (Hammarström 1994). Germany's auto industry has also taken a lead in combining new technologies with job redesign based on work groups. These new approaches involved considerable negotiation and cooperation between the powerful IG Metall union and German auto producers. In Australia, considerable restructuring of the automobile industry has occurred as the result of reductions in tariff protection. The survival of the industry, and a stronger export orientation, have been greatly facilitated by cooperation between the unions and employers in the upgrading of workers' skills and the introduction of more flexible work arrangements (see Lansbury and Bamber 1995).

For all these reasons, the automobile industry remains a central focus of analysis and national attention around the world. Unfortunately, although it recognized the importance of the link between employment practices and manufacturing practices, *The Machine That Changed the World* said very little about the human side of lean production. Hence, it is important to sort out the lean production debate by conducting further research and analysis of developments in a wide range of countries.

The auto industry is not unique in experiencing changes in employment practices. All industries exposed to global competition and changing technological possibilities are facing similar pressures to transform their employment practices in ways that are better attuned to the changed environment. Debates over the nature and implications of these broader developments motivated researchers from MIT's Industrial Relations Section to organize an international network of scholars to study these changes in various countries and industries. The first phase of this project compared changes occurring in national systems of employment relations in a set of industrialized (Locke, Kochan, and Piore 1995) and newly industrialized (Verma, Kochan, and Lansbury 1995) countries. We are now in the second phase of this work, in which teams are examining changes in employment relations within specific sectors across countries.

The first industry-level project focused on telecommunications (Katz and Darbishire 1997). The teams engaged in that study concluded that although the combination of technological change, deregulation, and emergence of new enterprises is producing significant restructuring of this industry and its employment practices in countries around the world, the pace and nature of the changes vary depending on whether a market-based or a labor-mediated and -negotiated adjustment process guides restructuring. The Anglo-Saxon countries (Australia, Britain, Canada, and the United States) generally took the market deregulation approach, while the European countries and Japan followed a more negotiated adjustment pattern. Mexico and Korea followed a third path in which the state played a strong mediating role in the restructuring process. The major differences observed in the outcomes of the restructuring were that less downsizing and displacement occurred when the labor-mediated and -negotiated adjustment models were followed than when a market-driven model dominated.

One important finding from the telecommunications study is particularly relevant to our work. In telecommunications, no single model of production or employment practices dominated the adjustment process, unlike the auto industry, where the lean production model has dominated debates about the nature of the changes. Still, the authors observed common trends toward greater work organization flexibility, employee participation, investment in skill development, and reductions in employment security associated with downsizing. Thus, these trends toward transformation of employment systems appear to be common across industries and countries. Yet considerable variation in practices and employment systems continue to exist as the competing pressures of cost cutting and downsizing versus gaining employee commitment and flexibility play out in different settings. These findings help put the data and results we will present on the auto industry in perspective.

In this study, we follow the same analytical approach developed in the larger project. As shown in figure 1.1, we focus on changes occurring in four sets of employment practices: (1) the way work is organized, (2) the process of skill acquisition and development, (3) the compensation structure and process, and (4) the staffing and employment security arrangements. Given the importance of union-management relations in the auto industry, we give additional emphasis to this issue here, viewing it as part of the broader governance process in the enterprise.

As suggested by figure 1.1, variations in employment practices are expected to be influenced by features of the external environment, by the broader institutional context—government policies and union-management structures at the industry and national level—and by the specific strategies of firms, unions, and governments. Indeed, disagreements over the relative importance of these different forces lie at the heart of the lean production debate. Those who believe lean production will diffuse in a singular fashion around the world believe that manufacturing and employment practices are determined solely by technical and market forces. Seen from this perspective, national or industry institutions or different strategies of firms or unions either do not matter or are misguided if they fail to adopt lean production. Critics of this view emphasize the need to examine how different institutions and individual actors use and adapt the features of lean production to address the interests of the different stakeholders in the industry and the economy. We will explore this debate in the chapters that follow.

In chapter 2, we take advantage of a unique set of survey data on assembly plant manufacturing and employment practices collected by John Paul MacDuffie and Frits Pil as part of the MIT International Motor Vehicle Program. They use these data and their deep knowledge of practices in different countries, companies, and plants both to describe and to analyze the pattern of diffusion lean production has taken to date. Then, in the chapters that follow, research teams from Japan, the United States, Canada, Germany, the United Kingdom, Italy, Spain, France, Sweden, Australia, South Africa, Brazil, and Korea use the framework outlined in figure 1.1 to present case studies of company- and plant-level practices in these countries. In the concluding chapter, we summarize these analyses and suggest future directions for change and adaptation of lean production and employment practices.

Figure 1.1 Framework for Analyzing Employment Practices

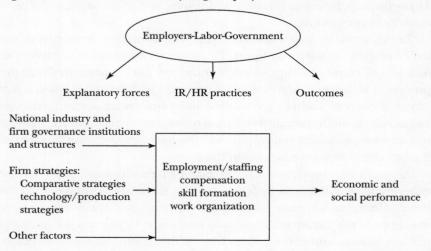

Source: Locke, Kochan, and Piore 1995:xxvii. Reproduced by permission of the MIT Press.

2 Changes in Auto Industry Employment Practices: An International Overview

John Paul MacDuffie and Frits K. Pil

In this chapter we sketch the outlines of recent changes in work practices and human resource policies in the international automotive industry.[1] The chapters that follow provide a closer examination of the dynamics of change in different national and company contexts, while also exploring the country-level details of the assembly plant data summarized in overview form here. In other publications, we have discussed how work and human resource (HR) practices affect productivity and quality, the institutional and cultural pressures that influence how these practices are implemented, and the determinants of who adopts new practices over time (MacDuffie 1995, 1997; MacDuffie and Pil 1996; Pil 1996; Pil and MacDuffie 1996a and 1996b). In contrast, our goal for this chapter is explicitly descriptive. By describing the patterns of work practices and HR policies that emerge from the comparative data, we hope to set the stage for the analyses that follow.

We start by providing a brief summary of the evolution of work practices within different production paradigms in the auto industry. Then we examine the current work practices and HR policies used in automobile assembly plants, drawing on the survey data from a sample of almost ninety such plants representing twenty countries and twenty-one companies as well as observations from our visits to more than fifty assembly plants in the last three years. First, we highlight regional differences, using means from the most recent round of data collection (1993–94). Next, we

[1] The International Assembly Plant Study is sponsored by the International Motor Vehicle Program at MIT, which receives financial support from the Sloan Foundation as well as almost every automotive manufacturer in the world. Round 1 of the International Assembly Plant Study was carried out from 1986 to 1990 by John Krafcik and John Paul MacDuffie at MIT, and round 2 was carried out by MacDuffie and Frits K. Pil from 1991 to 1996.

9

analyze the global forces that push toward convergence in work and HR practices and contrast them with the company-level factors that generate considerable divergence in the use of these practices within country or regional boundaries. Finally, we draw upon data from both rounds of the assembly plant study (1989 and 1993–94) to examine change over time in the adoption and utilization of new work and HR practices and the forces underlying these changes.

Evolution of Work Practices and HR Policies

While the early auto industry in Europe was dominated by craft principles of work organization, the overlapping principles of Taylor's scientific management and Ford's sequentially interdependent assembly line combined in the formative years of the U.S. auto industry to yield the powerful mass production paradigm. Mass production can be usefully summarized along four core dimensions: (1) an extreme *specialization of resources,* including narrowly defined tasks carried out by people and/or equipment dedicated to each task; (2) a *standardized product design* that can be produced in *large batches* to achieve economies of scale and minimize setup time, coupled with *large buffers* of inventory stock, repair space, and utility workers to prevent any interruptions in production; (3) a *centralized hierarchy* that handles the control and coordination tasks that accompany a highly specialized and narrow division of labor; and (4) a *separation of conception and execution,* so that all "thinking" work associated with production is specialized and isolated from the "doing" work (MacDuffie 1991).

Once the economic advantages of this approach, as implemented by Henry Ford, became widely known, these organizing principles quickly became the dominant model for the auto industry in the United States, but they also had a more gradual but still powerful influence on automotive company practice the world over. There was substantial variation in how mass production principles were understood and applied in other countries, however, and these variations persisted over time (Kogut and Zander 1992). In Europe, the persistence of craft traditions was the dominant cultural influence on the adoption of Taylorist work organization (Lewchuk 1988), and managers were less inclined (or less able) to wrest shop-floor control away from workers and union officials to centralize control and separate thinking from doing work. In Japan, constraints on the implementation of Fordist mass production (e.g., little opportunity for economies of scale because many companies were competing in a small market, fixed labor costs as a result of lifetime employment agreements) led in a different direction—toward the development of the alternative organizing principles associated with flexible or lean production (Cusumano 1985).

Thus, the evolution of "organizing principles" in the auto industry historically was marked first by divergence between "old" (craft production) and "new" (mass production) models and then by convergence toward the dominant mass production model, driven by its proven performance advantages. Despite the trend toward convergence, variation around the dominant model was generated by the presence or absence of certain conditions necessary to support mass production (e.g., demand large enough to support high-volume production) and by cultural, institutional, and organizational influences on the diffusion process.

This pattern is useful in understanding current developments in the auto industry. At the current time, we would argue, the dominant organizing principles in the industry are associated with flexible or lean production. Although mass production depends on there being large and stable markets to achieve efficiency through the highly specialized use of resources devoted to long runs of standardized products, flexible or lean production is based on the premise that being able to respond to more differentiated or fluctuating markets results in substantial competitive advantage.

As such, flexible or lean production inverts the four dimensions of mass production mentioned above: (1) more *general resources* are used (multi-skilled workers, general-purpose machines, fewer functional specialists); (2) *small buffers and lot sizes* facilitate the handling of a greater *variety of product designs* and hence support a market strategy of offering niche products and responding quickly to demand fluctuations; (3) authority is more *decentralized,* and there is greater lateral communication across functional boundaries and faster response time; and (4) there is a higher degree of integration of *conceptual activity with the execution of production tasks.*

The link between flexible or lean production and economic performance results, we would argue, form a distinct "organizational logic" that integrates bundles of "high-involvement" work practices and HR policies (also characterized as "high-performance" or "transformed") with manufacturing practices in pursuit of simultaneous improvements in productivity and quality (MacDuffie 1995). A flexible production plant reduces inventory levels and other "buffers," increasing interdependence in the production process and highlighting production problems. Dealing effectively with these problems requires motivated, skilled, and adaptable workers. By combining the reduction of buffers with the development of these workforce characteristics, flexible or lean production systems create the conditions under which innovative HR practices are most likely to yield effective economic performance.

Although the performance advantages of flexible production may provide some incentive for convergence in practices, we predict that considerable variation will remain around this increasingly dominant model, as was the case for mass production. One purpose of this chapter is to identify the conditions that facilitate the move toward flexible production and the cultural influences on that transition process.

High-Involvement Work Practices and HR Policies

As mentioned above, the data in this chapter (and in many of the chapters that follow) are drawn from the International Assembly Plant Study (MacDuffie 1991, 1995, and 1996; MacDuffie and Pil 1996; Pil and MacDuffie 1996a and 1996b), the most comprehensive comparative study of manufacturing plants ever undertaken in any industry. The study encompassed two rounds of data collection from an international sample of assembly plants, seventy plants in the first round and eighty-eight plants in the second round; forty-four participated in both rounds. The regional breakdown of plants in the sample is shown in table 2.1. Here we present regional averages from the entire round 2 sample in cross-section, while below we present changes in regional averages from round 1 to round 2 for the matched sample.

Table 2.1 Distribution of Participants in the International Assembly
          Plant Study

Regional Group*	Round 1 (1989)	Round 2 (1993–94)	Matched
U.S./N.A.	16	25	13
Europe	24	21	12
Japan/Japan	9	12	6
Japan/N.A.	4	8	3
Korea	2	6	2
Australia	6	4	3
South Africa	0	6	0
Other NEs	9	6	5
TOTAL PLANTS	70	88	44

*U.S./N.A.=U.S. plants in North America; Japan/N.A.=Japanese plants in North America; and NEs=new-entrant plants (includes Mexico, Brazil, Taiwan, and India).

Only a few plants in the world still operate along craft production lines, and these tend to be low-volume specialty producers or knockdown kit operations. Although there are a few exceptions, such as Volvo's Uddevalla plant in the early 1990s, most high-volume passenger car plants organize their work somewhere along the continuum between mass production and flexible production. To provide an easily interpretable overview of the work and HR practices used in each region, we created an index scaled from 0 to 100, in which 0 represents the plant closest to the mass production or traditional end of the spectrum and 100 represents the plant closest to the flexible production or high-involvement end. We distinguish between structural aspects of the organization of work (e.g., the use of work teams and other small-group activities organized for production-related problem solving, job rotation, the division of labor for quality responsibilities between team members and supervisors or quality-control staff) and a set of complementary or supporting human resource practices and policies (e.g., selection procedures, training, compensation).

We capture work organization aspects of the production system with the high-involvement work practices index, which reflects five specific work practices: (1) use of shop-floor "on-line" work teams, (2) use of "off-line" employee-involvement or problem-solving groups, (3) use of job rotation, (4) use of suggestion programs (number of suggestions, as well as percentage implemented), and (5) the decentralization of quality efforts (the degree to which production workers take direct responsibility for quality-related activities).[2]

We also created a corresponding index of HR policies that are complementary to and supportive of high-involvement work practices. This index includes criteria used in the selection and hiring of production workers; the extent of contingent compensation; the extent to which new and experienced employees receive training both on and off the job; and the extent to which there is status differentiation between production workers and managers. Table 2.2 describes how each of the practices in the HR index and the work systems index is measured.

---

[2]The work systems index is calculated by pooling the data, standardizing the data for each practice through a z-score transformation, and then additively combining the standardized scores. To have an index value that is easier to interpret, we apply a linear transformation to the sum of the z-scores, such that the plant with the lowest level of these high-involvement work practices has a score of 0 and the plant with the highest level has a score of 100. The distribution of the variable is unaffected by this transformation. The same procedure is used for the HR policies index.

Table 2.2 Overview and Operationalization of Variables in High-Involvement Work Practices Index and Human Resource Management Index

Variable	Description
High-Involvement Work Practices Index	Work structures and policies that govern shop-floor production activity and that foster worker involvement in decision making and problem solving. This is a composite index of the high-involvement work practices listed below. For each plant, scores on each practice were normalized across both time periods, summed, and then rescaled from 0 to 100. A low score indicates that a plant has few or no high-involvement work practices, and a high score indicates an extensive presence of such practices.
Elements in High-Involvement Work Practices Index	
Percentage of employees in teams	Percentage of employees in on-line teams
Percentage of employees in involvement groups	Percentage of employees participating in some type of off-line problem-solving team (e.g., quality circles, employee involvement groups)
Job rotation	Level of rotation at production worker level: 1=none, 2=trained to do multiple skills but do not rotate, 3=within teams, 4=within teams and across teams in same department, 5=within and across teams and across departments
Suggestions/ employee	Production-related suggestions per employee per year
Suggestions implemented	Percentage of suggestions implemented
Level at which quality control takes place	Level within the organization at which four key quality control activities take place: 1=production worker level, 4=specialists. Tasks considered: inspection of incoming parts, work in progress, finished goods, and gathering of SPC data

Table 2.2 Continued

Complementary HRM Practices Index	Organization-wide HR policies that are complementary to high-involvement work practices. Like the work practices index, this is a composite index that includes several HR practices. For each plant, scores on each practice were normalized across both time periods, summed, and then rescaled from 0 to 100. A low score indicates a plant that has few or no complementary HR practices, and a high score indicates an extensive presence of complementary HR practices.
Practices Included in Complementary HRM Practices Index	
Hiring criteria	Criteria used to select production workers, first-line supervisors, and engineers. This is a sum of various criteria; a lower number indicates a greater emphasis on using previous experience in a similar job, and a higher number indicates willingness to learn new skills, and ability to work with others.
New training	Index of new training based on annual training hours of new production workers, supervisors, and engineers: 1=0–40 hours of training for category receiving least amount of training. 3=80 hours+.
Experienced training	Index of training for experienced employees based on annual training hours of experienced production workers, supervisors, and engineers: 1=0–20 hours of training for category receiving least amount of training, 2=20–40 hours, 3=40–60 hours, 4=60–80 hours, and 5=80 hours+.
Contingent compensation	Index of the level and scope of pay for performance: 1 indicates no pay for performance; 6 indicates pay for performance at the individual or group level, and for production workers, supervisors, engineers, and managers. Intermediate values indicate some pay for performance for some of the employee groups.
Status differentials	Captures some of the surface indicators of status differences between managers and production workers. A score of 1 is given to each of the following practices—no ties for managers, a common cafeteria, a common parking lot, and a common uniform for all employees.

Table 2.3 shows the work systems index and its component variables for the full sample in 1993–94. In terms of the overall index, the Japanese plants are the greatest users of high-involvement work practices. Korean automobile plants are next highest in their claimed use of these practices, although other knowledge we have about developments in Korea suggests these data must be interpreted cautiously. The Japanese transplants in North America report somewhat lower levels of these practices than their mother plants in Japan but are still considerably higher than U.S., Canadian, and South African plants, which make the least use of high-involvement work practices.

Although the work systems index provides a general indicator of the use of high-involvement work practices, it masks key differences in what work practices are actually used. The utilization of work teams, for example, is extremely popular not just in Japan but in northern Europe, Korea, and even South Africa; unlike the plants in the other regions, however, the South African plants employ very few other high-involvement work practices. Likewise, the idea of work teams is not always understood in the same fashion across these regions. For example, the Korean producers all have relationships with Japanese producers and have attempted to mimic Japanese work practices from their partners. But although on the surface there may not appear to be much difference between the Japanese and Korean plants, the numbers belie fundamental underlying differences. Thus, although most Korean workers are in "teams," the average size of those teams is twenty-six employees, whereas plants in other parts of the world rarely have more than ten to twelve employees on a team. Indeed, Korean teams are really much closer to what would be considered standard supervisor groups than teams in most countries.

The extent to which work teams have influence and the issues over which this influence is exerted also vary dramatically from location to location. Table 2.4 shows team influence by area. As we can see, teams in most areas have significant influence in deciding who should do what job, but there is greater diversity in whether teams have a "say in how work gets done." Teams in North American plants have little influence over how work gets done, whereas teams in Japanese plants and Korean plants have much more say. In practices related to personnel issues, such as performance evaluations and grievances, teams in Japanese and Korean plants have some say. Teams in Japanese-owned U.S. plants differ from their Japanese counterparts in this respect, however, in that they have little influence in these areas. Teams in U.S.-owned plants in North America generally have a

Table 2.3 High-Involvement Work Practices by Region

Plant Ownership/Location	US/US	US/CA	JP/JP	JP/NA	EUR	USJP/EUR	New Entrant	KOR	AUS	S.AFR
Work Systems Index (100=high involvement; 0=low involvement)	32.9	30.8	78.4	61.8	56.7	52.2	54.8	71.3	54.0	31.1
Percentage of workforce in teams (all plants)	23	4	70	70	80	50	19	46	49	46
Percentage of workforce in teams if teams present	48	25	70	70	80	50	32	70	65	57
No. of plants in region with teams	9/19	1/6	12/12	8/8	9/9	11/11	3/5	4/6	3/4	4/5
Percentage of workforce in EI or QC groups	33	4	81	27	32	59	64	92	51	29
Suggestions per employee	0.3	0.2	23.2	4.0	1.1	0.7	7.2	37.2	1.2	0.1
Percentage of suggestions implemented	42	37	84	70	43	38	63	44	23	15
Extent of job rotation (1=none; 5=frequent, in and across work groups)	2.1	1.8	3.9	4.0	3.6	3.6	3.6	3.0	4.0	3.8
Responsibility for quality control (0=specialists, 4=production workers)	2.1	3.1	1.6	2.5	2.7	2.3	2.3	2.2	2.8	0.8

US/US=U.S.-owned plants in U.S.; US/CA=U.S.-owned plants in Canada; JP/JP=Japanese-owned plants in Japan; JP/N.A.=Japanese-owned plants in North America; EUR=European-owned plants in Europe; USJP/EUR=U.S.- and Japanese-owned plants in Europe; New Entrant=plants in Brazil, India, Mexico, and Taiwan (excludes Korea); KOR=Korean plants in Korea; AUS=Australian plants; and S.AFR=South African plants.

significant say in the selection of team leaders. This is not the case in most other parts of the world.

Teamwork is one means by which to foster flexibility and involvement on the part of the workforce. Job rotation is another. In the area of job rotation, we find that workers in most regions of the world rotate extensively, not just within their teams but across teams within a given department. Job rotation is still relatively uncommon in North American plants, however. The data for the U.S.-owned plants in the United States and Canada indicate that although workers are capable of doing other work tasks within their work groups, they generally do not rotate jobs.

Another way to foster worker involvement is through quality circles. Although these are extremely common in Japan and Korea, they have not really caught on in Europe or North America. Indeed, even the Japanese transplants in North America make little use of such off-line problem solving, although the transplants vary considerably in this regard. It is possible that like their American counterparts, workers at transplants believe that

Table 2.4 Team Influence by Region

Influence	US/NA	JP/JP	JP/US	EUR	KOR	AUS	S.AFR
Influence use of new technology on job	2.70	2.80	2.00	2.20	3.50	2.25	1.8
Who should do what job	3.10	4.30	3.13	3.35	4.25	3.50	3.4
The way work is done	2.90	4.30	4.13	3.35	4.00	3.50	3.2
Performance evaluations	1.30	3.20	1.38	2.30	3.50	2.25	1.4
Settling grievances or complaints	1.60	4.20	2.13	2.65	3.50	2.50	2.2
How fast the work should be done	2.20	2.70	2.00	2.25	3.00	2.75	2.2
How much work to do	2.00	2.40	1.63	1.85	2.75	2.50	1.8
Selection of a team leader	3.40	1.50	2.13	2.00	2.75	2.25	1.8

1=little to none; 5=much.

kaizen, or continuous improvement, can result in job loss (Young 1992). The employment security assurances of the transplants are intended to address precisely those concerns, however.

An alternative view comes from Martin Kenney and Richard Florida (1993), who suggest that the low level of quality circle and employee-involvement activity in the transplants reflects their newness and that the plan is to increase their use over time. Furthermore, according to Robert E. Cole (1979), employees in Japanese plants are more likely to view partici-pation in these "voluntary" small-group activities as mandatory because of management and peer pressure than are employees in U.S. plants. Much like their American counterparts, as well as plants in Europe and Australia, all but one of the transplants pay employees during the time their quality circles meet. In Japan, one-third of the plants report that teams meet dur-ing nonpaid time, and in Korea, more than half said that employees par-ticipate in quality circles without pay after the regular shift ends.

Yet another means to elicit involvement in work is through suggestion programs. Although many plants in all parts of the world have imple-mented such programs, they have not caught on in North America or Europe, and even in plants that have instituted quotas and other mecha-nisms to elicit worker suggestions, such as those in Korea, the implemen-tation rate for suggestions remains low. This is a drawback in that workers are more likely to get frustrated when implementation rates are low. By contrast, while the transplants have been building up their levels of sug-gestions more slowly, they have focused on high levels of implementation.

Table 2.5 shows that although Japanese plants tend to have significant worker involvement through such practices as teamwork and quality circles, they do not grant production workers much responsibility for quality con-trol, whether for the inspection of incoming parts, work in progress, and fin-ished parts or for tracking of statistical process control (SPC) data. (One of the reasons this does not happen for incoming parts is that plants in Japan do not inspect most parts upon their arrival.) The influence that Japanese workers have on quality is captured more effectively through the measures of their participation in quality circles and other off-line problem-solving activ-ities. Plants in other parts of the world allow for extensive production worker participation in the inspection of work in progress. Plants in Australia, as well as the Japanese transplants in North America, also make extensive use of pro-duction workers for the inspection of incoming parts. Canadian plants, which have generally avoided most aspects of high-involvement work prac-tices, claim to have driven responsibility for quality control to the lowest levels of the organization—although it is not clear how this extensive responsibility for quality coexists with traditional work organization.

Table 2.6 provides an overview of HR policies that help support high-involvement work practices. The index suggests that Japanese plants have high levels of these practices in place, but so do European and even Australian plants. In different analyses, we have found that the implementation of these practices is something of a precursor to the implementation of high-involvement work practices (Pil and MacDuffie 1996a). The Japanese transplants in North America score highest on the extent to which they employ supporting HR practices. In part, this is because of their extremely high levels of training and careful selection of employees. The transplants do not provide the same degree of pay for performance or seniority that is found in plants in Japan, however, reflecting their adaptation to the pay norms of the North American environment (Pil and MacDuffie 1996b).

As with the work systems index, the HR policies index masks the degree to which plants in any given region utilize the underlying practices. For example, the North American plants of the Big Three do careful selection but offer virtually no pay-for-performance programs beyond corporate-level profit sharing. There are also significant regional differences in training practices. Table 2.7 shows considerable variation in the topics offered during training of experienced production workers. Japanese plants provide great emphasis on interpersonal, statistical process control, and problem-solving

Table 2.5 Responsibility for Quality Control by Region

Responsibility	US/US	US/CAN	JP/JP	JP/US	EUR	KOR	AUS	S.AFR
Inspecting incoming parts	1.7	3	1.2	2.3	1.5	2.1	2.8	0.7
Inspecting work in progress	2.5	3.4	2	3.3	3.1	3	3.4	1.9
Inspecting finished products	1.6	3.2	1.4	2.1	2.4	2.2	2.6	0.9
Statistical process control	2.3	2.9	1.5	2.2	2.7	1.6	2.6	0.8
Quality control methods	0.5	0.3	0.4	0.7	0.6	0.6	0.5	0.5

0=specialist, 1=engineering, 2=supervisor, 3=skilled trades, 4=production workers.

Table 2.6 Complementary HR Policies and Practices by Region

Plant Ownership/Location Number of Plants	US/NA (26)	JP/JP (12)	JP/NA (8)	EUR (20)	KOR (6)	AUS (4)	S.AFR (6)
Complementary HR Policies Index (100=many; 0=few)	28.7	72.6	59.3	42.5	62.3	47.8	18.0
Percentage of workforce in teams if teams present	49.4	56.6	67.6	68.2	73.7	65.7	80.3
No. of plants in region with teams	9	12	8	19	4	3	5
Percentage of workforce in EI or QC groups	32.8	93.9	39.5	62.6	96.3	60.4	41.0
Suggestions per employee	0.3	69.1	5.3	1.2	83.5	1.4	0.1
Percentage of suggestions implemented	41.8	85.6	71.9	38.8	43.9	22.9	14.6
Extent of job rotation (1=none; 5=frequent, in and across work groups)	2.0	3.9	4.1	3.6	3.0	4.0	3.3
Responsibility for quality control/SPC (0=specialists, 4=production workers)	2.4	1.6	2.5	2.4	2.2	2.8	1.1
Responsibility for programming flexible technology (0=specialists, 4=production/skilled trades)	1.4	0.5	1.2	0.7	0.6	0.9	0.7

Table 2.7 Training of Experienced Employees (percentage of total training per topic) by Region

Topic	US/NA	JP/JP	JP/NA	EUR	KOR	AUS	S.AFR
Plant orientation	1.0	3.7	1.0	2.2	4.2	8.3	0.0
Basic skills	4.0	2.5	2.0	1.6	2.5	8.1	25.0
Interpersonal skills	5.9	23.3	6.0	16.6	9.9	6.2	33.3
Statistical process control	10.3	17.2	4.9	8.1	8.8	2.9	0.0
Problem solving	8.7	21.2	9.4	9.1	5.3	3.5	12.5
General technical skills	13.4	5.2	11.4	10.5	16.7	12.9	1.3
Specific technical skills	14.0	0.6	10.3	12.9	16.9	24.2	2.5
Production methods	15.9	9.5	22.4	20.1	19.8	12.5	19.2
Health and safety	18.8	10.1	18.7	5.1	10.8	8.5	6.3
Environmental policies	3.8	1.4	5.0	2.0	4.1	2.8	0.0
Other	4.1	5.6	9.0	12.0	1.1	10.0	0.0

Note: Column totals may not equal 100% owing to rounding error.

skills as a result of their extensive use of teamwork and quality circles/ problem-solving groups. Training relating to basic skills features prominently in South African plants, where the incoming skills levels of the workforce are low. Plants in most other regions of the world place a greater emphasis on technical skills and production methods, perhaps because they can rely on selecting workers who possess basic skills. It is noteworthy that both U.S.-owned plants in North America and Japanese transplants in North America provide similar proportions of training in health, safety issues, and environmental issues—possibly because the institutional and regulatory environments in which they operate are so similar.

In addition to training and pay for performance, work rules that permit flexible use of workers are also important in supporting such practices as teamwork and job rotation. One example of this flexibility is the number of job classifications in place. Table 2.8 shows the number of job classifications for both production workers and maintenance workers. The transplants have by far the fewest number—only one production worker classification and one or two maintenance worker classifications—while plants in Japan on average have approximately five to ten classifications for production workers and maintenance workers. By comparison, U.S.-owned plants in North America have an average of thirty-three job classifications for production workers and fifteen for maintenance workers; these represent greatly reduced numbers than in the past. The Australian plants most closely resemble the North American transplants (half of them are Japanese-owned). European plants are somewhat unusual in that they tend to have more classifications for maintenance workers than for production workers, although classifications are defined somewhat differently than in the United States.

Table 2.9 shows the differential between the entry-level pay for a given job and the highest possible pay for the same job. Although the transplants in the United States have few job classifications, they seem to be following the compensation norms found in their local environment. Their pay differentials for jobs for production workers and maintenance employees are almost equal to those of their American counterparts, although they have far fewer levels or job categories than plants in Japan or U.S. plants in America.

Global Forces for Change

Although we have been describing regional differences from a static perspective, it is important to recognize that major developments have occurred in the auto industry in recent years that have affected the use of work practices and HR policies. U.S. and European companies have set up joint-venture plants with Japanese competitors. Wholly owned "greenfield" plants, such as GM's Saturn and Volvo's Uddevalla, have provided a "clean sheet of paper" for companies to experiment with new work practices. First Japanese companies and now German companies have set up transplant facilities away from their home bases. Many existing plants have undertaken major changes in work organization when presented with both a carrot (the promise of new products or new investments in technology) and a stick (the threat of plant closure) by their companies. Most significantly, with the rise in legitimacy and understanding of Japanese-influenced lean production principles, there has been a greater shift toward so-called high-involvement human resource and work practices.

This shift at the global level is due to two key factors: (1) increased international competition as a result of the globalization of markets is providing

Table 2.8 Job Classifications by Region

	US/NA	JP/JP	JP/US	EUR	KOR	AUS
Classifications for production workers	33.6	8.0	1.2	6.3	10.7	2.5
Number of levels per classification	2.0	2.2	1.1	1.9	1.0	2.2
Classifications for skilled workers	15.0	5.0	1.4	15.9	10.3	4.0
Number of levels per classification	1.6	2.50	1.1	1.5	1.0	3.2

greater awareness of the importance of these practices for productivity and quality, and (2) overseas production facilities, some of them joint ventures, are providing insight into how these practices work. Various plant-level conditions are also inducing plants to adopt the new high-involvement work practices (see Pil and MacDuffie 1996a for a comprehensive discussion).

With respect to the globalization of markets, the sales of vehicles made by nondomestic producers (either imports or vehicles produced at transplant facilities) have captured an increasingly large share of the market in many countries. The share of non–Big Three vehicle sales in the United States rose from less than 1 percent in 1955, the peak year for sales in the postwar period, to 18.4 percent twenty years later (1975) to a high of 28.5 percent in 1991, before falling back to 25.9 percent in 1994. The import share in European and Japanese markets is considerably lower but climbing steeply, reaching 12 percent in Western Europe and nearly 5 percent in Japan by 1994 (*One Hundred Year Almanac* 1996).

Foreign direct investment by companies in overseas production facilities and distribution networks is higher than ever, so that Japanese companies operate subsidiaries in almost all parts of the world and U.S., European, and Korean companies operate manufacturing facilities outside their home regions. The development of cross-national strategic alliances has also occurred at an explosive rate as auto companies look for opportunities to learn from each other, to share the risks of technological development or expansion into new markets, to fill gaps in each other's product lines or distribution networks, and to build global economies of scale (Nohria and Garcia-Pont 1991).

To the extent that the globalization of markets brings more intensified competition for all automotive companies (whether or not they are global

Table 2.9 Pay Differentials in Japanese- and U.S.-Owned Plants

Pay Differential between Highest and Lowest Paid	Japan	Transplants	U.S.	Japan vs. Transplants*	Transplants vs. U.S.*
Production worker	204%	26%	25%	.01	
Maintenance worker	205%	12%	11%	.01	.05
First-line supervisor	117%	31%	52%	.01	.05
Manufacturing engineer	446%	130%	89%	.05	.1

*Mann-Whitney tests were done using two-sided confidence intervals.

competitors), it creates pressures for convergence toward whatever approach to work organization is most associated with market success. By the early 1990s, when industry recessions plunged such companies as General Motors, Mercedes-Benz, Volvo, and Fiat into crisis, the normative pressures to see lean production and its associated high-involvement work and HR practices as the "best-practice" route to recovery were very strong. Furthermore, with the discrediting of the "high-tech" strategy for achieving competitive advantage at General Motors and (to a lesser degree) Volkswagen and Fiat, the idea took hold that the new flexible technologies needed to be coupled with the organizational flexibility provided by lean production to be used effectively (MacDuffie and Krafcik 1992). Finally, lean production plants seemed better able to handle high levels of product complexity without incurring cost or quality penalties (MacDuffie, Sethuraman, and Fisher 1996)—a strategic advantage given the enthusiastic response of consumers to the proliferation of product offerings.

Globalization of markets has put serious competitive pressure on the old mass production model. The perceived performance advantages of lean production, together with evidence of its transferability, have given it powerful legitimacy as the new dominant model for auto manufacturing. Flexible automation offers considerable strategic advantages over fixed automation, particularly with respect to meeting the growing market demand for product variety, but is most strongly associated with improved economic performance when coupled with more flexible organizational practices (MacDuffie and Pil 1996).

The 1980s marked the interruption of a long period of stasis for the dominant model (mass production), during which new technologies and organizing principles took hold and the old model was slowly displaced. As we shall show, however, the path toward acceptance of these new organizing principles varied dramatically, both by region and by companies within regions. We turn now to a discussion of some company-level factors that have affected the use of high-involvement work and HR practices in North America, Europe, and Japan.

Company-Level Factors Affecting Adoption of New Work and HR Practices

This section focuses on the divergent forces across companies that underlie the substantial variations within the regional averages described above. At the same time, these company-level accounts will add contextual depth to the broad characterizations drawn from the regional data.

North America. We begin with North America, where the American Big Three companies of General Motors, Ford, and Chrysler began to encounter the various forces for convergence earlier than companies in Europe, largely because the large and open U.S. market drew earlier, more sustained attention from Japanese competitors. As the accounts below reveal, each of the Big Three faced one or more severe competitive crises between the early 1980s and the early 1990s. These crises prompted dramatic improvements in some areas of these companies, but they also sparked controversy between management and the UAW in other areas, or encouraged a certain conservatism with respect to making fundamental changes in the production system. We will consider the three companies in the order in which they experienced a severe financial crisis—first Chrysler, then Ford, then General Motors.

Chrysler faced its severe financial crisis in the late 1970s, when it nearly went into bankruptcy. Wage and benefit concessions and some loosening of work rules, negotiated with the UAW, became crucial to the company's recovery. But Chrysler's overall approach to work organization and the production system changed little at this time.

Chrysler's first experimentation with new forms of work organization occurred in the mid-1980s, a time of relative prosperity for the company, in the form of the Modern Operating Agreements (MOAs), which were implemented at two assembly plants and four components plants (Lovell et al. 1991; MacDuffie, Hunter, and Doucet 1995). The MOA initiative was bold in its reliance on collective bargaining as the means to achieve full-scale changeovers of existing brownfield plants, involving as it did the use of work teams, pay for knowledge, and the decentralization of quality responsibilities.

Implementation of the MOAs was extremely slow, however, since both corporate management and the UAW saw the agreements as primarily a labor relations initiative and not as central to manufacturing strategy. As such, initiation was often disrupted by labor-management disputes on other matters. At plants where the local union was unwilling to implement an MOA, Chrysler often introduced a Progressive Operating Agreement (POA), which focused on increasing the flexibility of labor deployment through the elimination of job classifications and work rules. Other U.S. plants were able to resist nearly all management efforts to make changes in the traditional system because they built extremely popular products and were running many hours of overtime each week. For example, the St. Louis plant building minivans voted against introducing an MOA repeatedly in the late 1980s and early 1990s.

MOA implementation was also affected by Chrysler's return to crisis conditions in 1989–91. This time, Chrysler's response focused on the reform of product development. It moved quickly to implement a "platform team" approach that enabled the company to develop successful new products in three years—matching or exceeding Japanese product development benchmarks. With the return of high market demand, particularly for the product segments in which Chrysler was strong (e.g., minivans), the company made a very successful comeback in 1993–94. There has been little effort, however, to build beyond the MOA experience to achieve broad changes in work organization at Chrysler's assembly plants. Persistent quality problems reveal that much scope for improvement still remains. At least so far, Chrysler's competitive ups and downs have had relatively little to do with changes in the company's approach to work organization in manufacturing.

Ford also faced a financial crisis in the early 1980s, and, in response, it began to consider introducing Japanese production systems. Ford had acquired 25 percent of Mazda in the late 1970s and had observed Mazda's efforts to adopt lean production, in which it followed the Toyota production system (TPS) as a model. According to Ford's top managers, the company's rigid structure, its emphasis on narrow functional specialization, and its adversarial labor-management relations contributed to its problems. Employee involvement and quality were endorsed as twin initiatives that could help the company overcome these organizational deficiencies.

Although Ford instituted less plant-level innovation than General Motors, it was more successful at changing labor relations at top levels. The effort to break down barriers between functional groups helped pave the way for more cross-departmental communication at the plant level and for more cross-training for workers. Finally, Ford's decision to focus heavily on quality improvement, with its "Quality Is Job 1" campaign, helped promote more decentralization of quality responsibilities from inspectors to shop-floor workers.

As Ford's fortunes began to improve in the mid-1980s, it became cautious about implementing more far-reaching changes in work organization, such as teams. In part, Ford wanted to preserve good relations with the head of the UAW's Ford department, whose public position was one of opposition to teams. Ford also knew from experience that the UAW was willing to allow considerable flexibility at the plant level as long as potentially controversial changes in work organization, such as the adoption of work teams, were avoided. Thus, although the changes in work organization at Ford were quite modest on the surface, they were more fundamentally linked to the quality-oriented strategy for competitive recovery than the more visible MOA changes at Chrysler.

Finally, in 1979, General Motors embarked on an ambitious quality of work life (QWL) program jointly with the UAW, emphasizing off-line QWL groups that addressed nonproduction-related issues in an attempt to boost worker satisfaction. At the same time, GM tried to open some nonunion "team concept" plants in the South (the so-called Southern Strategy) as well as at some greenfield plants around Detroit. The Southern Strategy failed almost immediately as the UAW successfully organized the new plants in Oklahoma City and Shreveport, Louisiana. To the UAW, however, teams had already become associated with an antiunion strategy. Team efforts in Michigan and elsewhere soon ground to a halt. The Fiero plant in Pontiac, Michigan, the most advanced of GM's team plants during this time, was the first to involve teams centrally in dealing with production-related issues. Its closing because of poor product sales prompted further skepticism about the value of teams from the union and workers alike.

GM had another opportunity to learn about lean production from its involvement in New United Motors Manufacturing, Inc. (NUMMI), its joint venture with Toyota. The NUMMI story is well known (Krafcik 1986; Brown and Reich 1989; Adler 1992; Adler and Cole 1993), so it will suffice to say that GM did a terrible job of learning from that experience. GM top management and engineers expected that Toyota's advantages derived from technology and that hiring back the workers and union officials from the former GM Fremont, California, plant would be a liability for Toyota. GM completely overlooked the different approach to organizing production work and the greater emphasis on worker skill and motivation as the source of NUMMI's impressive performance. GM exposed hundreds and possibly thousands of its employees to NUMMI during one-day visits, complete with a plant tour, but these visits did not reveal the different "logic" at NUMMI and, if anything, bred skepticism about NUMMI's value as a learning model.

The crisis at GM came much later than at Chrysler and Ford, in part because of the company's size and wealth. By the time its problems came to a head in the early 1990s, the company had lost so much market share and closed so many plants that it was in an extremely difficult position from which to implement new work practices. With staggering losses, big cost savings were needed quickly. Workers were cynical about management intentions, and trust was low. As a result, GM has taken a more "top-down" approach to lean production in the last few years, primarily through its Synchronous Manufacturing Program, which carries out process reengineering efforts (primarily driven by industrial engineering staff) at its plants.

Europe. In Europe, the movement toward lean production and high-involvement work and HR policies has been more recent and reflects the trend toward convergence to a greater extent than in the United States. Nonetheless, important differences have existed across companies, particularly during the 1980s, in such respects as the timing of the competitiveness crisis, perceptions of the best path to recovery, management strategies and union responses, and capabilities for learning.

By the mid-1980s, for example, Renault was facing a major competitiveness crisis and chose to embrace lean production as a way out of its difficulties and as an alternative (given its severe financial constraints) to making heavy investments in technology. This required the company to reach agreement with its unions, in both France and Belgium, on a new contract that allowed significant changes in work organization at its existing plants. Peugeot, in contrast, faced no such crisis. With its CEO leading the campaign within the European Community (EC) to keep Japanese companies from building plants in Europe or boosting their exports, Peugeot had little interest in adopting a Japan-influenced model and did not pursue the same kind of work restructuring through collective bargaining as Renault.

Also in the mid-1980s, Fiat was just reopening its Cassino plant, heralded as the most automated assembly plant in the world and a reflection of Fiat's intent (following a financial crisis in the late 1970s and a bitter strike that was won decisively by management) to reduce its dependence on workers (Locke 1992; Camuffo and Volpato 1995). Volvo, during this time, was preparing to open its Uddevalla plant, the most ambitious in a series of plants with sociotechnical designs—in this case, with no moving assembly line—intended to help it attract Swedish workers into manufacturing jobs and reduce high levels of absenteeism and turnover. Volvo was also continuing its efforts to implement off-line assembly and other sociotechnical design concepts in its other plants in Sweden, Belgium, and Holland (Berggren 1992).

Volvo's example was in turn influencing both Volkswagen and Mercedes in their planning of off-line assembly areas for new plants at Emden and Rastatt. Like Fiat, however, Volkswagen was also committed to a high-tech strategy to reduce direct labor in assembly, motivated more by a desire to utilize its highly skilled technical workers and improve ergonomic working conditions than by a move away from a reliance on workers (Jürgens, Malsch, and Dohse 1993; Turner 1991).

When a competitiveness crisis hit these four companies—Fiat, Volvo, Volkswagen, and Mercedes—in the early 1990s, each responded in a different way. Fiat abandoned its high-tech strategy and negotiated plans with its unions for a new plant (Melfi) that would utilize team structures (elementary technical units), performance-based pay, and other new forms of work organization (Camuffo and Micelli 1995). Volvo closed its two innovative sociotechnical plants, Kalmar and Uddevalla—in response, according to some observers (Hancke 1993; Berggren 1993), to pressure from Renault (briefly Volvo's partner in an alliance), which was convinced of the greater virtues of Japanese-style team structures. Volkswagen negotiated new arrangements with IG Metall and its works councils for working-hour reductions and pay freezes to minimize layoffs during a period of reorganizing of production and increased its utilization of "group work,"[3] building on pilot projects from the mid-to-late 1980s (Jürgens 1995; Roth 1995). Mercedes-Benz accelerated its move away from craft methods and boosted investments in automation, while backing away from the Volvo-influenced

---

[3]In the German context, many of those involved in the debates over new forms of work organization differentiate between "group work" and "teamwork." The former term is associated with high autonomy from both managerial oversight (i.e., "self-managing," with no supervisor) and technical constraints (i.e., a machine-paced assembly line), in the tradition of sociotechnical theory and many Scandinavian experiments, while the latter term is associated with Japanese-style lean production and is characterized as low in autonomy and dominated by management. These distinctions are less often observed in practice, in part because many companies choose to create their own terms for their group/team-based activities (e.g., elementary technical units at Fiat, work modules at Saturn).

production system at Rastatt and hiring a Japanese consulting firm to implement lean production at its new U.S. factory.

For the American-owned companies in Europe, company differences were also pronounced. As in the United States, Ford of Europe got a fast start in the early 1980s, with its After Japan program, on implementing employee-involvement activities directed at increasing quality and improving labor-management relations. But unlike Ford in the United States, these were boom years for Ford Europe, and the early experiments with work reorganization were short-lived. Ford had laid the foundation for more cooperative relations with its unions and works councils, however, enabling Ford Europe to revive some quality-oriented initiatives later in the 1980s (in connection with learning exchanges with Mazda plants) while proceeding cautiously (as in the United States) with teams and other new work structures.

GM of Europe, unlike GM in the United States, faced a severe financial crisis in the early 1980s that set the company on a path of learning about lean production. This strategic redirection resulted not only from the competitiveness crisis but from the appointment of new top managers, first Jack Smith and then Lou Hughes, who had helped set up the NUMMI joint venture and had become convinced of the value of lean production principles. Although there is still more variation in GM's plants in Europe than Ford's, GM has gone further than Ford in establishing more far-reaching reforms in work organization at some of its plants (Turner 1991).

For example, the most advanced lean production plant in Europe that is not Japanese owned is the new GM Europe plant in Eisenach, in eastern Germany, which is run primarily by young American and Canadian managers and advisers who formerly worked either at NUMMI or at GM's joint-venture plant with Suzuki in Canada (CAMI). The achievement of the Eisenach plant owes much to GM Europe's strategy of trying to replicate lean production principles developed elsewhere, without major efforts to reinvent or modify them, and to the transfer of managers with extensive hands-on experience with lean production to oversee the launch effort. The Eisenach plant has also benefited from its greenfield status and its workforce—workers from the former East Germany who have no previous experience in a traditional mass production plant and who have shown a strong interest in adopting "group work" (MacDuffie 1996).

To summarize, most of the European companies that faced competitive crises early in the 1980s pursued different strategies for improvement, depending on whether they were oriented primarily toward technology (Fiat, VW) or "people" (Volvo, Ford) solutions (Jürgens, Malsch, and Dohse

1993), whether they had adversarial (Fiat, Renault) or cooperative (Volvo, VW) relationships with unions and works councils, their past experiences with work organization reforms (especially at Volvo and VW), and the influence of "learning models" (e.g., Volvo's sociotechnical experiments for VW and Mercedes, Mazda's for Ford Europe, NUMMI's for GM Europe). GM Europe and Renault were the only European companies during the 1980s to make serious moves, companywide, toward lean production, as a result of the timing of their competitive crises, the orientation of their leadership, and their capacities for learning. Thus, it is only since the competitive crises of the early 1990s that the responses of the European companies begin to look more convergent.

Japan. Even in Japan, there has been substantial divergence across companies, although largely within the bounds of the lean production model. Toyota remains the leader in a variety of ways: it has the largest market share (both domestically and based on exports and sales from overseas production), has been most financially able to withstand the industry recession (because of its huge cash reserves), and is continuing to push forward with new plants and new production concepts. Takahiro Fujimoto and Takashi Matsuo (1995) have documented Toyota's shift away from a high-growth mentality toward a more balanced approach in which more attention is placed on the problems of attracting and retaining workers. First at its new Kyushu factory and subsequently on retrofitted assembly lines at its oldest assembly plant at Motomachi, Toyota has been willing to move away from supposedly sacrosanct principles of the Toyota production system to create a less physically demanding, more motivating, and more knowledge-intensive work environment.

For example, the continuous assembly line in these new or retrofitted Toyota sites is now broken into multiple short line segments, each corresponding to a major module or subsystem of the vehicle and separated by a small buffer of work-in-process inventory (with a capacity equivalent to five minutes of production time). The idea is to group together a set of tasks related to one "whole job" or "product" and to train workers to do all tasks and to understand the underlying product design and manufacturing process for that line.[4] It was the process of kaizen that slowly shifted job

---

[4]This way of organizing work bears a strong resemblance to the principles of job enrichment that were promulgated in the United States during the 1970s and 1980s (Hackman and Oldham 1980) and also to the sociotechnical principles applied at Volvo's experimental assembly plant in Kalmar during the same time period. Because it retains a moving assembly line and relatively short cycle times, it cannot be compared with the production concepts Volvo applied at its Uddevalla plant, mentioned above.

content at Toyota toward a set of unrelated tasks, as individual tasks were shifted from job to job in search of greater installation efficiencies or line balance. But Toyota managers believe that this new concept will provide new kaizen opportunities resulting from the more integrated knowledge that workers will possess about the product and manufacturing process in their section of the line. Furthermore, Toyota envisions a greater incidence of line stops, since it will be less intimidating for workers to contemplate stopping production for a limited section of the line as opposed to, potentially, the entire plant.

Beyond Toyota, there continues to be variation across the Japanese companies with respect to their internal organization of work and HR policies, although less variation than in the United States and Europe. The diffusion of Toyota's production methods within Japan in the 1970s resulted in considerable company convergence with respect to the most visible aspects of lean production, particularly the just-in-time inventory system and the use of formal work teams and quality circles. Sizable differences remain, however, in how well companies understand Toyota's innovations and in how successfully they have been able to maintain lean production practices in the face of various challenges, including industry downturns, increasing product variety, and major automation initiatives within the assembly area.

For example, Nissan's experience has been quite different from Toyota's. For many years, Nissan resembled U.S. companies in its emphasis on automation and economies of scale and its relatively traditional work organization (Cusumano 1985). Even after adopting much of the structure of Toyota's work organization, Nissan was much less successful at getting workers involved in kaizen activities. (As noted below, Nissan has had more success in this area in its U.S. and European plants than in its plants in Japan.) Nissan has also been among the Japanese companies hardest hit by the industry downturn of the early 1990s. Like Toyota, Nissan built a new plant on Kyushu island in the early 1990s that served as a showcase for new assembly automation and conveyance systems. This plant has run under capacity since it opened and has had difficulty with its automation. Furthermore, in 1993, Nissan became the first Japanese company in the postwar period to close one of its assembly plants—although all employees from the plant were redeployed elsewhere within Nissan and its affiliated group of suppliers.

Variation among the other manufacturers in Japan has been exacerbated in recent years for a variety of reasons. One consequence of the prolonged recession for the Japanese industry was a worsening of quality performance at some of the smaller automakers, often because of problems in their supplier networks but also traceable to their assembly plants.

At the assembly plant level, there was also a considerable reduction in the level of training provided to experienced employees from 1989 to 1993–94 by Japanese companies, primarily as a result of cost cutting, and increasing reliance on quality inspectors, rather than production workers, to handle key quality responsibilities. Both trends are deviations from these companies' past pattern of investing heavily in the skills and motivation of employees and a related dependence on production workers to take the initiative to improve performance.

Questions also are being raised about lean production in Japan (Cusumano 1994; Fujimoto 1994; Confederation of Japanese Automobile Workers' Union 1992), in light of the apparent end of years of uninterrupted growth and the emergence of various problems associated with the maturity of the industry (e.g., traffic congestion from just-in-time deliveries, difficulty attracting young Japanese to factory work, excessive product variety). Whether these developments are temporary, related to the recession, or reflect a more permanent shift is not yet clear. A related change worth following is whether Ford's move to exert more substantial management control over Mazda, which has been financially troubled since the end of the "bubble" economy, will result in any changes in work organization and HR policies at Mazda's two plants in Japan.

Company differences are also apparent when examining the transplant operations of various Japanese companies in the United States. Nissan yielded substantial authority to the first American manager of its Tennessee facility over such issues as plant design and ended up with the most space-inefficient plant in North America. In addition, many of Nissan's HR policies in Tennessee bear a closer resemblance to the U.S. nonunion model than to employment practices in Japan (Shimada and MacDuffie 1987; Pil and MacDuffie 1996b). Yet the Nissan plant in the United States, as well as the Nissan plant in the United Kingdom, have been the most innovative plants within the company with respect to employee involvement in continuous improvement activities. Toyota continues to manage the most effective of the unionized transplants, at NUMMI (the GM-Toyota joint venture), where it maintains an effective working relationship with the UAW local union despite a shift in the membership of the shop committee to include more members of the opposition People's Caucus. As noted in chapter 3 of this volume, Toyota's nonunion transplant operations in Kentucky and Canada have work organizations that are very similar to NUMMI's, accompanied by HR policies that represent a hybrid of Japanese, NUMMI, and local practices.

In contrast with NUMMI, Mazda made several mistakes in its handling of the union and the workforce when it opened its plant in Michigan. Management first built overly rosy expectations during an endless hiring and training process, then reversed its position on several key issues, such as training and use of temporary workers, during the pressures of the first year of production (Fucini and Fucini 1990). Among the smaller companies, Mitsubishi, Suzuki (in the CAMI joint venture with General Motors), and the Subaru-Isuzu joint venture have all had some difficulties simultaneously managing lean production and American/Canadian workforces at their transplant facilities (e.g., Graham 1995; Huxley, Rinehart, and Robertson 1995). As chapter 5 recounts, CAMI is organized by the Canadian Auto Workers (CAW), which has developed a clear policy against certain features of lean production. Tensions surrounding these issues, as well as unresolved pay grievances, led to a strike at CAMI in the fall of 1992—the first and only strike at a Japanese transplant in the United States to date.

Within-Company Divergence in Work and HR Practices

In addition to divergence across companies, several factors promote divergence in work practices *within* companies, including whether the plant is a greenfield or a brownfield facility, the strength of the market demand for the products made in a particular plant, and plant-specific arrangements with competing companies for collaborative "benchmarking" or joint-venture production. Companies typically institute the most comprehensive changes in work practices at greenfield plants. At many companies, the management philosophy for older plants is to attempt major changes in work practices only when there will be a "significant emotional event" (GM's term)—generally a corporate decision about investment and product placement—that will shake up employees and ready them for change.

Such management pressure is unlikely to be applied at a plant that is building a best-selling product and running at or above full capacity, given the risk of disrupting both economies of scale and profitability with an unwelcome initiative to change work practices. For example, Chrysler plants making the minivan have regularly been able to resist pressure from both top management and the Chrysler department of the UAW to adopt an MOA contract.

Finally, it appears that plants engaged in benchmarking comparisons inside and outside their company—an increasingly common phenomenon—are often more willing to share information with a competitor than with a plant within their own company, because of internal company rivalries over resources (including investments, promotion opportunities, the chance to hire new employees). This situation may contribute both to convergence across companies and to divergence within companies in work practices.

Changes over Time in High-Involvement Work and Complementary HR Practices

To examine change over time in the adoption and utilization of high-involvement work and HR practices, we present regional averages for the two rounds of the assembly plant study. (Confidentiality agreements prevent us from providing such data at the company level.) Table 2.10 presents data on changes in work and HR practices from the matched sample of forty-four plants participating in both rounds 1 and 2 of the assembly plant survey. The matched sample offers the most precise look at change in the same set of plants over time but for a small sample. These results are not much different from those found when the full 1989 sample is compared with the full 1993–94 sample.

The most striking trends evident in table 2.10 are the huge increase in European, new-entrant, and Australian plants in their use of small-group activities—both on-line work teams and off-line employee-involvement groups—and job rotation and in their reliance on suggestion systems. In contrast, small-group activities at the U.S.-owned plants in North America affect fewer employees than in any other region. Problem-solving activities (i.e., suggestions received per employee and the percentage of suggestions implemented by management) also remain low for the Big Three plants even as they increase for plants in Europe, the new entrants (NEs), and Australia (as well as for the Japanese transplants). Job rotation is the only practice to have increased significantly in all regions. Increased concern about ergonomic problems and repetitive strain injuries may provide a common motivation for the increase in job rotation across companies, rather than a commitment to job rotation as a way for workers to learn multiple skills.

Plants in Japan remain the most consistent followers of lean work practices. They do show some diminution in their adherence to certain practices, which seems most likely to be caused by the recessionary conditions in the Japanese auto industry that continued through 1993 and 1994. In contrast, the Japanese transplants in North America appear to be on a steady trajectory toward converging upon the practices of their counterparts in

Table 2.10 Regional Averages for Key Variables in Round 1 (1989) versus Round 2 (1993–94) of the Assembly Plant Study

Variable	JP/JP 1989	JP/JP 1993–94	JP/NA 1989	JP/NA 1993–94	US/NA 1989	US/NA 1993–94	EUR/EUR 1989	EUR/EUR 1993–94	NIC 1989	NIC 1993–94	AUS 1989	AUS 1993–94
High-Involvement Work Practices												
Percentage of workforce in teams	82	81	71	76	23	24	16	52	37	55	20	36
Percentage of workforce in employee-involvement groups	93	90	12	14	17	20	5	54	42	68	24	62
Job rotation (0=none; 4=lots)	3.8	4.2	2.7	3.7	0.9	2.1	1.8	3.9	2.2	3.7	1.7	3.7
Suggestions of employee	56	48	68	79	0.3	0.2	0.3	1.0	2.3	???	0.1	0.2
Percentage per suggestions implemented	91	90	65	68	22	34	15	49	39	59	8	6
Supporting HR Practices												
Contingent compensation (0=none; 4=extensive)	1.8	1.8	2.3	2.3	1.4	1.3	1.3	2.6	2.0	1.5	0	3.0
Status differentials (0=many; 4=few)	3.0	3.2	4.0	4.0	1.3	2.0	1.2	2.0	2.5	2.2	0.7	1.7
Training for experienced production workers (0=low; 3=high)	2.7	1.7	2.7	3.0	1.6	1.6	1.8	2.2	2.5	2.3	1.0	3.0

Japan, although the percentage of workers in employee-involvement groups and suggestions received and implemented remain considerably lower than in Japan.

These data reveal that the direction of the changes in work organization is clearly convergent toward high-involvement practices. The changes in Europe, NEs, and Australian plants can perhaps be accurately described as convergent in terms of the degree or extent of the change as well. We would argue that the appropriate reference point for assessing the degree of convergence for these regions is the Japanese transplants rather than Japanese plants in Japan. The implementation of lean production has been going on in Japan for more than thirty years, while implementation in the transplants as well as in any other plants that are moving toward lean production has occurred in the last five to ten years. For most of these variables, the difference in means when comparing the Japanese transplants with European, new-entrant, and Australian plants in 1993–94 is not statistically significant. But although Big Three plants in the United States and Canada may be converging in direction, their degree of implementation of flexible work organization clearly diverges substantially from the degree of implementation in other regions.

To examine complementary HR policies, we compare trends in the use of contingent compensation, the presence of status differentiators, and the level of training for experienced employees. In these areas, the European and Australian plants have been the most enthusiastic. Indeed, the Australian claim that its plants train workers for far more hours than plants anywhere else in the world probably reflects a temporary "catch-up" in the implementation of a new training qualification program negotiated between the industry association and the metalworkers union. Japanese plants in the United States have remained relatively constant in these HR policies, while Japanese plants in Japan have actually experienced a drop as a result of a reduction in training for experienced employees. The only trend among the Big Three plants is a move to reduce status differentials.

Whereas plants throughout the world could be classified relatively easily into lean or mass production categories in 1989, clustered around the extremes of the continuum between these two models, the picture was considerably different in 1993–94. Many more plants from nearly every region have implemented or expanded their use of some high-involvement work and HR practices. Relatively few appear to have implemented these practices to their full extent, however.

Impact of Past Performance on Adoption of New Practices

The wide variation in the amount and type of change in the utilization of new work practices within the international sample provokes some curiosity about the factors underlying that variation. We have explored this question elsewhere (Pil and MacDuffie 1996a) using data from the same matched sample of plants discussed in the previous section. One issue of particular interest was the impact of past performance on the adoption of new work practices.

There are conflicting perspectives on the impact of adversity, defined as poor performance, on a firm's behavior. Some literature suggests that poorly performing organizations become increasingly committed to losing courses of action; that is, they escalate their commitment (e.g., Staw 1976). Other literature suggests that poor performance is more likely to result in innovative change. Alfred D. Chandler (1962), for example, proposed that poor performance induces the search for new behaviors within organizations. More recently, Michele K. Bolton (1993) showed empirically for a sample of high-tech firms that those exhibiting substandard performance were more likely to alter how they conducted research than their better-performing counterparts.

Our data and our field observations suggest support for the latter view. Under conditions of poor performance, a company or plant is already inclined to view current practices as suboptimal. Even where the adoption of new practices represents radical (and "competence-destroying") change from traditional work organization—which may reduce the immediate benefit of new practices—poor-performing plants will find that the short-term differential between potential new practices and existing practices is not so great. As a result, the cost of change relative to maintaining the status quo is lower for poorly performing organizations than for average and superior performers, making change more likely. Thus, our working hypothesis was that the worst-performing plants would be the most likely to undertake change in their work systems.

Our empirical analyses provided mixed support for this hypothesis. Although our fieldwork strongly suggested that the worst performers were more likely to undertake change, regression analyses suggested that plants with worse quality (i.e., a greater number of defects per vehicle in 1989) were only somewhat more likely to have increased their use of high-involvement work practices by 1993–94. Worse productivity in 1989 was also associated with the adoption of high-involvement work practices, but that relationship was not statistically significant.[5]

More descriptive analyses, shown in table 2.11, indicate that both poor productivity and poor quality are associated with the adoption of high-involvement work and HR practices. The quartile of plants with the worst productivity performance was most likely to increase their use of high-involvement work practices as well as complementary HR practices; the same relationship held for the quartile of plants with the worst quality performance. Indeed, the quartile of plants with the worst performance in 1989 went from having the lowest levels of high-involvement HR practices in 1989 to having the highest level in 1993–94.

In a separate analysis, we examined the length of time since the plant adopted the new work practices in relation to plant performance. We found that those that had adopted innovative work practices many years earlier had the best performance, followed by new plants that had opened between round 1 and round 2 and employed innovative work practices from the start. Those plants that had implemented new work concepts the most recently had considerably worse performance in terms of both productivity and quality, even in relation to plants with traditional work practices that made little or no change from round 1 to round 2. Given that these new work practices represent a radical or competence-destroying change in many work settings coupled with the fact that it is often the worst-performing plants that increase their use of such practices, it is no surprise that these plants did not exhibit stellar performance in the short run. Table 2.12 shows the mean productivity and quality performance measures for plants in these four categories.

Table 2.11 HRM Index and Work Systems Index Rankings of Top-Performing versus Worst-Performing Plants, 1989 and 1993–94

Rank in 1989	HR index		Work systems index	
	1989	**1993–94**	**1989**	**1993–94**
Top-performing quartile	52	53	58	62
Intermediate 50%	41	49	27	39
Worst-performing quartile	34.5	56	25	50.5

[5]A potential cause for the lack of strong support for the performance hypothesis is collinearity among independent variables in the regressions on 1993–94 work practices. In the round 1 data, both the productivity and quality measures were very highly correlated with measures of both work practices and complementary HR practices.

Conclusions

While powerful economic forces related to the globalization of markets and the influence of foreign direct investment have promoted a certain degree of convergence across regions in work and HR practices, many factors across and within companies have led to continued divergence. (National-level factors also underlie the divergent trends, as the chapters that follow will emphasize, although we believe these factors are less important than in the past and are now superseded by more company-level factors that have a greater impact on plant-level work and HR practices.)

The results indicate that the auto industry worldwide is composed of four distinct groups of plants and companies: (1) Japanese-owned plants in Japan and overseas that were already following lean production practices and are (mostly) maintaining or (in the case of the transplants) deepening their use of those practices; (2) plants in Europe and some new-entrant countries (e.g., Korea) that are reporting rapid and comprehensive adoption of lean production practices in the past few years, following many years of adherence to traditional mass production practices; (3) U.S.-owned plants in the United States and Canada that, following some experimentation with new work and HR practices in the 1980s, maintained (or reverted to) more traditional practices in the early 1990s; and (4) plants in all regions that manifest some hybrid combination of mass production and lean production practices.

We close with questions about the future trajectory for each of these groups.

Stable and lean (Japanese-owned plants): Will the pressures facing Japanese companies in their domestic market lead to fundamental changes in how they

Table 2.12 Mean Productivity and Quality Performance Measures of Participants in Assembly Plant Survey, 1993–94

Timing of Changes in Work Practices	Productivity (hours per vehicle)	Quality (defects per 100 vehicles)
Traditional plants, little or no change (n=28)	23.0	74.9
Traditional plants, recent change (n=23)	28.2	73.7
New plants (n=3)	20.9	55.0
Long-time lean plants (n=18)	17.2	49.8

organize work and manage the employment relationship with their employees in Japan? If so, what will the implications be for how overseas plants in the United States, Europe, and increasingly new entrants are managed?

Rapid move to lean (European and new-entrant plants): How sustainable will the rapid moves by these companies toward the adoption and implementation of lean production practices prove to be? Will the strategic commitment of these companies to these practices remain constant? How much variation in the implementation of practices across plants will emerge?

Sticking with tradition (U.S.-owned plants in North America): Will these companies be able to sustain a push toward lean production manufacturing practices without eventually adopting high-involvement work practices and HR policies as well? How much of the current pattern of more traditional practices reflects the ambivalence of both union officials and managers about past experiences with innovative work and HR practices? How might future shifts in the dynamics and power balance of labor-management relations affect the current pattern of adoption and utilization?

Hybrids (assorted plants from various countries): Are plants with a hybrid mixture of practices simply in transition from mass production to lean production? Or have they established a "stable hybrid" that will endure as a distinctive model for how to organize work and manage the employment relationship? How many different stable hybrids (if any) will emerge? What national (cultural/institutional), company, and plant-level factors will support these new hybrids most successfully?

Although this chapter and those that follow are unlikely to provide definitive answers to these questions, they help identify the most promising clues in the present-day situation that indicate future trends. We turn now to the in-depth discussions of the situations in individual countries, which probe the national-level institutional and cultural factors driving similarities and differences in the work organization and HR practices of the auto industry throughout the world.

PART **II**

Bellwethers of Innovation in the Auto Industry

3

Japan: Beyond the Model for Lean Production

Mitsuo Ishida

Japanese automakers have been regarded as setting the pace for other automakers throughout the world since the publication of *The Machine That Changed the World* by James P. Womack, Daniel T. Jones, and Daniel Roos in 1990. Thus, research on the auto industry in countries other than Japan has focused on how to adopt lean production methods, how lean production has been revised, and other production methods that have developed as a consequence of difficulties in implementing lean production. An investigation of the situation in Japan, however, provides some alternative perspectives on these issues.[1]

The starting point of this discussion is a description of lean production as offered by Womack, Jones, and Roos (1990). Since the book was published, debate has centered on whether lean production is a new system that overcomes the problems associated with the monotonous, repetitive work typical of automobile assembly or whether more radical change is needed, namely, giving plants the authority to make decisions autonomously.

Fueling the "post-Fordism controversy" (Kyoya 1993) are two essential questions: what kinds of labor and work organization are required for a production system to operate efficiently, and how can workers be convinced to accept these requirements? Since acceptance is up to the workers, the way in which these requirements are accepted reflects cultural and

[1]The members of the study team were Mitsuo Ishida (Doshisha University Graduate School of Policy and Management), Norio Hisamoto (Kyoto University Faculty of Economics), Fumito Matsumura (Nagoya City University Faculty of Economics), and Hiroyuki Fujimura (Shiga University Faculty of Economics).

historical differences among countries. Specifically, how does one explain the acceptance of these requirements in Japan?

With respect to the first question, Womack, Jones, and Roos (1990) argue that because workers at lower organizational tiers are held responsible under lean production for seeking cost reductions, zero defects, and zero inventory, "most people—including so-called blue-collar workers—will find their jobs more challenging as lean production spreads. And they will certainly become more productive" (14). Womack, Jones, and Roos concede that workers "may find their work more stressful" (14) but that "lean production offers a creative tension in which workers have many ways to address challenges" (102).

Womack, Jones, and Roos (1990) do not disregard the importance of the second question. For example, their book contains the following claims: "Holding back knowledge and effort [under lean production] would swiftly lead to disaster" (53) and "To make a lean system with no slack—no safety network at all, it is essential that every worker try very hard" (103). If these statements are true, essential to lean production is a practice of ensuring that employees are encouraged to be involved. Yet the authors also note that "workers respond only when there exists some sense of reciprocal obligation" (99). Among the specific practices that the authors cite as necessary for such reciprocal obligation are "delegation of responsibility to the shop floor," skills training, evaluation of the resulting performance, and, above all, employment security.[2]

In *Alternatives to Lean Production*, Christian Berggren (1992) criticizes Womack, Jones, and Roos on the following grounds: so-called multiskilling is only "multitasking," which forces people to do various kinds of unskilled labor; the training periods are quite short; improvement is oriented toward further standardization of work, which can be characterized as Taylorism; and, finally, the difference between lean production and conventional Taylorism is that workers cooperate on making improvements.

Why then do Japanese workers cooperate? There are several reasons, among them the institution of postwar reforms, including employment security, a seniority-based wage system, the dissolution of status differences

[2]The authors of *The Machine That Changed the World* added that the seniority wage system was a condition for achieving a state of reciprocal obligation, referring to the case of Toyota. For this mechanism—the longer a worker remains an employee, the higher the cost of his or her labor—to be used successfully, there must be increases in skills and productivity to compensate for any rise in labor costs. It can be argued that this incentive will drive skills development. The seniority wage system is not suitable, however, for evaluating the efforts of individual workers. Since 1990, therefore, Toyota has tried to incorporate ability or merit elements into the framework of (but not in place of) the seniority wage system.

between labor and management, and the subsequent purge of militant trade unions. The last of these changes resulted in the elimination of entities that resisted rationalization through improvement, whereas the previous initiatives made it possible to procure agreement among general workers on new managerial policies. Against this historical background, Berggren argues, competition among Japanese workers for wages, even under the current personnel management system, weakens solidarity among them.

Although *The Machine That Changed the World* did not take into account the weakened positions of trade unions and competition among workers, that book and Berggren's evidence little difference regarding the perception that acceptance of the kinds of labor and labor organization required for a production system to operate efficiently cannot take place in the absence of reciprocal obligations. The relationship between a production system and a labor organization cannot be understood systematically without referring to management efficiency at the plant level. Hence, it is necessary to clarify the characteristics of wage and personnel management and labor-management relations that support the stable functioning of an efficient management system and ensure that such a system is accepted by the workforce.

Management of Production

One defect in discussions of the models of production followed by Japanese automakers, often called lean production methods, is that they disregard a method of plant management designed to combine delegation of authority to the shop floor with improvements in productivity and quality. The conventional view, as exemplified by Womack, Jones, and Roos (1990), is that productivity and quality will improve when the morale of workers improves, which occurs as a result of delegating authority. Productivity and quality will improve because problems will be swiftly addressed or fundamentally solved by workers if the only alternative is a delay in production. In other words, the conventional argument is that high worker morale and an efficient production system automatically guarantee good plant performance. Is this true?

At Mazda and Toyota, the key element affecting plant performance has been management by objectives by division. At Mazda, an important index for implementing such management has been cost; at Toyota, it has been efficiency. The final assembly workshop shall be used as an example.

Mazda sets and allocates per-car cost targets for each subsection within its plants. The semiannual results of subsections and larger units of organization are identified by comparing actual costs with cost targets and are expressed as deficits or surpluses. Costs and results are compared with the targets every month at the section, department, and plant levels. The monthly report meeting is an occasion to exert substantial control over line managers, including subsection leaders and those in higher positions, to pursue further cost reductions. The achievements of each division are directly reflected in the performance evaluations of section managers and their superiors. Individual evaluations of foremen (crew leaders) and chiefs (subsection leaders) are also indirectly affected by the results of cost performance. If a subsection's costs are above the cost target, it is unlikely that the individuals in the subsection will receive favorable performance evaluations.[3]

It is important to understand that each workshop will be leaner every year only if there is systematic management by objectives by division. For example, each subsection divides its cost targets into labor costs and other costs. If the reduction of labor costs is to be pursued on the shop floor, proposals could include reducing unproductive walking time, reducing the downtime frequency of line ABC, and so on. Proposals for reducing other costs could include reducing the frequency of oil spills on line XYZ, reducing the defective fabrication of guide holes, and similar ideas. These efforts are examples of kaizen, or the practice of continuous improvement.

The three or four crew leaders under the supervision of each chief are held responsible for achieving the cost reduction targets set by the chief through improvement plans. Before the chief is to attend a section monthly report meeting, the foremen consult with the chief regarding the progress of kaizen on the shop floor, as well as about any other problems.

Such management by objectives by division is synonymous with productivity improvement. If an objective to reduce costs by 10 percent is set, about 10 percent in reductions can be obtained through "improvement." The setting of feasible objectives for the next fiscal year is ensured through the frequent exchange of shop-floor information at the monthly meetings.

---

[3] Individual personnel appraisals of employees of Japanese firms usually consist of a semiannual short-term performance appraisal and an appraisal of individual ability from a medium-term perspective. The results of performance appraisals are reflected in twice-yearly bonus payments, and the results of ability appraisals are reflected in annual increments in basic pay and in promotions. Mazda's "performance evaluation" is equivalent to the performance appraisal described here.

Toyota's management by division is essentially the same. Whereas Mazda uses a monetary index of costs per car in monitoring performance, Toyota uses two indexes simultaneously: production efficiency and costs for each section within a plant. Simply expressed, production efficiency is standard time multiplied by the volume of production, the result being divided by total work hours. The production efficiency results of each section are circulated among all departments and sections every month and attract strong interest from line managers. Efficiency meetings and cost meetings are held systematically at company, plant, department, and section levels, and progress with respect to objectives is monitored monthly. The processes at section and lower levels are the same at Mazda.

What is remarkable at Toyota is the following. Formerly, the company used an efficiency index for each section directly responsible for production lines. Although the person-hours of these direct production line sections decreased smoothly with further automation, more personnel were needed for control and maintenance. Therefore, since 1992, the company has shifted to monitoring the efficiency of every section, including the person-hours spent on control and maintenance tasks.

The conventional explanation for productivity improvement as being the result of the increase in worker morale and the introduction of the new production system is inconsistent with actual plant management at Mazda and Toyota. Productivity is something that is planned and managed, and it must not be overlooked that the mechanism for applying relentless daily pressure on all personnel, including line managers, to achieve productivity objectives is an indispensable element of such planning and management.

Work Organization and Skills Development

The operations performed on the shop floors of Japanese automakers may be classified as operations to achieve division objectives (nonroutine operations) or as normal production activities (routine operations). The discussion so far has focused on the extent to which line operators conduct nonroutine operations. Nonroutine operations can be roughly divided into responses to mechanical problems and improvement activities aimed at reducing hours of work.

The general procedures for responding to mechanical problems are the same at Mazda and at Toyota. If a problem occurs, it is the operator's responsibility to activate an alarm to bring attention to the problem immediately. Shop-floor managers are the first to respond. At Mazda, these people are either team leaders or foremen, and at Toyota, they are either team leaders or group leaders (see table 3.1). If these supervisors cannot deal with the problem, they request help from the maintenance division. The responsibility of these shop-floor managers is limited to complying with prescribed procedures.

Improvement operations can be classified as developing improvement plans, adding minor equipment, or developing and implementing improvement plans without introducing new equipment. In the case of Toyota's final-assembly shop floor, improvement plans are developed mainly by section managers together with shop-floor engineers. The plans represent attempts to devise ways of reducing person-hours that involve investments to reduce labor and policies devised through brainstorming on the shop floor (and which involve small amounts of funds for minor equipment). Improvement comes through shop-floor brainstorming in which group leaders and team leaders play the main roles. In the survey we conducted for our study, one section manager commented that "it is impossible for rank-and-file workers to attempt an improvement as large as a reduction of one person."

Workers cannot commit themselves to improvement because they are busy performing line operations. They implement small portions of improvement proposals as part of the "one-second improvement" campaign. To eliminate a full person-hour or more, it is necessary to add automated equipment, an improvement effort led by group or team leaders. Improvement groups at both Mazda and Toyota built such equipment.[4]

Table 3.1 Organization of the Shop Floor at Mazda and at Toyota

Organizational Level	Mazda	Toyota
Subsection (kekari)*	Chief (shunin)	Production chief
Shop floor (shokuba)	Foreman (shokucho)	Group leader (kumicho)
	Team leader (hancho)	Team leader (hancho)
	General workers (ippan)	General workers (ippan)

*Section managers exist above the subsection level at both firms. Though there are few exceptions, generally chief or production chief mark the limit to which workers who are high school leavers can be promoted.

[4]Historically, Toyota's improvement group became separate and independent from a maintenance section through the spread of improvement activities. Mazda brought together skillful people from among line workers. We observed that Toyota's improvement group had

Thus, the main people involved and their relation to the above classification of improvement operations are (1) section managers, production chiefs, and engineers, who develop improvement plans; (2) improvement groups, which build minor equipment; and (3) group or team leaders, who develop and implement improvement plans without introducing new equipment. In general, workers play a rather modest role in the improvement process.

In that workers mainly repeat standardized tasks under the restrictions of cycle times, the Japanese system does not differ significantly from conventional Taylorism. Yet these standardized tasks include less waste. In this sense, the system is an extension of Taylorism. The following reservations must be fully considered, however. It is indispensable that team leaders, group leaders, and production chiefs be able to carry out improvement activities. These people are promoted internally from the general workforce. They need to develop their improvement abilities from the stage of being general workers through quality control and suggestion activities (no matter how modestly such activities contribute to reductions in person-hours). In this sense, these workers are capable of performing improvement work. In addition, the number of employees with ranks equal to or higher than team leader is 17,600; this is equivalent to 54 percent of the 32,500 employees with ranks equal to or lower than group leader.[5]

In a mechanical fabrication workshop, for example, where operation of the production line has been progressively mechanized, the normal tasks of workers amount to "baby-sitting" machines. Their primary responsibility other than checking quality and changing blades has been reduced to responding to machine problems. At a Mazda workshop where cylinder blocks are fabricated, a foreman noted that the emphasis is on developing workers' skill in "specifically identifying what is wrong based on the particular situation." Further automation will naturally increase the need for such skills.

---

higher levels of skill. A group of workers who specialize in improvement, which exists between a production line and a maintenance section, is more or less indispensable for carrying out improvement activities at a Japanese automobile plant. At Toyota, there were about ten people in the improvement group, as compared with a total of 320 employees in the final assembly section.

[5] The percentage is so high because nonsupervisory production chiefs, group leaders, and team leaders are assigned to these positions in recognition of their specialized skills. These people are engaged in the execution of changes in models, improvement activities, and engineering.

Remuneration Systems

The current Japanese wage system is a mixture of seniority and merit systems.[6] The seniority system had a strong influence over the wages of Japanese workers from the end of the war through the 1950s. Use of the merit system started to spread gradually in the 1960s.[7] Conflicts between the seniority system and the merit system became the main theme of the history of wage determination and administration.

The seniority wage system and the merit wage system have several implications with regard to lean production. The seniority system results in higher labor costs as the seniority of a worker increases, and employers expect that increased efforts from individuals will correspond to the higher costs. In other words, they expect workers to perform nonroutine operations. The seniority system has two weaknesses, however. First, it cannot prevent average workers from reducing their level of skill development or their work efforts. Second, it cannot compensate for individual differences in ability or effort. The purpose of the merit system is to overcome these weaknesses. If the morale of all workers is sufficiently high, however, and differences in ability can be adequately reflected in supervisory positions, there will be no consequences as a result of either the first or the second weakness in the seniority system.[8]

Changes in the environment, such as the development of individualism as part of workers' consciousness, shortages in positions, the emergence of individual differences as a result of there being higher standards for workers in higher ability levels, and so on provide incentives to use the merit system. Nevertheless, Japanese enterprise unions are wary of increasing competition among union members arising from wage differentials and auto manufacturers have therefore been very slow to replace the seniority system with the merit system.

[6]Unlike the situation in Europe and America, wage tables for white-collar and blue-collar workers in Japan are less differentiated. This is because status differences within companies dissolved as a result of the postwar labor movement.

[7]The diffusion of the merit system and its impact on labor-management relations are important in understanding labor-management relations in Japan. The process coincided with a relaxation of trade union restrictions on competition among union members with respect to wages and work efforts. For more details, see Ishida 1990.

[8]Management pursued the establishment of wage differentials corresponding to managerial positions in the 1950s, after the postwar turbulence. It was called pay for rank. The wages of general workers who did not assume managerial positions were determined by seniority and educational background, and no large differentials were based on performance appraisals. By contrast, the merit system establishes ability-based grades among these workers and also creates wage differentials among people of the same ability grade depending on the results of appraisals.

What are the specifics of the Japanese remuneration system? We will examine the specifics of how the seniority system and the merit system are combined at Toyota.

Since 1993, the monthly wages of workers (so-called blue-collar workers, including supervisors) have represented a combination of basic pay, pay for ability, pay for age, and pay for productivity. The weighting of these elements has been 40 percent for basic pay and 20 percent for each of the others.

Basic pay is the fundamental element in postwar Japanese wages. It is the sum of the initial wage, which is based on educational background, plus wage-level improvements, determined through collective bargaining (in the shunto spring labor offensive) at each firm.[9] If wage-level improvements consistently exceed the increase in initial wages, this element can be characterized as a seniority-oriented wage because senior employees receive more basic pay.

The important point is how wage-level improvements are distributed to individuals. Personnel with ranks equal to or lower than production chief are classified according to nine grades of ability qualifications. There are five ranks in each grade based on ability appraisals. An increase in basic pay is determined on the basis of the worker's grades of ability qualification and ability appraisal.

One characteristic of Toyota's wage system is the extremely small differentials in pay raises originating from appraisals. The major portion of the differentials arises from differences in grades of ability qualifications. Promotion to a higher grade of ability qualification is an important factor. Such promotions are based on seniority and accumulated ability appraisals.

Thus, not only does basic pay depend on seniority as a result of cumulative annual improvements to the initial wage level, but the distribution of wage-level improvements to individuals reflects promotions. As long as ability appraisals result in differentials in promotion, however, this basic pay has an aspect of the merit system.[10] Nevertheless, people in the same grade

[9]After the war, many Japanese firms determined basic pay by the following method: annual increments were granted before the spring negotiations; then the basic pay of the preceding fiscal year plus such annual increments for the current fiscal year were multiplied by percentages agreed upon in the spring negotiations. This was the basic formula for implementing the seniority wage system. Since Toyota does not have such an annual increment system, the company revises basic pay only through wage-level improvements. Even in this case, it is important to understand that the wage is based on seniority. If the wage-level improvement continues to exceed the initial wage increase, senior employees receive more basic pay.

[10]The ability grades of regularly recruited employees of the age of forty range from second to fifth among the nine grades.

receive pay raises that are not so different since the system tends not to reward those who remain at the same grade.

Pay for ability was introduced in 1990 with the intention of recognizing individuals' short-term "efforts." Pay for ability is not cumulative. This pay is determined in accordance with a table of performance appraisals consisting of five ranks for each grade of ability qualification. In that appraisals are performed annually, pay for ability reflects the results of these evaluations more directly than does basic pay. Nevertheless, the pay for ability differential within a given qualification grade is a few hundred yen, which is much less than the average among Japanese firms.

Pay for age was introduced in 1990, and amounts are prescribed for each age. Whereas the merit system was reinforced by pay for ability, pay for age is a clear expression of and an adjustment factor for the seniority system.

Pay for productivity is the product of a basic amount for each qualification multiplied by a coefficient based on the production efficiency of each section as explained above. Thus, pay for productivity can be viewed as group piecework. Group piecework was based on individual basic pay until 1993, when it was revised to more clearly reflect the merit system.

A few points are worth noting regarding workers' acceptance of this pay system. First, although the seniority system forms the basis of the wage system, worker effort cannot be obtained consistently without merit-oriented incentives. Second, incentive systems vary among firms. Toyota's is not typical. Wage differentials at Toyota are small for those with the same qualification grade, while promotions are given substantial weight. That is, incentive arises as a result of how personnel are managed rather than because of wages themselves, and pay for collective efficiency has been maintained.[11] Third and most important, the skills and attitudes of workers who support the underlying principles of lean production on the shop floor are properly evaluated in appraisals. At Toyota, "improvement ability," "ability to guide and teach," and "a sense of responsibility and cooperation" are valued as key factors in ability appraisals, along with "professional knowledge and skills." It is indispensable for the steady development of lean production that workers not only demonstrate improvement ability but impart this ability to subordinates and exercise

[11]Group piecework is not indispensable for implementing lean production. Among Japanese automakers, only Toyota has such a pay item. Although a system is necessary for managing production efficiency, many firms use individual personnel appraisals rather than group piecework to evaluate efforts on the shop floor. The reasons certain systems are being adopted are rooted in the histories of wage formulations and administration in particular companies.

self-control as members of an organization, without standing out excessively as individuals.

Labor-Management Relations and Enterprise Governance

One of the most important facts revealed above is that labor is remarkably individualized under the lean production system. It is inevitable with management by objectives by division on the shop floor that each shop-floor supervisor allocates nonroutine tasks to individual workers in accordance with their potential improvement abilities. Management has the exclusive authority over such allocations, and the incentives for the individual to accept this differentiated allocation of work are expressed in how this individual is remunerated based on his or her personnel appraisal. In other words, the so-called commodity of labor is bargained individually.

Another important fact is that lean production makes person-hour reduction a daily operation (no matter how nonroutine these efforts are) under the banner of continuous improvement. Put simply, person-hour reduction is rationalization, but plant management becomes stronger when rationalization is turned into a daily routine.

These two facts imply that the definition of trade unions in Europe and America primarily as organizations that engage in collective bargaining does not apply to Japanese unions. Further, the explanation that Japanese trade unions are organized by enterprise is inadequate. Although they are willing to have suborganizations at each plant, many European and American trade unions resist rationalization and personnel appraisals and commit themselves to bargaining collectively for the workforce.

The labor-management coordination and cooperation required to implement lean production cannot be assured without considering the structure of collective bargaining. The question here is how to ensure a persuasive argument for the dissolution of the collective bargaining structure. National characteristics are an important element in answering this question.

Postwar reforms are an obvious starting point in identifying these national characteristics, but one must remember that Toyota tried to reach a labor-management agreement on the basis of a rather individualistic social philosophy of "reward for effort" under the condition that lifetime employment and the seniority system should be maintained as a foundation of employment relations.

Japanese workers are not totally satisfied, however. In particular, there are four areas of dissatisfaction.

Staffing Levels. As the monthly production schedule changes, requirements for staffing levels also change. There is no problem if the staffing schedule indicated by the head-office personnel department is consistent with the staffing requirements of shop-floor section managers; however, workers must undertake heavier workloads if there are any discrepancies in calculations arising from utilization of paid leave, increases or decreases in the availability of support personnel, the availability of project personnel outside the production line, and so on. Someone from the plant-level branch of the union consults informally with the personnel group of the manufacturing department to address any problems prior to official central production meetings and personnel reassignment meetings.

Person-Hour Reductions. The union does not have any voice over person-hour reduction targets; however, it questions "unreasonable improvement." If shop-floor workers alert the union that one person will be eliminated when, in reality, improvement efforts cannot garner a reduction of even one person-hour, the president of the union branch discusses the situation with shop-floor department and section managers. The situation will usually be rectified if the union's claim is reasonable. Nevertheless, the important point is that there are few complaints about improvements. According to the president of one union branch in our survey, "That's because everyone regards improvement as part of their jobs."

Reassignment. Supervisors have the authority to decide who will be assigned to particular routine tasks (or stations) and how rotation will be done. The union does not have any voice in these decisions. Workers often regard assignments that are off the assembly line as desirable in terms of workload. Regardless of what workers feel about such assignments, however, their sentiments are not conveyed to the trade union. According to a branch chief, "That's because there are no expectations along the lines of 'ask and ye shall receive.' "

Personnel Appraisals. Although workers may have few complaints about job assignments or reassignments, they are sometimes dissatisfied with the results of appraisals and with decisions concerning promotions or upgrades. Such dissatisfaction is usually expressed indirectly as a perception of generalized unfairness, rather than as a specific grievance, and is resolved within the framework of a management mechanism called the appraisal adjustment meeting. These meetings are attended by production chiefs (the highest position held by union members), who are also primary appraisers. In other words, these meetings are outside the scope of labor-management relations.

Employment Systems and Job Security

The Japanese economy has experienced unprecedented changes since the end of the 1980s. These changes include the overheating that occurred in the early 1990s before the bubble burst, weakness in manufacturing industries caused by the long period of stagnation since 1992, and appreciation of the yen. It may be useful to summarize changes in the area of employment security during this unsettled time.

During the period of the bubble economy, changes were induced because of the tightness in labor markets (Fujita et al. 1995; Shimizu 1995). Young people also began turning down dirty, demanding, or dangerous jobs in the auto industry as highly paid work emerged in the service sector. Toyota sought to alter its production method by introducing a higher level of worker specialization at the No. 4 Tahara assembly plant, the Kyushu plant, and the No. 2 Motomachi plant. The innovations introduced by Toyota are summarized below.

Long assembly lines were broken up, so that three or four main lines were divided into eleven to twelve mini-lines, and, when possible, some tasks were transferred to sublines. An allowance of three to five cars was provided before and after the mini-lines to serve as buffers. Furthermore, a check-and-remedy process was introduced to enhance quality assurance on each mini-line. Each mini-line specialized in a particular system, such as the brake system, and the workers dedicated themselves to specific tasks. Finally, whereas tasks had previously been allocated to workers according to "baton time," workers in a given group now perform all related tasks to produce complete assemblies. It was thought that the new method might limit the flexibility with which task groups could be organized. Such flexibility had contributed positively to reducing the total quantity of people needed as well as to improving the ability to cope with production changes. To overcome potential problems, some tasks were designated as "transferable."

According to a survey report on the Tahara plant (Fujita et al. 1995), this innovative production method has resulted in improved productivity and increased worker motivation. Fewer corrections have been necessary later in the process as a result of an emphasis on self-contained task allocation. Furthermore, the time required to master a task has been shortened because all the workers in a group are involved in related work. The buffers before and after the mini-lines have reduced the psychological pressure on workers not to halt operation of the lines.

The lengthy period of economic stagnation and the high value of the yen also had a negative impact on employment in the auto industry. Automobile production peaked in Japan in 1990 at 13.49 million vehicles then fell steadily to 10.55 million vehicles in 1994. Labor adjustment to smaller production quantities had previously been achieved by reducing overtime hours and by natural attrition. The automobile industry has continued these practices since 1992 but has also used several other means of adjustment, which are discussed below.

Reduction in Use of Temporary Employees. Temporary workers are employed under contracts for three months, six months, or one year. Thus, the workforce is reduced if their contracts are not renewed. Toyota suspended this employment system in 1992, after recording a peak of 5,600 temporary workers in 1990 and, as a result, had no temporary workers in 1993 (*Mainichi Shimbun,* June 17, 1992; *Nihon Keizai Shimbun,* August 30, 1993). Mazda also employed temporary workers—a peak of 1,800 among its total of 14,500 factory workers in May 1992. The company entirely eliminated temporary workers by 1993. Tasks previously performed by temporary workers were done by 1,600 white-collar nonmanagerial employees who were transferred to factories (*Nihon Keizai Shimbun,* March 12, 1993). Similarly, Nissan had 3,500 temporary workers at the end of 1991 but none by 1993. Honda also suspended the hiring of temporary workers in July 1993 (*Nihon Keizai Shimbun,* August 30, 1993).

Layoffs. When the elimination of temporary workers was not sufficient to match labor to the level of production, manufacturers adopted layoff systems that specified a particular number of days per month for layoffs. Mazda had a companywide two-day layoff in November 1993 (*Asahi Shimbun,* December 10, 1993). It was reported that Mazda's Hofu factory continued its layoff until May 1994 (*Nihon Keizai Shimbun,* February 6, 1995). The market recovered in early 1995 but contracted again surrounding fears of declining exports caused by the appreciation of the yen. Mazda's head office factory began monthly two-day layoffs in April 1995, and its Bofu factory held several-day layoffs subsequently (*Nihon Keizai Shimbun,* April 8, 1995). Moreover, a monthly two-day layoff was implemented in July 1995 for indirect divisions such as those staffed by office workers (*Nikkei Sangyo Shimbun,*

May 31, 1995). Nissan's Tochigi factory, which specializes in luxury cars, held monthly four-day layoffs for a year and a half from November 1993 to May 1995 (*Nihon Keizai Shimbun*, February 6, 1995).

Outplacement. Nissan, which lost an estimated 160 billion yen (approximately U.S. $1.5 billion) in the first quarter of 1995, became the first automaker to implement an outplacement scheme. Following the closing of its Zama factory, two thousand employees were scheduled to be transferred to its Kyushu factory. But 120 of these employees were transferred to Nissan Shatai, an affiliated company, and were scheduled to take up employment there by 1997. Furthermore, more than half the employees of the textile machinery manufacturer Nissan Texis (which became independent of Nissan in 1993) were transferred from Nissan. Among them, 550 workers will change employers to Nissan Texis over the course of several years (*Nihon Keizai Shimbun*, February 21, 1995).

Medium-Term Manpower Reduction Plans. Reducing working hours and eliminating temporary workers was not enough to adjust labor in line with the extent to which production had fallen. Consequently, there was a need for medium-term plans to reduce the number of regular employees through natural attrition over the course of three years. Mazda, which posted a loss in 1993, planned to reduce its workforce from thirty thousand to twenty-seven thousand over three years. In 1994, however, Mazda received more applications than anticipated from workers fifty years and older seeking to participate in its early retirement with incentives plan, and it was estimated that the company's workforce would shrink to twenty-six thousand by the end of 1995. Mazda expects to further reduce the number of workers to twenty-three thousand during the three years beginning in 1996. By limiting recruitment, the total workforce is expected to contract by about one thousand annually because of natural attrition. The company anticipates redundancies totaling approximately three thousand in its office divisions and will continue to reassign workers from office divisions to factories and to transfer them to sales departments (*Nihon Keizai Shimbun*, November 11, 1995).

Nissan also recorded a loss in the first quarter of 1993. While implementing a three-year structural improvement plan since 1992, the company formulated another three-year plan to begin in 1996. Under the new plan it is expected that the company's total workforce will be reduced by six to seven thousand from forty-nine thousand as of March 1995, with annual natural attrition of approximately two thousand. Nissan believes it will have fifteen thousand redundant white-collar workers, of whom 20 percent will be reassigned to direct divisions or transferred to sales companies or affiliated parts manufacturers. Outplacement to these companies will be encouraged but will be dependent on the consent of the individual workers concerned (*Nihon Keizai Shimbun*, March 6, 1995).

Honda formulated a restructuring plan and decided to reduce its workforce from forty-three thousand to forty thousand over three years, while shifting production of its popular Accord and Civic models from Japan to the United States. With the annual retirement of twelve hundred workers, Honda's workforce will decline by one thousand every year if hiring is controlled (*Nihon Keizai Shimbun*, September 18, 1993). According to its three-year medium-term plan, which was begun in 1996, the staffing of affiliated dealers will be increased from nine thousand to thirteen thousand to boost domestic sales and three hundred head office personnel will be transferred to dealers. Furthermore, outplacement will be allowed if the individuals concerned agree to a change of employment (*Nihon Keizai Shimbun*, January 17, 1995).

Conclusions

The Japanese automobile manufacturers have implemented a wide range of strategies in recent decades to ensure that the organization of work in their assembly plants remains flexible and adaptable. Some researchers have questioned the degree of autonomy available to Japanese work groups to make decisions (e.g., Dohse, Jürgens, and Malsch 1985; Jürgens, Malsch, and Dohse 1993); however, the Japanese producers have introduced continuous improvements in productivity and quality, given extensive training to supervisors who play key roles in workplace change, and implemented extensive job rotation and work group activities to enhance the skills of the workforce. Aspects of the lean production system that Womack, Jones, and Roos (1990) have identified as characteristic of assembly work at Toyota, in particular, appear to be in a process of change. At the same time, some of the Japanese transplants in the United States and Britain that are using aspects of lean production have successfully introduced forms of management and work organization that have yielded much higher productivity rates and quality than the local manufacturers. Such changes will ensure that developments in employee relations and the management of production among Japanese automobile companies, such as Toyota and Mazda, continue to attract international attention.

4 United States: Variations on a Theme

Paul S. Adler, Thomas A. Kochan,
John Paul MacDuffie, Frits K. Pil,
and Saul Rubinstein

Labor-management relations, workplace innovations, and human resource practices play a pivotal role in the economic performance and competitiveness of the U.S. auto industry. Chapter 2 reviewed the second round of the assembly plant surveys and provides the best available basis for assessing the extent to which the manufacturing, human resource, work organization, and labor-management practices associated with lean production have been diffused in the United States relative to other countries. The overall picture to emerge from the surveys is that some U.S. plants are adopting key elements of lean production and the associated labor-management practices, but, in general, U.S. plants have not moved as rapidly as the European plants. The gap between Japanese plants in Japan and Japanese transplants in the United States on the one hand and U.S.-owned and -managed plants on the other has been closed slightly but remains significant. The survey results also show that differences between country averages hide considerable variations within countries and across plants of the same companies.

In this chapter we look more closely at several U.S. companies and plants in an effort to understand these variations. In doing so, we sharpen both our understanding of the process by which innovations in work practices are diffused, adapted to different settings, and modified in ways that produce new innovations of their own.

Various plants representing the full range of current practice in the United States are presented as separate cases. We start with the Saturn Division of General Motors since it represents the most radical departure from traditional production, organization, and employment practices found in any plant in the United States. This is followed by a comparison of Toyota's Georgetown, Kentucky, plant and the Toyota-GM joint venture known as NUMMI. The features implemented in these two transplants are compared both with Toyota's parent facility in Japan and, where relevant, with the traditional mass production practices typically found in U.S. plants in the past. We then discuss two plants that illustrate the mix of mass production and lean production practices found in the majority of the plants of the Big Three firms (GM, Ford, and Chrysler). We choose one from Chrysler (the new Jefferson North plant) and one from GM (the refurbished Wilmington plant), which together illustrate the processes by which U.S. firms are transforming their operations on a case-by-case (plant-by-plant) basis as new investments and models are introduced.

Saturn

From its initial stages of planning, conducted by a "Committee of 99" GM and UAW representatives, Saturn has been conceived of as a full partnership between the union and the company. The establishment of the Saturn Corporation, a wholly owned subsidiary of GM, was motivated by the desire to build and sell a small car in the United States that would compete well against imports. The decision to create an entirely new company in a greenfield site was made after GM's management concluded that the company could not competitively manufacture a small car in the United States under the existing labor contract and labor-management practices. Thus, in 1983, GM and the UAW began a joint study of the feasibility of starting with a clean sheet of paper, but one that built on data gathered from benchmarking experiences from around the world, in GM's most innovative facilities, and at NUMMI.

The Committee of 99 produced an organizational design that makes the UAW an institutional "partner" in consensus-based decision making from the shop floor to the senior management levels of the corporation. This structure makes Saturn the boldest experiment in comanagement in the United States today. The organization is overseen by a series of "decision rings" at the department, plant, or business unit, manufacturing policy, and strategic policy levels of the organization. Each ring consists of union and management representatives that meet periodically (usually weekly) to share information, consult on upcoming decisions, and make decisions.

The partnership organization has evolved beyond the initial twenty-eight-page collective bargaining agreement that outlined the basic principles governing the relationship and the team-based system of work organization. For example, at the department or module level, management responsibilities are shared by a union module adviser who is partnered with a nonrepresented management module adviser. Until 1994, jointly selected UAW crew coordinators had responsibility, along with their nonrepresented partners, for managing crews across several departments (the responsibility of superintendents in GM's more traditional plants). In 1994, as a result of a negotiated agreement, and in response to considerable pressure from rank-and-file workers, the fourteen UAW crew coordinators became elected officials with the authority to file grievances.

Other labor-management and human resource practices are also innovative. Saturn requires all employees to take a minimum of ninety-two hours of training each year. In 1995, 20 percent of compensation was contingent on completion of this minimal amount of training. In addition, more than 80 percent of the workforce is guaranteed employment security for life.

The Saturn work organization is based on self-directed work teams of ten to fifteen members who are cross-trained and rotate among all the tasks in their unit. Teams have responsibility for hiring new members and electing team leaders. Teams also have responsibility for quality assurance, job assignments, record keeping, safety and health, material and inventory control, training, supplies, and housekeeping. Modules encompass an average of five to seven teams and have weekly governance meetings at which teams are represented by their leaders.

The manufacturing system builds on the principles of the lean production model, including the need for team-based production, reduced buffers and just-in-time inventories, problem solving for continuous improvement, minimal job classifications, and a salaried wage structure. In some ways, however, the Saturn manufacturing system bears unique marks of its own. For example, the degree to which the union is involved in firm governance is clearly a significant departure from practice in both GM plants and in the rest of the industry, including firms engaging in lean production. Through the partnership arrangements, the union at Saturn is an important actor in decisions regarding supplier and dealer selection, choice of technology, and product development. Finally, the management structure, whereby 50 percent of the middle managers involved in plant operations are members of the UAW, challenges long-held beliefs about the separation of management and labor.

Saturn's task and job design represents an attempt to synthesize a European sociotechnical approach with the Japanese lean production system. Saturn teams have far greater decision-making autonomy than teams in Japan; while most lean production plants continue to rely on short job cycles of about sixty seconds, Saturn teams have organized jobs around cycle times that can extend up to six minutes; and in the assembly plant, moving platforms carry workers along with cars as they perform several different operations on the vehicle.

Saturn uses as its marketing slogan and logo "A Different Kind of Car, a Different Kind of Company." It thus builds on its partnership with the UAW and several other distinctive features, such as its fixed-price, no-haggle retail sales and service strategy, in positioning the company and its products in the minds of consumers. To date this approach has been very well received by the market. Within two years of its first production run in 1990 and each year since, Saturn achieved higher ratings in initial vehicle quality, satisfaction after one year of ownership, and service than any car in its class. According to the 1992 through 1994 J. D. Power surveys, only the Lexus and the Infiniti, two upscale models that cost three times as much as the Saturn, received higher customer satisfaction ratings.

Saturn's ratings for productivity and profitability are not as high as those for quality, however. Investment in product development, the plant, and equipment is estimated at $5 billion. In evaluating profitability, a question arises as to whether Saturn, operating at only 60 percent of its original business plan capacity, should amortize this investment alone or whether the rest of GM, which has benefited from Saturn's innovations, should share in its costs. (GM scaled back the original capacity plan and investment when the corporation was experiencing serious losses and cash shortages in the early 1990s.) Saturn generated its first operating profit in 1993 after putting on its third crew and being pressured by its GM parent to cut costs and move up the date targeted for it to make a profit. Bonuses based on financial, productivity, and quality goals were paid to Saturn employees in 1993, 1994, and 1995. The 1995 bonus totaled $10,000 for each UAW member, the maximum allowable under the contract.

Saturn remains a controversial organization within both the UAW international union and the GM Corporation. The UAW leadership and the leaders of the Saturn UAW local have been in conflict over a host of issues ranging from the adequacy of representation surrounding traditional union concerns to shift schedules, overtime and shift premiums, and other administrative matters. Political factions have also arisen within the local (similar to those that have developed within other UAW local unions), and each election of union officers since 1992 has been hotly contested. Membership surveys and focus group interviews have also documented the buildup of some dissatisfaction with the representation of individual workers' concerns by the union. This pressure led to the election of crew coordinators with authority to file grievances on behalf of individual workers. Thus, the union at Saturn continues to search for the right balance between partnership and participation in management and governance and traditional forms of employee representation and dispute resolution.

GM management has also been ambivalent toward Saturn. On the one hand, the corporation relishes the positive image that Saturn has achieved and has urged other divisions to learn from Saturn's experiences. On the other hand, although technical and marketing innovations have been adopted, there is little evidence that significant learning from or diffusion of the organizational principles being followed at Saturn has occurred within GM. Moreover, to date GM has committed funds requested by Saturn (and part of the original Saturn business plan) to design and build a second-generation model not in Spring Hill, Tennessee, but in an older plant in Wilmington, Delaware. (This development is described in greater detail below.) Thus, despite the positive publicity the UAW-Saturn partnership has received and its success in the areas of quality and marketing, the long-term financial payback to GM, along with the ambivalent support from both parents (UAW international and GM), leave the future of Saturn somewhat uncertain.

Saturn nevertheless exemplifies a new model of organization that goes well beyond the principles of lean production. More than any other U.S. case, Saturn illustrates the positive organizational partnership and employment system that can be created when a union with a vision participates in the design, governance, and management of the enterprise. Workers have a strong voice in traditional labor-management concerns as well as in broader managerial and strategic issues. Principles of teamwork, continuous improvement, quality, safety, ergonomics, and customer satisfaction are given high priority. Conflicts occur both within and across traditional labor and management boundaries but are managed and resolved in ways very different from those used during traditional contract negotiations or grievance arbitration processes. Thus, although Saturn's manufacturing policies are rooted in lean production principles, they introduce features that are responsive to worker and union concerns to expand their role in decision making through joint governance and comanagement arrangements.

Whether the limited profitability of Saturn to date means that some of the financial rewards will be redistributed across the different stakeholders at the expense of shareholders is still an open question and one that is likely to be the subject of considerable debate in the future. Whatever the outcome, Saturn clearly has served as an important opportunity for everyone in the auto industry (in North America and worldwide) to observe and learn from an organizational design and strategy that has pushed industrial and labor relations beyond the framework of lean production.

Two Japanese Transplants

As subsidiaries of multinational corporations, Japanese transplants face a range of alternatives between adoption and adaptation of the policies and practices of their parent companies (Abo 1994). In this section we compare two Toyota transplants—NUMMI in Fremont, California, and the Georgetown, Kentucky, plant, hereafter referred to as Georgetown—to illustrate some of the causes and consequences of these adoption/adaptation choices. Although NUMMI is a joint venture of GM and Toyota Motors Corporation (TMC), the day-to-day operations of the plant are under Toyota control. Georgetown is a wholly owned Toyota subsidiary.

A closer look at these subsidiaries is useful since it reveals first that at least in these two cases, the adoption/adaptation choices are differentiated across the various elements of the management system. Local management is tasked by Toyota headquarters with faithful implementation of the Toyota production system, but the other elements of the management system are deliberately tailored to local conditions. The former president of Georgetown, Fujio Cho, described the policy in these terms: "I told people here that the [Japanese] coordinators were teachers on production issues and TPS but that they were the students in the office areas such as Legal, Human Resources, and Public Affairs" (interview with coauthor Adler, 1994).

A comparison of NUMMI and Georgetown also reveals that the adaptations made by individual subsidiaries in the same host country can differ significantly. Most notably, NUMMI is unionized whereas Georgetown is not. A close analysis of their policies reveals other, more subtle differences. We briefly describe the histories of each of the two plants, then compare their human resource management policies.

NUMMI. NUMMI was created in 1983 as a joint venture between Toyota and GM, with its mission to produce small cars for sale by both partners. It has succeeded admirably.

The company took over the GM-Fremont plant, which had been closed in 1982 and had a long history of poor productivity, quality, and labor relations. Although Toyota was initially reluctant to work with the UAW, NUMMI agreed to recognize the union and to give priority to rehiring the laid-off workers. The initial 1985 collective bargaining contract embodied a very different role for the union than prevailed in the Big Three plants. The introduction stated that the union and management "are committed to building and maintaining the most innovative and harmonious labor-management relation in America." The union accepted the implementation of the Toyota production system, and management committed to a no-layoff policy.

Production began in 1984, and by 1986, with largely the same workforce and comparable equipment, NUMMI had achieved productivity levels almost twice those of GM-Fremont in its best years, 40 percent better than those of the typical Big Three assembly plant, and very close to those of its Toyota sister plant in Takaoka. It was also producing the highest quality levels in the industry. Through the early 1990s, the plant continued to excel in quality and productivity.

During those early years, worker satisfaction and commitment were high. Almost unanimously, NUMMI workers reported that they would not want to switch jobs if there were a Big Three plant across the street (Adler 1993; Holusha 1989). In anonymous biannual surveys of team members, the proportion of workers who said they were "satisfied with [their] job and environment" increased progressively from 65 percent in 1985 to 90 percent in 1991 and 1993.

In 1989, Toyota announced that it would invest another $350 million to expand the plant and begin production of pickup trucks. This led to the hiring of an additional seven hundred workers—selected from an applicant pool of nine thousand—which brought total employment up to thirty-seven hundred.

In developing its management systems, NUMMI followed a policy applicable to all of Toyota's overseas operations: local management was tasked with faithful implementation of the Toyota production system, but the supporting organizational systems were to be tailored to local conditions. Toyota defines its production system as encompassing *kanban* (just-in-time inventory control), production leveling, kaizen, visual control, *poka-yoke* (error-proofing), teams, and standardized work. Since the key components of work organization as described in chapters 1 and 2 (the use of teams, rotation, quality circles, suggestion systems) are part of the Toyota production system, it is not surprising that NUMMI's production system conforms more closely to the Toyota model than do NUMMI's human resource management practices (such as its compensation, status differentials, and training).

NUMMI's work practices resemble those at its sister plant in Takaoka. Takaoka has only one classification for production workers and one for workers in the skilled trades, whereas NUMMI has one classification for production workers and two for workers in the skilled trades. The differentiation of tasks between categories is significantly more rigid, however.

As in Japan, all production and skilled trades workers at NUMMI are organized into small teams of five to eight people. These teams have little autonomy. They cannot pace their work, since they are tied to the pace of the assembly line; and they have no role in hiring or firing or in any other higher-level decisions. These teams are, however, the key structure for job rotation and process improvement.

The aim of job rotation at NUMMI is to increase operational flexibility, alleviate boredom, and reduce ergonomic strain. The number of teams actually rotating has fluctuated. Initially, rotation was left to the teams, and many ended up not rotating. After a conflict over ergonomics came to a head in 1993, management made rotation a formal policy, and the practice has increased.

Quality circles (called "problem-solving circles," or PSCs) were introduced at NUMMI in 1991, making the program relatively new. NUMMI's PSCs are more truly voluntary than in Toyota's Japanese plants, although participation is expected of workers hoping for promotion to team leader positions. PSCs are structured as standing committees based on work groups (not teams, as in Japan). In an average month during 1994, 14 percent of NUMMI workers participated in the PSC program.

The suggestion system at NUMMI is very similar to that used at Toyota in Japan. The focus is on encouraging a high proportion of the workforce to submit a large number of small-scale suggestions. By 1994, well over 90 percent of NUMMI's workers were participating. More than 90 percent of suggestions are implemented, and although workers receive only modest financial rewards if their suggestions are implemented, they are given considerable symbolic recognition.

The supporting HR practices at NUMMI are relatively differentiated from the HR practices at Toyota's Japanese plants. NUMMI follows the Big Three/UAW wage levels very closely and also replicates the industry standard pay structure, unlike Toyota, which has an individualized pay system. NUMMI has no seniority/age component, no personal assessment, and no department performance bonus. Since 1991, NUMMI has had a gain-sharing program called Performance Improvement Plan Sharing that rewards workers for meeting improvement goals in plantwide quality and efficiency.

Under this plan, each worker received $700 in 1991, $645 in 1992, $733 in 1993, and $1,285 in 1994.

Like the other transplants surveyed by MacDuffie and Pil and discussed in chapter 2, NUMMI goes far beyond both Toyota and the U.S. Big Three in its suppression of visible status differentials. Managers at NUMMI have neither a separate parking lot nor a separate cafeteria and more often than not wear uniforms rather than suits.

The intensity of training for production workers at NUMMI resembles that found at Takaoka. But whereas Takaoka management encourages production workers to broaden their skills by planning moves from one area of the plant to another over a period of years, job changes at NUMMI are determined primarily by seniority and personal preference and thus resemble the more traditional American pattern (Brown and Reich 1995).

The industrial relations context of these practices is an important feature of NUMMI. Its collective bargaining agreement makes an explicit commitment to employment security, and NUMMI lived up to the commitment in 1987–88, when capacity utilization fell to less than 60 percent but no one was laid off. Workers were put into extra training programs and were put to work on kaizen projects and facilities maintenance jobs that had previously been contracted out.

Although UAW Local 2244 retains its affiliation with the international, the local's leadership cooperates with NUMMI management through an extensive structure of joint committees. There are weekly meetings between management and the union bargaining committee, weekly safety committee meetings, weekly meetings between section managers and committee people, and quarterly three-day off-site meetings between union and company leadership. The recent shift in the leadership of the local from the Administration Caucus to the People's Caucus has not significantly reduced the high level of dialogue and cooperation.

NUMMI's "problem resolution procedure" resembles Takaoka's in its emphasis on joint problem solving as the first step; but subsequent steps bring NUMMI's procedure into closer conformance with the traditional UAW model, including its use of third-party arbitration as the final step. The combination of an industrial union and a local that is involved extensively in planning and joint forums suggests that NUMMI represents a hybrid of Toyota and American traditions.

A key issue facing workers at NUMMI is whether their union is capable of playing the important role assigned it in this system (see Adler, Goldoftas, and Levine 1997). Local 2244 has accomplished a great deal for NUMMI's workforce. To mention just a few items: within the pattern set by GM-UAW settlements, the local has bargained effectively to add new benefits; NUMMI workers have no fear of reprisal for voicing complaints; and when workers became frustrated with perceived favoritism in management's selection of team leaders, the union negotiated a joint-selection procedure. Moreover, to the benefit of both workers and the company, the union voice has helped workers gain equity, credibility, and legitimacy—and has thus encouraged worker commitment and production effectiveness.

The conditions under which the local operates create some important challenges, however. First, the local cannot rely on the international to provide as much intellectual and material support as it provides to Big Three locals. For example, following the OSHA crackdown in the late 1980s, Big Three companies began addressing ergonomics more seriously, and corporate-level labor-management committees developed programs that were adopted in many plants—resulting in significantly better programs than at NUMMI (see Adler, Goldoftas, and Levine, forthcoming.) More generally, one has to sympathize with NUMMI's union leaders, who have been forced to invent their own way in a highly unusual labor-management system. It was not until 1992 that the international brought together the locals from the three unionized Japanese transplants.

Second, and related to the first challenge, neither of the two caucuses within the local has managed to elaborate a compelling interpretation of the role of the union at NUMMI. The Administration Caucus became comfortable in its new role as a participant in discussions about the policies that affect the plant's overall direction, but it has been less successful in convincing members that it will defend their interests in cases when conflict might be necessary. The People's Caucus, currently dominant in the local, has presented a more assertive profile, but it has not articulated a vision of how it will take advantage of the possible benefits of labor-management cooperation.

Third, the local has been partially paralyzed by internal conflicts. The relationship between the caucuses has been contentious and counterproductive. At the peak of intercaucus conflict, many union committees stopped functioning altogether, and longtime members voiced bitterness about the high level of acrimony at union meetings.

Fourth, and finally, the local has not had a tradition of fostering the kind of active internal democracy that seems required to capitalize on NUMMI's more cooperative form of labor-management relations. At NUMMI, more issues are open to union input than at Big Three plants, and many cannot await the traditional three-year bargaining cycle. The UAW tradition has been a somewhat top-down one: leaders lead, and members express their post factum assessments by voting them back in or out every three years. The union needs to invent ways to sustain more active, continuous involvement of the rank and file in governance of the local.

Toyota Georgetown. Toyota's Georgetown plant, part of the company's strategy for building capacity in the United States, was a successor to NUMMI and leveraged some of the lessons Toyota managers felt they had learned there. Whereas NUMMI was a joint venture, Toyota managers now felt they knew enough about the U.S. environment to operate a wholly owned subsidiary (formally called Toyota Motor Manufacturing). Further, whereas GM had imposed NUMMI's location and in doing so made union recognition a de facto requirement, Toyota chose to locate the new operation in a rural area and to stay nonunion insofar as possible.

Plant construction began in 1986, and volume production of the Camry began in 1988. Plant expansions were made in 1988, 1989, and then again in 1993 for the launch of the Avalon. Compared with NUMMI, Georgetown's products were in higher-margin, upscale segments, which afforded the plant more opportunity for automation. By 1994, total investment had reached more than $4 billion.

Hiring began in 1987. Georgetown management was extremely cautious to avoid the charges of discriminatory hiring leveled at other transplants. Nevertheless, compared with NUMMI, Georgetown was much more highly selective. There were some fifty thousand applicants for the initial three thousand jobs. Successful applicants had to make it through a total of eighteen hours of tests and interviews as well as reference checks. By 1994, total employment reached six thousand, and the total number of applicants over the period had been more than two hundred thousand. All the blue-collar and white-collar employees have at least a high school–level education, and more than 50 percent have some college. Only 2 percent have any background in the auto industry, however.

Quality and productivity have been very high—as high or higher than at NUMMI, and close to the world-class standards set in Georgetown's sister plant in Tsutsumi. Based on interviews and various objective indicators, it seems that worker commitment and satisfaction levels have also been high (see also Besser 1996).

The practices that undergird this success are broadly similar to those at NUMMI: rather rigid conformance to the core elements of the Toyota production system and plant-specific adaptations in the HR arena. Although work practices resemble those at NUMMI and Tsutsumi, some nuances are worth noting. First, rotation has been a more systematic practice for longer at Georgetown than at NUMMI. As at NUMMI, rotation was initially haphazard, but a surge in repetitive strain injuries within the first year of startup led management to insist on ergonomically balanced rotations as part of a comprehensive health and safety program.

Second, Georgetown started its quality circles program in 1989, sooner after plant startup than at NUMMI. Quality circles usually meet monthly on paid overtime, whereas at NUMMI they meet at lunchtime and management pays the workers' lunch. In an average month in 1993, about 40 percent of the Georgetown workers participated in a quality circle.

HR practices are somewhat more differentiated at Georgetown than at Tsutsumi. The pay levels and structure conform closely to the practice at NUMMI and at Big Three plants. Indeed, management regularly distributes comparisons of the wage rates of its team members and the rates at the Big Three. As of 1993, Georgetown ranked second—after NUMMI—for both production and skilled trades workers. There are two gain-sharing-type programs, one based on a percentage of the worker's pay and the other paying identical amounts. But notwithstanding plans to individualize workers' pay, so far this has not been done.

The most distinctive feature of Georgetown is its labor relations. Georgetown is nonunion and follows a conscious "union substitution" strategy (Kochan 1980). This strategy imposes real constraints on the plant since the UAW threat is real: there are workers in the plant who wear UAW T-shirts, and the UAW office in Georgetown leaflets the plant regularly.

The union substitution strategy is expressed in several ways. First, as we have noted, the pay levels and structure are patterned after the unionized sector. Second, Georgetown expresses a commitment to employment security, but whereas NUMMI's collective bargaining agreement specifies in considerable detail the company's commitment to a no-layoff policy, Georgetown's position is more nuanced. Fearful of the legal consequences of making an explicit commitment, and perhaps hoping to reserve for management a greater margin of flexibility in hard times, the Georgetown team member handbook describes "career employment" as a "goal" but emphasizes that it is "not a legal commitment nor a contract."

Third, Georgetown has an extensive set of mechanisms to identify workers' concerns and grievances. A "concern resolution process" parallels NUMMI's problem resolution procedure but affords employees no opportunity for representation and provides no recourse to third-party arbitration. Georgetown also has a twenty-four-hour-a-day message system called the Hotline for workers to register complaints, anonymously if they desire. There are also employee opinion surveys regularly (as at NUMMI), round-table meetings between team members and senior management, and managers' "lunchbox meetings."

Fourth, Georgetown's discipline process, its "corrective action program," is patterned after the "positive discipline" policy found at several "progressive" nonunion U.S. companies (Campbell, Fleming, and Grote 1985; Cameron 1984). The penultimate step is a day of "decision-making leave." The final step (for all cases but those of serious misconduct) is appearance before a voluntary peer review panel made up of three team members and two managers. Membership on the panel is voluntary and rotating. Its judgment is only advisory, and no third-party arbitration is available to the worker.

Corresponding to the challenges posed by the UAW to NUMMI's viability, Georgetown must manage the challenges and risks created by its union substitution strategy. First, apparently concerned about the legality of nonunion representative committees under Section 8(a)2 of the National Labor Relations Act, Georgetown management has not established any mechanism for "interest aggregation." As a result, it is difficult for management to channel frustrations that inevitably arise in adjudicating competing priorities and claims; and since wages are significantly higher than those available elsewhere in the region, dissatisfied workers stay on, resentful, rather than leave.

Second, over the longer term, and absent the challenge of a union, the commitment of managers to the underlying core values may dissipate. Most notably, managers recruited from outside (from Big Three auto companies in particular) bring with them values that are deeply ingrained and often autocratic; these values have to be changed and translated into the myriad details of everyday work and must take root there as new habits; under pressure to improve business performance, managers who have not completely "internalized" these new values are likely to revert to the more deeply ingrained older values.

So far, however, these risks are merely hypothetical. Copying rather closely the work practices of the Toyota production system but associating them with different human resource management systems, both Georgetown and NUMMI have achieved world-class levels of productivity and quality and so far have managed to sustain high levels of worker commitment.

Summary. NUMMI and Georgetown have adopted Toyota's approaches in some areas and in other areas have adapted Toyota's practices to fit both the American union and nonunion context. The transplants *adopted* most of Toyota's practices with respect to work organization and small-group participation. They also invested heavily in skills development and training, consistent with Toyota's approach in Japan. In the areas of labor and employee relations, however, considerable *adaptation* is visible. For the union setting at NUMMI, Toyota implemented its own version of a labor-management partnership that accepts the UAW as a shop-floor partner without going as far as Saturn's approach to comanagement and joint governance at intermediate and higher strategic levels of decision making. In its nonunion plant, Toyota adopted many practices found in American plants managed under a "progressive" union substitution approach. Not withstanding these differences, however, Toyota has been able to achieve high levels of quality and productivity in both these facilities. This suggests that there is considerable flexibility in the way high performance can be achieved using the lean production model.

Chrysler's Jefferson North Plant, Detroit

No Chrysler plant captures the juxtaposition of new approaches with very strong traditions better than the new Jefferson North plant in Detroit. This plant was the first new Big Three assembly plant built in southern Michigan in more than ten years. It opened in 1992 to build the newly redesigned Grand Cherokee, a luxury sport utility model that Chrysler had acquired as part of the Jeep family of products from the American Motors Corporation. Jefferson North replaced the Jefferson Avenue plant, which was one of the first five manufacturing plants established by Walter Chrysler early in this century and Chrysler's oldest plant (with the oldest workforce) by the time it closed in 1990. With its two-story main building and detached paint shop connected by an over-the-street conveyor, Jefferson Avenue faced staggering problems in production flow and logistics that impaired its efficiency considerably. Yet it had a strong reputation within the company for having a dedicated if feisty workforce and made an important contribution to Chrysler's comeback from near-bankruptcy in the early 1980s, when it became the first plant to build the Aries/Reliant "K" cars, popular and affordable family sedans.

Jefferson Avenue had a dramatic history of confrontational labor relations spearheaded by a series of charismatic local leaders who could successfully rally their memberships to resist management initiatives in various ways—including with wildcat and "work-to-rule" strikes. In the 1960s, Jefferson Avenue was the strongest base of support for the Dodge Revolutionary Union Movement, a radical splinter group that fought both management and the UAW establishment. Yet Jefferson's UAW Local 7 was quick to agree to wage and work-rule concessions in the face of the 1979 bankruptcy threat. Jefferson was also the first plant to vote to adopt the Modern Operating Agreement in 1986. (As mentioned in chapter 2, the MOA was established through collective bargaining, developed nationally and voted on locally, as a means for full-scale changeover of work and human resource practices at existing brownfield plants. The MOA involved the use of work teams, more flexible work organization, new compensation plans, and the decentralization of quality responsibilities and a heavy investment in training in technical and problem-solving skills. A joint union-management steering committee oversees the MOA implementation process.)

Although the MOA changes were intended to take effect even before the move to the new Jefferson North plant, early implementation was plagued by labor-management conflicts. For example, when Chrysler sold some parts plants that were part of its Acustar subsidiary without consulting with the UAW, the union insisted that MOA efforts at Jefferson Avenue be put on hold. As demand for the K car dwindled during the late 1980s, Jefferson Avenue received an even older model (Omni/Horizon) to build for a while. Then, in the fall of 1990, Chrysler decided that sales of this model were too low and announced that it was closing Jefferson Avenue earlier than planned—again without consulting with the UAW or Local 7. In protest, MOA training was canceled immediately.

Despite the turmoil surrounding the transition from the old to the new plant and the startup of the MOA, excitement about the new Jefferson North plant soon predominated. The shutdown period (during which Local 7 members received layoff benefits) provided ample time for extensive training, both in preparation for the MOA (team concept, pay-for-knowledge, reduced job classifications) and for the new technology that would be introduced. This training was complicated by the relatively low literacy levels among the Jefferson Avenue workers yet was received enthusiastically.

The launch of the new plant in January 1993 was accompanied by considerable fanfare and high spirits. The Grand Cherokee was heralded from the start and sales rose rapidly, so that by 1994 the plant was operating overtime five days a week.

By all accounts, the MOA has been well received at Jefferson North. In a survey of individual attitudes toward the MOA at six Chrysler plants, workers at Jefferson North were among the most positive, particularly about their experiences with teams. Also noteworthy was the high percentage of workers who agreed that the MOA was contributing to improved productivity, quality, and safety. Workers report relatively high participation in completing the "twenty team duties" that each team is expected to perform, and nearly all teams hold weekly meetings to work on these tasks. They perceive that they have more control over the scheduling of overtime and the layout of their work areas and greater freedom from close supervision.

When the plant first opened, training levels were quite high, so that most team members were learning the additional jobs they needed to know to advance under the "capability-progression-pay" (CPP) system. The atmosphere at the plant is also markedly egalitarian: there are common parking areas and a common cafeteria, and managers do not wear neckties. Furthermore, with Chrysler's profits soaring on the strength of sales of such popular models as the Grand Cherokee, workers at Jefferson North have received sizable profit-sharing bonuses in recent years—in striking contrast with the wage concessions they were forced to make just fifteen years earlier.

Although it has most of the visible structural elements of lean production in place, Jefferson North has been less successful at transforming daily work processes in the direction of continuous improvement. According to several indicators, the plant has had difficulty achieving high levels of ongoing problem-solving activities. Workers initially rotated jobs to learn the skills needed for pay increases under the CPP system, but rotation was stopped once most of them reached the top of the CPP pay scale. Subsequently, jobs on teams were allocated on an (unofficial) seniority basis according to difficulty.

After the initial surge of training, ongoing training activities have dropped considerably, in part because of scheduling difficulties created by the heavy reliance on overtime hours. The number of suggestions from workers is still very low, although a very high percentage of suggestions are implemented. And although the assembly line was set up to include various line-side "terminals" where production-related information could be punched in and accumulated, workers typically do not use them. Much of the attention to daily production problems is still undertaken by engineers and manufacturing staff. For the workforce at Jefferson North, which has the oldest average age of any assembly plant in the United States, the large amount of overtime makes the job sufficiently demanding that there is little incentive to put extra effort into problem-solving activities.

As many of the older workers at Jefferson North have reached the "thirty and out" retirement age, the plant has begun hiring replacement workers. An outside firm runs an "assessment center" that tests reading and math skills, evaluates interpersonal skills, and runs applicants through some group-based production simulation exercises. These workers are much more highly educated than the workers they are replacing—averaging more than a year of post–high school education, typically at a community college—but they enter at the pay level specified for new hires in the UAW contract. Chrysler gives these workers extensive training.

As of the spring of 1996, there were too few of these workers to tell how they will affect the dynamics in the plant. Early indications are that the older workers feel that the new, younger workers lack the work ethic that they have and are more likely to complain about their workload. Union officials accustomed to skirmishing with management now find themselves joining with managers each week for orientation and training of these new employees.

One issue that has concerned Jefferson North's workers is that few of the new hires are from Detroit and specifically that many sons and daughters and cousins of existing workers have applied but not made it through the rigorous selection process. Local 7 has made it a priority to create more job possibilities for the next generation in autoworkers' families, and in a recent agreement with management that avoided a potential dispute over outsourcing, each worker was given the right to give a referral card to one friend or relative that will give that person preference in the hiring process.

Chrysler management clearly has high hopes for the new hires. The company expects to be able to reduce supervisory levels—already at a span of control of one supervisor to forty workers—to a level of one per one hundred workers by the year 2000. In connection with redoubled efforts to bring lean production methods into its plants and improve product quality, Chrysler intends to boost the training given to new hires and to increase its expectations about workers' contributions to performance improvements. In the meantime, both plant management and local union officials may have their hands full managing a workforce that is divided generationally, that has different educational levels and different expectations, and in which one group has less attachment to the Jefferson North plant and its predecessor and fewer reasons to feel strong commitment to the company. Furthermore, new workers are likely to adopt the norms of the current workforce with respect to involvement in problem-solving activities. Thus, the tale of Jefferson North is partly one of successful transition of a brownfield workforce into a greenfield plant but partly the tale of how strong and durable the "old plant" mentality can be, even as new hires are brought in.

GM's Wilmington, Delaware, Plant

The workers at General Motors' assembly plant in Wilmington, Delaware, had as tumultuous a series of experiences in the 1980s and 1990s as those at Chrysler's Jefferson North, although the pattern of ups and downs was very different.

In the early 1980s, GM was the strongest company, in terms of market share and financial strength, of the Big Three. As part of CEO Roger Smith's campaign to "leapfrog" Japanese competitors with a "high-tech" manufacturing strategy, Wilmington was one of several GM plants chosen to receive massive investments in new capital equipment. By 1986, the retrofitting of Wilmington was complete and the plant began to build two new Chevrolet models—the midsize Corsica four-door sedan and the sportier two-door Beretta. At that time, Wilmington was one of the two or three most advanced GM plants technologically, but it continued to be constrained physically by an old two-story production facility containing its weld and assembly operations; the new paint shop was located in another building nearby.

It was not long before it became clear that Wilmington's advanced technology was not performing particularly well—not unlike other plants, such as Hamtramck, in Michigan, that were part of this high-tech investment group. Robots often failed to function as expected, misplacing welds or crashing into each other. Other new pieces of equipment, including the plant's fleet of automatic guided vehicles (which automatically carried parts from one workstation to the next on platforms guided by magnetic strips embedded in the floor), were subject to frequent breakdowns, boosting downtime and maintenance costs. The massive scale of the "high-tech" workstations, with huge machines hidden behind safety gates, created more distance, both physical and psychological, between different parts of the production process, thus impeding communication about production problems. The plant's quality lab, with its highly sophisticated equipment for testing dimensional accuracy, was a popular stop for visiting engineers but encouraged an "inspect-and-repair" approach to catching quality defects, rather than an emphasis on "getting it right the first time."

As a consequence of these problems, Wilmington's productivity and quality after the massive capital investment were lower than expected, even compared with other GM plants. According to industry observer Maryann Keller (1989), an internal GM cost study during this period in which the cost of building the Beretta was compared with the cost of building a similar Japanese car, found that the Japanese cost advantage was $3,611 per car.

To make matters worse, by 1989 and 1990, Corsica/Beretta sales began to dip precipitously, even though GM was selling more and more of these models through "fleet" sales to National Car Rental, a subsidiary. The line speed was slowed from sixty-one cars per hour to fifty cars per hour, and many workers were put into the jobs bank, established in the GM-UAW contract. Meanwhile, GM's overall crisis was deepening each year, culminating in 1991 in an all-time-low market share of 34 percent (down from 45 percent in 1981) and losses for North American operations estimated at $600 million a month. Pressured by a newly active board of directors, new CEO Robert Stempel quickly cobbled together a plan in December 1991 that called for shutting six assembly plants and fifteen other factories. By February 1992, the plant names were released and Wilmington was on the list—scheduled for closing by 1996.

The news came as a shock to Wilmington, where managers felt they had started to turn around the plant's performance problems. Beginning in late 1990, the plant had begun participating in two new corporate initiatives: the Quality Network, operated jointly with the union and focused on enlisting worker involvement in eliminating quality defects, and Synchronous Manufacturing, an engineering-designed program to introduce Toyota production system ideas into GM's manufacturing plants.

The "synchronous" effort, as it was generally called, had more support from the plant's management team, as well as a "champion"—a former hourly worker-turned-manager who was well liked in the plant. According to these managers, synchronous offered "a bigger bang for the buck" in process improvements than other GM programs. In-house training programs, begun in March 1991 and conducted by managers and engineering staff, emphasized ways to achieve cycle time reductions and identify the sources of quality problems. The union president backed the Quality Network program, which was designed to include a role for the union, but he largely withheld support for the management-initiated synchronous program—a state of affairs that continued until the election of a new union president in the summer of 1992.

The announcement that the plant would be closing motivated the Wilmington management team and workforce to intensify its search for ways to enhance plant efficiency and quality. Much that had previously been viewed as sacrosanct was put on the table as possibly requiring improvement. For example, engineers and manufacturing staff began examining the plant's high-tech equipment very critically. As one engineer said, "We used to set things up so that the equipment would never be idle but the people would have to wait. Now our view is that operators should never have to wait for the machine; the equipment should wait for the operator" (interview with coauthors Pil and MacDuffie). This created new incentives to find ways to organize the operators' tasks more efficiently and also highlighted unreliable and overly sophisticated equipment. In the words of the engineer, "We began to rip out equipment that was too complex and fill those jobs with people. We often achieved performance gains from this, in terms of labor productivity, despite adding people." In the weld shop, the removal of some massive, overengineered workstations allowed U-shaped lines to be set up. Whereas a worker might once have had the task of loading only the sophisticated machine, the U-line setup enabled workers to load a piece on one machine, then turn and cross the U to unload another machine, utilizing their time much more effectively. Workers were also able to become much more involved in the equipment layout and work method choices being made during the U-line redesigns.

As sales of the Corsica and Beretta picked up in 1992 and 1993, line speed increased but without an increase in the number of line workers. (Early retirement programs and retirements were helping thin the ranks of the workforce during this period; in fact, the jobs bank was emptied out rather than swelling, as usually happens during periods of productivity improvement.) Some workers who came off the line helped the plant deal more effectively with product variety issues by working in a "kitting" area, putting together "kits" with exactly the parts needed for a particular vehicle. Others worked in problem-solving teams to identify design-related issues that hurt the plant's performance (such as the very high amount of sealer being applied in the paint shop to reduce wind noise and water leaks and the very high number of different steering columns—put together with 117 differently numbered parts—that might have to be installed because of differences in option packages.

Another initiative, facilitated by the removal of bulky equipment, involved improving space utilization in the plant by consolidating and changing the layout of operations on the ground floor of the main production building, making it possible for tasks from the upper floor to be brought downstairs. By mid-1993, this project had been accomplished and the empty second floor provided ample space for two basketball courts.

The results of all these initiatives were impressive. By mid-1993, Wilmington's productivity was the best of all of GM's plants. Quality had improved as well, though it still lagged behind the average for Big Three facilities. Although Wilmington was still scheduled to be closed, plant managers and union officials alike were optimistic that they would be spared if they could maintain or improve their performance record. By this time, there had been a change in leadership at the top of the corporation, raising hopes that Robert Stempel's plant-closing decision might not be viewed as binding by new CEO Jack Smith.

Despite Womack, Jones, and Roos's (1990) forecast that there would be rapid convergence to lean practices among auto manufacturers worldwide, performance improvements at Wilmington did not follow the lean production template very closely. As of 1993, inventory levels for incoming parts had shrunk to very low levels and other in-plant buffers had also been reduced, but the plant had not implemented new forms of work organization such as teams and job rotation. Although workers were encouraged to suggest process improvements (and reached a level of one-half suggestion per employee per year), the implementation rate remained low, at about 30 percent. Some off-line problem-solving groups met regularly, but only about 5 percent of the workforce belonged to such teams. And although managers and engineers received lots of training through the Synchronous Manufacturing program, there was little accompanying training for production workers. Furthermore, much of the synchronous effort consisted of engineers and manufacturing staff carrying out "reengineering"-type analyses of production processes and proposing changes that would boost efficiency. The removal of unreliable or overly complex automated equipment was also primarily an engineering initiative.

In short, Wilmington's turnaround cannot be attributed to the adoption of lean production approaches, particularly with respect to work practices and human resource policies. It may be better understood as a top-down engineering-driven initiative that resulted in many of the problems of the original, flawed "high-tech" plant design being fixed, combined with the development of a climate that was highly motivational for managers and workers alike because of the threat of closing. That the union-management relationship became more cooperative during this period and that there was eventually union support for the synchronous initiatives may also be attributable to the crisis atmosphere, at least initially. Given this backdrop, it may be significant that most of Wilmington's performance gains were in the area of productivity and not quality. It seems likely that a more fundamental change in worker responsibility for quality might have been necessary for equal gains to occur in this area.

By 1995, the optimistic scenario for Wilmington's future appeared to be coming true. Wilmington had become the focus of intense interest as the possible location to produce a new model—an addition to the Saturn Division's product line that would be based on a platform developed by GM Europe (Opel) for its top-selling Vectra model. There were several important ingredients in this plan. Using platforms developed in one region as the basis for products manufactured and sold in other regions was a critical component of GM's efforts to streamline product development and identify potential "world car" models that could be produced (and sourced, with respect to parts) with great economies of scale. Adding a product built on an Opel platform to the Saturn product line would signal GM's intentions to integrate Saturn more tightly with its other product divisions.

With respect to work systems and industrial relations, it appeared that Wilmington would not adopt the innovative but controversial Saturn contract but would develop a variant of the traditional UAW contract that would provide more flexibility in the allocation of workers to jobs but would not mandate teams or other Saturn-like practices. In this way, the Wilmington plan would satisfy the (unofficial but widely acknowledged) agreement in the 1993 GM-UAW contract that GM would put some future small-car investment into a plant other than Saturn. It would also provide UAW president Steve Yokich with an opportunity to establish a clear, contractually based alternative to the "Saturnization" of GM's manufacturing plants.

In late 1996, GM decided to build the next-generation Saturn in Wilmington, thereby ensuring that the plant will remain open well into the next century. As expected, the union contract for the plant does not adopt the full set of principles and practices found in the Saturn agreement. Instead, the plant remains under the national GM-UAW contract. Local plant managers and union leaders are committed, however, to experimenting with new participatory approaches to managing the facility as the new product is introduced. Thus, the Wilmington plant has retained many traditional elements in its labor-management relationship, its organization of work, and its roles for managers and workers, even after its severe crisis. Although it can be expected to move beyond those traditions somewhat when the new product comes to the plant, Wilmington holds high potential to remain a "hybrid" operation that combines elements of mass and lean production approaches to employment relations.

Conclusions

The U.S. auto industry is on a path toward transforming labor-management relations, work practices, and human resource policies. This path leads away from a traditional, coercive, Tayloristic form of work organization, arm's-length collective bargaining, and personnel policies that keep strategic decisions and corporate governance separate from the institutions and practices of industrial relations and human resource management. The emerging new practices fit better than traditional employment practices with the features of the lean or flexible production system; however, strong forces in the economy, the legal system, and the values and strategies of both business and labor threaten to stall further progress on this path.

The transformation currently under way is not yet close to converging on a singular new mode of organization. Japanese transplants such as Toyota's Georgetown facility and NUMMI have more of the features of the Toyota production system than do other plants in the country. Saturn shares many of these features but goes well beyond all other organizations in its cogovernance and partnership features. Other plants of the Big Three vary considerably depending on their age, the extent to which they have been retrofitted with new technologies and/or product lines, and the nature of local-level union-management relations. Thus, for the foreseeable future, U.S. auto manufacturers will exhibit a wide mix of practices. As suggested by Womack, Jones, and Roos, the authors of *The Machine That Changed the World* (1990), this mix can be mapped on a spectrum from mass to lean production, but, as this chapter has shown, superimposed on this dimension are a host of plant-specific organizational characteristics that reflect each plant's history.

5 Canada: Continuity and Change

Pradeep Kumar and John Holmes

This chapter examines the restructuring of production and work systems in the ten assembly plants operated by the Big Three automakers in Canada (table 5.1), highlighting the diverse pattern of change in key human resource policies and practices and its impact on workers, the union, and industry performance. General Motors, Ford, and Chrysler have been engaged in a massive restructuring of their production and management systems since the early 1980s. This process has entailed huge capital investments in plant modernization and new technology, the introduction of lean production methods, more dependence on outsourcing and closer collaboration with suppliers in the design and delivery of high-quality component parts, workforce rationalization and downsizing, and a wide variety of changes in work processes and relationships with a view to improving productivity, product quality, and flexibility.

Since the North American auto industry has been highly integrated on a continental basis for nearly three decades, the pressures for change in Canada have been very similar to those facing the Big Three in the United States—namely, overcapacity combined with weak and uncertain product demand, the growing market share of Japanese transplants, changing consumer preferences, and the new trade and investment environment created as a result of the establishment of the continental free trade area under the North American Free Trade Agreement

The research reported on in this chapter was funded by the Social Science and Humanities Research Council of Canada under grant number 410-92-1101. We would also like to thank the management representatives and CAW officials at GM, Ford, and Chrysler who agreed to be interviewed and provided information for this chapter.

Table 5.1 Profile of Big Three Assembly Plants in Canada, 1995

Location	Car Plants						Truck Plants			
	Bramalea, Ont.[a]	St. Thomas, Ont.	Oshawa, Ont. #1	Oshawa, Ont. #2	Ste Thérèse, Quebec	Windsor, Ont.[b]	Windsor, Ont. (Pillette Road)	Oakville, Ont. #1[c]	Oakville, Ont. #2 (Ontario Truck)	Oshawa, Ont.
Company	Chrysler	Ford	GM	GM	GM	Chrysler	Chrysler	Ford	Ford	GM
Year of start	1987	1967	1955	1957	1965	1925	1975	1953	1965	1965
Current production line	Concord, Intrepid, LHS, New Yorker, Vision	Crown Victoria, Grand Marquis	Lumina/Monte Carlo	Lumina/Regal	Camaro, Firebird	Caravan, Voyager (minivan)	Ram Van, Ram Wagon	Windstar (minivan)	F-Pickup Trucks	Chevrolet C-K, Sierra
Current capacity	250,000	226,000	245,000	245,000	192,000	325,000	120,000	250,000	71,000	282,000
Line speed (units per hour)	66	60	65	65	51	70	26	66	38	50
No. of shifts	2	2	2	2	2	3	2	2	1	3
Total 1994 production in thousands	255.7	210.8	253.5	253.5	192.0	350.0	89.4	213.0	71.1	278.0

Total 1994 employment (hourly)	2,652 (2,434)	2,985 (2,724)	3,299 (3,095)	3,524 (3,306)	2,981 (2,739)	4,914 (4,591)	1,658 (1,572)	3,934 (3,596)	897 (779)	3,978 (3,715)
Labor productivity (worker per vehicle)										
1994	2.67	3.11	3.12	3.34	3.58	3.60	3.91	3.28	2.91	3.37
1992	3.03	3.39	3.76	4.43	3.88	3.75	5.19	2.80	2.93	3.14
1989	NA	4.16	4.87	4.87	5.51	4.39	5.17	3.24	3.30	4.04
Product quality rating										
—Within company[d]	1	5	3	5	27	2	13	19	2	17
—Within North America[e]	18	23	7	9	69	19	73	64	17	47
Degree of automation	High	Low	High	High	Moderate	High	Low	High	Low	High

[a] Plant was built in 1987 under American Motors ownership and acquired by Chrysler following the merger of two companies.
[b] Plant started producing minivans in 1983. Before that, it produced passenger cars.
[c] Plant was converted from a car assembly operation to an all-new midsize Windstar minivan plant in February 1994.
[d] Included in the survey were fourteen Chrysler plants, twenty Ford plants, and twenty-nine General Motors plants.
[e] Based on ratings of seventy-seven plants in the United States, Canada, and Mexico.

Source: Ward's Automotive Year Book 1995, Harbour 1992 and 1995, and unpublished data from J.D. Power and Associates' 1995 North American rankings.

(NAFTA).[1] The process of change, however–in particular, the nature and scope of changes in work methods and union-management relationships—has been very different in the two countries (table 5.2).

A key source of the divergence has been the difference in union response. Whereas the Big Three have been able to forge (to varying degrees) "partnerships" with the UAW to achieve flexibility in compensation and work arrangements and to foster a participatory enterprise culture, the Big Three have encountered considerable resistance from the Canadian Auto Workers (CAW) to the introduction of new forms of work organization and contingent compensation. The CAW maintains that it is not in the long-run interests of the workers to enter into a partnership with management and that managerial efforts to redesign work and reward systems could potentially undermine workers' rights, create intolerable working conditions, and erode the independent role of the union. While opposing partnership, the union does not rule out participating in "positive" workplace changes that "use workers' experience, knowledge and skills to produce good quality products and services in well-designed workplaces with the proper tools and equipment" (CAW 1993a:3). To this end, the union espouses the development of "close working relationships" with management, based on the explicit recognition of different interests and unequal power and the importance of maintaining an independent base from which to negotiate with management.

This mix of ideological resistance and pragmatic willingness on the part of the CAW to negotiate reforms that benefit both workers and employers has led to the development of a distinctive and realistic vision of workplace change in the Canadian auto industry, shaped by what is "feasible" rather than by what management deems to be desirable.[2] The corporate strategies of the Big Three are relatively uniform, centered as they are around variants of lean production. Their production methods and management systems bear a close resemblance to one another: focus on the increased use of outsourcing and just-in-time deliveries; reduction in subassembly processes and nonvalue-added time; integration of product and process development to include suppliers; rapid application of new computer-

---

[1]This integration dates back to 1965 when the Auto Pact between Canada and the United States was signed, which provided for duty-free trade in vehicle and equipment parts subject to certain safeguards for Canadian production and employment. Integration was further strengthened by recent comprehensive trade agreements, namely, the Canada-U.S. Free Trade Agreement in 1989 and NAFTA in 1993 (Holmes 1992).

[2]The concepts of "feasibility" and "desirability" in the context of workplace change are further elaborated in Walton, Cutcher-Gershenfeld, and McKersie 1994.

Table 5.2 Key Areas of Divergence at the U.S. and Canadian Big Three
Plants, 1995

Wages	In 1978, base wage rates for assemblers (in national currency terms) were almost identical at the Big Three plants in Canada and the United States. By the end of the last contract in 1993, however, base wage rates in Canada were $2.88 an hour higher than in the United States. This divergence can be attributed largely to the use of contingent compensation in the United States. Unlike the Canadian contracts, which provide for annual increases in base rates, the American contracts at GM, Ford, and Chrysler include a base rate increase in the first year, lump-sum "performance bonus" payments in the second and third years, and profit sharing in lieu of base rate increases. Profit-sharing bonuses vary by company, however, and have not totally compensated for the loss of earnings resulting from the abandonment of annual wage increases. New hires are paid 70 percent of the maximum job rate in the United States and progress to the normal rate in thirty-six months. In Canada, the new-hire rate is 85 percent of the maximum job rate. New hires reach the normal rate in one and a half years. Although wage rates in Canada are higher in national currency terms, total compensation per hour (in U.S. $) continues to be significantly lower than in the United States because of the lower cost of health-care benefits and the lower value of the Canadian dollar.
Paid Time Off	Canadian contracts provide for more holidays and vacation days (through a higher paid absence allowance) and a compulsory one-week paid time off in pursuit of the CAW goal of reducing annual hours of work. Although the U.S. collective bargaining agreements provide for fewer holidays and vacation time off, effective 1994, they include two weeks of summer vacation shutdown in July.
Employment Security	American contracts include more emphasis on job security provisions, such as the "Expanded Job Opportunity Bank" and "Secure Employment Levels," while Canadian contracts emphasize income security programs (e.g., indexed pensions, expanded supplementary unemployment benefits, early retirement incentives, and severance pay plans for voluntary termination of employment). In Canada, employers are required to give a one-year advance notice of a plant closing. In the United States, there are strong protections of placement opportunities for workers affected by closed or idled facilities.
Work Practices and Work Organization	American contracts have fewer job classifications and more formal team concept/employee-involvement provisions and provide for greater management flexibility in work

Table 5.2 Continued

	scheduling, shift work, job rotation, multitasking, and work assignments. Canadian contracts allow less management discretion, but changes in work scheduling and work arrangements are negotiated as need arises. Although there are far fewer formal contractual provisions for teamwork and employee involvement in Canada, there is considerable *informal* employee participation and communications on efficiency and quality issues.
Training	In the United States, training in all areas is conducted jointly by both the union and management. In Canada, training is delivered by the union in consultation with management. Contracts include provisions for joint training review committees to assess training needs and resources. Both countries have an extensive array of training programs. Canadian contracts also provide for social training (literacy and human rights training in addition to legislated health and safety training).
Union-Management Relations	American contracts, both at the national level and in many cases locally, provide for a formal pledge of union-management cooperation, jointness, and partnership in shop-floor governance, productivity and quality initiatives, outsourcing decisions, and training and education activities. The CAW is opposed to partnership with management, although it participates in several joint programs (e.g., orientation, apprenticeship training, health and safety, substance abuse and employee counseling, employment equity), and a few local contracts (e.g., GM's Ste Thérèse plant and Chrysler's Bramalea plant) include formal pledges of cooperation and commitments to "working together."

Source: Kumar and Meltz 1992 and 1993 *Contract Highlights,* CAW and UAW.

based technology; and the decentralization and delayering of management structures. Changes in work rules, work arrangements, and union-management relationships have tended to be diverse, experimental, incremental, and evolutionary, however, and characterized by both continuity and changes in past practices.

Where changes have occurred, they have been dictated by the concrete needs of both employers and employees and have reflected pragmatic considerations of survival and security of employment as well as the fulfillment of "previously underemphasized" worker interests and aspirations. For example, although the basic elements of the traditional labor relations system—the adversarial arm's-length relationship between labor and management, formula-like wage rules in multiyear contracts, centralized pattern bargaining and connective bargaining between plants, and the job-control focus linking workers' rights to detailed job classifications—have remained virtually intact, work rules and work arrangements in individual plants have changed markedly to make effective use of new technologies and to accommodate employers' need for operational flexibility. Investments in training, both social (literacy, human rights, and health and safety) and technical, have increased in response to the introduction of new technology and the changing composition of the labor force. Both the formal and informal incidence of work teams and problem-solving groups, to draw out the tacit knowledge and creative potential of workers, has also risen. In many Canadian plants, these employee-involvement initiatives have been associated with changes in management structure, in particular, reductions in the number of first-line supervisors. Similarly, the frequency of information sharing, union-management consultations, and employee communications has risen significantly.

Union-management relationships diverge considerably from plant to plant, however, ranging from relatively cooperative to bitterly antagonistic. The diversity is related to plant histories, management styles and strategies, the nature and demographic composition of the workforce, local union politics and leadership, and the personalities of, and personal relationships that exist between, plant managers and local union representatives. Plant performance appears to be highly correlated with these variations in labor-management relations. Where a close and well-developed union-management relationship exists, plant productivity is relatively higher, product quality ratings have been improving, and the industrial relations environment, measured by grievance settlement, absenteeism, and health and safety indicators, is better compared with plants in which workplace relationships are poorly developed.

Several conclusions can be drawn from the Canadian experience, which has been enriching and mutually beneficial for both the union and management. First, whatever the idealized vision of lean production, the nature and scope of workplace innovations depend crucially on the union response. Second, labor and management have different visions of work reorganization. Third, the actual forms assumed by these innovations are based on concrete needs, overlapping concerns, and the mutual interests of employers and employees and are pursued for pragmatic reasons.

Management has no immutable core values regarding work organization, other than the market imperatives of improving the bottom line. Fourth, change is guided by both management considerations of efficiency and flexibility and union concerns for equity, fairness, and security. Fifth, negotiated change is more stable than change dictated unilaterally by management. Sixth and finally, to participate effectively in shaping workplace reforms, unions have to be not only strong and independent and have leaders capable of taking risks and mobilizing workers around desired goals but able to articulate a clear vision, agenda, and strategy for change.

The Canadian experience further indicates that the Fordist system of labor relations, which has been a source of stability in the North American auto industry for more than four decades and has provided significant benefits to both workers and employers, does not need to be totally dismantled but can be modified incrementally to meet the efficiency and flexibility needs of management. When viewed in a comparative context (see table 5.3 for a comparison of the changes in selected elements of the work and reward systems in Canada, the United States, Japan, and other countries), the changes occurring in Canada shed light on the debate over whether there can be "one and only one best practice" with respect to human resource policies and practices within the broader framework of lean production.

The data in table 5.3 suggest that although Canadian plants perform very well with regard to productivity and quality, with the exception of devolving responsibility for quality, they rank low on every measurement of "modern operating" practices that many commentators argue are necessary for the attainment of high productivity and quality. The Canadian experience highlights the fact that although production and management strategies to achieve competitiveness are converging toward lean production in auto plants in North America, actual changes in work organization and relationships remain diverse and plant/enterprise specific and are strongly influenced and shaped by the distinct organizational/institutional culture and the history of labor-management in particular plants.

Overview of the Canadian Automobile Industry

The Canadian automobile industry is a high-value-added, high-productivity, high–labor cost industry noted for its high wages, generous employee benefits, good working conditions, and relatively secure employment. It is heavily unionized, and almost all union members belong to the CAW.

Table 5.3 Canadian Vehicle Assembly Plants in Comparative Context, 1993

	Canada (Big Three)	U.S. (Big Three)	Japanese Transplants (North America)	Japan	Korea	Australia	United Kingdom	Southern Europe	Northern Europe	South Africa
Number of plants surveyed	6	19	8	12	6	4	5	5	11	6
Productivity (hours/vehicle)	20.0	22.4	17.4	16.5	30.0	33.7	25.7	22.9	28.9	86.7
Work systems and HR policies Multiskilling (highest possible=100) Specializing=0	26.9	27.8	59.3	72.6	62.3	47.8	38.0	38.3	45.1	18.0
Percentage of workforce in teams	25.2	52.4	67.6	68.3	73.7	65.7	75.7	40.9	78.3	80.3
Percentage of workforce in EI of QC groups	6.1	38.0	39.5	93.9	96.3	60.4	66.4	40.9	66.3	41.0
Extent of job rotation (1=none; 5=frequent)	1.8	2.1	4.1	3.9	3.0	4.0	3.1	3.4	3.8	3.3
Responsibility for quality inspection/SPC (0=specialists; 4=workers)	3.1	2.1	2.5	1.6	2.2	2.8	2.4	2.1	2.6	1.1

Table 5.3 Continued

	Canada (Big Three)	U.S. (Big Three)	Japanese Transplants (North America)	Japan	Korea	Australia	United Kingdom	Southern Europe	Northern Europe	South Africa
Responsibility for programming flexible technology (0=specialists; 4=workers)	1.4	1.4	1.2	0.5	0.6	0.9	0.8	0.4	0.9	0.7
HRM philosophy (100=high commitment; 0=low commitment)	19.9	30.0	74.6	49.9	37.1	55.8	50.8	49.9	44.5	34.8
Contingent compensation (0=none; 6=extensive)	0.7	1.5	2.1	5.6	2.2	5.0	2.8	3.0	4.5	3.0
Training for new employees (0=less than 40 hrs./year; 3=160+ hrs./year)	1.6	1.7	2.5	2.7	1.8	2.5	2.4	3.0	2.2	2.0
Training for experienced employees (0=less than 20 hrs./year; 5=80+ hrs./year)	1.3	1.9	4.3	1.7	2.7	2.8	2.0	3.0	2.2	1.8

Source: MacDuffie and Pil unpublished data.

The CAW was formed in 1985, when it broke away from the UAW, which had been the dominant union in the industry in both Canada and the United States since 1935 (see Gindin 1995 for a history of the CAW). All production workers at the Big Three, CAMI, and Volvo plants are covered by collective agreements, whereas workers at the three Asian transplants, owned by Honda, Toyota, and Hyundai, are nonunionized (CAW 1994).

Although most Canadian auto plants are foreign owned, the automobile industry is a key industry in Canada and represents a significant segment of the auto industry globally. Since the continental integration of the industry under the Auto Pact in 1965, the industry in Canada has made impressive gains in production, trade, employment, efficiency, and product quality. Although it has faced serious international competitive pressures since the late 1970s as a result of escalating production costs and the rise of the Japanese automakers, it remains competitive in North America. Indeed, Canada has steadily increased its share of North American production of both light-vehicle assembly and component parts. The future outlook for the industry remains uncertain, however, because of the projected slow growth in demand for motor vehicles in the late 1990s, continuing problems with overcapacity, the growing competition from transplants, and the increasing importance of Mexico as a production site within the North American marketplace. Nonetheless, most analyses are optimistic about the continued competitiveness of the assembly sector in Canada (Industry Canada 1991 and 1992; *Ward's Automotive Handbook* 1994 and 1995; Holmes 1996). This optimism is based on the planned expansion of the production capacity of the transplants, the continued large investments by the Big Three in plant modernization and automation, new product mandates received by Canadian plants, the introduction of technologically advanced production and integrated supply management systems, the Canadian labor cost advantage over the United States, and the stable labor relations environment. The outlook for component parts manufacturing is less optimistic, because of the increasing competition from lower-cost plants in Mexico and the continuing rationalization by the Big Three of their high-cost parts facilities and operations (Industry Canada 1991; Holmes 1996).

Restructuring Strategy of the Big Three

The Big Three (including American Motors, which was acquired by Chrysler in 1987) had a virtual oligopolistic control over the Canadian industry until the early 1980s. They accounted for all of Canadian production and more

than four-fifths of Canadian sales. This situation changed dramatically in
the late 1970s, and between 1979 and 1982, the Big Three's share of
Canadian vehicle sales dropped from 86 percent to 69 percent. The share
of imports during this period climbed from 14 percent to 31 percent, while
the share of Japanese imports increased from 8 percent in 1979 to 25 percent in 1982. Over this three-year period, the Big Three suffered a dramatic
decline in production, sales, revenues, and profits.

Although the Big Three's production and sales recovered during the
period from 1983 to 1986, the competitive crisis further deepened in the
mid-1980s with the opening of the Asian transplant facilities, which have
continued to erode the Big Three's competitive position. Their market
share declined from 71 percent in 1987 to 64 percent in 1992.[3] The market share of the transplants went up from less than 1 percent in 1987 to 11
percent in 1994, and over the same period, the transplants' share of total
vehicle production in Canada rose from less than 0.5 percent to more than
16 percent. Competition from the transplants has been particularly serious
in the passenger car market, where their share has steadily increased, so
that by 1994 they accounted for 16 percent of sales and 25 percent of total
Canadian car production. Since the announcement in 1996 that Honda,
Toyota, and CAMI are planning capacity expansions of their plants, the
expectation is that the transplants' share of total production will be even
higher by 1998. Because of their lower benefits costs, high productivity, and
superior product quality ratings, the Asian transplants continue to pose for-
midable competitive challenges to the Big Three in Canada.

The Big Three have responded to this competitive crisis by significantly increasing capital investment in plant modernization and automation and by undertaking several initiatives to restructure their
production, supply, and management systems to enhance efficiency, flexibility, product quality, and cost competitiveness. The key restructuring
initiatives have included accelerated use of computerized manufacturing
technologies, such as CAD/CAM, robotics, programmable controllers,
automatic guided vehicles (AGVs), and monorail systems to replace traditional assembly lines; the adoption of statistical process control and
just-in-time inventory management; greater use of outsourcing and subcontracting as well as a more cost- and quality-effective sourcing of parts
and raw materials by developing new partnerships with suppliers based
on long-term contracts, a consolidation of the number of suppliers, sole

[3]The market share rose to 69 percent in 1993 and to 73 percent in 1994 because of a marked
decline in imports.

sourcing with preferred suppliers, and increased involvement of suppliers in product design and development; and the rationalization of management structures through area management, flat hierarchies, and new systems of work organization based on teamwork and employee involvement in decision making.

Between 1980 and 1995, the three companies invested more than $20 billion in the renewal of their Canadian plants and facilities through the application of state-of-the-art technologies and production systems.[4] Although the new manufacturing systems are called by different names at the three companies—Ford 2000 and the Modern Operating System at Ford Canada, Synchronous Organization at General Motors of Canada, and the Chrysler Operating System at Chrysler Canada—the overall framework and direction of change is the same and they all embody the lean production principles of the Toyota production system. These include the elimination of waste and the reduction of nonvalue-added time, use of just-in-time delivery and synchronous flow of components, parts, and raw materials; lead time reduction; rationalization of work processes, process variation reduction, and continuous improvement. There are significant variations, however, in the applications of new technologies and lean production systems among the ten assembly plants.

The work organization changes pursued by the Big Three are also similar, but, once again, work practices and policies vary depending primarily on the nature of the local union-management relationship. The agenda for work reorganization by the corporate management at all three companies includes greater management flexibility in work scheduling and work arrangements, increased effort through the adoption of flexible work rules and job boundaries, teamwork and employee involvement, and the development of more cooperative union-management relationships to reduce absenteeism, achieve better health and safety outcomes, improve productivity and quality, and promote an enterprise culture in which employees identify with corporate goals and objectives.

As part of their cost-cutting strategy, all three companies have been downsizing their workforces, through rationalization, plant closings, and/or consolidation of facilities. The Big Three employed slightly more than sixty-five thousand workers in 1994, compared with nearly seventy-seven thousand in

---

[4]GM has been the most aggressive of the Big Three companies in pursuing plant modernization and lean production. It has invested nearly $10 billion in new capital expenditures, including building the Autoplex in Oshawa—the largest, most modern vehicle complex in North America.

1985, the peak level of employment.[5] Over the same period, their total production of cars and trucks was up from 1,891,000 in 1985 to 1,915,000 in 1994, leading to significant gains in productivity.

Chrysler Canada has reaped the most benefit from workforce rationalization over the past decade. Although its overall employment has remained unchanged, the volume of production has increased by a dramatic 78 percent, from 390,120 units in 1985 to a record 695,122 in 1994, resulting in impressive gains in labor productivity. Ford and General Motors have not fared as well, largely because of their lower capacity utilization and consequent reduction in vehicle production. For example, General Motors' production of cars and trucks declined by 14 percent from 1985 to 1994, from 834,899 units to 723,490 units. Similarly, the volume of production at Ford of Canada was 25 percent lower in 1994 than in 1985. Chrysler Canada's superior performance relative to Ford and General Motors is attributed to the unusually high demand for its products, particularly minivans, resulting in spectacular increases in capacity utilization.

Union Response

The CAW has viewed the Big Three's restructuring strategy with skepticism and serious concern. As one union document notes:

> The differences between lean companies and other companies *are not found* in developments such as teams, suggestion programs, small group improvement activities, multi-skilling or the like. The biggest differences are found in practices such as the massive outsourcing (contracting out) of parts and final assembly. The outsourcing is done with low wages, insecure employment and fully using production capacity. Other differences are in technical developments such as the ease of making products (simple designs, fewer parts, quick assemblies). Most important, in terms of the labor process, is work intensification—tight work cycles, long hours, regimented work practices and signifi-

---

[5]The downsizing has been most pronounced at GM of Canada, where total employment went from 48,100 in 1985 to 37,519 in 1994. Ford reduced its employment from 15,500 to 14,300 over the 1985–94 period, while the Chrysler workforce has remained stable, at about 13,100 to 13,600. (Chrysler employed 13,356 workers in 1985. Employment rose to 16,000 in 1987, when the company acquired American Motors. Since 1987, employment has declined to 13,600 in 1994.) At each of the three companies, the salaried workforce has been reduced substantially. Production worker employment has either remained stable or gone up at both Ford and Chrysler but has declined nearly 25 percent at GM of Canada. In all three companies, workforce rationalization has been achieved without any involuntary layoffs.

cant managerial flexibility to use labour as it sees fit. It is here that lean production ends up (CAW 1993b:3; emphasis in original).

The union has come to the conclusion that the lean production strategy as pursued by the Big Three is an obstacle to achieving the fundamental union goals of "a more democratic workplace with more worker involvement and control and better working conditions" (CAW 1993b:1). In an effort to make the lean production system more responsive to workers' needs, the union has articulated an independent, alternate agenda that focuses on both continuity and change—continuity to preserve the basic elements of the postwar Fordist system of industrial relations and thereby achieve stability and order, and change to modify and ameliorate the lean production system as advanced by management to make it more responsive to workers' needs. The purpose is to "oppose lean production from a position of engagement and to work to change it through negotiations" (CAW 1993b:8).

The union emphasizes that significant improvements need to occur in four key areas to humanize the lean production system: (1) workplace and production standards, (2) training, (3) job design, and (4) union input into production decisions (CAW 1993b). The union believes that "the workplace should be characterized by a comfortable work pace—one that is sustainable" (CAW 1993b:9). This requires recognition that a comfortable work pace involves discretionary time and the possibility for workers to vary the job and the pace, an adequate relief staff, and a regulated (negotiated) process for changing job content and job times. The union emphasizes the need for improving the extent, distribution, and content of training through a guaranteed training time of forty hours a year and the joint control of training programs whereby the content is codetermined by the company and the union and delivery is based on the principles of adult education and, in particular, peer training. The union agenda on job design emphasizes the need for safe and healthy jobs, with deepening skills and expanded options, negotiated job mobility, and accommodations for injured workers. The union also wants expanded opportunities to discuss production issues from a union perspective. To summarize, the union agenda calls for the creation of (1) training committees to assess training needs and develop training programs; (2) ergonomics committees to improve the design of jobs and workstations, (3) technology committees that focus on the design, implementation, and effects of new technology and that argue for skill-based technical change; and (4) environmental committees to discuss environ-mentally sound products and production methods.

In the area of work reorganization, the CAW has sought to clarify the roles and responsibilities of teams and team leaders and to develop contract language around production standards and the provision of relief. The union's goal is to set some limits on the speedup of work and to push for workplace changes that use and enrich workers' experience, knowledge, and skills to produce high-quality products in well-designed workplaces. Although the union agenda is geared toward the defense and advancement of workers' rights and the improvement of their economic and social well-being, it has also been sensitive to and supportive of management needs to increase production flexibility and efficiency to gain competitiveness.

This pragmatic orientation led the union to participate in several work reorganization experiments (for example, at the GM Ste Thérèse and Oshawa plants, at the Chrysler plants at Bramalea and Windsor, at Ford Oakville, and, above all, at CAMI, a greenfield joint venture of GM and Suzuki in Ingersoll, Ontario). According to a CAW official, the purpose of these experiments was to learn "whether [the union] can have input into the changes that actually improve the life of workers and their working condi-tions." It appears that both the companies and the union have benefited from these experiments. The companies have realized that they can work around "the labels" and still improve their productivity and quality performance. As Harry Katz and Noah Meltz (1989) discovered in their 1987 survey of auto assembly plant practices, even though Canadian plants do not have formal team concepts or employee-involvement programs, management has been able to increase the flexibility of work rules considerably. Consequently, Canadian plants are rated high for both their economic performance and their industrial relations climate (see Kumar and Meltz 1992 for details). The data gathered in the most recent IMVP assembly plant survey, conducted in 1993 (table 5.3), the Harbour Report productivity rankings, and the J. D. Power quality ratings all point to the same conclusion: notwithstanding the differences in work practices and union agendas between Canada and the United States, Canadian assembly plants achieve consistently high rankings for economic efficiency and product quality. The positive working relation-ship was an important factor in substantial new investments recently announced by Ford and Chrysler and by GM in the mid-1980s.

For its part, the union has learned that it can pursue its goals and objec-tives effectively and can change production and work methods to the ben-efit of workers through participation and discussion based on a strong independent stance. Following the first-ever strike against a transplant, the CAW succeeded in persuading the Japanese management at CAMI to modify team concepts and practices and to accept union input into setting production standards. This event encouraged and lent support to those in the CAW who favor positive and proactive intervention in work reorganization (CAW 1992; for a detailed analysis of the CAW's interpretation of its experience at CAMI, see Rinehart, Huxley, and Robertson 1997.) The union has come to realize that workplace changes can be turned to advantage and, in particular, used as a tool "to make jobs more rewarding and workplaces more democratic" and as an "opportunity to develop a new activism in the workplace, an opening to mobilize . . . members around new—or at least previously underemphasized—needs" (CAW 1993a:5).

Workplace Changes

In this section, we discuss the extent and scope of the workplace changes that have taken place in the ten assembly plants that have been the focus of our recent empirical research. The analysis is based on information gathered from a systematic reading of the local collective agreements for each plant and other company and union documents but primarily from interviews conducted with management and local union officers at each plant and personal observations made during plant visits. The interviews and plant visits took place from May 1995 to January 1996.

The picture that emerges is that there has been both *continuity* and *change* with regard to workplace organization. We are firmly convinced that it would be grossly misleading to suggest that present-day work organization and labor-management relations in the Canadian assembly plants operated by the Big Three represent fundamental breaks from past practices. At the same time, it would be equally misleading to maintain that nothing has changed. Instead, the reorganization that has occurred can best be characterized as incremental and evolutionary. As mentioned earlier, although there are significant differences between individual assembly plants with regard to the extent of automation (table 5.1),[6] GM, Ford, and Chrysler have each sought to introduce similar manufacturing systems. We

[6]In our set of ten assembly plants, the highest levels of automation and modernization were found in the three plants that comprised GM's Oshawa complex; at Chrysler Bramalea and Windsor Assembly; and at Ford's Oakville Assembly plant. At the other end of the spectrum was the Chrysler Pillette Road plant, which built a twenty-year-old product on a "traditional" body fabrication line reminiscent of lines used in the 1970s.

have observed several elements that are common across all ten plants, regardless of the level of automation: a tremendous emphasis and drive to further standardize work; a drive to reduce nonvalue-added time; the redesign of workstations to reduce operator travel distance and the floor space occupied; production designed around one-piece flow, the elimination of off-line subassembly work, and a general reduction of work-in-progress; the development of JIT systems both within the plant and between the outside suppliers and the plant; and the incorporation of quality monitoring and continuous improvement methods into the production process. The implementation of these techniques has invariably and understandably led to significant increases in the pace and intensity of work.

These new manufacturing methods have been pursued most aggressively in the three car assembly plants operated by GM as part of the latter's synchronous organization strategy. This is reflected in the results of a recent benchmark study on working conditions conducted by the CAW (1996), which found that conditions were reported to be significantly worse with regard to work pace and intensity, workload, physical health risks, stress control, and autonomy at the GM plants compared with the other plants in the survey. Another feature common to several of the plants, and particularly those such as Chrysler Windsor Assembly and Ford Oakville Assembly, which build popular minivan models, is the push to increase capacity utilization through such methods as the adoption of alternative work schedules.

Our discussion of work organization will focus on team or group work, working-time arrangements, training, and the structure of labor-management relations, all areas in which change has taken place. To emphasize that the process is one not only of change but of continuity with past practices, we will first briefly outline two key areas in which there has been almost no change: pay systems and the internal labor market of the plant, which for the past half-century have been controlled by the job-control focus of postwar industrial unionism.

Pay/Compensation Systems. The traditional postwar annual improvement factor (AIF) plus cost-of-living wage-setting formula and uniform pattern bargaining continue to prevail across the unionized plants in the Canadian auto industry.[7] Unlike the United States, there are no contingent compensation schemes, such as lump-sum bonuses, profit sharing, or pay for

---

[7]For all practical purposes, this statement can be extended to include the Asian transplant assemblers as well since CAMI (itself unionized), Toyota, and Honda all set their wages in accordance with the prevailing union rates of the Big Three.

knowledge, at any of the Big Three plants in Canada. The only bonuses of any kind are the relatively small bonuses offered for good attendance or as incentives as part of workplace suggestion schemes.

Internal Labor Market. More like the situation in auto plants throughout North America, management in Canada would like to be granted much more flexibility with regard to assigning and reassigning workers among jobs and redesigning and reorganizing work across existing job boundaries. At the same time, management would like to have more power to restrict or reduce the amount of "job churning" that annually takes place within a plant's internal labor market as workers exercise their contractual rights to bid on other jobs. Such job churning results in significant training costs, impedes productivity, and can compromise quality. To these ends, management would like to see a reduction in the number of job classifications, weakening of the seniority system with regard to the assignment of workers to jobs or the assignment of overtime, the formal acceptance of job rotation, and restrictions on job bidding by workers.

In interview after interview that we conducted, managers acknowledged that they had made almost no progress toward achieving these objectives because of opposition from the union on the key issue of seniority. The CAW has fiercely protected seniority rights to ensure that workers can move over time from "bad" jobs to "good" jobs. The union has rejected formal job rotation in every plant. In plants such as Chrysler Windsor Assembly and Ford Oakville Assembly, it has retained the practice of opening every single job to bids by seniority on one day a year, and at the multiplant complexes at Windsor (Chrysler), Oakville (Ford), and Oshawa (GM), the union has successfully defended the "complex-wide" posting of jobs despite management's desire to limit job posting and seniority rights to individual plants within each complex.

The impact of complex-wide job posting can be quite dramatic. When Chrysler added a third shift at Windsor Assembly, for example, the majority of new openings were filled by workers with varying degrees of seniority from the Pillette Road truck assembly plant and new hires moved into the open jobs at Pillette Road, resulting in a very large number of workers who needed to be either trained or retrained. In 1994, the union at Ford Oakville refused management's request to establish separate bargaining units for the car and truck plants in return for a pledge of new investment in the truck plant. The union eventually agreed to some partial restrictions on worker-initiated moves between the two Oakville assembly plants.

Similarly, management in these plants has enjoyed relatively little success in efforts to reduce the number of job classifications. For example, at Chrysler Windsor Assembly, a 1986 proposal to introduce an alternative work assignment system, which included reducing the number of unskilled classifications from fifty to nine and of skilled classifications from sixteen to eight, was rejected, as was a 1993 proposal to introduce a combined "welder repairer" classification. The same is true at the Ford plants and at GM's plants in Oshawa. Only at Chrysler Bramalea, a new greenfield plant opened in the late 1980s, and at GM Ste Thérèse are there significantly fewer classifications.[8]

Work Groups and Teamwork. The issue of work groups and teamwork has been one of the most complex and controversial in Canadian auto plants over the last ten years and illustrates well our general argument about the nature of workplace change in the Canadian auto industry. Only one of the ten assembly plants—GM Ste Thérèse—mentions a formal team concept, referred to as the "work unit concept" in the collective agreement. The concept, negotiated in 1986 and designed to promote employee involvement and participation, was viewed as "the cornerstone of a new world-class agreement." Work groups are charged with responsibility for completing the assembly cycle, monitoring product quality, enhancing the work environment, providing assistance and training to fellow group members, and ensuring the repair and maintenance of equipment. At the other end of the spectrum, GM's Oshawa plants and all the Ford plants have completely informal mechanisms for employee involvement. In between are the Chrysler Windsor plants, which in 1994 negotiated a memorandum of understanding that allows for two new positions—those of "production coordinator" and "quality alert system facilitator"—which are intended to provide "leadership" and support for work groups.

Whatever the particular form assumed by these informal experiments, they share common characteristics. The groups are informal and experimental (in that they can be canceled by either the union or management on relatively short notice); their primary function is to focus on quality issues and they rarely if ever address productivity or continuous improvement issues; group or team leaders mainly help solve quality problems, deliver

[8]At Ste Thérèse, which had had a notoriously poor industrial relations record, the reduction in classifications occurred in 1986, when a new agreement negotiated under a threat of impending plant closure ushered in a new era of labor-management relations. This is the only example of this kind of change among Canadian assembly plants.

training, and provide relief to other members of the group but do not engage in matters pertaining to production standards; and the selection of group leaders or production coordinators and the absence of formal job rotation within the work groups enshrines the fundamental principle of seniority. Above all, the informally negotiated changes are seen to benefit not only management, by helping to reduce the number of first-line supervisors and nonvalue-added activity, but the union, by empowering workers around the issue of quality improvement, a mutual objective of both management and the union, while maintaining the integrity of the bargaining unit and avoiding the blurring of the relationship between management and workers.

Working-Time Arrangements. Although management has pressed for changes in work practices that would permit it to have more discretion and flexibility with regard to the scheduling of overtime, the union has not been very accommodating.[9] The CAW favors a strategy that would not only limit overtime but reduce the amount of time worked by individual workers so as to force the creation of new jobs, or at least the retention of as many existing jobs as possible. This policy has underpinned the union's resistance to the relaxing of mandatory overtime provisions and has also shaped its approach to the negotiating of particular alternative work schedules (AWSs) in plants where companies are seeking to maximize capacity utilization in the face of strong product demand. This is well illustrated by the negotiation in 1993 of the AWS for Chrysler's Windsor assembly plant, which builds the highly popular Chrysler minivans.[10] As a result of the introduction of the AWS, a third shift was added by moving to a six-day, three-crew, three-shift system that established a shorter workday (i.e., seven and a half hours) for full pay (eight hours). This locally negotiated outcome increased capacity utilization and provided more production flexibility for management while benefiting the union by requiring individual workers to work less time for the same pay and generating more jobs in aggregate—a minimum of 650—than alternative three-shift systems. As the union noted in a press release announcing the AWS:

[9]Provincial labor standards in Ontario provide individual workers with the legal right to refuse overtime beyond a forty-eight-hour workweek. With the advent of lean production, and particularly JIT techniques, the ability of managers to extend shifts on short notice to meet daily production schedules has become increasingly critical. After much local negotiation and the intervention of the CAW national office, a memorandum allowing some limited modification of the rules governing overtime at GM Oshawa was signed in 1994.

[10]An almost identical AWS agreement was negotiated in 1993 for the Chrysler Bramalea plant but has yet to be implemented.

The new third shift at the mini-van plant is a tremendous achievement for Chrysler workers, their families and the community. . . . We have shown that there is an alternative [to double-digit unemployment]. By more equitably sharing existing work, everyone will benefit. In addition, we are retaining work opportunities including the six-day production schedule and premium working hours for all trades. . . . Our members, families and the community will reap the benefits and you can be proud of what you have done.

Training. There has been a steady increase in the amount of training for workers in Canadian assembly plants over the last decade, and the union has not only negotiated minimum training time and joint control of training with management but has played a major role in the design and delivery of training. In contrast to the United States, where training in all areas is conducted jointly by both the union and management, in Canada training is delivered by the union in *consultation* with management.

Broadly, one can distinguish two types of training. The first type, which is related to restructuring, involves major technical and work culture training associated with major plant modernization projects and the launching of new models. Good examples would be the training provided by GM for the launch of the GM 10 and GM 400 new product programs at the Oshawa car and truck plants respectively or the construction of the new training center and "Best in Class" training program that accompanied the launch of the Ford Windstar minivan at the Oakville Assembly plant. By its very nature, this training tends to be cyclical and discontinuous, and its longer-term impact at some plants such as Ford Oakville has proven problematic. The second type of training is much more continuous and ongoing and encompasses such issues as quality, ergonomics, literacy, human rights, and mandated health and safety.

Labor-Management Relations. At the Canadian plants of all the Big Three companies, management has initiated changes that include a shift to area management, significant reductions in the number of first-line supervisors, and focused efforts to improve communications with and increase the flow of information to the employees on the shop floor. Because of the CAW's steadfast resistance to any notion of partnership with management, management has not succeeded in persuading the union to participate formally in joint decision making regarding production standards and related productivity issues. In areas in which it deems that management and the CAW have mutual concerns, however, such as training, ergonomics, employment equity, quality, and health and safety, the union has been more than willing to work with management through joint committees.

Although there are labor-management issues common to all ten plants, there is also significant diversity among them; in fact, there is probably more diversity among plants than among companies. This diversity arises from the autonomy and flexibility union locals have had to negotiate informal changes at the plant level and reflects such factors as the history of union-management relations at particular plants, the work cultures that exist among plants, and, an important consideration, the personal qualities of plant managers and the strength and stability of local union leaderships. We have been impressed, for example, with the Chrysler plants in Windsor, where a strong and excellent working relationship has developed between a union local with strong leadership and an enlightened management. These plants have undergone incremental informal workplace changes resulting in significant improvements in quality and productivity. At the same time, the union has successfully resisted efforts to introduce new work practices that would threaten seniority rights, and the union-management relationship has remained fundamentally unchanged and adversarial.

Conclusions

The preceding analysis suggests that by adopting both defensive and proactive strategies, the CAW has been able to articulate its own agenda, based on its awareness of its different interests and constituencies, while emphasizing the importance of developing a working relationship with management. We would not claim, however, that the CAW has a fully coherent position on such issues as training, work scheduling, and overtime or even, for that matter, how to deal with management's continued push to intensify the pace of work through its lean production strategy. At the same time, the CAW experience is worthy of examination in that the union has played an important role in guiding and strengthening the ability of the leaders of its locals to negotiate pragmatic changes in work reorganization at the plant level. The union's development of a cadre of strong local leaders and activists, its emphasis on the continuous education of the rank-and-file membership with regard to issues such as work reorganization, and the commitment to open and democratic communications within the union have all been central to the effort to shape the changes going on in the local plants and to link those changes to a coherent strategy on work reorganization at the national level.

The CAW experience confirms the conclusions Kevin Middlebrook reached that the organizational and bargaining strength of workers is "the central factor determining variations in the character of the restructuring process and its political and economic consequences for labor in different countries and production sites" (1991:276). Unions, therefore, have the option of either simply acquiescing to management's agenda or devising their own strategies for, what Berggren has called, the "selected synthesis of both lean and human-centered practices" (1992:255). Only a strong union movement, with an independent labor agenda, emphasizing, among other issues, the importance of strong national institutions, alliances, coalition building, and international solidarity, can effectively change the corporate lean production agenda, promote workers' interests, and defend workers' rights.

6 Germany: Implementing Lean Production

Ulrich Jürgens

S ince the lean production revolution began in Germany in 1991, major changes have occurred in industrial practices as well as in the country's system of industrial relations. This system is often characterized by the codetermination or strong role works councils have in influencing company and plant-level decisions. Although rights to codetermination are limited in scope, they cover issues that are central to the lean production discourse: regulation of the pay-performance link, allocation of working hours, overtime, personnel transfers, and dismissals. In other areas, such as personnel development, work organization, the working environment, and business and financial matters, works councils are entitled to be consulted (Müller-Jentsch 1995).

Instead of tackling the broad subject of how the rights of the works councils fit into the broader system of industrial relations, this chapter focuses on the significance of lean production to three areas of this system. First is the relevance of lean production to the Standort debate. Second is the controversial issue of implementation, specifically, the effects of lean production on employment matters. Third is how different companies have arrived at solutions to the challenge of how to deal with lean production so as to increase competitiveness and secure employment.

Standort Debate

The Standort debate centers on how working conditions in industrial companies in Germany compare with those in other countries. The employers took the offensive in this debate by criticizing the high wages, increasingly shorter working hours, high rates of absenteeism, high taxes, restrictions and rigidities caused by government regulation, and union power. The union and works councils countered with arguments about industrial peace, the high qualification levels of German workers, and Germany's strong competitive position in the world market, particularly in the 1980s. The Standort debate traditionally has been divisive and ideologically loaded and became even more heated when a subsequent debate arose over deregulation of labor law.

Given these heated conditions, labor and management welcomed the introduction of lean production principles, which served as a catalyst for compromises and the development of joint programs. Of course, both sides had other motives as well; employers hoped to deregulate certain areas that were codetermined, while IG Metall, the metalworkers union which represents the vast majority of employees in the automobile industry, and the works councils sought for greater influence over work design. Nonetheless, the top representatives of both sides recognized the human-centered qualities of the lean production system.

In the October 1992 issue of *VDI-Nachrichten,* a journal published by the Association of German Engineers, Franz Steinkühler, the leader of IG Metall at that time, offered his cooperation to Gesamtmetall, the employers' federation that represents Germany's automobile companies in collective bargaining, to "overcome obsolete forms of organization, be it on the shop floor or the company level. . . . After all, there is an increasing contradiction between detached hierarchies and bureaucratic control, the extreme division of labor and the neglect of workers' competence and creativity, not only with regard to the needs and desires of the employers, but also with regard to the requirements of a flexible and efficient production system" (4).

Within IG Metall, the guidelines that Gesamtmetall recommended to its member companies for implementing lean production were widely appreciated. These guidelines concluded by saying that "competitive companies depend on the creativity, engagement, and qualification of their employees. But only through the appropriate design of work and process organization and the right style of leadership can this potential be realized and further developed."

A Shift of Emphasis

The first phase of the lean production debate centered on group work or teamwork. In the second half of the 1980s, staff members of IG Metall, influenced by Volvo's newly opened Uddevalla plant, developed a concept for group work (Muster and Richter 1990; Roth and Kohl 1988; Turner 1991). The need to elect a team spokesperson and to develop sociotechnical requirements for teamwork were strongly emphasized. The employers' federation and management at Germany's auto companies had not thought much about teamwork before it was heralded as the "dynamic heart of the lean factory" (Womack, Jones, and Roos 1990:99). IG Metall's criteria for teamwork were therefore often accepted when discussions started between works councils and management on whether it should be introduced.

Only later did management begin to emphasize various features of teamwork, notably kaizen activities and team commitment to performance targets. The flattening of supervisory hierarchies and the creation of small, responsible management units designed to compete with outside vendors became increasingly seen as core concepts (Warnecke 1992).

In the more than five years since the adoption of lean production by German companies, major differences in the degree of emphasis on teamwork have become evident. Some manufacturers have achieved almost full integration of their workforces into teams, while others, as discussed in chapter 7, are in a pilot stage. The differences cannot be explained by blockades and controversies in the industrial relations arena, however. Rather, operations managers often hesitate to introduce far-reaching changes, while top-level managers have other priorities.

In every case in which teamwork has been introduced, the works councils have been involved through plant or company-level agreements, and joint steering groups have been set up to monitor the process. Thus, implementation has been a fully codetermined process. IG Metall refrained from providing central guidelines for teamwork, thereby allowing the local actors to experiment and develop their own solutions.

Lean Production during the Recession

The newly opened markets in Eastern Europe seemed to offer an ideal opportunity for German auto plants to implement lean production. The hope was that the adverse effects on employment would be offset by growth in production volume. This expectation was not realized, however. In fact, when the recession came in 1993, the additional capacity built up in East Germany (in the new Opel and VW plants and at Skoda) increased the pressure to reduce capacity. Most manufacturers thought personnel reductions of 20 to 30 percent were necessary.

Codetermination cannot hinder employers from reducing personnel, but it makes it a costly and cumbersome procedure. The primary selection criteria used by works councils for individual dismissal—age and seniority—often force the "wrong" people to go. To avoid such counterproductive effects, management and works councils prefer to look for alternative solutions, the two classical ones being to offer early retirement and severance pay to induce voluntary terminations and to shorten working hours through short-term layoffs. Both methods have been in use since the mid-1970s, and with both options, affected persons receive base income out of the unemployment fund of the public labor market administration and additional compensation from the companies to maintain their income levels at previous levels.

On this basis, the German auto industry practiced a lifetime employment policy throughout the latter half of the 1970s and the 1980s. Safeguarding against dismissals (for nonpersonal reasons) has been the number-one priority for IG Metall ever since. At the same time, the union never opposed measures aimed at rationalizing production, such as the introduction of new technologies. By demanding a shortening of the regular workweek from forty hours (1984) to thirty-five hours (1995), it tried to establish parameters for such measures that protected the principle of employment security.

By 1992–93, however, the double effect of the recession and the introduction of lean production measures could no longer be compensated for in the usual ways, since the workweek had already been reduced to thirty-six hours and the labor market administration had tightened the conditions required to "subsidize" early retirement schemes and had signaled that it had reached the limits of its financial capability to compensate for layoffs caused by shortened workweek schemes.

To keep up the pressure to improve costs and productivity and continue the use of lean production methods, works councils and management at plant and company levels at most of the German car manufacturers worked out agreements to secure the future existence of their production sites. These *Standortsicherungs* or location-guaranteeing agreements differed in the way this goal was to be achieved. Concessions could be made in wages and benefits; shop-floor commitments could be made to achieve improvement targets; or income could be reduced along with working hours. The next section discusses several such agreements.

Standortsicherungs Agreements

The Standortsicherungs agreements struck at Ford and Opel's German sites in 1993 and 1994 focused squarely on cutting costs. This could be done within the framework of the agreement reached between IG Metall and the employers' federation by paying part of the yearly wage increase specified in the agreement from funds set aside voluntarily by the companies for such items as Christmas bonuses and vacation pay.

In addition, the Opel agreement of 1993 stated that "to maintain competitiveness, plant costs [would] have to be reduced by at least 30 percent within the next three years" (agreement 18.11). To achieve this goal, the company and the works council agreed to three changes: first, the elimination or reduction of a range of wage allowances; second, a stepwise reduction in the rate of absenteeism to 6 percent in 1997 on the basis of a concrete action plan; and, third, to the formation of project groups at the sites to develop plans for cost savings that in sum should result in savings of amounts specified in the agreement. In exchange, the company committed to maintaining the existing production sites, detailing its future products and projects in each case.

The 1994 agreement (25.2) reached at Ford for "securing investment at Ford Germany" is similar to the one in effect at Opel. In exchange for wage concessions, the elimination of bonus payments and wage allowances, and the formation of joint project groups to work out further cost savings, management has specified its product and investment plans for each of the German sites as far as this can be influenced by Ford Germany.

The 1993 "agreement at Mercedes-Benz AG between the company board and general works council to improve the competitiveness of the production sites and to reduce personnel" (14.12) follows the same pattern as that at Opel and Ford but adds as an explicit goal the reduction of personnel. Both sides confirm their intention that this shall be achieved in a "socially acceptable" form through early retirement and offers of severance pay. When reduction targets cannot be reached by these methods at the local level, working-time reduction schemes are to be negotiated at each location, thereby allowing for flexibility with regard to changes in the volume of production. In exchange for the works council's cooperation in reducing personnel and concessions concerning the annual increase in pay (like those agreed to at Opel and Ford) and reductions in break times, management at Mercedes-Benz has agreed that there will be no dismissals for economic reasons and has given its approval to produce a new car line at the German assembly plant Rastatt and not at a location outside Germany.

The 1993 collective agreement at Volkswagen (15.12) aimed to achieve cost reductions by lowering wages and salaries in return for a 20 percent reduction in the workweek from 36 to 28.8 hours. By mid-1992, declining sales resulting from the economic recession and the impact of lean production measures made it obvious that large-scale redundancies could no longer be avoided. It was projected that thirty thousand (i.e., 30 percent) out of one hundred thousand employees would have to be cut as soon as possible if the company was to survive. Volkswagen had already reduced labor by almost that magnitude over the previous three years. Thus, early retirement packages were offered to workers as young as fifty-five. In addition, negative side effects of the company's early retirement policy combined with a hiring freeze had become evident. The early retirement policy had created an extremely uneven age distribution, so that a dramatic loss of workers with experience and competence occurred whenever those in an age group that had been hired in a good year left. This was just the opposite of what the "learning organization" approach would require.

In light of this situation, it became clear to the company as well as to the works council and IG Metall that the implementation of lean production practices—the introduction of teamwork, continuous improvement activities, and outsourcing of noncore activities—could not be upheld in the face of mass dismissals. Therefore, within a short time the company representatives and the works council/union agreed to the 28.8-hour workweek and the corresponding 20 percent reduction in income for all employees. Four points in this agreement are worth noting. First is its long-term character (it was originally to apply for two years but subsequently was extended in a follow-up agreement). Second is its strictness with regard to the goal of work sharing: overtime is to be compensated for by free time, and no overtime supplement is paid for work performed during the twenty-eighth to the thirty-fifth hours. Third is its egalitarian character: the terms of the agreement extend to all employees, including salaried staff and management up to the executive board. Fourth is the role of the works council in comanaging the reallocation of personnel between areas and functions, which had to be redefined to rebalance the operations. Being given this role was regarded as a major achievement by the works council; codetermination was thereby extended beyond what is stipulated by law, and management waived its prerogative to institute mass dismissals.

The reduction of weekly working hours by 20 percent did not suffice to meet the savings target of 30 percent, however. The remaining 10 percent was to be covered by a further reduction in working hours for two groups of employees. The first such group would have included newly certified skilled workers, who normally would become regular employees after finishing their apprenticeship. They would have started out working a twenty-hour week and then would have been phased in over four years until they were working a full week at their full income level. The second such group would have included fifty-five-to-sixty-three-year-old employees who were to be phased out in a similar manner. The retirement program did not work out, however, because it relied on the willingness of employees to enter into the arrangement. The same was true of another scheme that would have temporarily removed workers from the payroll by offering them the opportunity to spend three to six months in training, during which they would have received public unemployment funds. The training would have taken place at a newly founded "coaching company" affiliated with VW. The labor market administration was unwilling to finance these courses, however, and rejected the plan. Its rejection can be interpreted as a sign that the traditional German way of solving private and public problems cooperatively may be eroding.

Summary and Outlook

The common key element of the agreements in force at Opel, Mercedes-Benz, and Volkswagen is that the works council/union has accepted concessions that reduce labor costs in return for a guarantee of employment security. Employment security is seen as a prerequisite for implementing such lean production measures as teamwork and kaizen activities.

The agreement reached at Volkswagen clearly is the most far-reaching in safeguarding employment while allowing for lean production, even during times of recession. To achieve flexibility with regard to fluctuations in order volumes and to accommodate differences among sites and areas, the agreement of September 1995 allows for an increase in weekly working hours, up to 38.8. Workers who have an excess in their "hours savings account" may take time off with pay or continue to save the hours and use them later for extended periods of paid leave or to take early retirement.

The VW agreement served as a model for the general agreement reached between IG Metall and the employers' federation in the 1994 round of bargaining. The purpose of this agreement is to support the process within companies in the metal-related and electrotechnical industries to improve cost structures and competitiveness while avoiding further increases in unemployment. On the basis of this agreement, labor-management partners at company levels can agree to a reduction in regular working hours within a framework of thirty to thirty-six hours in general or in the case of certain operations, departments, or groups of employees. In each case, these levels can be exceeded or not attained as long as this is compensated for within a one-year time frame.

In view of these developments, it has become clear that codetermination was not an obstacle to the introduction of lean production during the first half of the 1990s in Germany. Rather, it provided a framework in which lean production practices could be maintained even in difficult situations. It has also become clear, however, that for it to support lean production, the union had its conditions. These conditions shaped the way lean production was implemented and the concepts and priorities that surrounded the process of change.

The VW solution was widely appreciated by the public, yet most German companies have not followed in the same direction. This solution offers new opportunities for flexibility in work that have not yet been fully recognized, but it also has its risks. It presents opportunities to labor and management insofar as it protects the human resources of the company from being devastated by cyclical mass redundancies. It also helps decouple the lean production process from fear of unemployment. Finally, and of major importance, it offers enormous flexibility with regard to changes in volume over the year and among different areas and groups within the company. The works council has largely waived its right to codetermination in cases of overtime, which has been one of its major sources of power in the past.

There are also risks associated with the VW agreement, insofar as it may reduce the feeling that the need for change is urgent and reinforce attitudes of complacency within the organization. Also, by reducing everyone's work time, it puts pressures on the firm to outsource, possibly beyond the limits of core competencies. Functions and projects that are critical for "time-based competition"—work in product development, process engineering, testing—might have to be done too much by outside engineering services. Finally, the shortage of employees and the frequent absences because workers are taking time off to compensate for overtime have created many everyday problems with scheduling meetings, reaching people, and transferring knowledge and information.

7

Germany: Labor's Perspective on Lean Production

Siegfried Roth

The development of the German production system is unique because of the importance of the skilled worker (*Facharbeiter*), trained through the so-called dual training system, which combines formal education and theoretical learning with a strong in-service training component in designated companies. The technical and philosophical orientation of this model owes much to the features of craft production and remained in force long after the advent and establishment of mass production. The skilled worker takes center stage in this model, and the worker's broad-based knowledge of materials, tools, machinery, processes, and products has enabled him or her to carry out a wide range of complex tasks without close supervision. As a result, skilled work in Germany has always been seen as multifaceted and integrated with other industrial labor and has not been subject to Taylorist fragmentation, supervision, and control structures.

As industrial development has proceeded in Germany, companies have therefore preserved elements of craft methods. Sectors with small product runs and client-oriented, individualized production have met the need for high quality and a high level of flexibility with self-regulation of integrated processes. Hence, in many sectors, semiautonomous groups are crucial elements in the way work is organized. In many companies, there was no need to define and institute such groups, since they often grew quite naturally out of the way in which skilled workers were trained. In the automobile industry, for example, some companies have group work structures that date back to the immediate postwar period; these structures have proved stable and resilient, although the label "group work" was a later addition. Typically, these structures have arisen specifically in areas dominated by skilled workers, where product runs are small, the products themselves are complex, and a high level of subject expertise is required. Informal group structures also existed—and still do exist—in Fordist mass production companies; here, they defy the principle of hierarchical control or maintain a seamless production flow on the basis of self-regulation.

Fearing loss of control, management has always viewed the use of semiautonomous groups as problematic. For management, the challenge has been to limit the relatively autonomous areas in companies by means of "expropriation" of expertise and by formalizing processes. By contrast, for employees, self-regulated skilled work and semiautonomous group work were part of the challenge facing them—that of loosening management control and keeping the emancipatory elements of working methods over which they had more say and greater influence. This controversial issue has been reflected in disputes concerning domination and the desire for more humane work.

With a few exceptions, German management has failed either to understand or to make full use of the enormous post-Taylorist potential of trained skilled workers. In the past, skilled workers—with the support of trade unions—maintained self-organizing structures that were often implemented in the face of restrictive management models. In this sense, skilled work has always been an inherent obstacle to Taylorist ideas in Germany.

That semiskilled industrial workers take skilled workers as their model for vocational identity and enthusiasm for training demonstrates the attraction for German industrial workers of organizing work in an integrated and self-regulating way. Horst Kern and Charles F. Sabel (1994) argue that in expanding the scope of old forms of organization, there is a release of the workers' potential. The discrepancy between the skills requirements and the existing training profiles of workers in the German automobile industry illustrates the human potential currently lying unused, and in all sectors of the industry there is a substantial skills surplus. By clinging to old forms of work organization, companies are failing to make full use of the existing skills potential available to them (Schumann et al. 1994). The situation in assembly work illustrates this particularly vividly; there, young skilled workers react to the underuse of their skills not with high rates of turnover (as in Sweden) but with absenteeism and underperformance.

Humanization of Work: A Superseded German Tradition

The demand for humanization of work runs like a thread through the history of German industrial production, representing a permanent struggle for improvements in working and living conditions. The thrust of the humanization movement is fundamentally the broadening of individuals' scope of action. "Liberation in work," on the basis of greater self-organization, means broadening the scope of workers' initiative (the horizontal element) but also the scope of decision making (the vertical element).

In Germany, humanization has always been addressed in the context of improved living conditions. As far back as the 1970s, there was discussion of using further cuts in working time to do this, but it was not until 1984 that IG Metall's collective agreement paved the way for the thirty-five-hour week.

Government initiatives aimed at humanizing work promoted company-level projects from 1974 to the early 1980s that sought to secure improvements in conditions not only for the workforce but for the companies themselves. Many projects provided valuable experience in the structuring of work, work organization, and the development of new technologies to replace the assembly line. The approaches taken included not only the implementation of such restrictive measures as lowering staffing levels and simple job rotation but forms of semiautonomous group work coupled with job enhancement. These experiments resulted in the use of buffers that broke the link between automated sections of production and the individuals doing the work. Manual jobs were also arranged so that they were independent of the line.

Experiments with group work based on the U-shape principle were proposed as early as the 1970s and combined job rotation and an improved scope of communication between workers with a high level of flexibility and short lines. The ideas were not put into practice, however, until the 1980s, when Toyota developed the U-shape principle as part of the Toyota production system, by which time the German experiments of the 1970s had long been forgotten.

Despite these positive initial experiences, for a number of reasons, the group work concept never got beyond the experimental stage. Many firms failed to take sufficient account of plant or company cultures; the concept was not developed in collaboration with employees but imposed on them; works councils frequently withheld their support, since the economic interests of the companies were being put first; and, in most cases, the central interests of the workers for better pay and better skills training were ignored. Although important and valuable information was gained, the experience had no impact on auto companies. Indeed, even in companies that conducted publicly funded projects, practically no management employees have any recollection of them. As we shall see, the group work concept was revived in the 1990s, however, this time because of union demands.

Break with Continuity in the 1980s

Although the humanization experiments of the 1970s had clearly demonstrated the cost-effectiveness of achieving a balanced combination of human labor, technology, and organization, the focus in the 1980s shifted solely to automation. Companies invested in new information and communications technology and flexible manufacturing systems—in short, in developing the computer-integrated factory—in the hope of offsetting Japan's competitive advantage. Although mechanization and automation did produce some improvements in productivity and quality, in purely accounting terms they often had a negative effect on companies' profitability and use of capacity. Production operations also were much more subject to downtime. The combinations of complex, flexible technology and traditional Taylorist organizational structures were clearly not the way to compete with the Japanese.

"Fossilized" Taylorism left a large number of computer-integrated factories in its wake. For at least the next ten years, the advantages of worker-oriented organization models, and especially the "learning-curve effect," could not be turned to competitive advantage. In many companies where technological approaches to problem solving had been centralized, chaos was not conquered but managed. Meanwhile, Japan was going down another path—that of simple, easy-to-master automation combined with the delegation of responsibility and clear organizational structures (such as kanban). The lean production debate, which was particularly heated in the German automobile industry, forced a radical change of perspective, however, and companies hoped for spectacular results if they coupled schemes to cut "excess fat" from their production systems with broad-based cost-cutting measures. The same radical energy that years before had been pumped into technological solutions was now being channeled into the allegedly best-practice solutions of lean production.

Many sectors of German industry are now struggling to keep up with the latest trends. The new Toyota and Nissan plants on Kyushu have already instigated "post-Toyotaism," whose central planks are more attractive work, greater use of buffers, reduction of just-in-time production, and greater automation. Takahiro Fujimoto (1994) has described this change as a shift from a "lean-on-growth" model to a "lean-on-balance" model. Although there are signs in Germany of a trend toward striking a balance between a productivity and a human orientation, the question of whether German industry will find its own way through a second "post-lean" phase remains open. If it does, then in the tradition of the movement to humanize work, it is likely to aim to achieve a balance between work that is both efficient and attractive.

So far, German management does not appear to be making such a radical shift. There are, however, a few promising exceptions of companies pursuing the principles of humanization, with the aim of giving workers greater scope of initiative while creating greater company efficiency at the same time (Tropitzsch 1994).

The second radical break with traditional concepts and expertise that occurred in the 1980s demonstrates the dilemma faced by German management. Success factors, experience, and expertise are often undervalued in Germany, yet management is open to possibly successful solutions from other social systems that do not share the strengths of the German system. It is in some respects a reflection of the problems of a postwar generation that mistrusts its own traditions and prefers to import solutions to its problems.

Move to Lean Production

The wide public debate surrounding the publication of Womack, Jones, and Roos's book *The Machine That Changed the World* (1990) highlighted qualitative competitive factors that had previously been given such prominence only in the German humanization debate. Many management representatives realized only at this point that a process of change was occurring in industry worldwide in which such qualitative considerations as workers' skills, motivation, and potential for creativity were becoming of increasing importance. Womack, Jones, and Roos's study mercilessly exposed weaknesses in the way management in Germany, and in Europe more generally, dealt with such matters.

The increasing competitiveness of the automobile industry in the early 1990s and the general disorientation of the German automobile industry's leaders in the production debate resulted in the Womack, Jones, and Roos study (1990) being hailed as a lifeline. The discussion of lean production dominated not only business and trade union circles but also public debate for months. From a company viewpoint, lean production seemed to offer an appropriate way of integrating widely differing and independent reorganization measures. Integrating concepts down the process chain both within and between companies seemed a good way of combining high productivity gains with improved organizational structures.

The unions held out great hopes that the debate would prompt a move away from excessive fragmentation of work, impenetrable management hierarchies, and bureaucracy. They saw awareness that self-responsibility and motivation were key elements in effective production as opening up new opportunities for coupling the humanization of work with industrial democracy, on the one hand, and with greater efficiency and competitiveness, on the other. The unions warned, however, that against the backdrop of increasingly intense competition companies should not see lean production merely as a way of making short-term savings by the familiar management device of using intensification of work and job cuts to cut costs. The unions, instead, demanded efficiency improvements in plant and company organization. These included the following:

> better information and communication, more rapid decision making as a result of flatter hierarchies, decentralization, and the strengthening of responsibility within areas of the companies and suppliers; greater integration of tasks and cooperation, for example, between development and production, between production planning and implementation, and, particularly, along the supply chain between companies (a "value-creation partnership"); the introduction of group work to broaden workers' influence and responsibility on the basis of self-organization; and continuous improvement based not primarily on staffing cuts and work intensification but on increased efficiency, improvements in working conditions, and ecological production methods (Roth 1992:36).

In the wake of the recession in 1993 and 1994, these hopes were largely dashed. Lean production was widely seen as a method of cutting excess fat in the traditional sense, and job cuts were the main way of overcoming the problems the automobile industry faced at the time. Even when there were signs of an economic upturn in the industry, thousands of jobs were still being cut, and many companies did not know how to meet their need for experienced skilled workers. Moreover, the workers who were retained were very disillusioned about the way in which new production concepts could be changed. Their experience was that of classic rationalization, carried out primarily at the expense of the workforce. Despite the claims made for lean production, the workforce was seen largely as a cost factor that had to be reduced. In most areas of the industry, there was no understanding that the workforce was a key resource for innovation that needed to be cultivated and promoted.

Myth of Japan's Lead in Productivity

The findings of the Womack, Jones, and Roos (1990) study were clear: Japanese automobile manufacturers were twice as efficient as their European competitors in such key areas as productivity and quality. This devastatingly simple message had both a galvanizing and a paralyzing effect on the German automobile industry. Long-overdue reorganization methods were implemented, regardless of how appropriate they were, but at the same time management panicked in the face of Japan's apparently substantial competitive edge. Management demanded immediate improvements in productivity, which in itself produced contradictions.

The findings of the Womack, Jones, and Roos (1990) study pointed clearly to the fact that changes in organization and the use of human resources could not be introduced overnight. Almost any attempts to implement organizational change and learning processes in the German automobile industry foundered on the need for short-term cost savings, however. Top management typically responded to demands from works councils and trade unions for real organizational change with comments such as, "Yes, of course, we want that, too, but we can't afford the time. We need to cut costs now, not in two or three years."

Awareness that the productivity gap between Germany and Japan was "not as dramatic" as had originally been assumed came from German comparative studies (Springer 1993) but went largely unheeded. In 1994, IG Metall carried out a joint study project with Japanese trade unions to draw up an exhaustive comparison of productivity in the German and Japanese automobile industries. Inter alia, they compared gross value added per employee in seven German and nine Japanese automobile manufacturers from 1981 to 1990. The figures were calculated both at 1990 rates of exchange and at actual past rates.

Average gross value added per employee amounted to 92,000 DM per year in Germany compared with 131,000 DM in Japan during the period 1981–90. These averages do not, however, give the whole picture. With an average figure of 184,000 DM per year, Toyota clearly leads the league, putting it substantially ahead of not only the German manufacturers but also the other Japanese manufacturers, whose figures range from 93,000 DM to 128,000 DM. For the German manufacturers, the range is between 85,000 DM and 102,000 DM. If Toyota is removed from the calculations, then over the 1980s, average gross value added per employee was 92,000 DM in the seven German companies and 112,000 DM in the eight remaining Japanese companies. In other words, over this ten-year period the eight Japanese companies were only 22 percent ahead of their German rivals in gross value added per employee, and only Toyota had a figure twice as high as that of its German competitors. Thus, the "100 percent hypothesis" put forth in the Womack, Jones, and Roos (1990) study was true of only one Japanese manufacturer.

Because of the large differences in working time in the two countries, gross value added per employee is not necessarily a very indicative index by which to compare Germany and Japan. Therefore, the researchers also compared gross value added per employee per hour worked. These figures showed that during the 1980s employees in Japanese auto companies worked an average of 2,189 hours each year, whereas the figure for the German companies was 1,599 hours. The figures are for actual annual hours including overtime. In other words, the German auto workers' actual working year was 31 percent shorter than that worked by their counterparts in Japan.

Using these figures, the researchers then calculated average gross value added per employee per hour worked for the 1981–90 period. They found that for all seven German companies, the figure was 58 DM per employee per hour; for all nine Japanese companies, 60 DM; for the eight Japanese companies excluding Toyota, 51 DM; and for Toyota, 82 DM.

The German average was virtually the same as that for all the Japanese manufacturers taken together and higher than the figure for the Japanese companies excluding Toyota, and this held at both 1990 and past rates of exchange. The gap between the seven German companies and Toyota was 29 percent, while the gap between Toyota and the remaining Japanese companies was 38 percent.

The conclusion from the study was that the productivity level determined by gross hourly product was about 10 percent higher for the German automobile companies than for the eight Japanese companies excluding Toyota (a range of 5 to 15 percent once exchange rate fluctuations are taken into account). Thus, Japan did not have a productivity lead over Germany, especially when one excluded Toyota from the group of companies one was comparing. Moreover, the gap had narrowed over the years between the German companies and Toyota—as Womack, Jones, and Roos (1990) suggested would occur—with the result that by 1990, even that gap was only about 22 percent.

Comparisons of gross value added and product per hour worked clearly illustrate that the cost advantages of the Japanese manufacturers can be attributed largely to economic and social conditions. Further, although length of working time has played a small part in the differences, the key factor has been the Japanese workers' longer working hours and lower hourly pay or hourly labor costs.

The differences in productivity between the Japanese and German companies suggest that the eight companies, excluding Toyota, would not be competitive under German conditions, that is, if their pay levels were higher and their working year shorter. If the extensive reorganization in the German automobile industry since 1992 is included in the equation (although to do so formally would require a new, updated comparison), there is strong evidence to suggest that the German companies have actually taken an even greater lead over their eight Japanese rivals, excluding Toyota. Strong currency and exchange rate movements affect the calculations for both countries, but it seems that the German industry is in a better position to offset the cost disadvantages of a strong deutsche mark than is its Japanese counterpart in relation to the yen.

Yet Germany's decisive productivity potential is being frittered away. A move away from short-term cost-cutting measures coupled with a shift toward long-term improvements in efficiency on the basis of the use and promotion of human resources would release even more potential and increase the competitive edge over Japan still further.

Later Developments: Group Work Becomes Universal

The broad-ranging debate around group work and the advent of internationally standardized concepts of group work on the basis of common skills took on a positive tone in late 1992 and early 1993, when most German automobile manufacturers began the transition to the universal implementation of group work.

In 1990, only about 4 percent of all production workers in German automobile manufacturers were estimated to be working in group work situations, most of them in pilot schemes. By 1993, this figure had risen to 9.5 percent, and within a year it had risen to 22.2 percent. Thus, by 1994, some sixty-nine thousand production workers were in groups, representing a doubling of the figure in twelve months.

Audi made the transition in 1994. That year, about 68.4 percent of its production workers were involved in group work, compared with only 7.7 percent the year before. The figure needs to be qualified, however, since most of these groups were newly established and had yet to move beyond the early stages of group allocation and the election of group spokespersons. As a result, members of these groups were not yet acquiring the skills needed to have complete interchangeability of tasks, as is typical of more mature groups. If the Audi figures are excluded from the calculations for this reason, then by 1994 about 17 percent of all auto production workers were working under conditions in which there was interchangeability of tasks and self-distribution of work.

The findings illustrate strikingly the wide gap between companies. While Opel and Audi have gone all-out to institute group work across the board and have experienced major internal difficulties as a result, such as spiraling demands for training, BMW, Mercedes, and Volkswagen have proceeded more cautiously. One could argue that Ford is acting wholly in character in relation to group work: it is leaving it to others to carry out the experiments and may follow at a later stage. Porsche is playing a rather special role in that although it does not officially have group work, its short product runs and high proportion of skilled workers mean that its workers tend to work in integrated ways already.

These company-by-company findings are disappointing and give pause for thought. For many years, IG Metall and its works council members have been fighting for the introduction of group work instead of managerial work allocation. Throughout the 1980s, management generally rejected such demands, yet in many areas of the automobile industry, works councils fought to have group work accepted into company planning, and management eventually, if painfully, was convinced of its advantages. But in spite of the evident improvements in efficiency with group work, most of the management representatives at German automobile companies have never quite shed their original skepticism and hesitancy.

Internationalization of Production Concepts: Pressure on the German Model

German trade unions have tailored their demands for new concepts of production to the principles of humanization and have drawn heavily on Swedish experiences with semiautonomous work groups. Many demands for liberation from the belt, long-cycle assembly of entire units, interchangeability of workers, and self-organization have been based on experiments at Volvo and Saab in Sweden. During the orientation and research phase in the 1980s, the Swedish model was used to design some of the pilot schemes in the German automobile industry. Management took very different views of group work at that time, however.

The Womack, Jones, and Roos (1990) study prompted a strong move in the direction of the Japanese experience of production, and the subsequent wide public debate focused on whether Japanese concepts could be transferred to Germany. The result of the tensions highlighted in the debate about Toyotaism versus Volvoism was the emergence of a third model. The opening of the Opel factory in a greenfield site in Eisenach marked the beginning of a trend toward concepts transplanted from North America.

These concepts are based not on the unique qualities of the skilled worker or the related skills profile of semiskilled workers but on more narrowly defined common skills. Work in such sites is typically very restricted, with short-cycle and belt-dependent tasks (cycles are usually of about sixty seconds), a total focus on production line work, limited scope for widening the tasks done by individuals or for rotation, and minimal integration of indirect functions into the line. Moreover, self-organization is limited to a very few areas. Completing the picture are strict rules on conduct, low staffing levels, and continual increases in pressure. One of the key features of these operations is the cycle of continuous improvement, a concept that dictates that high levels of performance should be stimulated by permanent "excess loading"—the need to produce more vehicles with the same level of staffing, among other things—and that the results of the process are incorporated into further standardization of work. The cycle then begins again, starting with the new standards.

The concept of excess loading is currently sweeping other German automobile manufacturers and is causing bitter disputes between management and works councils. The experiences with the Canadian transplant CAMI (Robertson et al. 1993a) and of Nissan UK in Sunderland (Garrahan et al. 1992) resulted in works councils and trade union officials, as well as a few managers, realizing that these production models were provoking huge resistance on the part of employees and that they were unsuited to the German environment. The most commonly criticized features mentioned in employee surveys conducted at CAMI were the large workload and employee disillusionment. Nonetheless, large numbers of German managers are attracted to these standardized and Taylorized forms of group work since they have always opposed group work schemes with high levels of self-organization and set greatest store in new concepts of production with ease of planning, transparency, and control.

Conflicts between Taylorist Structures and Self-Organized Group Work

Proponents of new concepts of production in the automobile industry are caught in a double bind. Against a background of internationalization, they must follow practices that have proved successful worldwide, yet they must also take their own structural conditions into account. In the German case, the focus has shifted to the international models, and this is producing distortions and loss of potential because of the mismatch between existing conditions and prescribed solutions.

The basis for any discussion of the appropriateness of concepts of production—alongside technical and organizational structures and market and competitive conditions—is their staffing and skills requirements and employee attitudes to work. If these factors can be considered as performance motivators, they produce interesting indicators of the line that concepts of production need to take.

Table 7.1, which compares motivators in Germany with those in Japan (Jürgens 1992), clearly illustrates that attitudes among German workers are changing; they are not "just doing a job" but are increasingly thinking in career terms, desiring jobs with interesting content, scope for decision making, and self-determination. Despite the auto industry's Taylorist structures, the skilled worker orientation of German companies has persisted for decades and it is this that determines employees' relationship with their work. This phenomenon produces a very strong identification with a quality product that goes far beyond identification with the company. This has no parallel in Japan.

In workforce surveys, German employees of all ages put "interesting work" at the top of their order of priorities, ahead of "good pay," and followed it with "a good company atmosphere." If their desire for interesting job content and independent production is satisfied through the use of appropriate semiautonomous work structures and workers are offered appropriate pay and a high level of job security, significant gains in performance can result.

A simple yet crucial conclusion can be drawn from this discussion. German workers are usually highly motivated if they have interesting jobs and a high level of self-organization. Many managers seek to release further reserves of productivity by means of complex motivational strategies, yet in doing so they miss the real point: the workforce is already fundamentally motivated. What management needs to focus on instead is eliminating

Table 7.1 Performance Motivators in Germany versus Japan

Germany	Japan
Interest in job content	Recognition through the group
Desire for self-determined work and self-responsibility	Prospects for career advancement
	Pay linked to appraisal
Pay matched to demands	Lifelong employment
Job security	

*de*motivating conditions. These are, basically, organizational, work allocation, and management structures, as discussed below in a comparison of group work and the Japanese system of kaizen.

The distinctions between Taylorized group work and self-organized group work in the German automobile industry are compared in table 7.2. There is a tension in companies between these two extremes that is manifested mostly between works councils and management but that also erupts between the two camps within management.

Approaches to Kaizen in the German Automobile Industry

There are two distinct strategic approaches to kaizen in the German automobile manufacturing industry: the expert-led process and the group-led process (table 7.3). The former is typified by an orientation to short-term results.

The focus of the expert-led kaizen process is prescribed, as are also, in many cases, the savings objectives. External moderators and supervisors formulate these objectives, which are couched solely in economic terms. Kaizen activities concentrate primarily on the production area and within that area on throughput times, transit times, and staffing requirements. Any gains in efficiency cannot be built upon, since any initial success is rapidly followed by disappointment. German employees react coolly to externally imposed processes, and their willingness to pass on what they have learned from their experiences is limited, especially when the gains in productivity accrue solely to the company and no part is passed on to the workforce. Not surprisingly, this approach failed very early on in several German automobile companies.

Experiences with the group-led approach have been very different. This approach is focused on achieving long-term and steadily accruing improvements in efficiency. Suggestions are made within a group context, and all group members play an active part in formulating suggestions. Moderators,

Table 7.2 Taylorized Group Work versus Self-Organized Group Work in the German Automobile Industry

	Taylorized Group Work	**Self-Organized Group Work**
Job Content	Limited scope; close link to line speed; belt	Broad scope; liberated from line speed; "boxes"
Integration of Functions	Limited; allocation to groups; training of specialists	High: all group members can train for tasks (maintenance, follow-up, quality assurance, logistics, etc.)
Self-organization	Low: most tasks prescribed by supervisors, with scope for consultation	High: planning and supervision of work processes; social affairs; self-management
Group "Speakers"	Deployed on release from operational duties; junior management level; act as supervisors	Democratically elected; work collaboratively; are not part of management; represent and coordinate the group
Group Discussion	Restrictive: low level of participation; no cover during meetings; restrictions on choice of topics to productivity issues	Half-hour to one hour per week; cover during meetings; free choice of topics, including economic and social issues
Policy on Performance	Permanent overloading; standardized operations; continual optimization of operations and time scale	Stable conditions; compromise on performance between group and supervisors; codetermination through works council

experts, and supervisors see their role as being supportive and acting as catalysts rather than as overseeing and controlling. Kaizen groups discuss not only productivity-related issues but the full range of social matters affecting the group. Employee willingness to help optimize production processes is high, especially where workers receive a share of the gains made.

German Successes: Group Work among Skilled Workers

Genuinely skilled work has been achieved in the past only in indirect production areas, such as maintenance and tool-making. In the wake of the technical modernization of production in the 1980s in such so-called high-

Table 7.3 Approaches to Kaizen in the German Automobile Industry

	Led by Experts	Kaizen: Led by the Group
Goals/Efficiency	Short-term goals, high level of "one-off" effects ("fast buck")	Long-term and steadily growing efficiency improvements
Scope	Prescribed: economic topics only	Free choice: social and economic topics
Means	Workshops, weekly at most	Continual group activity
Focus of Activity	Experts, supervisors	Group and group "speakers"
Productivity Gains	For the company, the aim is to "mine" the workers' expertise and ideas	Profit sharing and "equal exchange" principle
Motivation	Low: expertise held back	High: willingness to optimize
Works Council	Protector: passive or defensive role	Both protects and influences; active and constructive role

tech areas as body shops and mechanical production areas, previously indirect tasks, such as maintenance, quality control, supervision of production, and scheduling, were gradually integrated. It is significant from a labor relations perspective that in the capital-intensive automated areas, production was largely "reprofessionalized" when this happened. A new role gradually emerged, that of the system regulator, who uses his wide hybrid skills to ensure the smooth flow of automated production. It is clear that such jobs will become increasingly important in the automobile industry, where there is a world-beating combination of professional skilled work and flexible technology.

As professionalization of the production area grows, so will pressure on management and supervisors to develop decentralized and self-governing units, as well as to introduce more transparent decision making and greater employee involvement. The desire for such self-organization exerts pressure for reorganization along self-governing and company unit lines. This shift is very much in keeping with modular or fractional concepts of the factory (the "factory within a factory" approach). Examples from mechanical production within the automobile industry show that there is progress toward expanding the integration of indirect tasks, reducing line dependence, greater planning of tasks, and greater self-organization, accompanied by highly developed communications and collaboration with other sections of the company.

One example from the same sector that illustrates the high level of integration of indirect functions that were formerly kept separate are the new system regulators. They spend their time as follows: preventive maintenance, 33.2 percent; function supervision, 28.3 percent; tool-fitting, 11.7 percent; loading/unloading, 8.0 percent; measuring/inspection, 7.6 percent; tool-changing, 5.7 percent; repairs, 5.3 percent; follow-up, 0.2 percent.

In mechanical production, high levels of job satisfaction and job content, which are related to the employees' skills, have reduced absenteeism from about 10 percent or more to 3.5 percent a year on average. The economic spin-off is also dramatic. German industry is ranked among the best worldwide for yield of vehicles per hour and, more significantly, on a level with the most efficient Japanese plants.

What is most significant, however, is the effect group work concepts have on employees' working conditions. The high level of task integration and wide-ranging self-organization give workers scope. This, in turn, has positive effects on workers' performance, their management of demands, and their interpersonal links. The higher the level of self-organization, coupled with self-management of time and availability of cover (e.g., for group discussions and training), the higher the acceptance of and willingness to integrate workers, especially older and poorer-performance employees, into the group. Those with psychological or mental problems are also more readily accepted if employees have scope to organize their work themselves, distribute it as they see fit, and support each other flexibly. Detlef Gerst et al. (1994) show that this is borne out in surveys of worker satisfaction.

Use of the self-organized group work model in high-tech areas of the German automobile industry is increasing rapidly. The concept has moved beyond the experimental phase and is now widely established in plants across the industry. It is not, however, suited only to the automobile industry. In particular, companies in the mechanical and plant engineering and electrical engineering sectors are using a model they call flexible production islands. These islands are in fact work groups that are defined by a high level of self-organization. The goal is to achieve "autonomous complete processes" by means of systems teams trained and skilled in all areas of the work. More than four hundred companies in Germany have already adopted this system.

This approach to skilled group work is a specifically German adaptation that one would not expect to be successful elsewhere. It seems to be an example of intelligent production based on the self-organization principle and the skilled worker model.

In light of the new demands on auto manufacturing in Germany, skilled work is also changing. The emphasis is shifting to the development of not only specific job content skills but competence in processes and methods, as well as social competencies based on the principles of self-organization. A clear, uniform model is now emerging along the lines of self-organized skilled group work. Moreover, this model is becoming established *despite* management's reaction, rather than *because* of it.

Wasted Potential: Group Work in Assembly

In contrast to the advances in traditional areas of production, progress toward group work in assembly is very patchy. In the past, various structures were piloted, ranging from the simple expansion of tasks (with no change to line structures) to experiments with wide and enhanced job content separated from the line. It has been difficult to discern any trend so far, however.

Several schemes are still in operation that survived the pilot projects. These vary from advanced forms of group work that involve a wide definition of job content and separation from the line to short-cycle assembly belt work that has not improved the workers' conditions vis-à-vis job content or self-organization.

More recently, a trend has emerged in which group work is developing along clearly Taylorist lines. This is occurring characteristically in companies that introduced belt independence for preassembly work and have reverted to reintegrating the belt system. In one multinational, there has been rapid integration of belt independent, preassembly structures in the areas of engine finishing, door assembly, and body assembly into existing assembly lines. This eliminated jobs that took from seven to twenty minutes and replaced them with a single cycle speed of just sixty seconds.

This trend is also visible in the new greenfield sites in Germany. The original plan aimed at wide-ranging integration of indirect tasks is increasingly being reversed and indirect functions are again becoming the preserve of specialists working in groups. In one "showcase" company, repairs have been moved back to the end of the line, quality assurance is carried out exclusively by specialists, and maintenance is the preserve of a special group of employees. The belt cycle is usually about 106 seconds. In another new plant, follow-up and logistics are now the work of specialists and the works council has been notified of a new scheme based on a 90-second cycle. Originally, this plant was to have developed into a belt-free plant; now, the assembly work could be said to be in the process of being re-Taylorized. The trend runs counter to the wishes and interests of assembly workers, and it is evident from surveys that most workers are in favor of taking increased responsibility for indirect tasks, such as quality control, materials provision, and follow-up work and maintenance, and want wide-scale job rotation. The job content interest is so marked in most employees' minds that they are often willing to take on additional tasks, even when this could possibly mean job intensification and a heavier workload (Gerst et al. 1994).

The problem is exacerbated because there is only a slight increase in demand for skilled workers in automobile assembly, while there is a substantially increased pool of skilled workers who frequently work below their level of skills training. Some seven out of every ten trained skilled workers in the automobile industry are in fact working below their skills level. The frustration this causes is not being tackled by means of appropriate changes in working structures but is instead being overlooked in the move toward Taylorized group work.

Clearly, the majority of the German automobile manufacturers are following production models that were developed in North American transplants. High levels of performance are sought based not on job content and employee motivation but on narrow prescriptions for standardized, belt-dependent work. The low-level task integration and self-organization, compared with the high-level belt dependence, is having an overwhelmingly negative impact on the employees' working conditions. Tight time frames are leading to greater performance pressure. A lack of self-organization is resulting in a breakdown of solidarity (manifesting itself in the jealous guarding of attractive jobs; swaps are refused, and those who do not perform well are put under pressure to leave). Opportunities are lacking to develop group structures along social lines. As in a Taylorist system, the reality for the workforce is characterized by limiting jobs and constraining conditions. The gulf between growing expectations of work and employment and the realities of the actual systems is becoming increasingly wide. It has proved impossible to implement the aim of workers to be in control of their own processes of optimization and improvement.

The juxtaposition of emerging Taylorized group work structures and the last vestiges of self-organized group work in assembly is causing great tensions in Germany's auto companies. As this new phase begins, works councils and trade unions are having not only to defend their positive experiences of skilled group work in assembly but to fight for a reversal of current trends. The German production system, including the Taylorized group work model, makes neither industrial relations nor economic sense.

It runs counter in every respect to employee expectations and to the skills profile of German assembly workers. In other words, the huge potential to achieve job satisfaction, personal commitment, and improved efficiency is being wasted. Group work in assembly areas cannot be based on as wide a range of tasks as it can in high-tech areas. Yet there are certain basic principles that could be mapped on to assembly work. Greater self-organization, function integration, and job content will result in greater identification with work and release previously untapped potential. The way this issue is resolved holds the key to the design of assembly production in the German automobile industry.

Conclusions

Until now, strategies of production in the German automobile industry have been characterized by a zigzag course marked by radical breaks between constantly changing orientations rather than by continuity. Management practice has failed to take existing conditions adequately into account and has negated native strengths. Independent German models of success (group work in expert areas) have been generated not *because* of management practices but *despite* them.

It is essential to recognize the variety of developmental paths and learning processes that have been followed in the German automobile industry. The dynamics of group work among skilled workers show a development from skill and professional competence toward self-organization. Social and cooperative competence develop to the extent that room for action is allowed, but also to the extent that supportive training measures are provided. Group work in the assembly process, by contrast, is subject to restrictive conditions. The level of worker qualification under which tasks can be redistributed is lower than among skilled workers. In addition, Taylorized group work has become firmly established.

It is often impossible to start down the path of self-organization by improving skills or professional competence. Rather, conditions must be created to stimulate the development of social and cooperative competence, which can then be recognized as qualifications for further training. These qualifications include influence over the supervision of working processes, tasks given to personnel, and process organization; planning of training, vacations, group discussions, and short breaks; cooperation and coordination with prior and subsequent steps in the production process and shift changes; time resources for group discussions, training, and coordination; and influence over the setting of the conditions of work performance.

Experience has shown that the development of social and cooperative competence in the assembly area presupposes the availability of time (the form of which must be controlled by works councils) and initiates a learning process in which the employees make increasing demands to be involved in shaping the content of their work. For this reason, the expansion of skills or professional competence can take place at a later phase in the maturing process of groups. Stable social and cooperative structures of self-organization form the most suitable basis for this process.

There is no reason to give up hope even in the face of the Taylorized group work now established in many assembly areas. Current conditions are pushing in the direction of self-organization, but first it is necessary to clear the way of obstacles.

8

United Kingdom: The Reorganization of Production

Harry Scarbrough and Michael Terry

In their recent review of the adoption of lean production in the world auto industry, MacDuffie and Pil (1995b) develop an apparently paradoxical argument. They suggest that the increasing dominance of the forces of convergence toward lean production are likely to engender greater variability in the implementation of the model. In other words, convergence will result in increasing diversity around a dominant tendency. According to MacDuffie and Pil, there are two distinct sources for this variability. First, as a larger number of companies pursue the lean production model, variation in the rate of adoption increases—thereby becoming continuous rather than bimodal. Second, because of this increasing variability, it is harder to discern clear correlations between business strategy, organizing principles, and performance.

The following account of the Rover Group's implementation of lean production in the United Kingdom provides support for MacDuffie and Pil's argument. The Rover Group's experience exhibits both a shift toward the techniques, norms, and language of lean production yet simultaneously reveals a high level of inter- and even intraplant variability in practices around that central tendency. These findings also suggest a corollary to the MacDuffie and Pil argument. That is, increasingly elastic relationships between lean principles, business strategies, and economic performance in the convergence stage imply that the lean production model ceases to be the principal motor of change at this stage. Without a tightly recursive interdependency between lean production principles and economic advantage, lean production can no longer diffuse itself through its own self-generated momentum. In short, during the convergence stage in the spread of lean production, global explanations based on the differential effect of archetypal production models are no longer as helpful as accounts focusing on the context in which the change occurred. Thus, macro patterns of implementation increasingly have to be explained in terms of institutional context, regional and cultural differences, and so on, while micro patterns of change correspondingly revert to the dynamics of the plant-level "negotiation of order."

U.K. Context

The 1980s were a turbulent decade for British car producers. Between 1973 and 1989, car production fell by almost 26 percent, much of this accounted for by the Rover Group and its predecessor companies. During those sixteen years, Rover's output fell by 409,220 units, almost 47 percent of its 1979 level (Williams et al. 1994). At the same time, as table 8.1 shows, production in U.K.-based Japanese companies expanded rapidly.

For most of the 1980s, the managerial strategy at the Rover Group (formerly called Austin Rover and before that British Leyland) focused on achieving tighter control of the production process. In the 1970s, managerial control had been compromised by high levels of unofficial strikes, restrictive "demarcations," and other practices policed by strong, decentralized unions. Although cogent arguments were advanced concerning other reasons for the failure (investment strategy, marketing strategy, the management of production logistics), the dominant managerial and government logic of the early 1980s was that for British companies to survive, management had to recapture the unilateral right to manage, particularly the organization of work, staffing levels, and work pace (Williams, Williams, and Haslam 1987).

While weakening the unions and their control over production processes remained a key objective, managers in the car industry also began to talk the language of Japanization. Honda had set up a joint agreement with British Leyland and opened its own U.K. plant in 1989. In 1984, Nissan announced its intention to set up a U.K. assembly plant, which opened in 1986. In 1992, Toyota started production of motor vehicles in the United Kingdom. By the early 1990s, all the major U.K. producers had introduced elements of Japanese practices—forms of team- or cell-based work, the blurring of demarcations between production and maintenance activities, and some quality circle activities.

Ford's "After Japan" initiative, introduced from 1979 onward, was perhaps the most thoroughgoing of these initiatives, but by the mid-1980s, it

Table 8.1 U.K. Production of Major U.K.-Based Auto Producers, 1986–93

	1993	1992	1991	1990	1989	1988	1987	1986
Ford	271,793	302,146	339,270	329,597	382,581	375,542	386,698	346,267
Honda	32,139	1,001	—	—	—	—	—	—
IBC	41,327	31,210	3,222	—	—	—	—	—
Nissan	246,281	179,009	124,666	76,190	77,282	56,541	—	—
Peugeot	72,902	85,821	87,983	116,548	107,195	82,326	45,549	58,426
Talbot Rover	356,280	339,054	359,951	417,351	434,816	450,666	450,726	389,968
Toyota	37,314	—	—	—	—	—	—	—
Vauxhall	232,569	287,884	255,733	256,293	208,333	176,489	183,857	161,857

Source: Society of Motor Manufacturers and Trades (SMMT) 1996.

had already been branded a failure, having foundered in the face of hostility from the shop floor, unions, and lower/middle management alike (Oliver and Wilkinson 1992). Among the problems were that the systems being introduced were based on a language of commitment, involvement, and participation at the same time that many jobs were being lost, and as the unions saw it, they were excluded from bargaining. The irony, as at Ford, of introducing these changes unilaterally (Oliver and Wilkinson 1992) is clear.

As companies steered between the Scylla and Charybdis of managerial prerogative and Japanization, important changes were logged in work practices and human resource policies. Many plants adopted key elements of lean production, so that multiskilling, teamwork, and quality management became commonplace items on managerial shopping lists. Even Rolls Royce, surely the archetypal craft producer, instituted a wide-ranging program of change in work organization aimed at securing a leaner (relatively speaking) production process.

Many companies introduced such processes in the late 1980s/early 1990s, in several cases following failure, or only partial success, in earlier efforts at team-based communication or participation exercises. Associated with these changes have been significant alterations in the roles of supervisors, involving reductions, retraining, and redeployment. The reworking of shop-floor control and monitoring arrangements between "supervisors" and team leaders or their equivalent is significant in all cases. Where unions are strongly represented—as at all the brownfield sites—the unions appear to have accepted the new arrangements, in contrast with earlier periods, and some detailed attention has been paid to electoral procedures for team leaders and their relationship to union-based channels of communication and the handling of grievances. Both union density figures and institutional arrangements for plant- and company-level consultation and negotiation appear to have been maintained.

Although the lean production recipe was adopted widely across the U.K. car industry, the importance of variability within this overall pattern of convergence highlights the need to address the local and institutional context of the changes, both because significant variations remain in practice across the sector and because the design and implementation of even the most thoroughgoing lean practices are heavily influenced by the local context and the chronology of corporate change. This last point is well illustrated by the following account of corporate and plant-level change at the Rover Group in the period since 1979.

Rover from 1979 to 1992

For more than a decade from 1975, following a profits crisis, British Leyland was a state-owned corporation, having been nationalized by a government that felt that it was politically unacceptable for the only independent car producer in the United Kingdom to disappear. In 1979, the first formal joint agreement was reached with Honda over the production of four vehicles on a combined basis. In 1986, British Leyland became Austin Rover; and in 1988, it was returned to the private sector through its sale to British Aerospace (BAe) for £185 million (U.S. $300 million). In 1989, the name was changed again, to Rover Group Limited, and Honda acquired a 20 percent share of the company in exchange for Rover's acquisition of 20 percent of Honda's new U.K. manufacturing operations. In early 1994, BAe sold its 80 percent share to the German car company BMW for £800 million (U.S. $1,300 million). Honda, publicly angered by the way BAe handled the deal, reviewed and weakened its relationship with Rover almost immediately.

The effect of BMW ownership is still to be seen, but initial indications suggested that Rover plants would be managed with a high degree of autonomy, especially in the area of human resources and employee relations. At the time of our research in late 1994/early 1995, Rover was organized into six divisions, of which the largest, and the one of primary concern to this research, was Product Supply, within which all manufacturing activities were grouped, including the manufacture of large cars at Cowley, Oxford, site of our main intensive fieldwork.

Apart from the vagaries of ownership and control, Rover can be seen as an important bellwether of changes occurring across the U.K. car sector in the areas of human resource management and employee relations. Not only was Rover directly exposed to both the collaborative and competitive effects of the Japanese incursion in the 1980s, but its record of productivity improvements in the 1980s and 1990s was typical of the trend in many other firms. In 1972, a workforce of eighty thousand was producing nearly 700,000 cars. In 1981, seventy-seven thousand were producing 348,000. By 1984, however, forty-two thousand were producing 433,000, and by 1992, thirty-one thousand were producing about 420,000. Between 1990 and 1994, total employment fell from 41,700 to 34,200. Table 8.2 shows recent trends in sales and profits.

In the remainder of this chapter, changes at Rover will be addressed under seven headings: teamwork and work organization, changing work practices, team leaders, staffing and employment security, labor-management

Table 8.2 Sales and Profits/Losses (pretax, preinterest) at Rover, 1986–95

	Sales	Profits (loss) £ million	Profits (loss) $ million
1986	446,800	(356)	(570)
1987	476,900	28	45
1988	526,000	66	106
1989	509,500	64	102
1990	504,100	65	104
1991	470,000	(52)	(83)
1992	422,700	(49)	(78)
1993	442,745	56	90
1994 (est.)	460,000	120	192
1995 (est.)	475,000	150	240

Source: UBS Research Ltd., March 2, 1994.

relations, training and development, and compensation. The changes in each of these areas will be examined on the micro level, as revealed by an empirical study of Rover's Cowley plant, and as they relate to Rover's long-term corporate development.

Teamwork and Work Organization. Like many other U.K.-based car firms, Rover initially attempted to address its quality problems by grafting employee-involvement mechanisms onto existing forms of work organization. In 1986, an initiative known as "Working with Pride" introduced, among other things, "zone circles" and "zone briefings," designed primarily to foster communication and involvement. The initiative collapsed within a year, because, research suggests, operators and supervisors alike saw it as a waste of time and as a threat to the role of union stewards. The trade unions opposed the initiative (Smith 1988; Oliver and Wilkinson 1992) from the beginning.

In 1987, a total quality program was introduced with the objectives of "prevention not detection" and "right first time." As part of this program, all employees received four days' off-the-job training in total quality techniques ("Rover's 'New Deal'" 1992). A form of teamwork was introduced at about the same time, which gave foremen (first-line supervisors) responsibility for briefing groups of about thirty employees. In 1994, a senior manager argued in an interview that the total quality program represented Rover's view that "quality comes through ownership and continuous improvement by and of the workforce; managerial exhortation is not enough."

The details of the total quality program were later modified by eliminating the role of supervisor and distributing the workers into "cells" consisting of teams of about forty to one hundred employees each. "Cell managers" were managerial staff, but "team leaders" were shop-floor employees. Cells could request assistance from "facilitators"—production engineers or quality-control personnel, some of whom were displaced supervisors—on matters that required expert input. The cell management concept was put to Rover's unions and eventually they accepted the idea (Vernon 1994).

Changing Work Practices. The work practices and attitudes we observed in late 1994 at Cowley were heavily conditioned by the events of the previous two years. Between 1992 and 1995, workers not only participated in the introduction of two new models—the Rover 600 and 800—they witnessed radical rationalization of their production facilities. In 1992, a new assembly facility was opened, the number of factory units was cut from four to one, and the site's acreage was drastically reduced. Management was restructured, and many hundreds of workers were transferred to new jobs. Table 8.3 summarizes the overall effect of these changes.

In late 1994, the Cowley plant was producing five different models: the Maestro, the Montego, the Rover 600 and 800 series, and the MGR V8. Only the Rover 600 and 800 were produced in significant volumes, however, and although the changes taking place involved radical reconfiguration of the site, previous customs and practices were not obliterated entirely, as reflected in the average age of the workforce—forty-seven—and the workers' consequent awareness of previous regimes. Moreover, many of the changes in work practices could be traced to the development of the total quality initiative in 1987. Through "cascade" training exercises, this initiative eventually encompassed all managers, staff, and operatives. The total quality philosophy, with its emphasis on processes and customer-supplier relations, was closely implicated not only in the development of specific quality groups and activities, such as quality action teams, but in the restructuring of the Rover Group and the formation of the product supply business.

Rover's philosophy of total productive maintenance also has its roots in developments in the 1980s. These involved Rover management seeking to extend the responsibility of production operatives to encompass minor maintenance tasks, including the routine maintenance of robots. By 1994, this philosophy was well established at Cowley, helping to eliminate the

Table 8.3 Changes at Cowley, 1991–93

	1991	**1993**
Size of site	222 acres	114 acres
No. of associates	3,550	3,300
Vehicles per year	55,000	82,300
Cars/man/year	10.9	30.6
No. of suppliers	410	370

Source: Company documents.

involvement of maintenance specialists in many routine tasks, though not obviating the need for the specialist maintenance function.

By the mid-1990s, Rover managers at the corporate level felt that major improvements had been made in the area of employee involvement. They cited the success of the suggestion scheme, which had a 70 percent participation rate in 1991 and a 100 percent suggestion rate (number of suggestions divided by number of employees) in 1993, up from a 40 percent participation rate in 1989 and 1990. By 1994, there were more than one hundred discussion groups (Rover's version of quality circles) in operation and five hundred management-led quality action teams.

It also appears that direct communication between management and the workforce had increased significantly relative to the situation five to ten years earlier—when union representatives were a more central channel of communication. Line managers would stop the tracks once a month for half an hour to relay "core messages" to the workforce. In addition, senior managers gave presentations on major issues confronting the company.

Teamwork surfaced as part of the major changes occurring during 1991–92. Management discussed the issue with the Plant Joint Council (PJC) of trade unions as part of a wider agreement. The actual practice of teamwork was piloted in 1992–93 in low-volume production of the Maestro and the Montego.

By the end of 1994, most workers had been formed into teams, the average size being about fifteen, including one team leader and two spare operatives (the latter were notionally available for training but mainly covered during absences). The actual practice of teamwork varied between sections, however, so that Trim and Final Assembly (T&FA) was seen as much more advanced with respect to the adoption of teamwork than Body in White (BIW). Further, there was only limited penetration of teamwork practices into skilled work areas. These variations were seen partly as tech-nological effects: BIW and Paint offered a more constrained context for teamwork. But they also reflected cultural differences between work groups that had been distributed across several factory units (and before that dif-ferent companies) that had survived the site consolidation and relocation.

There were also conflicting interpretations of the teamwork that was in place. Management encouraged operatives to fill in their skills matrices, which were displayed track-side, but there was no plant-level monitoring of changes in matrices. Nor was there significant demand for job rotation from shop-floor workers. In effect, the extent of such rotation depended on the interest and enthusiasm of team leaders and managers.

A similar degree of variation applied to the pursuit of continuous improvement, which, as one production manager said, was "taken for granted." But even in the Trim and Final Assembly area, this was largely the preserve of cell support staff, who were dedicated to quality improve-ment tasks.

Cowley seemed to have a constrained form of teamwork. Management accepted that teams had little discretion in the production methods adopted. The old "man assignments" had been eliminated, but they had not been replaced by fully specified team assignments. Industrial engineers continued to specify process sequences in some detail. Thus, individuals were no longer clear about their own assignments, but the team's tasks were specified, with little scope for changing them. The prospect of teams exercising a degree of autonomy over the allocation of their "slug" of work was only a managerial aspiration—and that limited to one part of T&FA.

Team Leaders. Up to October 1994, team leaders at Cowley were paid £20 (U.S. $32) per week more than other assembly line operators. The selection of team leaders involved a process by which candidates (drawn from the team) had to pass math and English tests and then be elected by the rest of the members of their team. Management and the unions saw the roles of team leader and shop steward as mutually exclusive, and although the elec-tion of team leaders was obviously shaped by the interests and expectations of each group—for example, a few work groups were said to have resisted the team concept by electing weak leaders—there was no evidence that management manipulated the process to get the results it wanted.

The acceptance of team leaders by their teams and by local shop stewards followed the T&FA and BIW divide noted earlier. In the BIW area, one shop steward reported resistance to team leaders, especially from older workers, and one BIW team leader reported "hostility" on first being appointed. Another from a skilled area reported that his role was "more communications" than anything else. In other teams, however, particularly in T&FA, the team leader was seen as playing a genuine leadership role in representing the team to both management and the trade unions.

The cultural division between BIW and T&FA was reinforced by the differing technical implications of teamwork and the role of the team leader. The routine tasks of a team leader in the BIW area were close to those of the traditional foreman. They included making sure the line started at the beginning of the shift, recording absences, and asking team members to cover for absentees. Team leaders also performed such ancillary tasks as addressing safety concerns, ordering supplies, encouraging the development of total productive maintenance, ensuring that materials were available, and alerting the production manager of quality problems. Team leaders also covered, from one day per week to several days, depending on the area, when members of his or her team were absent.

In T&FA, by contrast, the role of the team leader was more extensive. One described his role as solving operators' problems—for example, meeting with the local shop steward on health and safety issues.

Practice was uniform in one respect: all team leaders were carefully exempted from any responsibility for discipline, which remained the prerogative of the supervisor and local cell manager. This distinction was maintained not only as a matter of management policy but because of pressure from below. One team leader who was reported to have taken detailed notes of the absences and work patterns of his team members was forced to give up the role when they discovered his notebook.

There is also evidence that the broader application of the principles of labor flexibility may have undermined some of the key tenets of teamwork. With the reduction in the number of factory units, for example, some maintenance workers were redeployed to production jobs. In some instances, this had the effect of disrupting existing team structures. Putting skilled workers onto the assembly line was an ad hoc response to the surplus of maintenance workers resulting from the site rationalization. This move was implemented only after careful negotiation to overcome worker resistance and involved a fixed rotation encompassing about fifty workers.

Cowley management had taken major steps toward removing the controlling presence of supervisors from the management hierarchy. In some areas, this seems to have been as much a change in style as in the structure of management: those foremen who became facilitators saw their responsibilities shift from pressuring the workforce to achieve targets to supporting teams and team leaders. Management admitted, however, that on occasion facilitators had been used to cope with a labor crisis on the shop-floor. In T&FA, facilitators were being further distanced from production pressures by relocating them into cell support groups whose responsibilities focused on quality issues and process improvement rather than on production volumes.

Staffing and Employment Security. In September 1991, Rover put forth a package to the unions called "Rover Tomorrow—the New Deal" in which the company argued for the need for continuing improvement to match world-best performance and to compete within a more deregulated European Community. The company declared that it needed "the maximum contribution of every employee, the removal of [any remaining] restrictive practices, and a commitment to single status quicker than originally planned" (Vernon 1994:19). The key to achieving this goal was job security—"Employees who want to work for Rover will be able to stay with Rover" (Taylor 1994:126)— since, as a senior manager argued, "conditions of absolute flexibility, the preparedness to acquire new skills, can only come about if we give a guarantee that we will not make people compulsorily redundant." Rover managers are keen to emphasize that this guarantee is dependent on employee preparedness to accept redeployment after appropriate training; there is no guarantee concerning existing jobs, and disciplinary dismissals can still be used. In fact, after the New Deal was implemented, the workforce in Product Supply fell from forty-two thousand to thirty-two thousand as a result of voluntary leaves and early retirement, although the job guarantee was maintained.

The key features of the New Deal package included the following: single status; a requirement of continuous improvement for everyone; flexibility, subject to employee ability to do the job, after appropriate training; (see also Taylor 1994); the introduction of a single-grade pay structure to replace a five-grade hourly paid and six-grade staff structure, so as to ensure that advancement would be "achievable by everyone through skill acquisition" (Taylor 1994:125); and the replacement of productivity bonus schemes with a bonus system related to attendance.

After negotiations, a slightly modified version of management's proposals (but retaining the key points noted above) was agreed upon overwhelmingly by the Joint Negotiating Committee (JNC), which now included representatives of all the unions for nonmanagement staff recognized by Rover. The proposals were put to the unions' memberships in a ballot and were accepted in a vote of 11,961 to 11,793 ("Rover's 'New Deal'"1992).

Senior management sees the New Deal both as a new initiative and as a consolidation of strategies that were partially developed or introduced without adequate attention to their integration. It emerged from a senior management group supported but not led by personnel/HRM specialists who argued that world-class performance and quality could be obtained only if employees were treated reasonably; hence, the emphasis on security and on eliminating what the company sees as "irritants," sources of intra-organizational differences in status and privileges, for example.

Several commentators have seen the New Deal as a highly significant agreement. Robert Taylor describes it as "an oft-quoted example of the new consensual approach to industrial relations apparent across British manu-facturing industry" (1994:122; see also "Lean Production—and Rover's 'New Deal'" 1992). Cowley is also widely seen as constituting perhaps the clearest example of a U.K. brownfield site that has set itself the task of "Japanizing" its industrial relations.

Labor-Management Relations. Labor relations at Rover and its predeces-sors over the period from 1979 to 1990 must be seen as an accretion of poli-cies. New initiatives and ideas were launched whose interrelationships were not always made explicit, at least to employees and managers on the shop floor. The New Deal was intended to cement cardinal elements of change in industrial relations, employment security, compensation, and work orga-nization. This agreement signaled a shift away from an industrial relations strategy centered on securing unqualified managerial control—a recurring theme in Rover's industrial relations since the dismissal of the leading union negotiator Derek Robinson in 1980—toward a conditional accep-tance of the union role. Although unions had been significantly weakened with respect to their ability to influence the details of the production process, Rover had made no outright attempt to eliminate unionism and stewards remained an important channel of worker representation on the shop floor. Union density remained relatively stable among manual grades, at well more than 80 percent, though there was some decline in union den-sity among white-collar workers.

At the group level, wages and conditions for all staff below management level continued to be settled through traditional collective bargaining channels; at the plant level, steward-based negotiation and consultation persisted. Further, Rover was prepared to go through extensive consultation with its unions concerning its total quality initiative. Following the upheavals at the start of the 1980s, unionism was accepted in its attenuated form and efforts were made to secure union agreement on the total quality initiative, but until the advent of the New Deal, the company did not always seek to involve unions actively in the processes of change.

More substantively, the relationships between Rover and the unions outlined in the 1992 deal reflected little that was novel. Several features—such as an agreement against any form of "unconstitutional" collective action (action taken before grievance procedures have been exhausted) and an agreement to refer any unresolved dispute to "binding" arbitration (a term that has no legal force in the United Kingdom but that implies a moral authority)—built on existing practice. The agreement did, however, replace Rover's two national negotiating committees—one for staff and one for hourly rated employees—with a single committee for both groups ("single-table bargaining"), led by a national official of the Transport and General Workers' Union (TGWU)—the largest union in the British auto industry.

The New Deal has revealed differences in perception and approach between the main unions at Rover—the Amalgamated Engineering, Electrical Union (AEEU), made up predominantly of skilled workers, and the TGWU. The Joint Negotiating Committee's acceptance of a slightly modified version of the deal was not matched by equivalent enthusiasm among local shop stewards, and, as indicated in the ballot, only a tiny minority of the workforce accepted the deal.

During the negotiations themselves, the unions were concerned about protecting those of their members who for reasons of age or other physical conditions may be unable to become "all-singing, all-dancing team members" ("TGWU's Response to Lean Production at Rover" 1993:11). But, with the exception of discussions concerning procedures for the election of team leaders, the unions appear to have made little contribution to the substantive heart of the New Deal proposals. Instead, they focused on the protection of their own organization and rights within the company. Publicly, the company is now fully supportive of its unions. In 1994, the then chairman stated that

> the fact that we have been able to enroll the trade union people at Rover in the company's mission and objectives has allowed us to move at a pace that would have been impossible without trade union collaboration, so we see the relationship we have with trade unions at Rover as a very positive thing for the company. Having the trade unions understand what the company's mission is in life

and working with us in partnership, we have been able to make tremendous strides in productivity and costs (Taylor 1994:123)

The New Deal endorsed the need for enhanced consultation between company and unions "to ensure maximum understanding of company performance, competitive practices and standards, product and company plans and all areas of activity affecting the company and its employees" (Rover company documents). Meetings to enable this to happen take place every six months. Although it still has vociferous union critics, from a historical perspective, the New Deal seems to represent a comparative transformation in the industrial relations of a company with a long-standing reputation for adversarial and bitter relationships.

At Cowley specifically, the change in the climate of employee relations has had as much to do with the massive physical and organizational changes of 1991–92 as with the New Deal agreement. So extensive were the changes at the plant that traditional union rivalries were set aside and the TGWU and AEEU worked together to set up the Plant Joint Committee, which by 1994 had become the major forum for the site's fifty-six shop stewards and seven senior stewards. Labor disputes, which had last flared up in 1987, were avoided even as significant reductions were made in the workforce. In the process of change, the possibility of complete plant closure, implicit in the site rationalization, tended to focus senior stewards' minds. As one of them said in an interview: "Our main objective is the security of the company we work for. As trade unions, whatever your aspirations, they become meaningless if the company isn't successful. We try both to represent our members and to think about the security of the company."

In this context, it is not surprising that the managing director of large cars saw trade unions as friendly persuaders in the process of change: "The trade unions were part of that persuasion process . . . turning historical attitudes of the trade unions to the positive attitude of being part and parcel of the business." He sought to turn the unions toward a more business-related role, which he believed would not conflict with their duties to their membership. This was not without some classic dangers. One of the senior stewards noted that the confidential meetings at which management supposedly passed on its strategic thinking were especially problematic: "We have to say to our members—trust us. . . . We're sworn to secrecy, and accused by union die-hards of selling out."

Plant unionists were equally uncomfortable when the company expected them to "deliver" an agreement on contentious issues. The question of temporary workers was a case in point. Although the Joint Negotiating Committee was initially opposed, Cowley stewards finally agreed to allow temporary workers to be recruited for twelve to eighteen months to meet the company's need to maintain low-level production on a couple of aging models, although the stewards did succeed in defining the terms and conditions for the temporary workers except for pension rights.

Training and Development. Training and development were seen as strategic issues at Rover. In 1988, the Rover Learning Business (RLB) was established as a separate division aimed at providing learning—not training—opportunities for the workforce. In 1990, RLB launched the REAL program (Rover Employees Assisted Learning), which provided every Rover employee with up to £100 (U.S. $160) for self-development learning. Currently, each major site has a development center that offers PC-based learning activities, and as of 1993, attendance was averaging well over one thousand associates per week.

The commitment to learning has been reflected in the philosophy of senior management at the Cowley plant. The managing director of large cars was loosely involved in setting up RLB and had committed his management team to providing two days of off-the-job learning for every employee. Progress was monitored through a quarterly meeting of the People Development Committee in the Large Cars Division.

In translating its positive commitment to training and development into an operational form, senior management had to contend directly with the pressures of production as responsibility for training and development activities devolved from the personnel function to line management. This inevitably created the possibility of patchy application of the corporate philosophy. Some team leaders were unhappy, for instance, with the amount of training they were receiving, complaining that an initial burst of training had not been followed up.

As for the informal aspects of training and development, there seemed to be limited scope for on-the-job learning given the existing production regime. Only one or two team leaders and managers felt that job rotation was being practiced extensively in their areas. Although one team leader claimed that each member of his team was capable of doing the work of any other team member, his perspective was the exception rather than the rule. In BIW, for instance, one shop steward claimed that the jobs—spot welding, straightening, and brazing—were too different for complete interchangeability to be achieved. One or two managers saw differences in individual competence as major constraints: "There are some of the people down there I would have reservations about doing more than one job," one manager said. More to the point, managers themselves paid limited attention to the job rotation issue. Even in T&FA, skills matrices were displayed at track-side, but there was no general incentive for team leaders or managers to ensure individuals acquired a wider range of skills. The team leader was simply responsible for ensuring that his or her skills matrix was up-to-date. There was general agreement, though, that the degree of job rotation was dependent on several variables, including the attitude of the team leader, levels of absenteeism, the innate difficulty of certain jobs, and the desire of the individual worker.

Compensation. The 1980 "blue newspaper" (covering manual workers) and the "green newspaper" (for white- collar staff), introduced at Rover in the wake of the Robinson sacking, finally ended the fragmented plant-level bargaining of earlier years. The same agreement introduced a new five-grade pay structure for hourly paid employees and a similar agreement for staff employees that reduced the number of job grades to six. These conventional grading-based pay structures remained relatively unchanged during the 1980s, but the New Deal prefigured their replacement with a single grading structure. In 1994, employees voted narrowly to accept the progressive introduction of a system with three new broad job classifications covering all previous hourly rated and staff categories. In 1995, this plan was finally implemented and assimilation is continuing.

The original proposals also included pay progression within each classification, based on individual performance, but it has been resisted by the manual unions. It has been accepted in principle but not yet implemented in practice with respect to Classification C, which includes staff such as personnel officers (for details, see Income Data Services 1995), whose pay scales were already merit-based. All other staff (i.e., those in the old hourly paid grades) are paid a flat rate, plus, where appropriate, shift premiums, overtime payments, and a recently introduced attendance-related bonus, all of which are bargained at the group level with the unions. A new profit-related scheme also went into effect in 1995; it paid about £500 (U.S. $800) to all staff. Managerial aspirations to some form of skills-based payment system have not been pursued strongly in the face of union concern about the arbitrariness of such schemes and the enhanced discretion they give to supervisors and managers. Nor have rewards systems been a central feature of the new approach at Rover.

Conclusions

This case study has highlighted the gaps between formal corporate policy and plant-level practice at Cowley. For example, although teamwork is now seen as an integral element of the work organization, we found that its practice was highly variable among and even within sections of the plant and much depended on the ability and initiative of cell managers and team leaders. Insofar as it is possible to generalize, this was for the most part a constrained form of teamwork, in which team leaders had a relatively restrictive role. Even some of the cardinal features of teamwork were shrouded in ambiguity. Thus, not only was one team operating without a leader, but even where leaders existed, there were several interpretations of their role.

These gaps between policy and practice can be interpreted in several ways: they may be a product of the untidy process of evolutionary change; evidence of a gap between management rhetoric and hard-nosed practice; or an example of the contrapuntal relationship between formal and informal organization. Focusing too hard on these gaps, however, is to risk not seeing the wood for the trees.

As soon as we lift our gaze to the wider ensemble of changes occurring at Cowley, the lack of uniformity and the apparent contingency of shop-floor practices can be seen in a different light. Production practices are nearly always governed by some form of "adhocracy," and this is clearly reflected in our data. There is no sign of a major effort to impose even a formal uniformity on every detail of work organization. Adhocracy does not imply randomness or anarchy, however, but responsiveness to specifically predefined actions and events. Thus, the adhocracy we observed was built into a wider production regime that privileged production pressures at the Cowley plant over, say, the preservation of demarcations. Indeed, senior Rover management argued the virtues of leaving things imprecise, allowing for local emergence of practice within an overarching ideology and organizational paradigm.

The sociotechnical interventions that helped to establish the new regime were only part of the overall pattern of change. Important changes in employee relations, brought about by both the New Deal and a societal shift in union power, not only helped to secure management's prerogative in imposing change but established the relationship between plant performance and employee job security as at the heart of management-union bargaining. From a managerial standpoint, such considerations are often viewed in terms of the supporting role HRM policy plays in the development of lean production, a role that is part of an "organizational logic" that connects HRM to a lean form of work organization (MacDuffie 1995:200). The Cowley case suggests that the construction of this logic is not simply an analytical point but a political project in which logistics, work practices, and employee relations are welded into a seamless whole that installs the ad hoc pressures of production as an overriding constraint on the discretion of management, unions, and workers alike.

The role of unions in this process remains problematic. Although the emphasis on plant performance articulates a long-standing issue in management-union relations, and enhanced employee performance and discretion have been union demands for many years, the strategic shift in employee relations is a major challenge for unions. Whether or not the new production techniques constitute a form of work intensification and enhanced managerial control, the adhocracy of the new regime constitutes a problem for unions as organizations that seek, in the interests of their members, to standardize and specify practice. If the classic output of collective bargaining is rules—formal and informal—the implications of a system that seeks to avoid precise rules are profound. If, on the one hand, as it is sometimes claimed, a de-Taylorization is taking place not only of production but of the managerial labor process, rule setting through bargaining over work relations becomes problematic. If, on the other hand, what is happening is merely work intensification in a period of acute labor weakness, the picture is more straightforward. Unions have a significant role in this process; as organizations with profound leverage over opinions and ideas, their position—between opposition to new work practices and embracing and pushing for their extension—remains important.

The point has already been made that the driving ideological force of the need for company survival through performance is contingent. The period in which Rover—and most U.K. manufacturers—introduced their quality and performance-driven packages (the late 1980s and early 1990s) was one of acute crisis. The need for change was evident from the closures and redundancies occurring everywhere. If these conditions were the drivers of change, and of its acceptance, among unions as well as managers and employees, what happens to these adhocratic systems if and when moments of stability and success occur?

9 Italy: Changing the Workplace in the Auto Industry

Arnaldo Camuffo and Giuseppe Volpato

The purpose of this chapter is to interpret, from an evolutionary perspective, recent developments in work organization and human resource management policies at Fiat, one of the world's largest automobile manufacturers. We will assess why these changes mark a radical transformation from the traditional organizational paradigm.

During the 1980s, while Japanese car manufacturers were outperforming their competitors (Womack, Jones, and Roos 1990), Fiat was successful, thanks to lean production. During this period, Fiat consolidated its leadership in the domestic market by producing a few fast-selling cars, maintained state-of-the-art automated manufacturing, and implemented work flexibility. All of this was made possible because of an aggressive industrial relations system that emphasized managerial unilateralism and concession bargaining (Becchi and Negrelli 1986; Kochan, Locke, and Heye 1992).

In the early 1990s, however, the dramatic recession affecting the automobile industry worldwide revealed imbalances in Fiat's strategy. The Turin-based company reacted by designing a comprehensive strategic and organizational system marked by new relationships with suppliers and dealers, massive investment in new product development and manufacturing plants, and a new organizational model. Fiat also undertook a massive restructuring of its plants, which involved reducing the number of production workers as well as employees in central staffing and services. This strategy was successful. By the mid-1990s, Fiat was profitable again, gaining increased market share in all the major European markets.

Fiat's Organizational Heritage

The early history of Fiat featured a gradual introduction of mass production and the Fordist paradigm. Unions were weak and the market was growing, a situation that enabled the company to implement a successful union-restraint strategy (Volpato 1978 and 1983). During the 1950s and 1960s, Fiat consolidated a "twofold specialization" approach; that is, it focused on the domestic market and on small cars.

The end of the 1960s was a period of full employment and social pressures, as well as market crisis, and Fiat's union-restraint strategy came under attack. Discontent grew among the workers, living costs were rising fast, and massive immigration of unskilled workers from southern Italy generated social tensions. Fanned by a wave of political resentment, the unions united, and in the "hot autumn" (*autunno caldo*) of 1969, strikes broke out. In the meantime, the oil shock and Fiat's specialization in the domestic market created a financial crisis that reduced investment and prevented renovation of the outdated product line.

Managerial Unilateralism and Union Demise (1980–85)

In the early 1980s, sales at Fiat dropped significantly, leading to layoffs and a tense industrial relations climate. In 1980, 20,500 workers (about 15 percent of the workforce) were supported by the *Cassa Integrazione Guadagni* (CIG), the state redundancy fund. As Fiat began its huge restructuring, the company was in the position to negotiate tough concession bargaining policies with the weakened unions. After years of personnel policies focused on collective (firm-union) transactions, new attention was given to individual relations and specific segments of the workforce. The most relevant concern for Fiat was to develop a set of personnel policies aimed not only at satisfying the key needs and expectations of employees but at legitimating management and restoring its hierarchical authority over decisions about the organization of work, compensation, and mobility criteria within the internal labor market (Camuffo and Costa 1993). Union density decreased from 32.5 percent in 1980 to 20.5 percent in 1986 (Kochan, Locke, and Heye 1992).

After 1980, bilateral industrial relations were reduced to a few issues, such as matters affecting employees returning to work after being supported by the state redundancy fund. The unilateral model of industrial relations expanded the scope of managerial decisions (Locke and Negrelli

1989). For some years, major technological and organizational innovations were introduced in a noncooperative way and with a substantial aversion on management's part to procedures aimed at greater union involvement.

Concession Bargaining and the Highly Automated Factory (1985–89)

In the mid-1980s, the combination of the growing market demand and the return of workers supported by the redundancy fund had a strengthening effect on the bargaining power of the unions. Industrial relations became increasingly based on union concessions to managerial pressures for internal firm flexibility (Locke and Negrelli 1989), but the union played an instrumental role in the flexibility strategy (e.g., the introduction of a third shift and collective overtime).

At the same time, Fiat pursued an automation-based strategy that was initially very successful. The know-how developed at Termoli in manufacturing the fully integrated robotized engine was fully formalized in the highly automated factory concept, which became a new organizational paradigm. Thus, technological and organizational know-how successfully developed and implemented in engine manufacturing were applied to assembly, namely, the redesign and restructuring of the Cassino assembly plant. There were problems with the implementation of this strategy, however, because management underestimated the critical role human resources play in the performance of a manufacturing division.

The Integrated Factory (1990s)

At the end of the 1980s, Fiat launched a total quality management program that involved group activities, relationships with suppliers, and the dealers' network. As the recession took hold, however, this plan was modified to take into account the firm's need to restructure and downsize. Managing these contradictory goals represented a major challenge.

To understand how Fiat's comprehensive change in strategy affected industrial relations, human resource practices, and work organization concepts, it is necessary to focus on its most important organizational project: the development of its integrated factory (IF), which originated as part of an attempt to correct some of the mismatches that emerged in the highly automated factory at the Cassino plant.

Basic to the development of the integrated factory is the concept of integration. The emphasis is on achieving organizational flexibility, coordination, and improvement. Automation ceases to be the only driver of productivity. At Fiat's IF, organizational, industrial relations, and human resource management choices were rediscovered as key constituents of the firm's competitive performance. According to Fiat HRM director Maurizio Magnabosco (1993 and 1994), this was a radical change and a discontinuity in Fiat's management philosophy. Since work organization is recognized as a key competitive factor, the role of industrial relations and human resource management policies also tends to be strategic. As a consequence, the role played by Fiat's HRM department began to change.

Fiat's goal in developing its IF was to achieve improvements in productivity and quality by maximizing product manufacturing efficiency, systematic monitoring, and control of logistics. According to Fiat management, these results will be reached, and the related investment (implementation, training, and so on) will be paid off, in only a few years.

The key principles of the IF model are that the organizational structure is process-based rather than function-based and there is integration of operations (direct work) and production engineering (indirect work), a lean organizational structure, decentralization by means of relatively autonomous and self-regulating manufacturing cells—so-called *unità tecnologiche elementari* (UTEs), or elementary technological units—and labor participation and involvement.

Organizational Structure and Work Organization

The best way to analyze the IF is by examining the following dimensions: the plant-level organizational structure, work organization, recruitment, training, compensation, and industrial relations. The section that follows addresses the first two dimensions. The other dimensions are discussed later in the chapter.

In the integrated factory, substantial delayering and decentralization are designed to take place within the plant's organizational structure. "Macro sets" of activities are allocated to operational units by aggregating what were previously machine shops. Parts of former central staffs, such as workers in maintenance and materials planning, are decentralized at the level of operational units. Thus, each operational unit becomes specialized in two areas: operations and production engineering.

In Fiat's IF, production engineering represents a rather decentralized pool of technical competencies, working as a support to operations. Through delayering, two out of seven hierarchical layers were eliminated, including the so-called *capireparto*, the traditional shop steward figure. The delayering results in cost reductions and more horizontal (less hierarchical) coordination.

The key element of the integrated factory is the elementary technological unit, which governs a process (a technological subsystem) in which such activities as prevention, variance absorption, self-control, and continuous improvement are carried out, in order to achieve the firm's goals of quality, productivity/costs, and service. Production workers are assisted in a ratio of 1:10 or 1:30 by highly skilled workers (integrated process operators, integrated process conductors) whose tasks are quality improvement and personnel training (not hierarchical supervision).

UTEs vary in size according to the area where they are formed. In components and engine manufacturing, the average size is twenty to thirty workers, whereas in body assembly they may include forty to seventy workers.

The main objective of the UTEs is to devolve solutions to problems at the lowest possible level. Resources and skills are distributed so that problems may be solved as and where they occur. Product and process quality improvement are facilitated by systematically incorporating organizational learning in the workplace.

UTEs relate to one another in a supplier-customer way. Every UTE is managed using an information system made up of diagrams showing indicators for product and process quality, costs, productivity, workers' skills, and maintenance. Most of these indicators are common (so-called institutional indicators); others are customized and defined according to the specific needs of the UTE. This complex information system, which makes possible so-called *gestione* ("vista"), or management by sight, is composed of subsystems covering quality control, manufacturing performance measurements, and so on. Each subsystem includes such instruments and indicators as defect ratios, Pareto and Ishikawa diagrams, CEDACs, flag systems, labor productivity ratios, and radar charts. These elements contribute to overcoming information inequalities between managers and operating personnel and to providing transparency to the organization. Besides management by sight, other management techniques, such as statistical process control, are being implemented to control microprocesses.

Job and skill profiles within the integrated factory are different from those in the highly automated factory. Among the new organizational roles are that of the CPI or integrated process conductor, for every twelve to fifteen workers, in final assembly, and the OPI, or integrated process operator, for every twenty-five to thirty workers, in other areas. Their main tasks are to provide workers with training, prevent problems, and provide information on quality. They intervene in the manufacturing process when necessary and deal with informal work organization matters, with the aim of achieving process improvements. Process improvements occur by means of suggestions or other interventions, such as job assignments. Although they have no hierarchical authority over workers, CPIs and OPIs absorb part of the organizational complexity inherent on production lines and, by helping to coordinate production, reduce the workloads of UTE chiefs.

Within production engineering, several new jobs have emerged. These include the line technologist, whose task is to help the UTE chief with training and meeting time and cost targets; the technology specialist, whose task is to diagnose and solve technical anomalies; and the product/process technologist, whose tasks are to maintain continuous improvement, process reliability, and product quality, as well as to participate in new or modified product engineering.

At Fiat, a team at the shop-floor level is composed of technologists (one or more), the UTE chief, a procurement manager (sometimes), and a maintenance and quality specialist. The team's tasks are to identify and solve problems. Once the problem has been discussed, line people intervene, with the support of specialists. The teams monitor complex interdependencies and may draw on employees with specialized skills when problems arise in a segment of the system.

Teams at Fiat are very different from those at Mercedes and at Volvo. Those at Fiat are not semiautonomous, self-managing work groups. They are more dependent on technicians and are at a somewhat higher hierarchical level than line workers (who are not formally included on teams). At Fiat, teamwork takes place within each UTE, and meetings are held between the UTE chief, the conductors or operators, maintenance people, and technologists.

Technologists and maintenance people, although assigned to UTEs, report to production engineering. They report only functionally to the UTE chief. Thus, personnel policies, such as systematic training, job rotation, skill evaluation, and performance appraisal, are managed by the UTE chief.

Another noteworthy aspect of Fiat's restructuring is the relocation of white-collar workers and offices. Particularly in greenfield plants, most white-collar workers have been moved to the shop-floor level, close to operations. The implication is that there is better integration of tasks and improved internal services.

Crisis of the Early 1990s

The organizational innovations underlying the IF model will not contribute to increased quality and performance if the unions do not cooperate (Bonazzi 1993; Pessa and Sartirano 1993; Rieser 1993). Innovative industrial relations are necessary not only to facilitate and speed up implementation but also to avoid the negative implications of a recession like the one in the early 1990s, which can damage the restructuring effort.

The new bilateral relationship between management and the unions, initiated at Fiat in the mid-1990s, was rooted in the 1980s, when managerial unilateralism and concession bargaining dominated Fiat's industrial relations. A turning point, a sort of "last event" for Fiat's concession bargaining model, was the firm-level union agreement of July 1988, which linked wage increases to firm performance. It marked the move toward the more cooperative industrial relations system of the 1990s.

Fiat's competitive situation has rapidly worsened since 1990, forcing firm-level industrial relations to become more complex for several reasons. First, break-even points needed to be lowered and competitiveness enhanced by cost reductions, the externalization of activities, and downsizing, not only in manufacturing units but also, and especially, among white-collar workers and central staff and services personnel.[1] Second, the strategy of simultaneously restructuring and downsizing some plants and areas of activities while building new plants and investing in other areas of activities requires the design and implementation of different and segmented industrial relations policies. Third, unemployment has made Fiat's decisions concerning redundant workers extremely critical, especially in such areas as Turin, Milan, and Naples, where the social impact of such decisions can be very severe.[2] Fourth, an accord concerning union representation at the firm/plant level was signed at the national level on December 20, 1993, that gave workers the right to elect two-thirds of their representatives (the other third is appointed by confederal unions) to factory/firm councils. The signing of this accord was an important step toward industrial democracy. The reduction in union density during the 1980s was in part due to a lack of union democracy and a progressive detachment of workers from their representatives, who were centrally appointed by

---

[1]Several articles by the vice president for human resources of Fiat, Enrico Auteri (1991 and 1994), address this increasing focus on white-collar workers and on the shift from a traditional, bureaucratic organizational structure toward a flatter, network-like model characterized by delayering, a wider span of control at each level, and externalization of support activities.
[2]The number of Fiat employees decreased from 107,774 in 1990 to 95,587 in 1992. The number of people supported by CIG was at zero in 1990 but soared to 5,083 in 1992.

national unions. With the exception of the Mirafiori and Rivalta assembly plants (where an election to choose the members of the works council Consigli di Fabbrica took place in 1988), workers in most Fiat plants had not chosen union representatives directly since 1980.

As the political situation changed in the early 1990s, Fiat's industrial relations became more characterized by their innovation. There have been several important landmarks in this history.

A March 27, 1993, accord concerned the introduction of a night shift on the production line for the Punto model.[3] The accord basically entailed an exchange: the unions would allow greater manufacturing flexibility, while Fiat would commit to maintaining the Turin area as the core of Italian automobile manufacturing in the future.

A June 11, 1993, accord governed the Melfi and Pratola Serra plants in southern Italy. An earlier accord concerning the two plants had been signed in December 1990, but the 1993 agreement is more relevant here because it represented a new approach to industrial relations at Fiat (Grassi 1993) in four areas.

First, the accord introduces a scheme based on three daily shifts, operating eight hours per shift (with reductions and flexibility at the end of each shift) for six days a week. This scheme is applied for two subsequent weeks to each worker. The third week he or she works for only three days.

Second, the accord contains two main innovations with respect to work organization and cycle times. Work times can be redefined every three years, even without major changes in technology or product. Further, the work flow on production lines can be stopped to prevent or solve quality problems, but production lost because of line breakdowns has to be recovered within the shift, even if there are cycle time reductions. On the whole, these innovations mark a radical modification of the rules set by the August 15, 1971, accord on work organization.

Third, compensation packages for the Melfi and Pratola Serra workers are more flexible than for other Fiat employees. Minimum national wages are applied to workers in Melfi. In addition, the accord makes workers eligible for a competitive prize, partly fixed, partly contingent on productiv-

---

[3]The Mirafiori assembly plant was (together with Cassino) one of only a few European plants (about five out of fifty) that had three shifts and operated for five days a week. In general, there are significant variations in the shift and working hours at Fiat plants: Rivalta operates two daily shifts, each of eight hours in length, five days a week; Cassino and Mirafiori (with minor differences) operate three shifts of eight hours each, five days a week; Melfi operates three shifts of eight hours each (with pauses), six days a week. This difference from plant to plant is another element of the aforementioned "segmented" industrial relations policies Fiat and the unions have implemented.

ity measures.[4] The prize is awarded monthly and can account for a significant fraction of the whole compensation package.

Fourth, the accord introduces bilateral consultation between union representatives and managers at different levels—company, plant, and operational unit. Matters they may deal with include the prevention and conciliation of strikes and conflicts, monitoring of the competitiveness prize, training, equal employment opportunities, and health care and safety.

In summary, the June 1993 accord represents the basis for a new industrial relations model at Fiat. Most of all, management's awareness that work organization is critical to remain competitive implies a new, strategic role for the unions. Industrial relations policies are therefore aimed at setting up a framework and set of rules whereby organizational flexibility can be fully developed. Thus, the agreement is clearly a sign of a more collaborative attitude on the part of both management and the unions.

The IF is not yet a fully participative model, in that it has been autonomously developed without union involvement. Nevertheless, the unions have been playing an increasingly important role in the implementation of the emerging organizational paradigm and are also "institutionally" involved in the old plants (e.g., Rivalta) by means of a consulting committee (instituted in October 1990), through which the firm reports to the unions about quality and productivity improvements, and by means of a participation committee, which teams up plant managers, quality managers, and union representatives to facilitate worker participation. These committees are helping to create a positive internal climate, allow for the development of trust among the actors, improve communication by reducing information inequality among the parties, and allow for clearer interpretation of the new organizational concepts by language sharing.[5]

---

[4]This prize is awarded based on several productivity indicators. Fiat managers choose, according to competitive and market needs, the set of indicators that best fit the situation. These indicators are used to evaluate UTEs, operational units, or the entire plant and concern such matters as absenteeism, workforce efficiency, equipment efficiency, quality, and product mix.

[5]For example, although a very militant minority of FIOM-CGIL ("Essere Sindacato"), one of the confederal unions, was very resistant to change in the old plants (Mirafiori, Desio, and others) during 1991, other unions understood the opportunities opening up at Melfi. FIM-CISL, for instance, proposed and discussed with the other unions the possibility of implementing an industrial relations model at Melfi similar to the one being followed at Saturn-GM. Obviously, FIM-CISL envisioned the Melfi plant becoming the site for a pilot experiment that would be extended to other sites later on. Considering the problems facing Fiat's unions, especially concerning issues of "democracy" (e.g., the election of factory councils—which have not been renewed for a decade in many Fiat plants—with stronger "voice" for the base and a lesser presence for union bureaucrats), Melfi can be seen as an increasingly important influence on the evolution and modernization of Fiat's unions.

A February 20, 1994, agreement constituted another step toward new industrial relations at Fiat. The 1992–93 market recession had been so severe that the company had used all the "bonus" available from the ordinary state redundancy fund (fifty-two weeks in two years) to decrease production levels and absorb the social effects of overcapacity. At that point, Fiat asked the ministry of labor for a declaration of crisis status, which would give the company access to a special redundancy fund. Fiat submitted an industrial plan to the unions and to the ministry of labor as background for negotiation. The plan included the allocation of present and future production to its various plants and the required reductions in head counts.

After long negotiations and with the mediation of the minister of labor, Fiat management and the unions reached an agreement in February 1994 of national importance, given the number of plants and the people involved. This agreement stipulated that, in addition to relying on funds available through CIG, as Fiat had done during the restructuring of the early 1980s, redundant workers and overcapacity would be managed by means of: early retirements,[6] reductions in working hours,[7] and mobility within the firms of the Fiat Group.

A total of fifty-two hundred workers took early retirements in 1994, and fourteen hundred did so in 1995. These included, for the first time in Fiat history, approximately twenty-eight hundred white-collar workers. Working-hour reductions involved approximately eighty-six hundred workers. The wage reductions were only partially absorbed by the workers because of the intervention of Fiat and the state. The agreement also introduced a national-level union-management committee to discuss the organization of work and market trends.

On the whole, the February 20, 1994, accord represented another step toward innovative industrial relations. Moreover, it confirmed the strategic use of industrial relations policies by Fiat to improve competitiveness. That the accord was submitted to workers for agreement via a referendum held

[6]Technically speaking, redundant workers do not take early retirements. Rather, they are first supported by the CIG. Their names are then placed on special "mobility lists" (mobilità lunga ex L.n.223/91 and D.L. n.90/94) through which, thanks to contributions from both Fiat and the state, they get an unemployment subsidy until they reach retirement age.

[7]In contrast to Volkswagen's policy (Hartz 1994), which realized an average reduction of 20 percent of working time against reductions in complementary compensation, paid holidays, and so on, Fiat has "solidarity contracts" (Contratti di solidarietà ex L.n.236/93); that is, wages lost because of working hour reductions (from 30 percent to 80 percent of total working time) are partly made up for by the firm and partly by the state. For instance, at the Alfa Romeo Arese plant, fifteen hundred jobs and forty-five hundred workers will be working under solidarity contracts.

at the plants before signing was also a way to introduce innovative and participative procedures on the union side.

A New Focus for Recruitment and Training Policies

During the time of labor redundancies and layoffs, staffing did not represent a problem, except at the new plants, namely, Melfi and Pratola Serra, which introduced innovative recruitment policies. Here, the selection criteria are extremely rigorous and the recruits are young. No new employee at Melfi is older than thirty-two. In selecting both line workers and plant-level professionals, the emphasis is not only on skills and learning potential but on the psychological and social traits of the candidates. Loyalty, a cooperative attitude, and the ability to interact and absorb stress are only a few of the traits Fiat is looking for.

Fiat's recruitment policies are aimed at avoiding mismatches between new hires and the company's new organizational philosophy, with its emphasis on flexibility, teamwork, cooperation, and so forth. To operate most efficiently, the company needs not only highly qualified and skilled workers (at the Melfi plant, UTE chiefs are often engineering graduates, and CPIs and technologists have impressive skills) but also people with interpersonal skills and flexibility, given the tasks and responsibilities that come along with the new delayered structure. Emphasis has been put on recruiting not only young but well-educated workers (in Melfi and Pratola Serra, 10 percent of the employees will be college graduates). This will probably affect cultural values and social behaviors (e.g., union related) within the factory.

This focus on recruitment is associated with a new effort in training. If careful selection of candidates results in reduced levels of labor turnover and workers with increased motivation, Fiat is likely to perceive greater investment in training as more worthwhile.

The introduction of new work practices has also boosted training expenses. For example, training expenses as a percentage of salaries were 0.75 percent in 1990, versus 0.55 percent in 1992, while, on average, 43.3 percent of the employees were involved in training programs in 1990 compared with 47.9 percent in 1992. The highest percentages were at the new plants.

The new organizational model also emphasizes on-the-job training and teaching by doing, especially by CPIs and OPIs. This effort is huge, but it is difficult to assess whether workers who have been operating under the old organizational model will be able to acquire the skills required to work under the new one.

For its new plants in southern Italy, Fiat developed a training system rooted in the training program pioneered at Termoli. This new system has been carefully engineered and designed. Agreements and partnerships with local technical schools have also been established to codesign educational programs.

Compensation: A New Fuel for Participation and Commitment

Throughout the 1980s, Fiat's labor costs grew, as a result of wage indexation, collective bargaining at the national and firm level, and the company's compensation policies. These increases were covered by the productivity gains realized with the implementation of the highly automated factory (at least in engine manufacturing). As market demand weakened in the late 1980s, however, management began thinking about how to make compensation and wages more flexible.

Wage scales under the new integrated factory model have to be redesigned, and this poses important problems concerning internal equity. Given the firm's objectives of high quality, low cost, and efficient delivery, greater worker participation and involvement become more crucial under the IF model. Thus, new incentives are required to gain people's commitment and trust, to overcome information deficits, and to align the firm's and workers' goals.

Quality circles, which were initially developed in the assembly plants in the 1980s with the unions' acquiescence, fostered some increase in worker participation. The circles were made up of eight to ten assembly workers who attended circle meetings after hours and without compensation. Participation, quality circles, personal involvement, and incentives were then linked together in a 1991 agreement, so that both quality circles and individuals were awarded with "quality prizes" for their suggestions. This incentive scheme was applied to the six hundred quality circles in the Fiat organization and, on an experimental basis, to fifteen thousand blue- and white-collar workers at the Rivalta, Termoli, and Cassino plants. Suggestions were presented to UTE chiefs, then reviewed and, if applicable, prizes were awarded by a plant-level union-management committee. Ideas were grouped into four main categories: product quality, working methods, input/energy cost savings, and equipment efficiency. This suggestion system is not in place at the Melfi plant, where making suggestions is considered an integrative part of workers' tasks and doing so affects compensation only if they are awarded competitiveness prizes at the aggregate level.

Delayering a Mammoth

Delayering requires a great deal of cultural change. The traditional shop-floor authority-based setting (vertical communication, hierarchical coordination, and so forth), which generally inhibited cooperation and horizontal information flows, is replaced by integrating mechanisms, such as teamwork, within UTEs. The success of such a shift depends not only on the coherence of the organizational design but on the attitudes and behaviors developed by both managers (especially UTE chiefs) and workers. At Rivalta, for example, CPIs and OPIs, who should be an integrative part of the team, do not always have the time, inclination, and motivation to participate. This is probably because of the large size of the UTEs, especially in assembly shops (Camuffo and Micelli 1994). In fact, the span of control of the UTE chief is very wide, and CPIs and OPIs tend to behave as assistants (hierarchical figures) to the UTE chiefs. This pattern is reinforced in the plants. UTE chiefs were previously shop stewards (*capisquadra*) and had long seniority, and many CPIs and OPIs were shop steward assistants. At the Cassino plant, for example, 60 percent of the UTE chiefs were previously capisquadra.

Another key feature of the IF is the decentralization. Decision making is supposed to take place at the lowest possible organizational level. But despite the intentions, contradictions arise. For instance, the IF model includes the Japanese practice whereby workers can and should stop the assembly line to solve problems as they occur. This does not happen systematically, because of resistance on the part of both workers and plant managers, who tend to maintain traditional hierarchical practices. Thus, workers seldom stop the lines. Operational unit chiefs and plant managers continue to decide when to stop the line, and concerns about achieving quantity goals tend to dwarf attention to quality.

The degree of decentralization differs across plants. For example, although the IF model specifies that the management of supplies be at the UTE level, this is true at only a few plants (Melfi, for example), while at others, such as Cassino, the management of supplies is still at the operational unit level.

Contrary to those who see the IF model as maximizing organizational transparency and eliminating information inequalities (Bonazzi 1993), production workers sometimes ignore the complex system of information displayed in every UTE, probably because of time pressures and difficulties with readability and updating. The workload is perceived as too heavy to allow systematic use of all the instruments that are part of the model, which in some cases are seen as "useless paperwork." Moreover, especially when the workforce is old and unskilled, interpreting all these sophisticated management techniques causes frustration and misunderstandings. Finally, team redesigns, changes in job assignments, and modifications in cycle times aimed at increasing workers' output put much pressure on workers.

As Giorgio Cerruti and Vittorio Rieser (1992) have pointed out, data about quality are sometimes disguised or not detected and a process of self-regulation and certification of UTEs for quality measures is theoretically required but only rarely occurs. CPIs and OPIs also express frustration about these issues. On the one hand, they are expected to encourage teams to solve the problems they detect on the line, but, on the other hand, CPIs and OPIs are not always actively involved in problem diagnosis and solving, which is carried on by technologists and UTE chiefs. Further, CPIs and OPIs sometimes misinterpret their role and behave like quasi-hierarchical figures, like traditional assistants.

Teamwork also differs across plants. In some, such as Cassino, much emphasis is put on the formal convocation of UTE teams, on the bureaucratic structure of meetings, and on their formal aspects. In other plants, such as Melfi, UTE teams meet informally and spontaneously when required. Meetings are considered useful, but nobody cares about formalities or how many meetings are held.

Overall, the structural changes occurring at Fiat plants are conspicuous from a quantitative perspective. From a qualitative standpoint, hierarchical coordination has been dampened by integrators and other horizontal coordinating mechanisms (teams, management by sight, and so on). The new model mainly affects workers at higher hierarchical levels (middle managers and UTE chiefs), while only a small percentage of workers such as CPIs and OPIs have experienced significant transformations of their roles.

Recruitment and Training Policies

Both Fiat management and the unions are aware that implementing the IF model requires time and a generational change in the workforce as well as in middle management. The average age of Fiat workers increased during the 1980s, and age was one of the criteria used in determining outplacement when the restructuring began in 1994.

Tenure is strongly related to resistance to the reorganizing effort (Pessa and Sartirano 1993). Fiat's top management has estimated that approximately 30 percent of its shop stewards cannot be requalified as either UTE chiefs or professionals (technologists and so on). Voluntary separation with financial compensation is quite common (Pessa and Sartirano 1993). In other words, it seems as if the desire for turnover, among both workers and managers, will be the ultimate driver of organizational change.

The most important selection criterion for CPIs and OPIs, other than age, is interpersonal skills (communication, collaboration, and so forth). These jobs require a great deal of flexibility and much overtime. There are some cases of unmet expectations among the new CPIs and OPIs, caused by discrepancies between what they have been trained to do and what they are asked to do in the workplace. Many of them, as well as some UTE chiefs, feel underutilized and have higher salary and career expectations than Fiat can meet, which provokes some turnover. Furthermore, plant and operational unit managers often perceive and deal with CPIs and OPIs as if they worked under the old structure and had traditional assistant roles.

The effects of training are difficult to ascertain. Most training is given to workers in new jobs, and most other workers are only superficially involved. Routine training entails a two-hour weekly meeting in which participants are told about changes related to the introduction of the IF model. Although direct workers are subject to rotation and higher responsibility, including self-certification of operations, union representatives argue that this selectivity in training is evidence of a lack of substantial change in Fiat's attitude and commitment to fully developing its workers' potential (Follis, Pessa, and Silveri 1991).

Fiat's flatter organizational structure raises concerns among workers about career paths and professional development. The potential impact of training on quality and productivity cannot be realized if there are not real opportunities for career progression and horizontal mobility. Indeed, under these conditions, demotivation and turnover can result. At Fiat, the strict separation between operations and production engineering remains a problem.

Compensation and Quality

The new organizational model poses serious challenges to the reward systems. Because of the rigidities it inherited from the 1970s, Fiat put much effort throughout the 1980s into widening wage differentials among the classes in the national-level job classification scheme. Ad hoc compensation policies were designed for shop stewards, professionals, and middle managers with the explicit intention of also reconstructing the hierarchy among jobs.[8] The IF model seems to require very different policies, however. Delayering implies less hierarchy and thus less vertical wage differentiation. The new professional figures, together with the continuous changes in the organization of work and the application of the team concept, make it impossible to rigidly attach compensation to jobs. Knowledge, competencies, and performance are becoming the new drivers of the reward system. Moreover, the need for highly skilled workers implies that a concentration of the workforce will be in the central and higher classes of the job classification scheme.

As a consequence, the wage differentials between classes at Fiat seem to be narrowing, while wage differentials within each class seem to be widening, as a result of pay-for-knowledge, pay-for-capabilities, and pay-for-performance initiatives. Flexible compensation packages have been only partially implemented. A contingent pay scheme included in the July 18, 1988, agreement, linking pay increases to firm performance, failed because of disputes over the details of the mechanism. The indicators of firm performance determining the collective bonus, called the *premio performance gruppo* (PPG), declined because of market downturn. Currently, the unions are still disputing the bonuses and related performance indicators. The bonuses paid between 1989 and 1992 were basically fixed.[9]

The reason the contingent pay scheme failed is that neither the firm nor the unions were really willing to bear the risks of exogenous factors. Despite the new industrial relations approach that seems to be emerging, attempts to shift risks to the other party (union or management) can create the basis for noncooperative union-management relations.

In some cases, wage increases take the form of spot bonuses; in other cases, permanent increases. For shop stewards and middle managers, pay increases are linked to a management-by-objectives system, in which the objectives include volumes, quality, rates of absenteeism, and rates of injuries. Annual bonuses represent up to 20 percent of monthly wages (after results evaluations). This part of the salary becomes permanent after four years.

[8]The ratio of the average salary of workers included in the highest level of the job classification scheme (seventh super) and the average wage of workers included in the lowest (third) was approximately 1.3 in 1977 and 1.72 in 1993.

[9]The value of the PPG index decreased from 1.03 in 1990 to 0.976 in 1992. The average PPG-related bonus was Italian £1,396,000 in 1990 and decreased to £1,344,000 in 1992. As already noted, it turned out to be a kind of fixed bonus. On the whole, the PPG hardly reached 3 percent of total labor costs.

Other reward policies are linked to quality circle activities.[10] With respect to the relationship between individual incentives and quality improvement, the experimental stage of the suggestion system, from 1991 to 1993, yielded encouraging results.

Rates of participation in Fiat's suggestion system at the end of December 1992 are shown in figure 9.1. Cross-plant comparisons of union membership and participation in the suggestion system are a rough means of understanding the reason the situation is so diversified across plants. Even allowing that such comparisons are difficult and data should be interpreted very cautiously, figure 9.2 shows an inverse relation between union density and the percentage of workers involved in the suggestion mechanism. In other words, the higher the density, the lower the participation in the suggestion system appears to be. This relationship is not so neat and clear, however. Furthermore, data often hide very different situations, and

Figure 9.1 Participation in Suggestion System at Fiat Auto, 1992

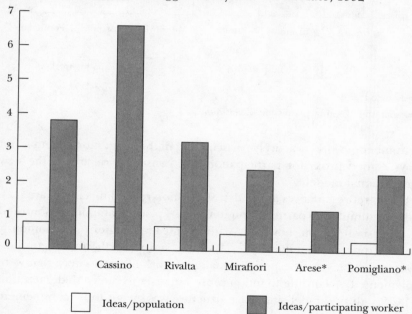

*Alfa Romeo Plants.

Source: Fiat Auto. Used by permission of Fiat Auto.

[10]On the whole, quality circle-related incentives have been marginal, since in 1993 they represented only 0.02 percent of total labor costs.

Figure 9.2 Relationship between Union Density and Participation in
Suggestion System at Fiat Auto, 1992

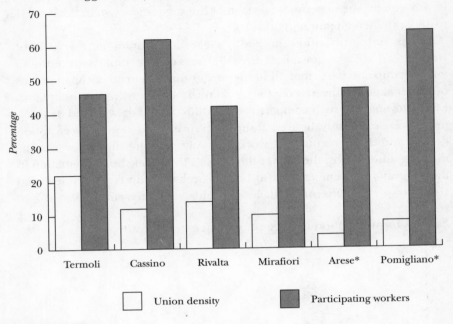

*Alfa Romeo Plants.
Source: Fiat Auto. Used by permission of Fiat Auto.

the number of workers actively participating in the suggestion system is not
always a good proxy for participation and consensus regarding the new
organizational model.

Union representatives argue that suggestion-related incentives are ineffective in stimulating participation in the workplace. Fiat unions sponsored
the suggestion system, however. At the plant level, unions autonomously
instituted prizes (mountain bikes, TV sets, and so forth) for suggestions
about particular issues, especially quality of work life and safety, that were
implemented. According to union representatives to the confederal union
FIM-CISL, this "parallel" incentive structure was meant to be complementary and not to conflict with that of Fiat.

It is noteworthy that at the new Melfi plant an incentive scheme in
which individual workers were asked to submit suggestions was developed
but has not been implemented. Suggestions are requested, collected, evaluated, and applied, but their impact from a compensation standpoint is on
the competitiveness prize only. This approach is consistent with the empha-

sis on teamwork at Melfi. Individual incentive structures can hinder cooperation, especially where task interdependencies are high (Itoh 1992).

Industrial Relations Ambiguity

For Fiat, the IF model does not represent a means whereby the company
and the unions will codesign the work organization. Rather, the project is
anchored on managerial prerogatives. As a consequence, union involvement and consensus have been sought and pursued only during the period
of implementation, not, for instance, as at Saturn, during the design phase.
Thus, although Fiat management is aware of the importance of the need for
union consensus, this awareness has not yet been fully translated into a new
industrial relations model. Further, this resistance, rooted in the company's
heritage and history, negatively affects the company's capacity to implement
the new model. In fact, implementation requires new rules, mechanisms
whereby the work is organized, and human resource practices that are possible only when there is an innovative union-management relationship.

There seem to be signs that union-management cooperation is increasing at Fiat. Management seems willing to push for the workers' and the
unions' active involvement in the process of organizational restructuring
(Cerruti and Rieser 1992). For example, the union-management committee at the Rivalta plant solved many problems in product quality and work
organization related to the start of production of the Croma model.

Production of the Croma was transferred from Mirafiori to Rivalta in
early 1992. Immediately, problems arose. Together with other unions such
as FIM, UILM and FISMIC, FIOM-CGIL suggested holding a management-
union committee meeting every week. The committee faced and solved
quality problems, including decisions about line stops, workers' mobility,
the integration of workers moved from Mirafiori, the redefinition of cycle
times, and saturations. Interventions were made on matters of layout and
tools, and the committee solved disciplinary problems involving 120 workers who were reaching a production target of only 40 to 60 percent by
reducing the number of cases to twenty.

These positive industrial relations experiences seem to have increased
since the signing of the June 11, 1993, and February 20, 1994, accords.
The massive dependence on CIG (fig. 9.3) during the last years has
resulted in labor-management tensions, however, especially in Milan and
Naples, because of the militancy of several unions. The effects of this situation are uncertain because, for the first time, white-collar workers at Fiat
see their job security jeopardized. Hence, the issue of job security is

another issue that could potentially hinder the adoption of the new organizational model.

On the whole, Fiat's unions are cautious in evaluating management's
efforts. They are satisfied about the quality effort, the training programs,
and the new incentive schemes, because they represent a major discontinuity with respect to the technology strategy of the 1980s. Yet union leaders fear layoffs and plant shutdowns. The new plants in the South and the
increase in production in Poland and Brazil, among other foreign locations, may portend the shutdown of older plants (the Lancia plant at
Chivasso was closed in 1992). Fiat's recruitment policy, which is resulting in
a high turnover among older workers, also weakens the unions' presence.

The question of the destiny of the workers being supported by the CIG
and of those on mobility lists is especially troublesome. In Volkswagen's
case, the working-time reduction strategy seems clear: Volkswagen has to
reduce labor costs to become more competitive and reduce the number of
paid holidays, decrease complementary compensation, and so on. As

Figure 9.3 Employment and CIG-Supported Employees at Fiat Auto,
1987–92

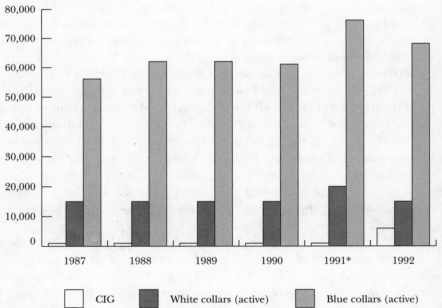

*Alfa-Lancia was absorbed by Fiat Auto in 1991.
Source: Fiat Auto. Used by permission of Fiat Auto.

demand recovers, workers who have been laid off will be reintegrated, depending on their skills. In Fiat's case, the restructuring strategy is ambiguous, partly because of corporate strategy but also because of the different quality, skills, and commitment of the workers supported by the state redundancy funds.

Hence, the evolution of firm-level industrial relations remains complex and multifaceted. For example, industrial relations at Fiat seem to be more cooperative and open, but strikes and absenteeism are increasing for the first time in a decade. Union density indicators have not declined, however, as they did in the 1980s (Kochan, Locke, and Heye 1992). Rather, they show some signs of increasing (fig. 9.4) and for blue-collar workers have almost reached their 1980 level. The union entropy coefficient increased, however,[11] suggesting a state of increased disorder, which corresponds to

Figure 9.4 Union Density at Fiat Auto Plants, 1990–92

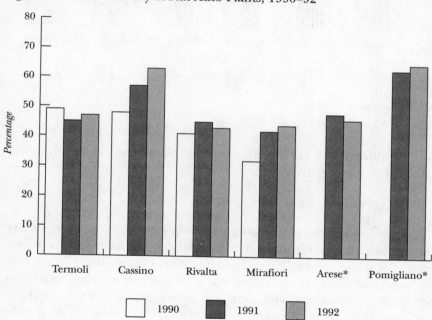

*Alfa Romeo plants.

Source: Fiat Auto. Used by permission of Fiat Auto.

[11]The entropy coefficient is defined as: $\sum_{i=1, 2, \ldots, n} Qi \log 1/Qi$ where Qi = union membership (share of total) of union i. It measures the dispersion of union membership.

Figure 9.5 Entropy Coefficients Based on Union Density at Fiat Auto Plants, 1990–92

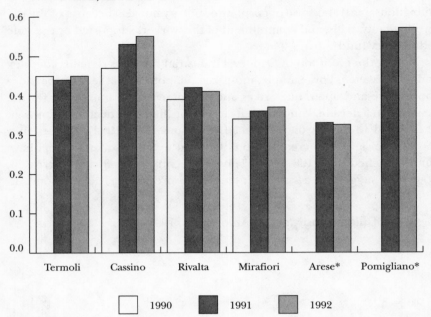

*Alfa Romeo plants.

Source: Fiat Auto. Used by permission of Fiat Auto.

the difficulties unions are undergoing at the macro level, especially in the industrial sector (fig. 9.5).[12]

Conclusion

The organizational model emerging at Fiat represents a major discontinuity with the past, despite the difficulties the company has faced in implementing it. The design of the IF organizational model proves that Fiat learned the lesson that advanced technology has to be carefully matched with innovations in organizational and human resource practices and that these innovations have to be implemented systematically, as a coherent set of policies. As a result, the key issue facing Fiat is having "smart people around the machine" and, even more important, participating and committed people.

[12]The increasing entropy is evidence of the fragmented situation among unions. In 1987, the FIM had a major split within its ranks. Separatists were led by Audres Tiboni, who created another union, the SIDA. The new union achieved a strong following at the Cassino plant. Anarchical fractions of the union movements have continued to emerge.

10 Spain, France, and Italy: Mediterranean Lean Production

Arnaldo Camuffo and Stefano Micelli

This chapter expands on the case study in chapter 9 by comparing the evolution of lean work organization and human resource practices in three Mediterranean companies: SEAT in Spain, Renault in France, and Fiat in Italy. We argue that the three automakers have generated an original and idiosyncratic evolutionary pattern that we label "Mediterranean Lean Production." (Kenney and Florida 1993).

Despite the enormous differences among the three firms, some features of their new organizational models are similar. In particular, at the plant level, Fiat, Renault, and SEAT have implemented original yet similar forms of work organization. Team leaders or newly designed first-line supervisors continue to play a crucial hierarchical role, principally in automated contexts, and especially regarding human resource management.[1] In other words, while substitutes for hierarchies (Lawler 1988) and horizontal coordination are usually considered the organizational core of lean

---

[1]The concept of team leader is a very ambiguous one. In this chapter, the term is used to convey its broad meaning, that is, to refer to the person governing a group of people, on the basis of acknowledged competence and/or appointed authority. The ambiguity stems from the fact that the concept of teams itself is rather fuzzy and has different meanings in different firms (Mueller 1994). Even management literature distinguishes between teams and work groups. Jon R. Katzenbach and Douglas K. Smith (1993), for example, characterize work groups as having a strong, clearly focused leader and individual accountability. The group's purpose is the same as the broader mission of the organization. The group has individual work products for which it is responsible, is expected to run efficient meetings, measures its effectiveness indirectly by its influence on others (e.g., financial performance of the business), and discusses and decides issues and delegates. By contrast, teams have shared leadership roles and individual and mutual accountability. Each team has a specific purpose that the team itself delivers. The team encourages open-ended discussion and active problem-solving meetings and measures performance directly by assessing collective work products. Finally, it discusses, decides, and does real work together. This summary suggests that, at least according to this

or postlean auto manufacturing, we argue that hierarchy is still crucial and that the human resource management activities performed by team leaders are the real drivers of personnel commitment and, eventually, of quality and efficiency.

A flatter, teamwork-based, management-by-sight, decentralized organization tends to redefine yet emphasize the role of hierarchy. This does not mean, as some rather radical interpretations of lean production seem to propose (Babson 1992; Robertson et al. 1993b), that the traditional concept of supervision and control has survived Fordism and integrated itself into the new production system. Nor does it mean that emerging production systems are pure and simply homogeneous and consistent with Fordism. Multiskilled workers and self-organizing teams represent important solutions to emerging management complexity even if they do not completely solve coordination problems. As shown in figure 10.1, the functions of first-line supervisors are not to command and control but to communicate, negotiate, empower, and offer incentives.

Evolutionary Trajectories of Fiat, Renault, and SEAT

While Fiat was defining its new organizational model (see chapter 9), Renault was deeply engaged in defining and implementing a somewhat French lean production system. From 1985 to 1987, Renault faced a financial crisis that almost resulted in bankruptcy. George Besse, the new CEO, launched a comprehensive restructuring program aimed at cost cutting

Figure 10.1 Key Functions of First-Line Supervisors under Mediterranean Lean Production

- Balancing workloads across team members
- Managing information flow and asymmetries within organizational units
- Facilitating systematic training and continuous improvement
- Managing internal and external interfaces (boundary-spanning role)
- Adjusting the degree of perceived equity of the incentive structure
- Appraising personnel performance and signaling opportunities for horizontal and vertical mobility as skills are developed and accumulated

definition, the term *team* is misused in most cases. Other distinctions are the basis on which team leaders are appointed (election by peers or formal appointment by management) and its stability (rotation and so on). According to this distinction, Fiat, Renault, and SEAT have work groups. This is true even of German automakers. For further discussion of the issue, see Murakami 1995. Throughout this chapter, the terms *team* and *teamwork* will be used in a broad sense; and *team leader* will be used interchangeably with *first-line supervisor*.

and lowering break-even points. The company stated its independence from political power and ceased cooperating with the Confederation General du Travail (CGT), the most influential Marxist-oriented union. Besse gained the commitment of top and middle managers, imposed priorities vis-à-vis efficiency, and launched cost-cutting projects that continued to develop in the following years.

As at Fiat, quality became a fundamental concern at Renault in the late 1980s. Outsourcing increased in importance, and codesign activities were developed with suppliers. The employment system and industrial relations changed, ending an era of privileged relations with CGT. HRM initiatives concentrated on massive reskilling programs for blue-collar workers to facilitate implementation of total quality management (Freyssenet 1993).

The diverse and scattered organizational experiences and innovations achieved in the automobile industry during this period began to be standardized and rationalized in the 1990s. At the same time, group work was progressively transformed from a social issue (plants had often been seen as social laboratories) to an organizational issue. Teams, once conceived as solutions to improve the quality of life of workers, became the main organizational building block to implement the principles of lean production.

SEAT's new organizational model reflected its multicultural development; in other words, the implementation of the German approach in Spain. After the acquisition of Volkswagen (VW) in 1986, SEAT was involved in a complete reorganization designed and implemented by German management. In 1987, VW launched a new plant project in Martorell and started developing two new models, the Ibiza and the Cordoba, in order to update traditional products (based on Fiat designs)[2] and to achieve a stronger presence in international markets. This transformation also involved reducing and simplifying SEAT's distribution network.

Martorell now represents SEAT's most important production plant. The Zona Franca plant, the other manufacturing unit, keeps producing the Marbella model, but its relevance is declining. On the one hand, the Martorell plant is the result of Wolfsburg technological know-how. On the other hand, it embodies the Japanese approach to the management of people, quality improvements (for example, the so-called *stand de calidad*, in which statistical process control and other quality-related measures are displayed), and the application of logistics components management (Economist Intelligence Unit 1993).

[2]Before 1986, SEAT belonged to the Fiat group.

From an organizational standpoint, SEAT management adopted concepts, tools, and procedures developed in German automobile factories. For example, as the result of its successful application at VW, the VW version of kaizen, KVP II, was transferred to SEAT. Today, the plant organization and management systems at SEAT are significantly different from those of the past, at least in some shops and for some lines.

Seeking Integration through Elementary Organizational Units

Although Fiat, Renault, and SEAT each developed its own organizational models, starting from different premises, similarities exist among the three programs. All of them, for instance, engaged in a process of delayering to obtain a more responsive and flat organizational structure. Similarly, production engineering and operations were decentralized and placed at the department, not the plant, level.

The rest of this chapter analyzes various production lines at Fiat, Renault, and SEAT: for Fiat, the lines at the Cassino (Tipo and Tempra models) and Melfi (Punto) plants; for Renault, the two different lines at the Flins plant (the Clio and the Twingo models, respectively); and for SEAT, the two lines at the Martorell plant (the Ibiza-Cordoba and the Toledo models, respectively). Although these production lines do not completely match one another and are not homogeneous, a comparison yields rich insights. The Tipo, Clio, and Toledo production lines represent good examples of how the new organizational scheme is applied in brownfield settings—that is, how the principles of the new work organization affected existing procedures, roles, and competencies. The Punto, Twingo, and Ibiza production lines, by contrast, were conceived and realized from a totally new perspective. Thus, the manufacturing process segmentation, training programs, and personnel recruitment policies were fully coherent with requirements of the new organizational scheme.

New Plant Organization

Fiat's, Renault's, and SEAT's plants have been substantially delayered and decentralized. Former sectors were divided into operational units by aggregating traditional machine shops. SEAT is like Fiat, so that each operational unit is articulated and specialized in two areas: operations and production engineering. Production engineering represents a decentralized pool of technical competencies, working as a staff of operations.

At Renault, decentralization is pushed even further. Not only is the department chief responsible for operations and engineering, but engineering has also been drastically reduced and its resources relocated to a lower level of operations or to other units, such as quality control or total productivity maintenance groups.

Through delayering, Fiat and Renault eliminated two hierarchical levels, while SEAT did away with one level. At Fiat and Renault, included in the delayering process was the elimination of the shop steward position, the most traditional hierarchical figure in auto manufacturing. According to IMVP plant survey data, Fiat's Melfi, Renault's Flins, and SEAT's Martorell plants have a lower than average number of hierarchical levels (table 10.1). Flat organizational structures require more horizontal coordination and less vertical supervision. Hence, mutual adjustment becomes the prevalent means of coordination within and between units (Thompson 1967; Mintzberg 1979).

Elementary Organizational Units: The Keystone of New Organizational Models

Fiat's HRM department defines a *unità tecnologica elementare* as a unit that governs a segment of the production process (a technological subsystem). In UTEs, prevention, variance absorption, self-control, and continuous improvement all take place in an effort to achieve the firm's goals of quality and productivity. Renault's *Direction du Personnel et des Affaires Sociales* defines its *unité elementaire du travail* (UET) as a group of multiskilled and

Table 10.1 Hierarchical Layers at Fiat Melfi, Renault Flins, and SEAT Martorell Plants

Plant/Area	Mean	Median
Japan/Japan	7.9	6.0
Japan/N.A.	6.5	6.5
U.S./N.A.	6.2	6.0
Europe	7.1	6.0
New entrants	6.9	6.5
Australia	5.7	6.0
Fiat Melfi	5	
Renault Flins	5	
SEAT Martorell	6	

Sources: Plant interviews and Ittner and MacDuffie 1994.

polyvalent workers, in charge of a part of the whole production process and supervised by a group leader. Finally, SEAT management, in analogous terms, defines its *grupo de trabajo* (GT) as a team that manages a specific segment of the production line, whose responsibilities include volume, quality, and maintenance.

In all three companies, the main purposes of these groups are as follows. The first objective is to solve problems at the lowest possible level. Resources and workers with various skills are available so that problems may be solved as and where they occur. The second objective is to facilitate improvements in products and processes by systematically incorporating the results of organizational learning. Each unit establishes client-supplier relationships with other units, downstream and upstream. Each problem caused by a unit must be solved by its personnel or with the support of central units. Thus, each unit is self-regulating and can certify the quality of the activities it performs.[3] Managers from the three companies claim that organizational structures based on teams result in leaner and smoother manufacturing processes, better job assignments, flexibility enhancement, process improvements, and lower costs.

Every unit is managed and coordinated by a complex information system and is composed of subsystems whose focus is quality control, manufacturing performance measurement, and so on. In addition to management by sight, management techniques such as statistical process control and total productivity maintenance (TPM) are implemented to control microprocesses.

The tasks of team leaders or unit heads can be described in terms of both their internal activities and their external activities.[4] The former refers to the relationships and the resources located within a cell, whereas the latter refers to interfaces with other units or organizations. Internally, team leaders manage human, technical, and financial resources so as to obtain results they have negotiated with their superiors. Team leaders conduct meetings and group activities to make explicit the objectives of the cell, maintain control of the main production parameters, prevent line breakdowns (ensuring equipment is functioning and parts are available), decide

[3]Although elementary organizational units are similar to some degree to work groups, although not teams in the strict sense proposed by Katzenbach and Smith (1993), they differ from semiautonomous groups derived from the sociotechnical tradition. These, in turn, were experimented with during the 1970s in many German (e.g., Opel) but also French (e.g., Renault) and Italian (e.g., Alfa Romeo) plants under pressure from unions (IGM, CGT, and CGIL) seeking quality of work life programs.

[4]UTE, UET, and grupo de trabajo chiefs correspond to the previously defined first-line supervisors or team leaders.

how to use the assigned budget (for example, for technical interventions), and supervise personnel training. In regard to interfaces with the rest of the plant and outside the organization, it is important to underline the impressive boundary spanning the leader's role. Leaders normally interact with other upstream and downstream units in order to solve production and quality problems. They negotiate objectives with superiors, they interact with technology and maintenance specialists to repair important technical breakdowns and adjust to changes, and they manage or govern supply flows.

Differences in Integration of Specialists and Team Leaders' Span of Control

The organizational schemes implemented by the three automakers are similar in many regards, but there are at least two crucial differences in their organizational structures. The first difference concerns the integration of technicians within elementary operational units (EOUs), especially in automated contexts, when technical breakdowns and maintenance can radically affect the team's global performance. Renault defines the EOU as a comprehensive team in which technicians and other specialists are fully integrated. These technicians, who report to the UET chief, are responsible for implementing TPM, and their task is limited to first-level maintenance. Relevant breakdowns and other technical problems are solved by the engineering unit that is staffed at the *département* level.

By contrast, the link between UTE chiefs and technology specialists/ maintenance people remains functional at Fiat and at SEAT, where specialists still report to production engineering units. They intervene within the UTE when necessary. Technicians at SEAT focus on second-level maintenance, while coordinators and system controllers operating within the *grupo* are constantly involved in first-level maintenance. Within the Fiat model, UTE teams are conceived as *integrators* (Lawrence and Loersch 1967; Galbraith 1977), that is, as enhancing horizontal coordination and information sharing.

The differences between plants should not be overestimated, though. In the Spanish and French plants, management imposed rules that clearly define different activity domains: the intervention of EOUs is limited to specific tasks and technical problems. Also, time assigned to individual and collective problem solving is strictly regulated. In the Italian plants, organizational design is still evolving according to dynamics within the UTE and the operational units. Whenever possible, technicians belonging to the unit staff become dedicated resources to one or two EOUs, developing not only knowledge and competencies on specific segments of the production line but also providing specific functional links with the first-line supervisors of the EOU.

In all three cases, the rationale is to distinguish between first- and second-level technical activities (reengineering and maintenance) according to their complexity. First-level operations, which strongly influence the economic and qualitative performance of production lines, should be managed by stable teams that develop a deep contextual knowledge of the process. Second-level operations are assigned to specialized groups at a higher hierarchical level to fully exploit the general and abstract knowledge of engineers and technicians.

A second important feature differentiating Fiat's UTEs from Renault's and SEAT's EOUs is the unit chief's span of control. EOUs at Renault and SEAT are comparatively smaller in size than Fiat's UTEs, which facilitates the human resource management role of the EOU chief. At the Flins plant, UET chiefs are in charge of analyzing and diagnosing personnel training needs. Once a year, they make formal performance appraisals of every worker in the UET. They also are responsible for motivating personnel and solving personnel problems. Furthermore, when asked, they are supposed to suggest candidates for promotion or for early retirement and layoff. SEAT supervisors are required to undertake the same functions, even if reforms are far from being fully implemented.

Fiat's UTEs are larger, especially in operational units in final assembly. The span of control of UTE chiefs remains very wide, and personnel functions are partially accomplished with the help of CPIs and OPIs. On the whole, HRM activities have become more centralized, although each operational unit has a *repo*, who reports hierarchically to the plant HRM manager and functionally to the operational unit chief. The repo is in charge of coordinating HRM policy and information systems.

Team Leader's Role

A common feature of the new organizational models at Fiat, Renault, and SEAT is that emphasis is placed on organizational design and human resource policies as competitive factors. Despite the differences in their evolutionary patterns, all three firms have evolved from a stage in which technology was considered the main driver of productivity. All introduced new forms of work organization during the 1970s not as the result of their awareness of the need for a new competitive strategy and HRM practices but as the most appropriate defense against union demands or social pressures. Consequently, new forms of work organization were not considered an important part of a competitive strategy.

The implementation of the new organizational models based on UETs, grupos, and UTEs represented an important discontinuity in the strategies of these three companies. The new models can be read as comprehensive attempts to make plant-level organization more transparent, to facilitate the exchange of information, and to allow for the sharing of experiences and knowledge among employees. Organizational transparency makes possible systematic reductions in the rents and costs associated with information inequality, which inevitably produce contrasts and conflicts. Teams and management-by-sight techniques should reduce opportunistic behaviors, favor self-control, and ensure the degree of horizontal communication necessary to solve problems as they arise.

Managers and scholars have often emphasized the importance of techniques and managerial tools that activate organizational learning. The almost simultaneous diffusion of all the (often Japanese-derived) management-by-sight instruments in many auto manufacturers is evidence of the important role nonhierarchical coordinating mechanisms play in organizational design. Nevertheless, the analysis of these three cases shows that first-line supervisors play a crucial role in implementing these changes and in eliciting cooperation within the organization. Managerial activity is crucial in developing competencies and building commitment among workers through training, communication, performance appraisal, compensation, conflict resolution, quality circles, suggestions, and so on.

Listening and Negotiating

Among the activities team leaders engage in at the shop-floor level are negotiating with workers to ensure their commitment and participation, which are essential if the company is to take full advantage of the potential of the information systems, integration mechanisms, and coordinating devices available. What does a team leader negotiate with his or her workers? First, he or she negotiates the acquisition of informal knowledge, which workers, especially technicians, accumulate in day-to-day activities. Second, he or she negotiates the commitment of the workers to the continuous improvement of quality standards and manufacturing efficiency.

The importance of situated knowledge (Lave 1988) seems to emerge in all the new organizational models. The competencies of graduate engineers in production engineering departments are wider and more flexible than those of technicians in elementary organizational units. The theoretical knowledge of the engineers provides a general systematic comprehension of how the different production segments work and interact with each other.

By contrast, only technicians operating in EOUs develop "situation-specific" knowledge. For example, they acquire particular confidence in dealing with equipment, and this allows for faster and more effective interventions. Looking systematically at machine breakdowns and evaluating the limits of equipment in daily activity, technicians gain an advantageous position that enables them to solve specific technical problems and provide suggestions to improve the efficiency and reliability of technology.

Generic line workers develop situation-specific knowledge, too. Although supporters of lean production emphasized the possibility of incorporating this individual know-how into organizational knowledge, by means of suggestion systems, kaizen activities, and the like, only part of the tacit skills that workers accumulate on the line results in innovations in local processes. More often, the *escamotages* ("rules of thumb") workers learn are used to reduce saturation and workloads and are not aimed at improving efficiency. This shows that management is not able to limit workers' autonomy and discretionary behaviors and that workers' commitment has its own price.

In this context, it is important to emphasize the value of the human resource management activities team leaders perform. Often these include taking a more flexible approach to working hours, holidays, and so on. A UET chief on the Clio production line commented that a North African immigrant worker asked for permission to take his wife to the doctor. Because of his religious beliefs, he could not let her go alone. The UET chief allowed him to leave the factory two hours before the end of the shift and undertook work on his behalf. The chief maintains that since then, nobody has refused to work during lunchtime when asked.

Managing relations with technicians is more difficult. They tend to master technical equipment and prefer to keep up their specialist knowledge rather than contribute to the global performance of the EOU. Keeping this in mind, a UET leader at the Flins body-welding shop allowed his technicians to call department specialists in the case of breakdowns only after all possible solutions had been explored. Given the time available to the UET technicians for problem identification and solving, greater pressure was put on the external experts. This informal policy represented an indirect incentive for them to cooperate with the UET technicians, who, in turn, appreciated the chief's decision and reciprocated by improving the results of their UET.

The integration of technicians with the other members of the team depends both on the degree of automation and on the technicians' capacity to learn. In all the plants surveyed, teams were rather well established in automated units (body welding, painting), whereas their implementation appeared more difficult in traditional shops (assembly). Technicians operating in automated units easily integrated themselves in the group because of their contribution to line reliability. In fact, their efforts directly resulted in both improvements in organizational performance and continuous individual learning.

Individual and organizational learning have their costs, however. Trial-and-error activities on the job require time and resources. Formal and informal meetings, solutions that do not work, and time taken in repairing technical breakdowns are all sources of costs for first-line supervisors. More generally, leaders who have no extra time available and feel strong pressure to achieve short-term results face important problems in undertaking team-building activities.

Thus, it is important that first-line supervisors manage resources (flexible hours, minor incentives) with the goals of creating and maintaining cooperation within teams. This calls for cautious, sometimes ad hoc maneuvering of HRM variables at the shop-floor level. For example, training and team meetings "on the spot" are very important. They enable the unit leader and technicians to explain interdependencies among different parts of the production system, how a single operation affects the activity of other workers downstream, and, from a more general point of view, the logic and costs of the entire system. What is most important is that ordinary production workers are actually part of a group and that they can legitimately ask questions and negotiate their role within the organization.

Brownfield versus Greenfield Sites

Although the training effort realized by firms is important, training does not imply coordination per se. Knowing the interdependencies that link the activities of a factory can certainly stimulate a cooperative attitude, but it is hard to believe that attention to quality and production suffices to create a cooperative group. What matters is that team leaders must take into account the needs and concerns of workers to gain their commitment. The role of the team leader is complex and requires a mix of various competencies and resources that is rarely found in traditional settings.

The full importance of the team leader's profile emerges if traditional settings are compared with innovative ones. As chapter 9 made clear, the implementation of Fiat's integrated factory has relied, as far as UTE chiefs are concerned, on former shop stewards. In spite of the massive training programs that these workers undertook to acquire the new skills, former team leaders, who are now UTE chiefs, maintain traditional behaviors and, in some cases, openly resist change (Cerruti and Rieser 1992). In other cases, the UTE chiefs misinterpreted involvement techniques, such as the suggestion system. At the Cassino plant, they seem reluctant to assume their new responsibilities. At the Melfi plant, by contrast, the situation is different. UTE chiefs have been carefully selected and trained, they have managerial and technical capabilities, and they are able and willing to make important decisions, such as whether to stop the line, autonomously.

At the SEAT Martorell plant, first-line supervisors of the body-welding unit are generally new, young, highly skilled employees. In assembly, by contrast, the majority were previously shop stewards at the Zona Franca plant in Barcelona. Older *supervisores* are resistant to change and keep dealing in traditional ways not only with their subordinates but with their superiors. To encourage autonomous decision making on the Ibiza-Cordoba assembly line, there are stickers on all telephones that say, "Don't phone your boss if possible." Former shop stewards sometimes feel abandoned and find it difficult to cope with the new organizational dynamics.

The situation is analogous at Renault. On the Clio lines of the Flins plant, UET chiefs, who formerly were line workers, had major problems developing interpersonal skills and managerial competencies. Workers complained about poor communication concerning technological improvements, product quality problems, and new management techniques. Many workers also remarked that their superior was not capable of representing and defending them, while others complained that the chief was not integrated within the group.

These remarks shed more light on the complex role of UET chiefs and explain why Renault emphasized the importance of the selection process for this job. Some problems were overcome by recruiting chiefs from engineering and technological areas, whose importance has gradually but constantly been decreasing during the last few years. Such a cross-functional career path placed priority on managerial and interpersonal skills over technical competence. For the Twingo line, young candidates were selected and trained to fill team leader jobs. The selection criteria included commitment, capacity to relate well with others, and entrepreneurial initiative. Results seem to confirm the validity of this approach.

Economic Performance and the Creation of Groups

The creation of teams as the new building blocks of organizations is the result of a strategic choice that rejects the traditional emphasis on group work as an organizational solution to improve the quality of life of workers. Teams were originally designed to decentralize decision making on quality and reliability issues. Nonetheless, the social dimension of team-building activities at Fiat, Renault, SEAT, and elsewhere has acquired a somewhat unintended relevance. Where team leaders succeeded in listening and negotiating with their subordinates and improving their units' performance, the perceived equity of the incentive structure increased. In these cases, the leader's role evolved and resembled that of spokesperson (a leader representing and acting on behalf of the group). A technician of a Flins UET said: "Our chief is a good one. When there is a meeting [to negotiate objectives with the operational unit chief], he knows how to defend our interests!" The technician was not just saying that the first-line supervisor was no longer the traditional boss. Rather, to the technician, the team was a precise entity, its boundaries actually mattered, and it had a holistic and a systemic nature.

First-line supervisors seem to become good leaders when they act as an integrative part of their teams, rather than as part of the hierarchical chain. Nonetheless, team leaders still play a hierarchical role. They manage resources that are fundamental to workers and technicians, and in this sense their effective power has been increased. From this standpoint, teamwork and the role of the first-line supervisor in these Mediterranean plants differed from other versions of lean manufacturing as it is applied, for instance, in northern European countries.

Conclusions

Notwithstanding the strong differences that characterize their evolutionary patterns, Fiat, Renault, and SEAT have successfully started to implement a new organizational model. These new models incorporate several features of lean production, with the aim of making the organization more responsive, quality focused, and cost-effective. Although it is difficult to overestimate the importance of such instruments and techniques, hierarchical roles are still crucial, even at the lowest levels, in activating workers' commitment.

The function of this hierarchy has changed substantially, however. Team leaders are not required to reward conformity and to punish anomalous behavior as long as line workers execute procedures and routines effectively, as specified by engineers and line technologists. The main task of team leaders now is to involve people in the production process, build commitment, and facilitate organizational learning in order to improve production and quality standards. Such an effort requires not only interpersonal skills and natural leadership but resources and managerial tools. As a consequence, the team leader's power is not grounded on traditional bureaucratic authority but on his or her capacity to negotiate, exchange, and share information and commitment with subordinates. That is when teams become more than people simply working together.

Overall, the organizational schemes implemented by Fiat, Renault, and SEAT cannot be considered the result of the application of lean production techniques to Italian, French, and Spanish plants. Rather, they reveal original traits that should be considered from an evolutionary perspective. In other words, the specific role played by team leaders appears to be partly related to the historical backgrounds of the three firms. A hypothesis that is worth further investigation is that these differences in the roles of team leaders are related to the history of labor relations at the firm level.

In the future, the terms of exchange between these firms and their workers will probably become more complex and articulated. The redefinition of hierarchical relationships is probably the first step of a global redesign of an employment relationship whose main traits are still evolving and seem difficult to specify. For the time being, team leaders are an important building block in establishing trusteeship and a new cooperative attitude inside formerly traditional factories with antagonistic labor-management relations.

More generally, the new organizational schemes at Fiat, Renault, and SEAT mark a discontinuity with Fordism and with an obsolete conception of hierarchy. Contrary to the illusions of some scholars, however, neither flexible automation technology nor lean manufacturing management systems in and of themselves make the factories transparent and self-regulating.

11

Sweden: The Volvo and Saab Road beyond Lean Production

Göran Brulin and Tommy Nilsson

This chapter provides an account of the changes in work organization on the shop floors of Volvo Torslanda and Saab in Trollhättan, the main assembly plants of the two Swedish car producers. In 1991, management at Torslanda, in Gothenburg, launched the KLE program, the Swedish acronym for "quality, precise delivery, and economy" (QPE). One year earlier, Saab introduced a similar program in Trollhättan.

We conducted approximately twenty interviews with people at all levels of Volvo and Saab—from company managers to operators on the shop floor—and with trade union representatives. Our objective was to understand the meaning of such new concepts as lean production and lean enterprise in these companies. Our empirical research focused on changes at Volvo Torslanda and Saab in Trollhättan in the production departments, the integration that occurred between the production departments and the research and development departments, and the changes in employment relations that followed.

The product and process development work has changed at Volvo Torslanda and Saab in Trollhättan in a few important respects (in line with the ideas put forward, for example, in Clark and Fujimoto 1991). The reorganization of the product and process development departments and their integration with the production departments will not be discussed here, however. Nor will the merits of the lean production concept be debated (see Williams et al. 1994), although we are aware of the objections to lean production that could be made.

Paradoxically, the introduction in the 1990s of new production concepts paralleled the closing of Saab's Malmö plant and Volvo's Kalmar and

Uddevalla plants and thus the discontinuation of these sociotechnical experiments. It is worth remembering, however, that none of Volvo's and Saab's alternative production plants was closed because quality or productivity was declining. Instead, what forced these plants to close was the rapidly decreasing capacity utilization caused by the crisis in the auto industries (Berggren 1992). Management at the Volvo Torslanda plant claims that it is using the experience gained at Kalmar and Uddevalla. Furthermore, Volvo has now reopened the Uddevalla plant, together with a British partner, albeit for special production.

The most noteworthy result of our empirical investigations is that it seems possible to foster work development for operators on the line. At this level it appears to be more productive to break away from strict Taylorist work organization. Similar ideas seem to have taken hold at some new Nissan, Honda, Mitsubishi, and Toyota plants. The physical working environment has been improved, cycle times are longer, and assembly work has been broken up into "mini-lines" with buffers (Nomura 1992; Rehder 1994). The QPE activities at Volvo and Saab are only a minor part of the total work, however. It is difficult to determine how much working time, in addition to assembly work itself, these activities consume.

Unlike the metalworkers union at Saab, the local branch of the union at Volvo accepted the cessation of the sociotechnical experiments and is attempting to create conditions for job development for its members within the framework of the line system. Although the change in the organization of work has been questioned, both the local unions have accepted layoffs. The largest layoffs have been at Saab. From 1988 to 1993, employment in Trollhättan was cut from 9,800 to 5,300. Total employment in Saab Automobile contracted from 15,800 to 6,500. At both Saab and Volvo, however, criticism of the permanent understaffing is emerging.

Work Groups in Volvo's Production Departments

The concept of QPE work organization was developed jointly by employers' and employees' representatives of Volvo, and in 1991 QPE groups started work in the production departments of the Torslanda factory. According to the developers, work groups should be customer-oriented. The aim has been to replace departmental relations with customer-supplier relations on the shop floor as well as in the entire organization. The long-term objective is for the groups to be responsible for a range of work tasks. Thus, in addition to their actual assembly work, the groups are expected to be responsible for quality (which includes control of their work input), materials supply, and some personnel administration and to participate in process development, instruction/training, and planning. Each group appoints its own leader. Thus, there is both lateral and vertical integration.

The QPE group work strategy is that work groups should gradually take over tasks that were formerly considered outside the domain of the assembly line. This applies both to tasks that affect production technology (such as balancing the line), planning, quality work, and maintaining contact with suppliers, traditionally done by white-collar workers, as well as tasks done in off-line workshops, such as maintenance and materials supply (i.e., lateral integration). In short, the members of work groups must be flexible. To a greater or lesser extent, they must each be able to carry out almost all of the group's various work tasks. Learning these tasks takes a relatively long time, however.

Group members are also part of a network. Thus, they may become involved in establishing a structure for a number of groups to address quality problems, for example, or in coordinating development work with engineers in the factory or in a pilot plant.

It is also assumed that work groups will reflect on problems in production. They must also conduct follow-up analyses of their work. This may involve calculating key ratios or the number of faults per body, the amount of scrap, working hours, and so forth. The objective is to remove the boundaries between operational work and white-collar work that is closely linked to production. According to one projection, the manufacturing operators carry out at least 10 percent QPE work and 90 percent manufacturing work during their total working hours. Another internal projection gives these proportions as 20 percent and 80 percent.

In practice, development has been uneven during the more than six years since the QPE project has been in operation. There are differences in the levels of development between the workers in the body shop, the paint shop, and final assembly. This makes it difficult to make an overall assessment of the current situation. At first glance, it appears that the level of development is higher for the work groups in the body and paint shops than for those in final assembly. At the same time, there are examples of work groups in the body shop that found it very difficult to develop, while there are groups in final assembly that have made progress toward the objective.

The differences between the groups may be an illusion. It is clear that the work of the groups in the body shop and the paint shop is better structured than in final assembly, although this structuring has come largely from above. In final assembly, more than in the other two shops, efforts have been made to introduce results-based management, in the sense that the groups themselves must decide the way they are to be structured. This takes time. If this interpretation is correct, it is possible that, given a little more time, the work groups in final assembly may develop at least as far and become as motivated to apply the QPE strategy as the groups in the other shops.

Management has been concerned that losses in productivity may result because the work groups set their own goals, but this assessment may be unfounded. An internal survey carried out in the final assembly plant by a group of production technicians indicated that the efficiency goals set by the work groups were stricter than those set by management.

A major benefit of the new system has emerged as a result of the introduction of and emphasis put on the concept of internal customer-supplier relationships. If, for example, a quality problem arises in one part of the assembly process that may be assumed to have arisen in the preceding stage, the work group that identifies the problem initiates rapid feedback. The member of the group who is responsible for quality or the group leader has an important role in this transaction. In some cases, an investigation may be undertaken, which some work groups can carry out themselves.

Almost all the work groups perform some improvement work. Sometimes this is as simple as housekeeping, while in other cases it is more sophisticated and is carried out in project form. There may be a project to install new equipment, for example, or to address an ergonomic problem. Most work groups are also responsible for day-to-day planning, including who is to do what, and administer the work group's time reports. In final assembly, the work groups perform detailed balancing of their respective assembly stations, after the production technicians have completed the main balancing procedure. Some work groups have a great deal of influence on the recruitment of new members to the group, while in other groups this is entirely in the hands of production management.

A noticeable change has been the move toward long balance times in final assembly, which results in longer cycle times. Balance times of no longer than two minutes used to be common, while many work groups now have balance times of ten to fourteen minutes. Many work cycles now include two balance times of this length. Thus, work cycles are between twenty and twenty-eight minutes. Work is in progress on making balance times even longer.

For many reasons, progress has been slow in introducing group work at Volvo. As an expression of the inertia in the social system, maintenance staff are reluctant to become part of work groups. The most efficient solution would probably be to put the maintenance function in the work group organization as part of the flow. According to the QPE work group representatives, this arrangement would also give the work groups more opportunities to be flexible in production work.

Another problem is that some production managers and product workshop managers find it difficult to delegate responsibility and authority to the work groups. They appear to still have a traditional hierarchical view of work on the shop floor. Thus, in some work groups, only the group leaders do QPE work, and they behave as traditional supervisors.

That QPE work is only a minor part of the total work program is particularly evident in the final assembly phase, where there is still an extensive amount of hands-on labor. Assembly work nowadays involves less walking alongside the line, however, since there are more carriers at which the work is done. Often workers ride with the car on the line. In the paint shop and particularly in the body shop, there is less hands-on work because of the high degree of automation of the processes, for example, paint spraying and welding.

In general, the changes in work organization have been linked to profound changes in the production system and technology. For example, stamped sheets are delivered just in time from the Olofström plant four hundred kilometers away from Torslanda. Safety storage as well as delivery control have been abolished. Although the objective of "no-hands production" has not been reached in the new body shop, there is a high degree of automation. This is also true of the paint shop.

Work Groups at Saab

Saab introduced work groups, initially called autonomous groups, in Trollhättan at the beginning of the 1970s. Discussions soon started on whether the line system should be broken up and side assembly at permanent stations be developed. In the 1980s, this organization was introduced in some parts of production, mainly in the paint shop. Changes were also made in this direction in the body shop and in final assembly.

By the mid-1980s, work development had more or less come to a standstill. According to a union representative, most operators "just stood there and tightened bolts." There was some work rotation, but it was unsystematic. An occasional assembly line worker was able to solve certain simple problems on his own initiative, but few such workers took on responsibility for improving efficiency in the work flow. To a large extent, work was still directly controlled by the foreman. On matters of quality, workers relied on quality controllers and adjusters on the line, who also took responsibility for a great deal of the assembly faults and faults from the subcontractors. Errors related to the design process were not dealt with until a long time after they occurred. Assembly line workers look back on the work of that time as being extremely inefficient. It was also boring and physically wearing.

At the beginning of the 1990s, following an agreement between management and the local metalworkers union, a program called QLEH was introduced for assembly work. Q stands for quality, signifying that the work group itself must be responsible for the quality of work. L is for lead-time reduction, which means that the work group should work on eliminating any interruptions in work flow. E is for economic efficiency, meaning, among other things, that the work group must rebalance the work so that unnecessary operations are eliminated, and H is for human resources development, meaning that the skills of the work group members must be developed so that the group gradually becomes more self-regulating.

The introduction of QLEH meant that work supervisors, each of whom was responsible for a section of the assembly line staffed by between ten and twelve operators, disappeared. Instead, production leaders were introduced, with responsibility for three to four work groups, or a total of thirty to fifty operators. The production leader is responsible for meeting production goals, the reliability of deliveries, the budget within his production area, and the development of employees. Thus, he has overall responsibility for the operation but not detailed control, which was within the scope of responsibility of the old work supervisors. Instead, there are work group leaders, who oversee each work group on the line.

According to the conceptual thinking behind QLEH, each work group should have no more than two leaders, formally appointed by its respective production leader. The union and management are not in agreement on this point. The union would like to see many people rotating through this function and have each group appoint its leaders. In practice, however, leaders are appointed in a process of consultation between the group and its production leader.

Each work group also has an "andon"person. The person in this function rotates within the group, offering assistance when problems arise on the line. The assembly workers call for the andon via a system of signals from the line but without stopping the line, as happens at Toyota. If the problem is caused by a fault in a component, it is the job of the andon to contact arrival control, which in turn contacts the supplier. The work group itself determines the details of the andon function.

Unlike the situation at Volvo, Saab has focused on achieving short balance times. The assembly line balance has ranged from two to three minutes, depending on capacity utilization. Each assembly line operator in a work group carries out one balance during a longer period and then changes to another work task, so that he or she carries out a total of five to seven balances. In management's view, this arrangement results in higher productivity.

Since work groups are responsible for quality, a large number of adjusters and quality controllers were taken off the assembly line when QLEH was introduced. There used to be six control gates on the final assembly line and special controllers on the line, but now there are none. Most of the members of the most highly developed work groups can carry out other QLEH tasks, such as detailed balancing, day-to-day planning, improvement work, and some administration (e.g., recording the time worked).

Job development is achieved by, among other things, rotating workers between different tasks, and workers' development is charted in a skills matrix. Efforts are made to achieve a high degree of flexibility, at least with respect to the assembly work itself. In most work groups, almost everyone can do all these various tasks. With respect to QLEH work, rotation is not as advanced. The new group work organization has meant that there are no longer any buffers in final assembly. In the past, there were a number of stations where work pieces could be taken to one side if problems occurred or if the work group wanted breathing space.

Several work groups do their own follow-up work. They record the number of faults per one hundred cars. They also record interruptions measured in minutes and the amount of scrapping used as a measure of efficiency. The work groups also prepare statistics on the number of suggestions for improvements each person has submitted. The groups are also empowered to approve leaves of absence for work group members of up to four hours a week.

Each work group has a half-hour meeting once a week, which provides an opportunity for reflection and a chance to consider ways to improve the efficiency of the operation. At Saab, much emphasis is placed on the standardization of work, and work sheets are used as part of this process. In some groups, the members themselves rework these sheets in an effort to further standardize operations. Members also instruct new work group members on how to read the work sheets. Everyone must work in the same way; tools and materials must be put in the same places and so on. Formerly such standardization was done by production technicians, but now the workers themselves must do this work.

Assembly workers think that the standardization of assembly work is good in all respects. The job is easier, less stressful, and less physically wearing. In the words of one worker, "To stand and bang a rubber mallet hundreds of times an hour to put components in place wears out your wrists."

A network has been formed among the work groups. The work group leaders and andon people from different work groups meet from time to time to discuss problems related to the quality of assembly work. The network extends both to work groups within a production leader's area and to groups from different areas. Some groups, particularly those in engine and gearbox assembly, have direct contact with the suppliers in Södertälje and Gothenburg, respectively. Many assembly workers want more such contact to expand the improvement work to these subdeliverers.

Each assembly station has a "wall" on which the work group records the time spent on different operations. One purpose of this wall is for the group to get the optimal balance in its area. If one operation has a shortfall in time and another has a surplus, they should be evened out. Another purpose is to reduce the overall time taken for assembly by eliminating unnecessary time. Some trade union representatives think that assembly line workers should not be involved in improving the efficiency of their own work, but many assembly workers think that since efficiency must be improved, it is an advantage that they do this work themselves. They also think that by being involved, they can influence the pace of efficiency improvements and the arrangement of balances, and it makes them better prepared to discuss efficiency-related matters with production technicians.

In most work groups at Saab, the total working hours devoted to QLEH work is no more than about 5 percent. The 95 percent of their time spent in on-line assembly work includes some work on improving efficiency, however. Hence, people think about improvements and discuss them with their coworkers while doing the assembly work or taking short breaks.

Training and Skill Development

Recruitment and training of new employees are handled with far more care at Volvo as a result of the introduction of the QPE work organization. The new technological demands along with the demands to improve quality are also relevant.

The body shop has more highly educated operators than any other department, whereas final assembly has fewer highly educated workers than any other area. The body shop now asks that operators have at least an industrial technical education and preferably a diploma from a four-year upper-secondary technical school. The reason for this is that the body shop has more technically advanced equipment and the work there is more dependent on the workers having vocational knowledge than in assembly, for example. One important reason for employing well-educated personnel is that the expectation is that they will demand more complex work assignments. In addition, workers who are well educated tend to be more motivated to take initiatives and to expand their skills.

The body shop is not the only area of Volvo Torslanda where the recruitment policy has changed. In principle, all production units are supposed to recruit operators who have attended an eleven-week training program that is provided in collaboration with the county labor board. It is a very general introductory program, which includes an opportunity to practice work at Volvo Torslanda firsthand. The program includes training in certain technical skills and the basics of QPE group work, as well as other introductory information.

Those who are responsible for the training admit that there may be difficulties if the employees are too well trained since assignments still mainly involve assembly work of relatively short cycles. Using questionnaires, personnel in training maintain continuous follow-up on the effects of and workers' attitudes toward Volvo's educational ventures. They have found, for example, that there is growing discontent among workers that there is no room in the daily routine to do what they have been trained to do. Even in the body shop, there are quite a few simple manual assignments. These assignments are sometimes even more simple and have even shorter cycles than the manual assignments in the old body shop.

At Saab, the introduction of the QLEH system has resulted in a more extensive form of training than before. Most people get a basic four-to-five-week course plus about two weeks of training in an experimental workshop. This training is mainly in how to build a car, but aspects of production technology, quality assurance, and safety at work are covered. There are also continuation courses that cover such topics as production technology, quality technology, economics, and programming. The most advanced course is primarily for people who are earmarked as group leaders and for other people whom the production leaders have singled out to become technicians. These people represent a small percentage of the workforce as a whole.

Labor-Management Relations

Volvo has obviously been more innovative than Saab at generating work development on the line. Two examples are the efforts to create long balance times and to channel tasks not traditionally done by assembly workers to on-line work groups. Saab is perhaps the more interesting case, however. Because of the very severe crisis and pressure from the new owner, General Motors Europe, Saab planned to introduce an almost textbook form of team organization. When faced with reality, however, it seemed inefficient to imitate completely Eisenach or NUMMI in such a small production unit. Thus, a pragmatic attitude among management makes the differences between Volvo and Saab appear to be less great; even the work groups in Saab are given additional work tasks.

Contrary to the attitude of the local union at Volvo, the local union at Saab has been extremely dissatisfied with the new work organization. QLEH did not turn out as the union expected. First, the union was defeated on the issue of work group leaders, who are formally appointed by production leaders, not selected by group members, as the union wanted. Second, the volume of QLEH work for work group members has been lower than originally anticipated. Third, the union is skeptical about whether work groups should be doing work to improve efficiency. Fourth, there is criticism that the line system has no buffers.

A growing number of Volvo workers claim to feel stressed and disappointed, particularly those in the paint shop who are working on sealing. There has been a changeover in the paint shop from work on permanent stations to assembly line work. Other workers also report that their work has become more stressful. The speed of the line has not been increased, but the workday has become less porous, partly because of the absence of buffers and because workers are doing QLEH work. The workday is constantly filled with work tasks.

In contrast, the feeling at Saab is that the working environment has improved overall since the introduction of work groups. There has been a substantial reduction in ergonomic problems in recent years. Most of the "from-below-upward" work has been eliminated in the final assembly line and is now found only on the engine line. At many stations, the cars can now be tilted. Another innovation is that most people no longer walk alongside the line to do assembly work. Instead, they ride alongside the line on a kind of carrier on which the car is mounted. This makes assembly work far easier. Off-line assembly has decreased constantly, however, which has disappointed the local union at Saab. It has therefore terminated the 1992 agreement on development, which, in the union's view, contained many good ideas but ones management did not appear to follow up on.

The program developed by the national metalworkers union to modernize the organization of work and make it compatible with the demands of a competitive and flexible production system has served as a guide for local unions. This program has been interpreted differently by the local unions at Saab and Volvo, however. The concept of work development conveys the change on behalf of the trade unions from a solidaristic wage policy to a solidaristic work policy (Swedish Metalworkers Union 1989). According to this program, a constantly learning work organization must have semiautonomous (quasi-supervisorless) groups (i.e., QPE work groups) with authority to request better tools, machines, and changes in organizational design. These groups must be supported by a participative infrastructure that is flexible and less oriented toward bargaining than traditional automobile manufacturers. Work development is a general instrument that the local bodies are to use to create a work organization in which repetitive jobs are abolished and employees are trained to perform better and more productive tasks. The process toward work development shall be supported by new pay systems that reward great and wide skill within the organization.

Pay Systems

At Volvo, a new wage model has been created that is radically different from the old contract system. The basic idea is that there is a ladder of development, and an operator's pay is determined by the complexity and variety in the assignments he or she executes; in other words, the more assignments a worker performs and the more difficult they are, the better the worker is paid. According to the agreement between the local union and Volvo, since the beginning of 1995, the career ladder consists of six levels. A metalworker starts as a trainee for four weeks. After that, he works as an assembler at the "base level" for four months. Then he is qualified to be a licensed assembler. A period of assembly work and training follows in which he is trained to do all the tasks assigned to his work group's production area. After a year, he is supposed to become a licensed resource person. After another year, with further training, he can become a licensed specialist within such areas as production engineering, quality analysis, and education/training. The final step of development is to become qualified as a group leader. Because this system has been in operation for only a short time, it is still difficult to evaluate its practical implications.

Workers are also eligible for a group bonus, which depends on the quality of the work performed by their group as a whole. The bonus can represent a maximum of 10 percent of a worker's basic wages. Workers also receive an individual bonus, which can amount to a maximum of 10 percent of their basic wages. This is decided on by the production leader and depends on the operator's level of activity at work, willingness to cooperate and take initiative in suggesting changes, and so forth. Finally, workers receive a bonus that depends on Volvo's financial results. Everybody gets the same percentage share. The aim of this wage model is to motivate the operators to take on more assignments (i.e., to widen their areas of competence) and to take initiatives that will lead to improvements in production and the preservation of high quality.

The pay system at Saab has also changed. It is now graduated so that the more work tasks a worker performs, the higher he will be paid. There are six levels in the system. In the union's view, the system is rather ineffective because of the signals it sends. Most group members—that is, all the people who are not group representatives—do not benefit very much from this pay arrangement. Thus, group representatives are at level 6, while the majority of employees are at level 3. It takes about two years to qualify for level 6. Employees are also eligible for supplementary payments depending on the amount of time they have worked in the company, and there is a system based on the degree of difficulty of the work and a system that favors the craft workers in the subframe factory, the operators in the paint shop, and the maintenance staff.

Conclusions

The Swedish experience demonstrates that it seems to be possible to create work development for operators on the line, at least those employed in the upper-market segment occupied by Volvo and Saab. In combination with decentralization of the wage-formation process, the new forms of work organization may strike at the heart of the bipartite Swedish industrial relations model (Brulin and Nilsson 1991:330). These changes may result in the integration of blue- and white-collar workers locally and therefore weaken national union solidarity. In the long run, they may also undermine the solidaristic wage policy.

The current aim of the Swedish employers in the manufacturing sector is to conclude a collective agreement regulating codetermination, wages/salaries, and working conditions (working hours, fringe benefits, and so on) for all employees at one plant, thereby forming single-status workplaces as a first step toward single unionism (Brulin 1995). The Swiss-Swedish company ABB in Sweden has been a precursor of so-called coworker agreements. Volvo has also put forward a proposal concerning a coworker agreement. According to the employers, it is not the saving of transaction costs and contractual procedures or even increasing competition and demarcation disputes that force this measure but the changing requirements of production. The vertical division of labor and its corresponding union organizations do not fit with modern production.

Representatives of the different blue- and white-collar unions reject the demand for coworker agreements, arguing that the changes in work organization are still not sufficient. But even the unions are beginning to see the point where the traditional division between blue- and while-collar workers becomes an obstacle to productivity improvement and work development. Certain steps have been taken at the central (national) level to equalize the different agreements. This move indicates that the new forms of work organization in the Swedish automobile companies and the rest of the manufacturing sector should be perceived as something beyond lean production as such.

If the new pay system at Volvo turns out as anticipated, there will be an integration of blue- and white-collar work that certainly will exceed the Taylorist traits inherent in the lean production model. As a result, assembly line workers will have a more challenging but no less strenuous workday.

12 Australia: Restructuring for Survival

Russell D. Lansbury and Greg J. Bamber

The impact of the Japanese manufacturers' distinctive production techniques is evident to varying degrees in all Australian auto assembly plants. All four current manufacturers in Australia—General Motors Holden (GMH), Ford, Toyota, and Mitsubishi—have more or less embraced the rhetoric of lean production as part of their strategies to overcome long-term problems. But other forces have also created pressures for change. The Australian government has sought to provide stimulus for improvement in the industry through changes in trade and tariff policies. Each of the auto manufacturers has responded to these changes. In particular, employment relations practices are foci for reform and innovation.

Although only a minor player on the global scene, the auto industry in Australia is a major contributor to the country's manufacturing output. The combined assembly and components industries employed 6 percent of the manufacturing sector's total labor force and contributed 5 percent of the manufacturing sector's value added. But although the auto industry represents only about 1 percent of Australia's gross domestic product, it sources inputs from a wide range of industries within the economy.

The auto industry in Australia comprises three sectors: passenger vehicle manufacture, components production, and specialist importing. As shown in table 12.1, the number of employees engaged in components

We are most grateful for the help we received on this project from the Australian automobile companies and unions and from Christie Breakspear, Chris Briggs, Ed Davis, Hayden Fox, Mark Shadur, Bill Scales, and David Simmons. Tom Kochan, John Paul MacDuffie, and Frits Pil have also been very helpful in the context of the MIT International Motor Vehicle Program, with which our study is affiliated.

production has declined by approximately 2,300 since 1989. The number employed in passenger vehicle manufacture has fallen by more than 13,500 during this period, and it is now a smaller sector than components production. This chapter focuses on the passenger vehicle manufacture sector in an attempt to compare the Australian experience with the case studies from other countries and International Motor Vehicle Program data.

Each of the auto companies in Australia tried various approaches to employee involvement and participation over the past two decades in an attempt to improve productivity, quality, and industrial relations. Yet these activities were generally short-lived, in certain cases giving the impression that such activities were fads. They were subsequently replaced by other programs, such as quality circles at Toyota and Mitsubishi and natural work groups at Ford (see Simmons and Lansbury 1996).

Management complained that union representatives exhibited a lack of positive support for these changes (see Lansbury and Macdonald 1992). But, not surprisingly, the unions had become cynical about management's lack of long-term commitment to genuine employee participation (Lever-Tracy 1987 and 1990). Managers argue that changes in the direction of lean production result in greater integration of the new production systems and employee-participation programs (as evidenced by the greater autonomy afforded work-area teams within the workplace) and may therefore have a more lasting impact (Shadur and Bamber 1994; Shadur et al. 1994).

Following the closing of several plants in Australia and in response to an apparent decline in the Australian auto industry, the federal government announced its Passenger Motor Vehicle Manufacturing Plan in 1985 (known as the Button Plan after the former minister of industry, Senator John Button). One of the aims of this policy was to encourage major structural changes within the industry. The Button Plan became a driving force in the reshaping of the Australian auto industry.

Table 12.1 Employment in the Australian Automobile Industry in Selected Years, 1989–95

Sector	1989	1991	1993	1995
Passenger-vehicle manufacture	33,558	26,639	23,067	19,754
Components production	26,357	24,835	21,820	24,023
Specialist importing	2,190	1,774	2,247	1,547
Total	62,105	53,248	47,134	45,324

Source: Department of Industry, Science and Technology 1996:88.

Under the Button Plan, tariff protection for the auto industry was gradually reduced. From 1985 to 1992, the nominal tariff rate on imported autos and components was lowered from 57.5 percent to 36 percent. In 1991, the government announced that the program of tariff reduction would be continued until it reached 15 percent by the year 2000. Quota restrictions on imported autos were abolished in 1988, and the local content scheme for components manufacturers was removed in 1989. As a consequence, local manufacturers are faced with stronger competition from imported vehicles in their domestic market, which has brought the need for international competitiveness sharply into focus.

The demand for autos in Australia is closely related to the state of the economy. Hence, there was a sharp decline in the number of units produced locally during the early 1990s because of the depressed economic conditions. Between 1990 and 1992, there was also a 20 percent increase in sales of imported vehicles. Since 1992, however, local production has recovered in line with the economy. Nonetheless, as shown in table 12.2, in 1995 production of passenger vehicles was 17 percent below the 1990 peak and 6 percent below production levels in 1988. The major area of improvement was the number of units exported from Australia, which increased from 2,352 in 1988 to 23,424 in 1995. The value of exported component parts has also grown strongly: in 1988, they totaled $635 million, whereas in 1995 they totaled $1,288 million.

A 1996 report by Standard & Poor's gave the Australian auto industry only a D rating, which put it on the fourth rung of a five-rung ladder, even though it noted the industry's improved performance in recent years. Standard & Poor's questioned whether the industry could remain viable unless it was more integrated into global components sourcing and developed niche export markets. The report also noted that the major auto companies were generally pessimistic about growth in the domestic market

Table 12.2 Passenger Motor Vehicle Production in Australia by Volume and Value in Selected Years, 1988–95

	1988	1990	1995
Domestic market (units)	328,893	350,653	288,960
Export market (units)	2,352	26,808	23,424
Total volume (units)	331,245	377,461	312,384
Wholesale value (A$ billion)	5.12	6.39	6.73

Source: Australian Productivity Commission 1996:114.

as well as their chances of winning a greater share of export markets. Imports accounted for 44 percent of the domestic market in 1995 and are expected to rise to 70 percent by 2000.

Soon after its election in 1996, the Liberal-National Party Coalition government announced that it would review the post-2000 car plan to determine whether tariff reductions should be continued and to explore how Australian auto manufacturers could gain greater market access in the Asia-Pacific region. Even though Asia has the fastest-growing auto market in the world, it also tends to have the highest levels of protection. It is very difficult, therefore, for Australian-based manufacturers to expand their share.

Australia's Changing Product Markets

Since 1985, the Australian auto industry has undergone significant structural change. Under the Button Plan, the five manufacturers that collectively produced thirteen models were to be reduced to no more than three companies with a much smaller model range by 1992. Nissan ceased manufacturing and closed its assembly plant in 1991 after incurring heavy losses for successive years. By 1995, there were only four auto producers in Australia, all foreign owned (see table 12.3).

A linking of the manufacturing activities of Toyota and General Motors established a joint-venture company, the United Australian Automotive Industries, in the late 1980s. To some extent, this was inspired by the success of NUMMI, their joint venture in the United States.

After a few years of experiments with "badge engineering," in 1996 the Toyota-GM venture was dissolved. Toyota had been successful in increasing its market share in Australia in the early 1990s and had opened a new plant in Melbourne in 1994. This consolidated and expanded production it pre-

Table 12.3 Major Motor Vehicle Manufacturers in Australia, 1995

Company	No. of Production Facilities	No. of Employees	Total Motor Vehicle Production*
Ford	2	6,300	101,731
GMH	1	5,772	107,326
Toyota	1	3,800	60,547
Mitsubishi	3	5,000	44,548

*Includes vehicles for export.

Source: Standard & Poor's, 1996.

viously performed at two older plants in Melbourne. This new assembly plant provides an opportunity to evaluate the operation of the leanest production system yet attempted by any car manufacturer in Australia. It may also fuel criticism, however, from commentators who have argued for an alternative, "human-centered" approach (see Berggren 1993).

Automobiles sold in Australia have several sources of origin. The Australian-based manufacturers sell vehicles that are assembled locally. In the past, some of them assembled vehicles in Australia from completely knocked down (CKD) kits that were manufactured offshore. Successive governments encouraged locally manufactured CKD imports as a way of developing local industry. Recent government policy, however, has assumed that local assembly is a low-skill operation offering minor economic benefits. Consequently, tariffs on CKD kits have been increased to parity with vehicles fully manufactured overseas. The importance and size of CKD imports has thus diminished as a result of changing government strategies. The closing of Ford's Sydney assembly plant in 1994 was a direct consequence of this change in policy. The remainder of the market consists of vehicles fully assembled overseas. Local manufacturers and other overseas manufacturers import vehicles in a completely built-up (CBU) state.

The annual production of automobiles in Australia declined from 377,461 units in 1990 to 312,384 in 1995, although there has been a small but steady growth since 1992 as domestic consumer demand has recovered. A minimum production of 100,000 vehicles per model is generally considered necessary to achieve benefits from economies of scale. Only two of the Australian plants operate at this level, and domestic vehicle production in 1996 was 25 percent lower than in 1989. Production of vehicles for export totaled only 23,424 in 1995, which was a slight decrease from the previous year. This was due to a decline in exports by Mitsubishi and the end of the Ford Capri program, which had been aimed at the North American market. Nonetheless, GMH and Ford are optimistic about expanding their Australian production. Moreover, Toyota and Mitsubishi have announced plans to expand their export market through the year 2001 (Department of Industry, Science and Technology [DIST] 1995:16).

Although the export market for fully assembled passenger motor vehicles has not grown substantially in value since 1990, the value of exported components did increase significantly. The total value of components was $1.1 million (Austral. $) in 1994 compared with $0.6 million for vehicles. Among the most valuable components are engines manufactured by the General Motors Holden Engine Company for export to Korea and

Germany. By contrast, the largest share of automotive exports were to New Zealand (27 percent), followed by the United States (18 percent) and Japan (13 percent) (DIST 1995:23).

The relative performance of the local producers is given in table 12.4. Between 1987 and 1993, Ford, GMH, and Nissan all lost market share, whereas Toyota and Mitsubishi enjoyed increases. In the early 1990s, Toyota led the market for all vehicles in Australia, but Ford regained leadership of the auto market in 1995, despite a decline of 2 percent in the sales volume of locally produced vehicles in 1991–92. Ford's sale of imported autos grew substantially from 1991 to 1993, helping it to increase its overall market share to 21.5 percent in 1995. Two-thirds of all car imports were brought in by importers other than local producers, however. Among such importers, Mazda had the largest market share at 5 percent. Toyota and Mitsubishi were adversely affected by the stronger yen, and in 1995 Toyota lost market leadership to Ford.

The relative market share of imported vehicles has increased significantly. The market share of locally produced vehicles was 84.5 percent in 1987. From 1987 on, however, the number of locally produced vehicles has fallen steadily both in market share and sales volume. In 1993, these vehicles comprised only 63.1 percent of the market, while local producer imports totaled 11.9 percent and other importers achieved 25 percent (Automotive Industry Authority [AIA] 1994:82). Even though sales of exports have grown strongly to $1.78 billion in 1995, the automotive trade imbalance has deteriorated since 1988. In the six years to 1994, sales of automotive imports more than doubled, from $4.33 billion to $9.2 billion.

Since 1985, prices of locally produced vehicles have increased significantly more than the consumer price index, and imported vehicle prices

Table 12.4 Shares of the Australian Automotive Market Held by Local Manufacturers in Selected Years, 1987–95

Company	1987	1989	1991	1993	1995
Ford	28.6	24.5	20.6	20.9	21.5
GMH	18.7	16.5	16.8	17.4	19.7
Toyota	20.6	18.8	21.5	21.7	18.8
Mitsubishi	11.8	11.9	11.3	13.7	10.1
Nissan*	9.3	11.3	10.0	4.7	3.8

*Nissan ceased manufacturing in 1991.

Source: Standard & Poor's, 1996.

increased slightly more than local vehicles. In 1984, an Australian six-cylinder automatic sedan cost the equivalent of twenty-three weeks' average wages, while in 1993, a similar vehicle cost thirty-three weeks' average wages (AIA 1994:26).

During the period from 1985 to 1993, the quality of locally produced vehicles also increased considerably. The average number of faults per vehicle declined, and the range between the best and worst models narrowed significantly. In 1985, the highest level of faults was 4.4 per vehicle, while the lowest was 2.1 faults. By 1993, the highest fault rating was 2.1 and the best was 1.3. This substantial improvement occurred in locally manufactured vehicles, while the levels for imported cars remained reasonably consistent. Although the gap is much narrower than in the past, on average, the quality of imported cars is still marginally better than that of the local product, but the best Australian models now boast substantially higher levels of quality than some imported models. The quality range for imported models in 1993 was between 1.6 and 0.7 faults per vehicle (AIA 1994:16–18).

The Australian car industry has experienced relatively low levels of profit performance for many years. Local producers claim to have achieved aggregate manufacturing profitability in only three years of the past decade, and combined losses since 1985 have totaled more than $1 billion. The aggregate return on sales for manufacturing operations in 1993 was only 0.8 percent, although the return was 1.7 percent for the total range of activities. This compared with an aggregate return on sales of 2.6 percent for the three major producers in the United States (General Motors, Ford, and Chrysler) in that year.

Optimistic forecasts are that the performance of the automobile industry will improve as the Australian economy recovers from the recession of the early 1990s. It is also anticipated that the industry will reap the benefits of restructuring and rationalization that it has pursued in recent years. By 1995, for example, the industry was producing only six models in only four assembly plants, whereas it was producing thirteen models in eight plants only seven years earlier. Recent annual sales are at about the same level as in the early 1970s, and local production is likely to grow only slowly in the foreseeable future unless the market for exports increases substantially.

In the face of severe international competition, the continuing viability of the car industry in Australia is the subject of much debate. The exit of Nissan from local production is evidence of the problems the industry faces. The increasing market share for imports is putting pressure on the remaining Australian manufacturers. Yet there are signs of improvement. Increases in quality and exports may symbolize the success of recent reforms. Approximately $4 billion of capital investments have been made since 1992, representing plant upgrades and additional capacity plans by the major producers. These investments have been largely predicated on fostering increased export sales. Toyota, for example, expects $600 million in export sales by the year 2000. Optimism should be tempered, however, by international data that suggest that the Australian manufacturers are starting from a long way behind their overseas counterparts, which are also improving their performance.

The International Motor Vehicle Program has provided a wide range of comparative data on vehicle assembly plants in Australia relative to their counterparts in Japan, the United States, and Europe (see Womack, Jones, and Roos 1990; MacDuffie and Pil 1997). At the time of the first survey in 1989, the Australian plants had comparatively low levels of productivity, low levels of automation, high labor turnover, relatively few hours of training per employee, and low levels of multiskilling. Between 1989 and 1993, some of the ratings improved. Training levels rose significantly, for example, although productivity rates remained the second lowest, better only than South Africa's, of the countries surveyed (see table 12.5).

In a survey of the impact of microeconomic reform on the auto industry in 1996, the Australian Productivity Commission confirmed that although manufacturers had improved their performance, they remained substan-

Table 12.5 Productivity Rates of Auto Manufacturers Worldwide, Measured as Hours per Vehicle, 1989 and 1993

Location of Producers	1989	1993
Japan (Japanese firms)	16.8	16.5
North America (Japanese firms)	21.8	17.4
Canada	NA	20.0
North America (U.S. firms)	25.1	22.4
Europe	36.7	25.6
Asian newly industrializing countries*	38.8	29.5
Australia	38.8	33.7
South Africa	NA	86.7
Others	NA	28.3

*Includes Korea, Taiwan, Malaysia, etc.
NA=Not available.

Source: International Motor Vehicle Program, International Surveys, 1989 and 1993.

tially behind all major regions in the labor hours required to assemble a standard passenger vehicle. The commission argued, however, that this is only a partial productivity measure and could give a misleading impression of overall performance. It also claimed that the results should be considered in the context of Australia's relatively low cost of labor. By 1993, noted the commission, Australian labor costs per standard vehicle were substantially lower than those in the United States and marginally lower than those incurred by Japanese plants in Japan. Although exchange rate movements had contributed to these results, they were also the outcome of enterprise bargaining and other labor market reforms undertaken during the early 1990s (Australian Productivity Commission 1996:88–111).

The IMVP research shows a link between the level of automation and productivity. Automation, measured as a percentage of automated assembly steps, was found to account for about one-third of the differences in productivity between plants worldwide. The Australian plants surveyed in 1989 were in the lowest automation category (9 to 14 percent automated steps). The highest level of automation in any of the Australian plants was 13 percent, compared with 34 percent for the Japanese plant with the lowest level. Hence, there was a clear "automation gap" between Australian and Japanese plants.

The IMVP study also showed that significant improvements in productivity could be achieved by moving from low to moderate levels of automation, but since 1989 only modest increases have been achieved in the Australian plants. In 1993, it took an average of 33.7 hours to produce a vehicle in Australia, versus 16.5 hours in Japan. Similarly, inventory levels averaged 4.4 days for plants in Australia in 1993, compared with only 0.6 days in Japan. This reflects the much greater use of just-in-time methods in Japan than in Australia, where the "tyranny of distance" mitigates against the full adoption of JIT.

Some of the Australian results from the 1993 IMVP survey appear to be ambiguous. Reform was certainly being implemented, and significant improvements can be seen. Nevertheless, local vehicle manufacturers were still handicapped by much lower production runs and smaller output volumes. The average output in Australia was 49,012 units per plant in 1993, compared with 168,000 units at Japanese-owned plants in the United States. Australia produced only 312,384 vehicles in 1995, compared with 7.7 million vehicles in Japan. This makes it difficult for the Australian producers to achieve economies of scale and to justify high levels of automation.

A 1995 study by the federal government's Department of Industry, Science and Technology forecast low but sustainable growth and increasing competitiveness for the Australian car industry. It noted the industry's dependence on an essentially stagnant domestic market and that Australia has one of the oldest fleets of cars in the world (DIST 1995:43). The new globally oriented vehicle manufacturers will produce a common "platform," including engines, with minor variations in the body to suit local tastes. Under this scenario, it has been argued that perhaps the best the Australian industry can hope for is to become "a small but interesting niche in the overall reshaping of the global plans of the vehicle multi-nationals" (Dodson 1995:28).

Employment and Industrial Relations

Total employment in the Australian automotive industry fell from more than sixty-two thousand in 1989 to less than forty-six thousand in 1995. Some of this decline was a consequence of production cuts during 1991 and 1992, when volumes fell by 26 percent. According to the AIA, the production cuts were due partly to a loss of market share in the face of increased import competition and rationalization and partly to a decline of 13 percent in the overall market (AIA 1994:66). Local producers also introduced restructuring measures to improve their efficiency and productivity. The subsequent closing of Nissan, Ford, and Toyota plants contributed to further job losses, but these were at least partially offset by increased production by Mitsubishi and by the new Toyota plant.

In 1993, the largest occupational group within the passenger motor vehicle production sector consisted of assembly and process workers, who accounted for 63.8 percent of the workforce. Qualified tradespersons were the next largest group, with 13.1 percent. The industry is male-dominated; women comprise only 10.5 percent of all employees.

Since 1991, there has been a decline in labor turnover. In earlier years, the average annual turnover was regularly more than 35 percent. In 1991, turnover fell to 5.5 percent, however. It rose marginally in subsequent years and was 7.5 percent in June 1993 (AIA 1994:69–70). The reduction partly reflected the economic recession during the early 1990s. Incremental reductions in labor turnover since then may reflect growth in the economy. It is hard to estimate what proportion of this reduction is due to initiatives within the industry. Reforms such as more selective recruitment practices, increased training opportunities, more flexible work organization, and better communication policies may have contributed to the reduced levels. It is important to the industry that the level of turnover remain modest, so that investments in training and capital are not discouraged. Whether industry initiatives have been successful in arresting turnover will become apparent as the economy improves and employment opportunities increase.

In the past, the auto industry was regarded as strike-prone (Bramble 1993). In recent years, however, there has been a reduction in industrial disputes in the industry (see Lever-Tracy 1990; Rimmer 1992). The number of workdays lost per thousand auto industry employees was very low in the 1990s—well below the levels during the 1980s and before. Recent disputes have been concerned mainly with negotiations over enterprise-level or workplace bargaining, as employers have begun to push for greater flexibility and productivity improvements. A rise in the number of workdays lost, combined with a decrease in the number of workers involved, shows that the remaining industrial action has been localized, which may also reflect the processes involved in enterprise bargaining.

Ninety percent of the unionized employees in Australia's automobile industry are covered by the Australian Manufacturing Workers' Union (AMWU), which was formed in 1995 as a result of an amalgamation of several unions in the industry. The AMWU now includes the former Vehicle Builders Employees' Federation (which organized most production workers), the Association of Drafting, Supervisory and Technical Employees (which organized most technicians), and the Metal and Engineering Workers' Union (which covered most workers in the skilled engineering and maintenance trades). Several other unions cover clerical workers and electrical tradespersons. Among vehicle producers (and large components suppliers), there is almost 100 percent union coverage below management levels. There has been a decline in the proportion of clerical workers who are unionized, however.

The Australian Council of Trade Unions (ACTU) has played an important coordinating role between the unions in the automobile industry. Nevertheless, since the 1995 amalgamation, the ACTU has tended to play a less prominent role.

Although there is no longer an industrywide award, there is a high degree of coordination among employers. The trend in the 1990s, however, has been toward decentralized enterprise bargaining, whereby individual employers conduct separate negotiations with the unions and conclude agreements that are specific to each company. Although there are variations in the content and timing of these agreements, there are still similarities in the terms.

Industrial relations developments in the auto industry during the past decade should be seen in the context of broader changes in Australia (Lansbury and Niland 1994). Strong economic growth from the mid- to the late 1980s enabled the labor market to expand and levels of unemployment were reduced. Deteriorating economic circumstances, including severe balance-of-payments deficits, caused the consumer price index to rise to 8 percent in 1989–90. During the early 1990s, the government reacted by tightening fiscal policy, thereby achieving lower levels of inflation but creating a sharp downturn in the economy. This caused real wages to decline and unemployment to rise to about 11 percent by 1993. Although unemployment levels improved, the value of real wages continued to decline in the mid-1990s.

Since 1991, Australia's wage policies have been changed to encourage enterprise bargaining. This was a major change in the direction of a less centralized approach to industrial relations. The then federal labor government explained its support for this approach, despite its previous caution: "Encouraging and facilitating more bargaining at the workplace level is a logical extension of [the] reform process. . . . Such bargaining must be done freely and jointly, however, and in ways which do not damage the public interest" (Cook 1991:16).

Although each of the Australian auto manufacturers negotiated its own enterprise agreements and it is too early to draw firm conclusions, the parallel processes that were followed could perhaps be seen as an Australian form of quasi-"pattern bargaining" (cf. Katz and Kochan 1992). In the United States, typically the main union in an industry picks one company as a target, then seeks to impose a copy of the resulting labor-management "contract" on the other companies. Each of the companies' experiences has been reasonably parallel in Australia, not only because they were induced to follow an explicit pattern set by the AMWU but also because senior human resource/industrial relations managers met regularly and otherwise kept in close touch with one another. Such coordination between firms was understandable, for they were all operating in the same (fairly small) product market and were subject to the same national industrial relations regulations dictated by government policies and national wage case decisions.

Since 1990, each of the auto companies has concluded a series of enterprise agreements with the unions. The first round of agreements was very similar in form and content across the companies, but subsequent rounds have begun to reveal differences in approach. Thus far, the unions have succeeded in ensuring that the general features of the agreements remain similar, particularly with regard to wages and conditions of work. By contrast with American pattern bargaining, however, the unions in Australia have not generally sought to pick on one company as an explicit target. Rather, they have tried to confront all the companies more or less simultaneously. It will be interesting to see whether enterprise bargaining leads to greater variation among the companies over time as the parties gain more experience with the process.

Employment Relations Policies and Practices

Representatives of the auto manufacturers, the unions, and the government traveled to Japan, the United States, Germany, and Sweden in 1988 to examine alternative approaches to work organization, career paths, training, and employee participation. The group concluded that production and maintenance decisions should be decentralized, while skills acquisition and career development should be promoted to facilitate the creation of a skilled and flexible workforce, and that jobs should be broadly based rather than based on narrowly defined tasks. The group's report set the agenda for workplace reform and greatly influenced the pace and direction of the industry's program of restructuring (Mathews 1992). To obtain input and cooperation in the process, seminars were held with shop stewards and employees (Hudson 1988). The information derived from these consultations and research formed the basis for negotiations to establish cohesive career structures, determine the training required, and develop transition mechanisms between the old and new job classification structures.

To gain a perspective on the ways in which key employment relations policies and practices have changed in the Australian auto industry since the mid-1980s, data were collected during the period 1992–97 from the four vehicle manufacturers: Ford, GMH, Mitsubishi, and Toyota. Interviews were conducted with a sample of managers at corporate and plant levels, union representatives (full-time officials and shop stewards), and plant-level employees. The interviews focused on five employment relations practices but also included some questions that reflected current concerns in the industry, particularly the trend toward enterprise bargaining. Data from the Australian Workplace Industrial Relations Survey (Callus et al. 1991), which examined more than two thousand workplaces, were also used.

Although employment relations activities should not be treated in isolation from broader issues, such as the international economic environment in which the firms operate (cf. Bamber and Lansbury 1993), it is helpful to examine specific policies separately. Many aspects of industrial relations and human resources are interrelated (such as work organization and skill formation) and are influenced by other policies (such as business strategies) developed in other areas of each enterprise. Nevertheless, to provide a means of discussing change systematically, the following pages will examine work organization, skill formation, remuneration/compensation, employment security and staffing arrangements, and enterprise governance.

Work Organization. Since the 1980s, there has been a change in the Australian auto industry from rigid and closely defined job specifications toward more flexible forms of work organization. This has been assisted by award restructuring, which has reduced the number of job classifications in many areas and broadened the range of activities undertaken by particular categories of workers (Macken 1989). For example, employers are placing greater emphasis on the need for employees to be multiskilled so that they may undertake a wider variety of tasks and assume a wider range of responsibilities. Significant progress has been made in this regard in many "blue-collar" areas. As one manager explained, "We now define jobs on the basis of skills rather than tasks."

Although demarcation problems have persisted between certain craft areas, some new areas of friction have developed between blue- and white-collar workers, especially as the scope of blue-collar jobs has expanded to absorb tasks previously performed by clerical, supervisory, and even professional staff. As one manager noted: "While blue-collar jobs are becoming more flexible, white-collar and supervisory jobs have remained rather rigid. . . . Supervisors feel threatened as blue-collar workers are able to manage their own areas."

According to managers in the auto industry, teamwork has been a major objective in each of the four companies, but the realities are less clear and there are differences in the conception and application of teamwork at different plants. Teamwork was well developed in certain areas, such as two of the engine and plastics plants, but was less developed in other areas, particularly on assembly lines (see Mathews 1992). In some cases, there was resistance to teamwork on the grounds that it undermined existing work practices. In other cases, the concept was not understood by those who were required to implement the new strategies, which had usually been designed by managers located beyond the workplace.

The implementation of teamwork is a contentious issue between the AMWU and the employers. Union representatives alleged that managers were unwilling to permit teams to operate autonomously and sought to use teams in a manipulative fashion. They also expressed concern that teams did not have decision-making powers over such matters as the selection of team leaders. In general, managers acknowledged that the design and implementation of teamwork have proved to be more difficult than anticipated, but most argued that teamwork was a key element in achieving lean production and would continue to be pursued as a major objective.

Skill Formation. Management in each of the companies indicated that until recently most skills were still acquired on the job, without a planned program of training and development. In general, however, the companies were demanding higher levels of education and skills before a job was offered. Furthermore, since the introduction of the Vehicle Industry Certificate (VIC) in 1991, as well as federal government initiatives regarding vocational training (Carmichael 1992), all new employees have been required to undertake formal training on the job to acquire necessary competencies.

Promotion is increasingly based on skills acquired and on demonstrated levels of competencies. This trend has been fostered by award restructuring, which places greater emphasis on skills-related wage systems and on the VIC. The economic recession, which gave employers a wider range of people from which to choose, also fostered these developments. As shown in table 12.6, the average hours devoted to training auto workers in Australia during 1993 appeared to be high by international standards, particularly for new employees.[1]

The VIC was introduced with the support of the employers and the unions to formalize the training process and recognize skills acquired (table 12.6). It is anticipated that career progression by individuals in the auto industry will ultimately depend on their having passed all stages of the VIC course. So far, these requirements appear to have been applied to a much greater extent to blue-collar workers; white-collar employees appear to lag behind in this regard.

Female employees expressed concern that they found it difficult to take advantage of the VIC course, especially since some of the course work was provided after hours. Union officials argued that some of the

[1]When this survey was conducted, the Australian auto employers were trying to implement the VIC; this may have induced comparative "overreporting" of hours spent on training.

Table 12.6 Training Measured as Average Hours per Production Worker in Auto Firms Worldwide, 1993

Location of Producers	First Six Months of Employment	Experienced Employees
Japan	386.7	54.1
North America (Japanese firms)	186.0	192.6
Canada	56.3	16.7
North America (U.S. firms)	71.7	66.6
Northern Europe	121.5	46.1
France, Spain, and Italy	352.0	63.8
Australia	396.8	86.8
U.K.	121.0	80.0
South Africa	151.2	131.4
Korea	222.7	41.3

Source: International Motor Vehicle Program, International Survey, 1993.

companies were in breach of equal employment opportunity requirements by not providing female employees with easier access to courses during normal working hours since family responsibilities prevented them from participating otherwise.

Since embarking on more extensive formal training at the workplace level, managers have discovered significant problems with literacy and numeracy in the workforce, which has long included a high proportion of non–English-speaking immigrants. Extensive remedial education programs were necessary to raise the level of basic education before skills development programs could be introduced. Even when this was undertaken, some groups of employees still appeared to experience considerable difficulty in coping with the learning demands that were placed on them.

There has been considerable variation among the companies in the speed and extent to which they have introduced the VIC program. Ford was a strong supporter of the VIC when it was introduced. Union officials, however, complained that some of the other auto companies were less enthusiastic than Ford about encouraging their employees to undertake VIC training courses.

Despite the efforts to upgrade skills, companies have not been keeping pace with training requirements, particularly as new technologies have introduced higher levels of complexity. Although managers in some companies feel they are keeping pace in the blue-collar areas, they have had to "buy in" more highly qualified professional and technical personnel from the external labor market. The skills that are required have also been changing from narrow and specific to broader and deeper, which has required tertiary-level qualifications as well as on-the-job learning.

Remuneration/Compensation. From 1983, when wage indexation was reintroduced nationally, until the latter 1980s, pay differentials became progressively compressed. With the national introduction of a two-tier approach to wage negotiations in 1987, however, pay differentials appeared to widen again. Further, for many years wage rates were uniform throughout the industry, but since the late 1980s, the emphasis has shifted from a centralized approach toward a greater emphasis on enterprise-level bargaining, albeit still within the framework of arbitration.

There appears to be a widely held perception among workers in all Australian auto companies that their real wages are relatively low compared with those in some other sectors. This undercurrent of dissatisfaction has the potential to undermine the innovations that have accompanied the introduction of the VIC. A significant proportion of workers expressed the view that the new skills-related pay levels associated with the VIC are inadequate recognition for the improvements in quality and productivity that they have achieved. In this context, it is not easy for companies to recruit and retain high-quality employees.

There has been much international debate about the desirability of performance-related pay and other variable or contingent pay schemes (e.g., Milkovich and Wigdor 1991). Ron Callus and his colleagues (1991) reported that about 39 percent of workplaces with five or more employees, representing 34 percent of the total Australian labor force, had performance-related pay schemes for nonmanagement employees. The wholesale and retail sector had the highest proportion, whereas less than 1 percent of the workplaces in the public administration sector used such schemes. The most common schemes used in Australia were those in which pay was explicitly linked to measured output, such as payment by results (Callus et al. 1991:44).

In the auto industry, there has been some tentative movement to award performance bonuses, particularly for managerial staff. GMH's most recent enterprise agreement included such a bonus, but in general the proportion of the total wage that has been related to performance has remained very small.[2]

[2]In June 1996, the unions at GMH called a stop-work meeting to protest the company's refusal to pay a 2 percent increase based on productivity levels. The unions argued that the decline in productivity was due to factors outside the workers' control.

The main change in the wage system in Australia's car industry has been toward skills-related pay associated with the VIC. This approach has served to emphasize the value of skills acquisition rather than individual or group performance. This approach may have been adopted because it is easier and less contentious to measure the acquisition of skills than individual or group output. In one plant where a performance-related bonus had recently been tried, it was felt that it created divisions among workers and hindered attempts to create a corporative team-oriented environment.

In some firms in other industries, there has been a change in pay arrangements to reduce the differences between managerial and nonmanagerial employees. At several of ICI's chemical plants, for example, annualized salaries have been introduced for all production employees (Mealor 1996). Among workers who were formerly on weekly salaries, the movement to annualized salaries involved the absorption of overtime and other penalty rates.

There have been much-publicized moves in such operations as the Japanese transplants in North America and in the U.K. car industries toward single-status employment. This approach has also been adopted at Toyota's new Melbourne plant (Shadur and Bamber 1994); however, the other car manufacturers in Australia have not implemented this strategy.

Nor have profit-sharing schemes been widely used in Australian manufacturing enterprises. Callus et al. (1991) indicate that in workplaces with twenty or more employees, 8 percent, covering 7 percent of all Australian employees, had profit-sharing schemes. Share ownership schemes were somewhat more popular; 13 percent of workplaces, covering 17 percent of employees, had such schemes. These schemes were most prevalent in the finance and related sector, where they were found in 19 percent of enterprises, covering 21 percent of employees. None of Australia's four auto companies has such schemes, although they are under discussion.

Employment Security and Staffing Arrangements. Given the rise in unemployment to a record level of more than 11 percent in 1992, job security has been high on the employment relations agenda. The number of employees in Australian auto manufacturing declined significantly between 1985 and 1995. Following the widespread redundancies during previous economic recessions, particularly in the mid-1970s and early 1980s, most unions had negotiated redundancy agreements and had retrenchment clauses inserted in their awards by the industrial relations tribunals. The federal government also strengthened the laws on unfair dismissal and redundancy (McCallum, McCarry, and Ronfeld 1994).

All but one of the auto manufacturers implemented voluntary redundancy programs in the early 1990s. In most cases, union representatives accepted the right of the employer to implement redundancies as long as natural attrition was used and the process was voluntary. The focus of union action was mainly on ensuring that agreed-upon procedures were followed and that employers paid redundancy payments that were agreed to under the award. When Nissan, Toyota, and Ford closed plants in the early 1990s, the main union succeeded in obtaining relatively high redundancy payments but was unable to prevent job losses. The exception was Mitsubishi, which concluded a no-redundancy agreement in the late 1970s, after it took over Chrysler's plants, and which therefore provided greater job security.

Employers used several different procedures to adjust labor requirements to the decline in demand for locally produced vehicles. These included, on a temporary basis, shorter working hours and longer holidays, with commensurate reductions in pay. In some cases, managerial and other nonunionized staff were requested to work without pay on their rostered days off. Job transfers and redeployment were also used to fill positions vacated by laid-off employees. During our interviews, employers indicated that the unions' cooperation in these matters had recently improved. Union representatives commented that this was due, in part, to the willingness of union members to take the redundancy payments rather than risk losing their jobs, perhaps with less compensation, at a later stage if their plant closed. There was little enthusiasm among employees to resist the redundancies, as long as they were voluntary and there was adequate compensation. Most companies conducted their redundancy programs in cooperation with the unions, usually paid higher redundancy payments than were required in the award provisions, and sought to avoid arbitration if possible.

Faced with much upheaval and job insecurity over the past decade, many workers in the auto industry have become rather demoralized and fatalistic about the future. Policies of no *compulsory* redundancies provide little comfort to workers in an industry in which the number of employees has fallen dramatically in recent years. Where employees were offered a higher degree of job security, as at Mitsubishi, the company claimed there was a greater degree of commitment by the employees to the company and a greater degree of willingness to engage in workplace change.

There has been a steady increase in the past decade in the number of part-time, casual, and temporary workers in the Australian labor market as a whole. In 1995, approximately 25 percent of the Australian labor force was employed on a part-time basis, compared with less than 10 percent in

1970. The increasing number of part-time and casual employees has helped to reduce the average workweek to 31.6 hours; however, 20 percent of employed persons were working an average of more than 49 hours per week in 1995 (Norris and Wooden 1995).

In the auto industry, more than 90 percent of the workforce was classified as regular, full-time employees in 1995. All the manufacturers indicated that a small but increasing range of jobs were being "contracted out" and that they were seeking to have such arrangements included in enterprise awards. Although only a small percentage of current positions are subcontracted, these include office services, catering, accounting, sales, and various engineering and technical activities. Several managers mentioned that they were investigating which other "noncore" functions of their businesses could be assigned to contractors.

Enterprise Governance. The election of a Labor government in Australia in 1983 revived interest in industrial democracy and employee participation, which had briefly flourished in the early 1970s and then declined as the result of political and economic changes (Lansbury and Davis 1990). In the 1980s, there was arguably a more favorable context than before. The post-1983 accord between the labor government and the ACTU stated that there must be "continuous consultation and cooperation between the parties involved over economic, industrial and social matters." It also noted that "consultation is a key factor in bringing about change in industry. This consultation will be extended to industry, company and workplace level" (Australian Labor Party/ACTU 1993). These sentiments were subsequently endorsed by the Confederation of Australian Industry (CAI), which had joined with the ACTU in issuing the *Joint Statement on Participative Practices* (CAI/ACTU 1988).

At the time of our interviews, each of the auto manufacturers had introduced some form of employee involvement since the mid-1980s, but none offered workers significant influence over key management decisions. Most schemes focused on problem solving and employee suggestions for improvements in the production process. Unions generally played little or no role in strategic decisions. Some of the managers claimed that senior union officials were consulted on major decisions that had implications for the workforce, but they said this generally occurred only when management chose to do so. There were no formal mechanisms for consulting with unions or their representatives about strategic decisions. In general, the overseas parent company was consulted to a much greater extent about strategically important issues than were employees or their unions.

Employee participation in decision making appeared to be most advanced where there was extensive teamwork, requiring workers to be well informed and equipped to make decisions. The extent of implementation of employee-involvement schemes varied among firms and plants, however. At Ford, for example, an employee-involvement program was implemented in the 1980s, which, at its peak, covered approximately 30 percent of the workforce throughout the company. At one Ford plant, there was almost full coverage, while at others it remained marginal (Lever-Tracy 1990). By the mid-1990s, however, the program had been transformed into a "natural work-group" scheme and included stopping the line for a thirty-minute discussion session on a weekly basis (Simmons and Lansbury 1996). None of the other car companies sought to introduce such a system of employee participation, but all used other involvement techniques, including information sharing and quality circles.

Consultative committees were used in each of the four firms, as required under the national program of award restructuring (Lansbury and Marchington 1993). The effectiveness of these committees varied, however. Not surprisingly, the most successful committees tended to be in plants with high levels of employee involvement, though relatively few managers appeared to have moved beyond consultation toward involving their employees directly in decision making. Several respondents noted that success required strong commitment by management to genuine forms of consultation and employee involvement. As of the beginning of the 1990s, across Australian industry more generally, only 14 percent of workplaces, covering 40 percent of the total workforce, had consultative arrangements (Callus et al. 1991:135).

The moves toward lean production have generally been initiated by the production function, where employment relations considerations have been secondary. Thus, most human resource/industrial relations managers have tended to react to changes elsewhere rather than initiate major strategic changes themselves.

Conclusions

The auto industry in Australia has introduced significant changes in work organization, as manufacturers have moved away from formerly rigid job definitions to more flexible approaches to work design that utilize teamwork.

Similarly, skill formation has been an issue of major importance and has been assisted by the award restructuring and enterprise bargaining programs. Progress on these issues has been greater, however, among blue-collar employees, who have been the focus of more workplace reform than white-collar employees. Although there has been a transition from a relatively centralized system of determining wages to one that is related more closely to skill levels, progress at the enterprise level is uneven. In most firms, performance-related pay is confined mainly to senior management, and there is little evidence that gain sharing or similar programs are being implemented for the majority of employees in the auto industry. Greater attention has been devoted to implementing redundancy schemes than to developing innovative pay systems.

Two explanations have been advanced regarding the changes in employment relations policies and practices worldwide (see Locke, Kochan, and Piore 1995). The first explanation focuses on the increasingly competitive environment and new technologies that are inducing firms and unions to experiment with new production systems and employment practices. The second explanation emphasizes the changing roles of institutional arrangements and public policies.

Both explanations have application to the changing nature of employment relations in the Australian auto industry. The reduction in tariff protection by the Australian government combined with global strategies of foreign-owned auto manufacturers have led to a more competitive environment for the domestic industry. In addition, all the manufacturers have introduced elements of lean production in their assembly operations, although these have been more extensive in some plants (such as the new Toyota Melbourne plant) than others.

Enterprise bargaining and other labor market reforms have resulted in a more decentralized approach to industrial relations in the Australian auto industry. New technologies have been introduced that have improved efficiency, yet the level of automation in Australian assembly plants remains low by international standards. Furthermore, despite significant reductions in employment over the past decade, the level of staffing is not as lean as in many other industrialized market economies.

Although the Australian auto industry appears to have adapted a number of "new" employment relations practices, these are by no means uniform across plants and companies. In the area of union-management relations, there is a less adversarial approach than in the early 1980s, and the unions have exhibited a high level of cooperation in response to management-initiated changes in work organization, skills development programs, pay systems, and workforce reductions. Work design is more flexible, multiskilling has been successfully introduced in some areas, and teamwork is increasingly utilized. Yet tasks on the assembly line generally remain rather narrowly defined and teamwork is implemented mostly in off-line areas of production. Although supervisors have been replaced by team leaders and coordinators, in most plants the autonomy of work groups remains rather circumscribed. The involvement of workers in decision making and consultative processes is also limited in scope, although this also varies among plants. There are no local examples to rival the innovations of Saturn or Uddevalla.

Although there is some evidence that Australian auto plants favor a productivity enhancement approach that involves the application of broad lean production principles, as evident at the new Toyota plant, most Australian plants remain neo-Fordist in their orientations. This may be largely explained by the struggle of the industry to survive and the cost-minimization strategy that most manufacturers have adopted.

The recent success of Toyota and Mitsubishi in gaining export orders and the incorporation of both the Ford and GMH plants into global production operations may signal better prospects for Australian manufacturers in the future and a corresponding boost for the local components industry. If the new investments in plant and technology are sustained, Australian auto manufacturers may be able to further develop new and more diverse approaches to employment relations that will support post-lean production systems. In this scenario, the Australian industry would supply high-quality niche markets both locally and internationally. A more pessimistic alternative is that vehicle manufacturing in Australia is approaching its demise and only the components sector will survive in the long term.

PART III

Emerging Economies and Lean Production

Part IV

Emerging Economies
and Legal Reduction

13 South Africa: The Struggle for Human Resource Development

Philip Hirschsohn

Although Womack, Jones, and Roos (1990) recognized that existing institutions might inhibit the diffusion of lean production, they failed to anticipate that the breadth, depth, and pattern of diffusion are influenced by differences in economic, political, and social contexts. The South African experience suggests that the production conditions of a developing economy and the presence of a powerful union with a well-developed alternative vision of how to create a viable assembly industry are important in shaping the employment practices and outcomes in auto manufacturing. Moreover, differences in management strategies and local plant- and firm-level industrial relations trajectories are sources of diversity rather than convergence.

Where the industry is protected from international competition by tariff barriers and export activity is limited, firms are likely to respond to domestic competitive pressures only. Over time, shifts in government policy from import substitution to export promotion are likely to increase the importance of meeting international productivity standards. This chapter argues that the diffusion of international best practices to firms operating in protected markets is influenced by the extent to which the firm competes in export markets or is integrated into global commodity chains and whether the firm is directly controlled by a foreign multinational that is directly exposed to international competitive pressures.

I would like to thank numerous managers and shop stewards at Toyota, Volkswagen, and Gabriel in South Africa. Additional thanks to Anthony Black, Gavin Hartford, Richard Locke, and Thomas Kochan for their helpful comments on earlier drafts of this chapter. The research for this chapter was funded by the International Motor Vehicle Program at MIT.

Trade unions are seldom, if ever, portrayed as enthusiastic initiators of reorganization and restructuring as a way to protect their long-term interests. The South African case is exceptional because the union movement, rather than management or the state, provided the vision and drive to transform the auto assembly industry into a world-class competitor as the economy emerges from an era of isolation. Drawing on ideas from progressive European and Australian union movements, the National Union of Metalworkers of South Africa (NUMSA) developed a package of policies that were founded on what I call democratic human resource development principles. NUMSA initiated industry-level negotiations, concluded national agreements on work reorganization, training, and multiskilling, and reinforced its position through powerful shop-floor and plant-level negotiations. Although NUMSA does not have the capacity to implement the industry agreements, it has shaped the context in which auto firms in South Africa can develop competitive strategies and has constrained the range of possible approaches to reorganization.

Macro Context

Following a pattern typical of semiperipheral countries, in the 1960s South Africa introduced import-substitution strategies that led to the proliferation of local manufacturers of auto components and vehicles.[1] The import-substitution policy required moderate but increasing local content in the 1970s and 1980s (Bell 1990) and until the early 1980s remained unquestioned as the domestic market grew (see table 13.1). The increasing requirement to invest in local content, a sales collapse in the mid-1980s, a persistent economic crisis, and growing political isolation halved the number of assemblers to seven. Three German-owned assemblers and four South African–controlled assemblers currently produce thirty-nine car and light commercial vehicles from original equipment manufacturers (OEMs). With a market of only 300,000 to 400,000 units in 1994–95 and seven assembly plants, the industry is overtraded and inefficient by world standards, although sales in 1995 were almost 25 percent higher than 1994 volumes.

[1]Automobile production industries in semiperipheral countries developed initially by providing additional markets and subsequently as locations for low-cost production. As the industry became more global in scope, first European and later Japanese producers began to challenge American producers, and the dominant players established plants in the major markets. With the exception of South Africa, production capacity shifted spatially during the late 1970s and semiperipheral countries became increasingly integrated into the global operations of multinationals as production centers for the export market (Jenkins 1985).

Table 13.1 Unit Sales of South African Auto Assemblers

	Passenger Cars	Commercial Vehicles	Total
1960	98,800	20,400	119,200
1970	201,900	95,700	297,600
1980	277,100	127,700	404,800
1981	301,500	152,000	453,500
1983	272,800	132,300	405,100
1985	204,300	101,000	305,300
1987	200,800	108,300	309,100
1989	221,300	131,300	352,600
1991	197,700	110,300	308,000
1993	193,700	104,400	298,100
1995	236,600	140,200	376,800

Source: National Association of Automobile Manufacturers of South Africa.

In the late 1980s, South Africa finally began to place greater emphasis on export-oriented manufacturing (Oberhauser 1993). To enhance international competitiveness and save foreign exchange, the state increased local content requirements, which could be achieved by sourcing locally or by exporting. Assemblers, however, remain protected from international competition by high, albeit steadily declining, tariff barriers.[2] Despite a significant growth in exports, serious questions remain about their economic viability as export subsidies are effectively built into domestic vehicle prices.[3]

Because it produces no indigenously designed vehicles, the South African auto industry remains heavily reliant on foreign multinationals for access to the export market and technology.[4] Components firms and assemblers are being linked more closely to global producer-driven commodity chains, but integration has been hindered by the industry's dependence on comprehensive licensing agreements, which limit exports; the country's

[2]Tariffs and excise duties on fully built-up vehicles (FBUs) were reduced from 115 percent to 80 percent in September 1994 and to 65 percent in July 1995.

[3]Industry exports, including catalytic converters and other components, increased almost threefold between 1991 and 1995 to more than U.S. $900 million, compared with imports of about U.S. $4 billion in 1995.

[4]To the limited extent that local technical capacity increases in developing countries, it tends, first, to develop within subsidiaries of multinationals and is exploited within the firm's global network rather than within the local economy, and, second, is based on modifying international technology (Jenkins 1985). South African assemblers still receive detailed drawings, information on the nature of the materials to be used, quality-testing standards, and production methods from their foreign affiliates and pass them on to domestic components suppliers (Bell 1990).

remote location as a potential supplier to JIT production systems; and indigenous ownership, which leads to the worst of both worlds—limited integration into global commodity chains and dependence on foreign technology (Black 1988 and 1993).

Formulation of Tripartite Industrial Policy

In recognition of the problems facing the industry, in late 1992 the government appointed the Motor Industry Task Group (MITG), composed of representatives of unions, assemblers, components suppliers, and government, to consider a long-term strategy for the industry. The MITG addressed the need to ensure the industry's growth and thereby develop human resources and create employment opportunities; minimize the use of foreign exchange; reduce the number of models; encourage the industry to become more productive and increasingly competitive internationally; and reduce tariffs so as to meet the obligations of the General Agreement on Tariffs and Trade (GATT).

In August 1994, the first phase of the tariff-reduction process was implemented by the new government, which plans to accelerate the task group's tariff-reduction proposals to bring imported competition into the local market.[5] To comply with the latest GATT regime, the government will not offer the incentives the MITG recommended to rationalize the industry's model range. The lack of consensus between assemblers and components suppliers and within the two sectors frustrated attempts to develop a universally acceptable industry response to the government's proposals. As a result, the process of formulating a tripartite industrial policy degenerated into a free-for-all in which each sector and firm lobbied in its own interests.

NUMSA's Vision for Industrial Policy and Democratic Human Resource Development

A defining feature of South Africa's industrialization since the mid-1970s has been the emergence of a powerful trade union movement (Cooper 1991). Rapid industrial growth created a new black working class concentrated in

[5]Whereas GATT required South Africa to halve its tariffs to 50 percent by the year 2002, the MITG recommended the removal of excise duties and the progressive reduction of tariff protection to 45 percent by 2002 and the introduction of incentives to rationalize domestic production by encouraging the manufacture of high-volume models. The government decided to reduce tariffs on FBUs to 40 percent by the year 2002. Duty on components will reduce 75 percent of the duty on FBUs.

large-scale industrial sectors. The emerging union movement found one of its most receptive audiences among semiskilled black autoworkers.

In 1987, six auto and metal unions merged to form NUMSA, which subsequently played a critical role in shaping the auto industry's future. NUMSA's active participation in tripartite trade and industrial policy deliberations, in centralized collective bargaining in the assembly, components, and other auto sectors, and in plant-level negotiations necessitates the adoption of an integrated perspective on industrial policy, industrial relations, and human resource development.

In 1989, NUMSA used its shop-floor militancy and organizational strength to force all assembly plants to join the National Bargaining Forum (NBF), a national industrywide collective bargaining forum for the assembly sector. NUMSA then initiated a debate on restructuring the industry. NUMSA's approach was influenced by developments in the Australian metal industry and the German auto industry. In contrast to the lean production model, this human resource development strategy "entails the introduction of more participatory forms of work organization and the use of new technologies which bring benefits to both capital and labor. This economic growth path is premised on a strong trade union movement participating in the process of industrial restructuring. Multi-skilling, active labor market [policies] and life-long job-security are some of the human resource benefits which accrue to workers in this new accord between capital and labor" (Kraak 1992:404).

NUMSA's proposals seek to improve the industry's competitiveness by making changes in the work process and by ensuring the formal recognition and enhancement of unacknowledged multiskilling, the legacy of job reservation, low-volume production, and product differentiation (Adler 1993). By insisting that illiterate workers receive adult basic education (ABE) as the foundation to develop their skills and enhance their capacity as citizens, NUMSA is borrowing bits of hard technology and social innovation, adapting conventional notions of multiskilling to local conditions, and creating something quite different from the original concept.

In "Restructuring," an in-house document written in 1993, NUMSA has argued that all parties—assemblers, components manufacturers, and unions—need to participate in developing a long-term strategy to develop a "world class industry capable of meeting the changing demands of the domestic market while maintaining a high export profile in order to provide employment growth. Performance benchmarks, based on issues such as export growth, skill formation and quality measures, should be put in place in order to determine the rate of reduction in tariff protection. Incentives should be available in order to assist companies and regions to restructure and adjust to changing patterns of location and employment."

As necessary prerequisites for growth and competitiveness, the Congress of South African Trade Unions (COSATU) and NUMSA's multi-level strategy to establish a nationally coherent system of training is integrated with policies to transform adult education, labor markets, and economic restructuring (Bird 1992). Vocational training is an integral component of a strategy of restructuring focused on job reorganization to facilitate greater democratic worker participation and the reorganization of work into broad-banded skill categories characterized by multiskilling and career paths progressing up a defined skills ladder (Kraak 1992). NUMSA's democratic human resource development strategy, a key subject of annual auto industry negotiations since 1991, has provided a framework within which assemblers must approach work reorganization.

The 1991 National Bargaining Forum agreement was a landmark. The parties committed to the long-term growth and viability of the industry, the protection of employment, the improvement of quality, and the negotiation of work reorganization to ensure international and local competitiveness. For employers, the agreement marked an attitudinal shift from adversarialism toward codetermination. For NUMSA, it reflected its acceptance of responsibility for the industry's future and its commitment to a struggle over control of production (Bethlehem and Von Holdt 1991).

Work Organization, Training, Grading, and Compensation

The existing work organization in the South African auto industry is characterized by conventional production methods, hierarchical managerial structures, and relatively narrow job descriptions. Because of the lack of trust between management and workers, management's inability to tap workers' intellect, and workers' extremely strong loyalty to the union, NUMSA believes that it has to be the key driver of participation structures if work reorganization is to gain worker support (interview with national organizer Gavin Hartford, January 1995).

In line with COSATU's policy that skill-formation programs should maximize internal and external labor market flexibility (Bird 1992), the 1991 NBF agreement provides for competency-based modular firm-level training that is recognized across the industry so that skills are portable and provide workers with career paths from general to specialized skills. Modular training is linked to the broad-banding of grades, which were reduced from thirteen to five between laborer and artisan, and two grades were added higher than the artisan level. In addition to particular workplace skills, the modules lay the basis for career-long learning, enabling workers to keep pace with technological change. To determine the scope and content of education and training programs for the industry, the NBF established the Automobile Manufacturers Industry Education and Training Board (AMIETB), which is jointly controlled by the Automobile Manufacturers Employers' Organisation (AMEO) and NUMSA and financed by employers.

NUMSA's compensation strategy is closely linked to its approach to training and skill formation in that it provides incentives to workers to continue learning (Bird 1992). The 1993 NBF agreement thus provides that progression through the first four grades will be based on the completion of certified competency-based training modules at each skill level, regardless of whether the skills are utilized. The NBF agreement prescribes the relationship between skill levels, module training requirements, and pay differentials (see table 13.2). Whereas previous agreements specified the minimum pay for each grade, the pathbreaking 1995 NBF agreement provides for the phase-in of standardized industrywide pay rates over a three-year period.

Adult basic education forms an integral part of NUMSA's strategy because of the extremely high levels of illiteracy among South African workers and the importance of literacy in sustaining a democratic society.[6]

Table 13.2 National Bargaining Forum Agreed-upon Relationship between Skill Levels, Training Requirements, and Wage Differentials, 1993

Skill Level	Qualification	Number of Modules	Minimum Wage Differential (in U.S. $)	
1	Certificate 1	20% artisan	$2.51	
2	Certificate 2	40% artisan	$2.77	10%
3	Certificate 3	60% artisan	$3.04	10%
4	Certificate 4	80% artisan	$3.35	10%
5	Artisan certificate or AMIETB equivalent	100% artisan	$3.68	10%
6	Multiskilled artisan	120% artisan	$4.05	10%
7	Technician	140% artisan		

[6]Survey data from Volkswagen suggest that among production workers the functional illiteracy rates are higher than 70 percent.

Adult education should provide basic skills and "a deep understanding of the world of work and production . . . and technical, analytical, logical and organizational skills to operate more creatively and independently . . . [since] problem-solving skills . . . are best developed in the context of providing a general education" (COSATU 1992). Employers have committed to providing adult education so that all workers will be functionally literate (equivalent to nine years of schooling) by the year 2000.

Although an NBF agreement outlined the principles and framework for the establishment of the AMIETB, implementation was problematic. NUMSA emphasized the importance of developing portable skills and national competency standards, but some employers were concerned about losing their competitive advantage by sharing their training and skill-development strategies. Perhaps the most significant hindrance was the initial failure to establish a permanently staffed structure for the AMIETB to secure agreement on the competencies required to complete each of the constituent modules. The appointment of a permanent AMIETB secretariat and workshops with Australian unionists and employers on their auto industry's competency-based training system helped the AMIETB overcome these bottlenecks, and in late 1995 the parties finally reached agreement on the detailed competency standards required for each module. In 1996, union-management teams in every plant began to implement a process of recognizing prior learning by assessing the current skills of every operator in the industry.

Factors Influencing Diffusion of World-Class Practices

The transfer of managerial techniques and technology to semiperipheral countries is usually hindered by traditionally hierarchical and authoritarian managerial regimes, underdeveloped human resource capacity (both managerial and labor), and intense shop-floor conflict. Evidence from South African components firms suggests fairly extensive piecemeal, rather than in-depth, adoption of such Japanese management techniques as quality circles and just-in-time systems (Maller and Dwolatsky 1993).

Although the lack of competitiveness (table 13.3) of the South African industry may be attributable primarily to protectionism and inefficient investments (Black 1993), evidence from the three cases discussed below also suggests that the adoption of lean production principles will facilitate restructuring and improve productivity.

Table 13.3 Characteristics of South African Auto Assembly Plants versus Plants in Other Regions

Performance Hours	Japan	Europe	Newly Industrializing Countries	South Africa*
Productivity (hours/vehicle)	16.8	36.2	41	50
Quality (assembly defects/ 100 vehicles)	60.0	97.0	72.3	194
Size of repair area (% of assembly area)	4.1	14.4		15.1
Workforce in teams	69.3	0.6		2.5
Job rotation (0=none, 4=frequent)	3.0	1.9		1.5
Suggestions/employee	61.6	0.4		0.1
Number of job classes	11.9	14.8		32.0
Training of new production workers (in hours)	380.3	173.3		50.5

*Data are preliminary from three manufacturers. Quality data are based on manufacturers' own measurements rather than on customer surveys.

Sources: Womack, Jones, and Roos 1990 and Faull and Van der Riet (manufacturing/production consultants).

The cases suggest three explanations for the pattern of diffusion. First, because firms respond to the strategies of their leading competitors, diffusion is most likely to occur in firms that are integrated into global commodity chains or that compete directly in international markets. Second, since diffusion is more likely within firms, diffusion is more likely to subsidiaries of multinationals than to independent domestic firms. Third, where unions have a powerful presence on the shop floor, diffusion is more likely if union and management have compatible strategies than if they are in fundamental conflict.

Toyotaism without Cooperation

Toyota South Africa, which established an assembly plant in Durban in the early 1960s, remains under local managerial and financial control, although Toyota Japan bought a minority share in 1996. Annual production of about ninety thousand vehicles makes it the market leader and one of the largest Toyota plants outside Japan.

Manufacturing System. Labor-intensive mass production combined with external Toyotaism is a pragmatic response to the high cost of imported capital equipment and low labor costs in South Africa. Robots are introduced only when necessary for health and safety reasons or where human access to weld points on large panels is not practical. Although a modified version of the Toyota production system was introduced in the mid-1980s, management believes that the industrial relations and political environment has not been conducive to its operation. Initial successes in reducing inventories have been part of the TPS's undoing, and buffers between plants, which had largely been eliminated, have had to be increased to two days.[7]

The implementation of kanban supply is constrained since shipments of Japanese CKD kits are received only every two weeks. From the early 1980s, however, Toyota began demanding that local suppliers deliver several times daily and suppliers from other regions deliver daily or every two days. The number of suppliers was halved between 1983 and 1988, longer supply contracts were introduced, and engineers were sent to supplier plants to ensure quality standards, introduce the Toyota production system, and provide systems support. Suppliers, particularly those in the Toyota stable, relocated near the Durban plant (Duncan and Payne 1992).

Work Organization. In the early 1980s, before the unionization of Toyota, several Japanese-inspired participation and suggestion schemes were introduced to enhance quality and productivity.[8] In recent years, management has struggled to maintain interest in these programs, participation has declined, and the principles have not become an integral part of daily production routines.[9] Workers receive only token recognition for their suggestions (a key ring and a mug for three siyacabanga improvements, a T-shirt for more) and generally refuse to participate in suggestion programs since their ideas are

[7]For example, while I was discussing the topic with management, a local kanban supplier, which delivered at four-hour intervals, had gone on strike, thereby threatening to hold up production.
[8]Quality circles operate on a voluntary basis to address quality, maintenance, safety, cost reductions, and workplace improvements (Dewar 1990). Kaizen is a management-driven, project-based system focused on improving operating standards and involves few operators or supervisors. *Eyakho* (Zulu for "my own") aims to improve quality standards by getting operators to identify production problems and approach the supplier up the chain so they can resolve the problem jointly. *Siyacabanga* ("I/we think") encourages the development of ergonomic improvements in the working environment, narrowly defined, focusing on such aspects as access to materials and tools.
[9]In a production workforce of about 5,500, 225 employees made eyakho presentations in 1993. Only fifty-six quality circle teams of four to five members each are currently active.

typically refined by managers, who estimate the savings and pocket the rewards (Nattrass 1991; Toyota Shop Stewards Council [SSC] 1992).

Multiskilling is practically nonexistent. Job rotation is optional but not a common practice since there are no incentives to participate in it; workers perceive that it is used only in cases of absenteeism (Toyota SSC 1992), and management believes that "blacks like repetitive tasks" (Nattrass 1991; Southhall 1985). Waiting for the conclusion of the NBF framework agreements inhibited the pace of work reorganization since the NUMSA local refused to allow multiskilling until the AMIETB finalized the modular skills training agreement and the agreed industrywide pay-for-skills compensation system was in place. Disputes persist over whether leaders in teamwork experiments should be elected by team members or selected by management, although both sides agree that team leaders spend too much time substituting on the line and neglect other duties.

The extent to which first-line management has abdicated control on the shop floor, and the workforce asserted it, is demonstrated by the common practice of workers in the press shop taking a few hours off the line to sleep or play cards while others in the area carry the full load. This practice persists despite the resultant quality problems. Management believes these breaks are acceptable only if production schedules and quality standards are met.

Governance/Labor-Management Relations. Although the level of industrial conflict was below the rates in the industry in the late 1980s and early 1990s, recent intensification of shop-floor tension and wildcat strikes have forced management to roll back some Japanese-inspired initiatives.[10] The lack of an industrial relations department helps to explain why labor-management relations have deteriorated and why shop stewards identify the extremely slow process to resolve grievances through established procedures as a key reason that the levels of nonprocedural industrial action have been so high.

According to workers who were interviewed, management has decentralized the human resources function to the plant level and perceives industrial relations problems as "tacked on"—the result of "bad human

[10]Excluding brief stoppages, the company had four strikes in 1986–91: four days in 1986; ten days in 1989 over Toyota's initial refusal to join the NBF; two days in 1990; and eleven days during the 1991 industrywide strike. In 1992, Toyota lost almost three months' production and fired six thousand production workers. In 1993, nonprocedural strikes were only sporadic. In 1994, however, the tempo of industrial action escalated and in a letter to the union, management claimed that approximately twenty serious wildcat strikes had occurred between February and April. Twenty-eight days of production were lost before the five-week industrywide strike.

resource management." A fundamental lack of trust lies at the heart of the conflictual union-management relationship, and an us versus them attitude is pervasive on both sides on the shop floor (Nattrass 1991). Shop stewards openly express their perceptions that the predominantly white management is racist and authoritarian, and some managers have even acknowledged that this is the case.

Management agreed to join the NBF only after a series of work stoppages in 1989 and, given management's desire for strategic independence and Toyota's weak industrial relations, remains extremely wary of recognizing a permanent important role for the NBF. Meanwhile, the continued use of conventional mass production practices, which conflict with NUMSA's strategy, and lack of progress in implementing the NBF agreement fuel conflict on the shop floor.

Training, Compensation, and Employment Security. Toyota has begun offering adult basic education classes and is reorganizing all training on a modular basis in preparation for the implementation of the AMIETB training structure, which is expected to motivate operators to pursue the new career paths available to them. Although operators currently receive some on-the-job training and basic orientation, orientation is expected to include background on the organization, team activities, an explanation of the kaizen philosophy and quality circles, and training in basic operational skills.

Given the centralized bargaining structure, there is relatively little scope for Toyota to establish its own compensation policy, which is an important reason management has expressed discomfort with the NBF. Production peaked in 1990 and subsequently remained relatively stable, but Toyota has often been unable to satisfy demand because of industrial action. Although management had to agree to a shorter workweek in the mid-1980s to meet its commitment to job security, security has not been an issue in recent years.[11] High levels of unemployment and relatively high wages have resulted in an average tenure of sixteen years, but there is no evidence that this stability has been leveraged to Toyota's benefit.

Conclusion. While Toyota built its success on marketing and production, it has neglected human resources and industrial relations. The lack of managerial initiative in introducing innovative human resource practices since the advent of trade unionism can be explained by the lack of pressure to support diffusion. First, Toyota's concentration and strength in the domes-

[11]Toyota has never retrenched, although six thousand workers were dismissed during the 1992 strike; all were subsequently rehired.

tic South African market has desensitized it to international competitive pressures, which, some managers believe, has bred an unhealthy parochial view. Second, local management was independent and not subject to pressure from Toyota Japan. Third, local management faces militant union members on the shop floor who are frustrated by authoritarianism and the failure to implement NBF agreements.

Regional political instability and allegations that factional conflict and a disruptive radical faction in the local union account for the heightened industrial conflict provide management with convenient excuses for failing to address the shop-floor problems at their source. In late 1994, top management and the shop stewards, but not front-line management, participated in a weekend retreat to begin to build a new relationship based on trust and cooperation. As a result, the parties agreed to adopt the Volkswagen model. Given the extent of the shop-floor hostility, this process of building a more cooperative relationship must include first-line managers, who feel threatened by the progressive erosion of their authority. Both sides need to commit time and resources to ensure that they actually begin to address problems of racial polarization.

Despite losing market share because of poor industrial relations, a serious crisis may be necessary; Toyota can no longer rely exclusively on product strengths transferred from Japan to force a change in workplace and human resource practices. At this point, neither side appears ready to make the necessary commitment. As the facilitator of the 1994 weekend retreat concluded in his report: "There is a tendency within Toyota to define Strategic Focus Areas and then to try to [address them] with limited intellectual capital. This will invariably result in failures and frustration."

VW: Contested Codetermination

Although a wholly owned subsidiary of Volkswagen AG (VWAG), Volkswagen South Africa (VWSA) was not integrated into VWAG's international production and marketing network and served only the domestic market until it began exporting in low volumes to China in 1992.[12] To secure its future, VWSA needs to justify to VWAG that it warrants further investment and integration into its global commodity chain. German-style codetermination has influenced management's approach and suggests a way forward for a partnership with NUMSA based on adversarial cooperation.

[12]In contrast, plants in Mexico and Brazil became important production bases for exports in response to government export-promotion strategies (Doleschal 1992).

Because of South Africa's economic isolation and tariff protections, VWSA management had developed a siege mentality, focusing on domestic political and labor problems and largely ignoring international competitive developments, and was unprepared for a major cultural shift toward a system founded on equity and the skilling of labor in place of the previous low-wage strategy.[13] Now, however, local union leaders and management talk the language of world-class performance, although differences remain between management's vision of codetermined lean production and NUMSA's concept of democratic human resource development.

Governance/Labor-Management Relations. The militancy of VWSA's black workforce is linked to the politicization of the eastern Cape, where the plant is located, the recruitment of workers hardened on political unrest, and powerful shop steward structures that developed in the late 1970s. The human resources director believes that "negotiations must take place between strong representative groups, who have the ability to honor agreements and build relationships of mutual trust." This approach is predicated on a high level of involvement by the shop stewards and a system of consultation, negotiation, and compromise that recognizes the realities of the power structure (Smith 1990). Judith Maller (1994) suggests that through their collective power, workers and NUMSA exercise extensive control on the shop floor, reminiscent of British unions in the 1970s.[14] The potential for shop-floor conflict is heightened by the conservatism of the local white community, many of whose residents are employed at VWSA.

In the late 1980s, VWSA and NUMSA established joint committees to promote discussions and communication on strategy, human resource policies, and production issues. Under pressure from VWAG, whose management was concerned that the levels of industrial conflict had become unacceptable, in November 1994 VWSA and NUMSA concluded a comprehensive agreement to extend participation through codetermination practices.

In adherence with the agreement, weekly business unit meetings are held to address operational issues and related matters, and monthly Plant Committee meetings resolve business unit disputes, negotiate agreements

---

[13]Information on VWSA is based on interviews with management and shop stewards in January 1995.

[14]With an extensive network of experienced full-time and part-time shop stewards, NUMSA exerts considerable power on the shop floor, communicating through regular lunchtime meetings with workers. Part-time stewards are de facto full time and have become an integral part of the authority structure, and supervisors are often bypassed when union lines of authority are used to communicate with the workforce (Maller 1992).

on operational and plantwide issues, and review quarterly financial, marketing, and quality performance. Unresolved operational and policy issues are addressed by the company-level Negotiating Committee, while strategic issues are discussed at quarterly meetings of the Joint Union-Management Executive Committee.

VWSA's codetermination structures are an integral part of a broader strategic agreement that recognizes that world-class competitive performance requires investments in automation, human resource development, and the restructuring of work organization, with job security guarantees. The agreement also fosters flexibility, promotes multiskilling and training, provides for innovation in work organization, and marks the codification of a shift in management and shop stewards' attitudes. It is too early to judge how effectively the message has been conveyed to the shop floor.[15]

Manufacturing System. As is the case at Toyota, the degree of automation at VWSA is low because capital investments are not justifiable for economic reasons. A few robots have been deployed where required to ensure quality standards or because complications arose when labor-intensive production methods were used to produce complex parts. Despite limitations imposed because components are sourced from Germany and management is "inbred to have buffer stocks," buffers have been reduced significantly in recent years and there is increased emphasis on coordinating logistics with suppliers, some of whom supply directly onto the line.[16] Given the unreliability of South African suppliers and the complexity of the plant, management seeks a balance between the need to hold safety stock, customer needs, access to local and international supplies, buffer holding costs, the risk element, and the systems support capacity.[17]

In contrast to Toyota, VWSA has adopted the VWAG strategy of concentrating on the core business by contracting out important subassemblies to "logistical suppliers" (O'Brien and Karmokolias 1994). To improve operational efficiencies and achieve economies of scale, VWSA is also

[15]To heighten awareness among employees of the opening of markets, the impact of GATT, and other issues related to competitiveness, VWSA used a highly innovative and popular medium of industrial theater, involving operators and other employees as actors and script writers. Repeated performances were held at the end of 1994.

[16]Buffers between the engine plant and final assembly have been reduced by 300 to 400 percent down to 2.5 hours, while stockholding of engine components was cut by 50 percent to two days' production in 1994.

[17]For example, fifty-four types of engines are produced. On the A3 line, there are now eight types with one thousand derivatives, down from thirteen types and three thousand derivatives three years ago.

planning to reduce the number of platforms and the complexity of the plant and to seek further export business and is bidding to produce a low-volume right-hand-drive model for international markets.[18]

Work Organization. Management has not attempted to institute quality circles because of operator and union resistance, but it recently introduced off-line cross-functional KVP[2] (continuous improvement process) teams to address shop-floor problems. Although 15 percent of the operators have participated in week-long KVP[2] workshops as elected representatives of their work areas, continuous improvement is not integrated into daily activities. As Siegfried Roth has argued in discussing VW in Germany, there is evidence that KVP[2] is a short-term "instrument of rationalization" (1992:14) and that continued worker participation thus hinges on job security provisions.

Job reservation, which excluded blacks from all jobs occupied by whites, has left a legacy of incompetence at VWSA. Although their power was diminished with the advent of unions, white supervisors retained control over promotions, and management has "tolerated, if not encouraged, a system of informal patronage that has corrupted the relationship between, on the one hand, skill, education, and desire and, on the other hand, the chances of promotion" (Adler 1993:58). Racial politics plagued recent attempts to establish production teams with dedicated quality and logistics support. White quality assurance staff were unwilling to give up traditional roles as arbiters of quality. Functional integration led to confrontation with black operators, many of whom had higher education levels and were no longer prepared to accept without question the authority of white staff.

Glenn Adler's (1993) research suggests that low production volumes and product proliferation account for a marked degree of tacit multi-skilling because of the range of operations performed. Although classified as unskilled, many operators have informally acquired mastery over a wide range of jobs. In that NUMSA has not imposed cumbersome work rules, these cross-trained operators have provided management with a degree of flexibility at no cost because their skills have not been formally recognized and they have not compensated for them.

The need to address the retrogressive consequences of these practices underlies the current approach to work organization, training, and skill

---

[18]According to management, this VWSA plant is the most complex in the world. The number of parts used has already been reduced from twenty thousand to eighteen thousand. By reducing the number of platforms, currently five, and subcontracting, VWSA plans to reduce the number of parts to 13,500.

development and the process of assessing and recognizing existing skills and competencies. The 1994 agreement recognizes the importance of flexibly deploying workers so as to balance staffing requirements and facilitate career development and training. As one level of management is being eliminated, all managers, superintendents, and foremen are undergoing assessments of their eligibility for area manager or team leader positions. The failure of almost half those tested to make the grade is testimony to the patronage and incompetence Adler has identified.

Training, Skill Development, and Job Security. Pilot team projects have failed because they were rushed into implementation and because of problems with line layout, operator training, and supervisors' attitudes. Although committed to multiskilling, skill-based grading, and broad-band pay schemes, NUMSA is skeptical about the productivity benefits of teamwork. Nonetheless, multitasked teams, rather than the semiautonomous work groups NUMSA favors, were used for a short period on an experimental basis on the new Audi line.

Cycle times on the Audi line are about twenty-five to thirty minutes at each workstation. Experienced operators completed three months of full-time adult basic education and multiskilling training before the line became operational. All operators completed core modules in teamwork, problem solving, quality control, routine maintenance, and safety and housekeeping, as well as specialized technical modules, and for the first time they will be responsible for quality control.

VWSA has agreed to provide adult basic education to the entire workforce by the year 2000 to upgrade literacy levels to the equivalent of nine years of schooling. In 1995, up to 20 percent of workers were expected to participate in full- or part-time adult education classes. Management now restricts new hires to those with school-leaving certificates, although the union argues that VWSA has a social obligation to hire a cross-section of the workforce since blacks have been denied educational opportunities because of apartheid.

Between 1993 and 1995, VWSA reduced its workforce of eighty-four hundred by almost 15 percent, although direct labor increased by 10 percent. Following severe cutbacks among salaried staff and hourly paid indirect workers, restructuring led to the elimination of a level of supervisory management. Productivity improvements have been significant; daily volumes increased from 213 to 260 units per day between 1992 and 1994 and to 340 units in 1995. NUMSA has accommodated VWSA's ongoing strategic outsourcing of noncore functions, and the 1994 agreement provided for negotiations on each outsourcing decision and guaranteed the job security of hourly paid employees through 1995. In some cases, such as the outsourcing of seat assembly, the decision has been tied to the selection by VWAG of a global logistical supplier (O'Brien and Karmokolias 1994).

Conclusion. The introduction at VWSA of German-style decision-making structures and innovative human resource practices in its pathbreaking 1994 agreement can be attributed to three explanatory factors, all of which tend to support diffusion: VWSA is under increasing pressure from VWAG to enhance performance managerially and financially; although concentrating on the domestic market, VWSA has the potential to become integrated into VWAG's global commodity chain if productivity levels improve; and NUMSA believes in adversarial cooperation as the basis for workplace transformation.

Since NUMSA has lost many of its most experienced officials to Parliament, government, and business in recent years, management is concerned that the union may lack the capacity to respond to initiatives as pressure from VWAG to improve efficiency increases. Shop stewards are on a rapid learning curve to cope with the changing demands and shift their focus from political to productivist trade unionism. The critical determinant of the success of this project will lie in NUMSA's ability to retain membership support through the reorganization.

Gabriel: Adaptive Cooperation

South African components suppliers must produce a large range of relatively small volumes to meet the original equipment manufacturers' (OEM) and aftermarket requirements (Duncan and Payne 1992).[19] Gabriel, which manufactures shock absorbers, has exploited this flexible specialization capability by adopting lean production techniques without making significant capital investment.[20] In anticipation of the need to become increasingly competitive internationally, Gabriel is successfully targeting the foreign aftermarket, based on its wide range, high quality levels, acceptable prices, and small niche market capabilities (Black 1993).[21]

---

[19]Relative to market size, there is a proliferation of OEM models, and the average age of the country's registered vehicles is now twelve years, resulting in a large aftermarket for outdated models.
[20]In addition to cited sources, information comes from interviews with managers and shop stewards in August 1994.
[21]Exports of parts and complete components to Australia, India, Italy, Latin America, and the United States now amount to 20 to 25 percent of output and continue to grow.

Gabriel's U.S. parent, Arvin, has aggressively imposed JIT-based reorganization (Black 1993) by setting targets rather than prescribing solutions. Given the limited sharing of technologies between subsidiaries, management has been forced to learn and adapt rather than implement packaged solutions. Substantial gains in productivity and reduced costs have resulted from the extensive implementation of Japanese production processes and work organization systems. Following an initial confrontation, reorganization has been based on negotiation and increasing cooperation between management and NUMSA.

Manufacturing Systems. Gabriel gradually introduced JIT and reorganized production, guided by an Arvin industrial engineer. Once an experimental assembly cell had shown significant productivity improvements, production was reorganized into functional cells and subsequently into product cells, almost eliminating work-in-progress buffers. Lot sizes and setup times were radically reduced, enhancing flexibility and productivity, which doubled between early 1992 and mid-1994, measured in units/person/day.[22] Gabriel also reengineered its accounting and information systems, shifting from materials requirements planning to an order-driven visual-based kanban system, creating a culture of communication in which, as one manager said, "all singing to the same sheet of music" was essential because kanban is people-dependent and requires continuous discipline.

Work Organization, Training, and Compensation. Quality inspection, basic maintenance, and setting functions are the responsibility of operators, who also suggest adaptations that can be made to machinery to reduce setup times (Black 1993). During each day workers rotate between operating machines on which they have certified competence. Continuous improvement is achieved by action teams made up of operators, engineering maintenance staff, and toolroom personnel (Industrial Strategy Project 1994).

Prior to introducing cellular manufacturing, every worker received two weeks of full-time training, covering business processes, quality awareness and detection, and specialized skills in statistical process control, measuring instruments, and reading engineering drawings. To develop self-directed work teams equipped to continuously improve processes, workers

---

[22]Machine setup times were reduced from 30 to 120 minutes to 2 to 10 minutes (Industrial Strategy Project [ISP] 1994). Production flexibility has been enhanced as lot sizes were reduced from five hundred to one thousand units to fifty to two hundred units, even in the case of larger orders. Line balancing is now an important focus of attempts to improve productivity.

received two weeks of full-time training in employee involvement and total quality production systems (TQPS). TQPS training provides cross-functional teams with the "vision of an engineer" for a week, enabling them to address and solve small shop-floor process problems.

Workers' flexibility and skill acquisition have been steadily enhanced as a result of the shift from functional to product cells. Workers receive on-the-job training on each machine in the cell in four stages: basic operation, inspection, setup, and competence to train others. In line with NUMSA's demand of pay for skill, operators who have been certified to operate, inspect, and set up several machines are promoted to the second job grade. Those who can train others on several machines qualify for the third job grade and promotion to team leader.

Workers initially complained that work intensity increased under the cellular system and that multiskilling had resulted in "people working harder, not smarter" (Black 1993:92), and they feared possible skills saturation. Leaders of NUMSA now believe that multiskilling is educationally beneficial since workers have recognized the benefit of having extensive skills in the event they are retrenched.

Plant-level negotiations at Gabriel determine actual wages, which are significantly higher than industry minimums. Gabriel shares its strategic plan, sales volumes, and pricing information with NUMSA and seeks to set wages on the basis of its international competitive position, rather than affordability. Management has negotiated lump-sum amounts for wage increases, leaving it to NUMSA to determine the distribution between job grades. In line with NUMSA policy, those in the lowest grade receive at least 60 percent of artisan levels. In addition to an industrywide bonus, equivalent to two weeks of wages, workers are eligible for monthly plantwide production and annual plantwide performance bonuses, as well as annual and quarterly attendance bonuses, which the union supports to develop consciousness of the importance of increasing productivity.[23]

Governance/Management-Labor Relations. When NUMSA was founded in 1987, the local was restructured, shop stewards replaced worker representatives, and tension between the newly militant union and old-style management increased, culminating in a nonprocedural strike in 1989. Although many workers were subsequently rehired, 250 workers were dis-

---

[23]An annual bonus of one week's pay for 97 percent attendance is supplemented by quarterly bonuses for 100 percent attendance.

missed during that strike. The same conflictual attitude was evident when management introduced the first production cell. NUMSA prevented the formulation of the cell by declaring it was in dispute with management and threatened to take Gabriel to court for its unilateral changes in working conditions. Management came to recognize the importance of securing union cooperation, however, and a pattern of consulting operators and shop stewards became firmly established.

In response to pressures from Arvin and counterdemands from NUMSA, management initiated wide-ranging retrenchments, cost-cutting measures, and efficiencies throughout the firm. As a quid pro quo, job security guarantees were negotiated before the full-scale implementation of cellular production.[24] Consequently, no workers will be retrenched because of productivity improvements arising from the introduction of Gabriel's total quality production system.

The replacement of old-fashioned managers, who were unwilling to adapt, was critical to introducing the fundamental cultural change of working cooperatively with the union. The union is now provided with extensive resources, and a full-time shop steward was introduced in 1992. Extensive consultation and cooperation occur on a daily basis, and the union-management partnership is critical to the success of the ongoing process of reorganization and deepening multiskilling.

Is Lean Production Likely in the South African Auto Industry?

Given the auto industry's long-standing protection from international competition, the shift in government policy to lower tariffs and export promotion will be a critical determinant of the future of the industry in South Africa. The limited attempts at reorganization by assemblers reflect the difficulty of emerging from an era of politicized industrial conflict and a siege mentality into one demanding cooperative responses to international competition. NUMSA's farsighted approach will undoubtedly facilitate the industry's transition to a more competitive regime.

The three cases in this chapter support my hypotheses concerning the factors that affect the depth of diffusion of innovative practices. First, the Gabriel case suggests that diffusion is more likely where firms compete internationally than where firms compete primarily in protected domestic

---

[24]Layers of management were removed, salaried staff were decreased roughly in proportion to cutbacks among hourly paid operators, and management perks, such as the number of company cars, were reduced (Black 1993).

markets. Second, evidence from VWSA and Gabriel suggests that pressure from a multinational parent to perform encourages diffusion. Third, given NUMSA's powerful shop-floor presence, the VWSA and Gabriel cases suggest that diffusion is more likely if the union and management have compatible strategies than in cases such as Toyota where no basis for cooperation exists.

Achieving levels of productivity that are competitive in the international market requires the adoption of a systemic bundle of human resource principles and practices (Kaplinsky 1995; MacDuffie 1995). The lean production ideal type cannot be transplanted, however, without recognizing the distinctive institutional and social context in which it was developed. Furthermore, the specificities of national institutions, industrial contexts, and local strategies and conditions create distinctive configurations in each plant.

Although NUMSA's framework embodies a systemic bundle of human resource development principles that will constrain managerial choice, a single pattern in workplace transformation is unlikely to emerge. Some assemblers are subject to direct managerial control by their German parent, while indigenously controlled licensed assemblers are only indirectly influenced by their Japanese OEMs. Product market strategies and the local balance of power also influence the adoption process.

The adoption patterns described may be interpreted as a systemic sequential process in which firms such as VWSA are later starters than firms such as Gabriel. The observed differences may also reflect firms on fundamentally different paths (Kaplinsky 1995), whereby firms such as Gabriel are capable of systemic utilization while others, such as VWSA and Toyota, are constrained to particular techniques by industrial conflict or management's "intellectual capital." These cases thus provide no conclusive evidence of an indigenous adaptation of the lean production model.

Gabriel shows the potential productivity and human resource benefits of implementing an integrated bundle of innovative human resource and low-tech flexible production principles without making major capital investments in advanced technology. The VWSA-NUMSA codetermined institutional framework provided the model for works council–type structures that have been introduced under the country's new labor law. Although Toyota may still be competitive in a protected market using the modified Toyota production system, its potential performance improvement appears limited without some local union cooperation and human resource innovation consistent with the industry agreements.

Resolving Tensions between Industry Agreements and Plant Innovation

Important questions remain concerning the relationship between NBF agreements and company-level initiatives. Two schools of thought seem to exist within the Automobile Manufacturers Employers' Organisation concerning NUMSA's role in restructuring the industry. One camp sees the NBF as preventing leapfrogging, setting minimum standards, and providing enabling frameworks on work reorganization, multiskilling, and training. The other camp sees the NBF as constraining each firm from improving its competitive position through plant-level negotiations or unilateral management action. Given these differences in industrial relations philosophies and plant-level sophistication, AMEO struggles to achieve consensus and its relations with NUMSA reflect this tension. The balance between competition and cooperation within AMEO will remain extremely delicate and not easily resolved, particularly given the overtraded nature of the market and expectations of a shakeout between producers.

The slow pace of reaching an agreement on training within the Automobile Manufacturers Industry Education and Training Board highlights the tensions between firm and industry strategic choices. Some assemblers are ambivalent about cooperative industrywide initiatives. Because they believe that their competitive advantage rests on human resource development, they have been reluctant to reveal details of their training programs. Initial progress was slow because union and management nominees participated on only a part-time basis and they had fundamental disagreements over whether AMIETB should design training modules or merely specify the performance standards required for certification. Once a permanent AMIETB secretariat was established, the detailed input of experienced Australian unionists and managers provided both AMEO and NUMSA with a concrete example that formed the framework that could be adapted to local conditions. This lengthy process suggests the continuing difficulties both management and labor are experiencing in trying to translate NUMSA's democratic human resource development policies into practical reality.

For NUMSA, the NBF agreements may be inconsequential if it is unable to develop the capacity among local officials and shop stewards to engage plant management effectively in negotiations about reorganization and restructuring. The 1995 agreement provides for shop stewards to receive training in production engineering, work organization, quality performance, and human resource issues to address this problem. Although shop stewards have finely honed skills in conflictual collective bargaining, the more cooperative style of engagement required to ensure world-class competitiveness may not prove particularly appealing or marketable to union members. Moreover, if NUMSA pushes NBF agreements too forcefully and too rigidly, it may provoke the defection of one or more assemblers from the NBF.[25]

A Role for Industrial Policy

Although the Ministry of Trade and Industry is reforming the trade regime to comply with GATT and intensify competitive pressures on the industry, the results of restructuring may be economically undesirable without a coherent industrial policy framework. The Motor Industry Task Group proposal to establish a statutory Motor Industry Authority to monitor industry performance, encourage development, and promote change that will improve industry efficiency was not implemented, but an informal Motor Industry Development Council (MIDC), comprising all major interest groups, was set up in 1996. The MIDC cooperates closely with the recently established motor industry directorate in the Department of Trade and Industry and provides a forum to monitor the implementation and impact of the state's tariff-reduction reforms and to formulate policy proposals for the industry as a whole. Although the MIDC is a welcome initiative, the capacity-building process is hamstrung by the state's inexperience in industrial policy and lack of industry-specific knowledge.

The MITG sent a group abroad to examine changes in industrial relations and work organization and subsequently proposed an institutional framework to develop the skills required to adopt innovative human resource/industrial relations and manufacturing practices. The establishment of tripartite-controlled extension services and training organizations to provide shop stewards, union officials, and line management with formal programs in industrial relations, workplace change, and the challenge of international competition and industry restructuring is critical to successful restructuring.

Buoyant domestic sales in 1995 may generate complacency and temporarily divert attention away from the industry's poor productivity levels, although restructuring is easier during a growth phase. There is an urgent need to give content to the capacity-building proposals and to the AMIETB modular training framework to ensure that the progressive lowering of tariff barriers does not dissipate into a mess of uncoordinated liberalization and industrial conflict.

[25]During the 1996 NBF negotiations, this possibility almost became a reality. Mercedes-Benz remained a party to the NBF agreement but concluded a separate local agreement with NUMSA on wage increases.

14

Brazil: The Diffusion of a New Pattern of Industrial Relations Practices

José Roberto Ferro, Afonso Fleury, and Maria Tereza Fleury

The industrial relations system in Brazil's auto industry has been undergoing significant changes in the last decade whereby confrontation is being replaced by negotiation and cooperation. Various factors have shaped this new framework for employee relations. These include a process of democratization that has facilitated the reorganization of the labor unions, changes in the nature of competition as a result of economic liberalization, new industrial policies that have emphasized tax reductions for vehicles, and the diffusion of lean production principles.

Companies are increasing communication and negotiation channels, adopting real wage increases, and introducing massive training programs, new concepts of work organization, and productivity and quality programs. Labor unions have gradually refrained from using purely confrontational strategies to allow for more negotiation with companies. Unions are also becoming directly involved in the setting of new policies for industry. Higher levels of wages and reduced labor turnover have contributed to stable employment. There has also been significant growth in domestic production and market volume as a result of greatly increased efficiency from 1992 on.

Previous comparative studies of industrial relations have tended to emphasize differences among countries. For example, Michael Poole (1988) argues that diversity may be explained by such subjective factors as sociocultural values and political ideologies, as well as structural differences. Within this framework, national characteristics would prevail throughout all the companies and organizations, imprinting certain styles and practices of industrial relations.

Robert E. Cole (1985) is guided by similar assumptions in his comparison of the differences in small-group activities in Sweden, Japan, and the United States. He shows how national politics, historical and structural differences, as well as more subjective considerations, such as the incentives and motivations of labor and management, influence the diffusion of quality circles and related small-group activities.

By contrast, our study found that plant-level industrial relations have a relative degree of independence from national cultures and institutional frameworks, which provide basically the opportunities and constraints by which companies set their own policies. Companies tend to transfer successful practices internally within their own units, although they are shaped, during the diffusion process, by both national influences and managerial attitudes and values.

In this chapter, we discuss the cases of the Brazilian units of General Motors and Mercedes-Benz. The former case highlights the changes occurring in the production and human resources arenas whereby the company is developing new production strategies based on NUMMI manufacturing practices and associated industrial relations practices and concepts. The latter case focuses on the labor-management process of negotiating over work restructuring.[1]

Overview of the Brazilian Auto Industry

The Brazilian auto industry began in the 1920s when Ford (1923) and GM (1925) built plants in São Paulo to assemble completely knocked down vehicles. After World War II, auto imports increased dramatically, leading to a rise in import tariffs. The government was urged to set a policy to promote local industry. Thus, until the mid-1950s, an import-substitution policy was followed that required high levels of local content and foreign capital in exchange for a protected market.

During the 1960s and 1970s, the auto industry enjoyed substantial production growth following major investments by many companies, including mainly VW, Mercedes, Scania, Ford, and GM and later Fiat and Volvo. Expectations of continued success were frustrated in the 1980s when stagnation in production prevailed following a national economic crisis and the consequent shrinkage of the domestic market. Improved performance in the export market, however, helped minimize the negative consequences of this period. Thus, export volume increased from 157,000 units

[1]This chapter is based on two previous papers: DIEESE 1995 and Fleury and Fleury 1995a.

in 1980 to 345,000 in 1987. It then declined until 1992, when it started to expand again. Argentina, which bought 41 percent of Brazil's total exported vehicles in 1994, became Brazil's most important market.

In 1990, a major change occurred when a policy of economic liberalization opened up domestic markets for international competition. At that time, the industry had a major competitive problem, as well as very old products and an extremely low productivity level (Ferro 1992). In 1993 and 1994, however, there was significant production growth, resulting in increases of 30 percent and 14 percent, respectively, in each of those years. This is detailed in table 14.1.

One of the most important reasons for the noticeable growth was a new government-implemented policy known as the Camara Setorial (Sectoral Chamber), which established a tripartite arrangement among government, auto companies, and labor. The Camara Setorial defined a new set of strategic goals for the auto industry on such matters as production volumes, investment programs, wage agreements, taxes, and profit margin reductions. A "popular" car regime was implemented in 1993 in which companies were given major tax breaks for producing 1,000-cc-engine small cars.[2] In 1994, the small-car segment represented 48 percent of the total market, and the share of popular cars was 37 percent.

In the meantime, the imported vehicle market had been growing exponentially, from 10,000 units in 1990 to 80,000 (5.7 percent of the market) in 1993. In 1994, imports more than doubled again, reaching 190,000 units (13 percent of the market).

During 1995, government policy changed again. Import tariffs were increased from 20 percent to 70 percent, and a quota system was introduced,

Table 14.1 Motor Vehicle Production in Brazil, 1990–94 (in 000s)

	1990	**1991**	**1992**	**1993**	**1994**	**1995**
Cars	663	705	816	1,100	1,250	1,300
Light commercials	184	201	197	224	251	240
Trucks	51	49	32	48	64	70
Buses	15	23	24	19	18	22
TOTAL	913	978	1,064	1,391	1,583	1,632

Source: Associaçao Nacional dos Fabricantes de Veículos Automotores (ANFAVEA) 1990–94.

[2]Also included were the VW Beetle and the VW Kombi wagon.

which created great turbulence. The total export volume in 1995, however, was 380,000 units.

Following the process of economic liberalization, companies with assembly units have emphasized the development of programs aimed at improving productivity and quality. Although the Brazilian auto industry has lagged behind other world producers, it has been modernizing product lines, and there were more product launchings from 1990 to 1994 than in the entire previous decade. Production processes and technologies have improved with increases in automation levels.

Structure of the Assembly Industry

All the vehicle assemblers in Brazil are subsidiaries of foreign companies. In the car segment, Ford and VW separated after the dissolution of the Autolatina joint venture, which had united the two companies in Brazil and Argentina from 1987 until 1994. After the separation, VW gained market share, thanks to its success in the small-car market with its Go! Ford's last position in market share has been the result of its not having a small car. Fiat has been the fastest-growing company, acquiring market share from all the other assemblers. It doubled its market share from 1990 (15 percent) to 1994 (31 percent). General Motors, although it has been losing market share because of a weaker volume presence in the popular car segment, has been very aggressive in updating its product line. It currently has the most modern product line and has greatly improved its profitability, quality, and productivity.

In the commercial vehicles segment (buses and trucks), Mercedes continues to dominate, although it faced much competition from Autolatina, whose performance in the light and medium truck segment had been impressive. Scania and Volvo concentrate on the heavy truck and bus markets.

Initially, there was a concentration of assembly plants and suppliers in the suburbs of São Paulo, in an industrial belt called ABC, and this created

Table 14.2 Brazilian Automotive Industry Performance, 1991–95 (in 000s units)

	1991	1992	1993	1994	1995
Production	960	1,070	1,390	1,590	1,630
Total domestic sales	787	764	1,131	1,397	1,728
Imports	16	24	70	190	368
Exports	192	342	332	380	263

Source: ANFAVEA 1990–94.

a strong labor movement in this region. Following the decentralization of the industry in the 1980s, however, new entrants such as Fiat and Volvo were installed in the states of Minas Gerais and Paraná, respectively. VW and GM built new plants in Taubaté and São José, respectively, more than sixty miles from the city of São Paulo. As a result of the wide dispersion of new plants, the labor movement became fragmented in its actions and policies, despite the creation of national labor associations.

Industrial Relations in Historical Perspective

There has been an explicit attempt in the Brazilian auto industry to develop a more cooperative and trustful relationship between labor and management. New concepts in the areas of work organization, job design, compensation policies, and employee representation have all influenced management practices.

The industrial relations system in Brazil has its roots in the Getulio Vargas dictatorship (1937–44) and the foundation of a corporatist system influenced by the Italian fascist system of collective rights legislation, government control, minimum wages, monopolistic representation, and compulsory taxes. The military coup in 1964 represented a setback for the unions, which had been permitted to show some muscle during the democratic process that followed World War II. Until the late 1970s, the union movement was banned as part of a prevailing "anticommunism" ideology and workers unions were weak during this time period.

Since the beginning of mass production in the late 1950s, industrial relations policies in the Brazilian auto industry have emphasized the traditional Fordist-Taylorist pattern of work organization, characterized by standardization, highly fragmented jobs, job-oriented skills, formalized recruitment, high turnover, and authoritarian relationships, particularly at the workplace level (Humphrey 1984; Ferro 1989). These policies represented a rupture from the paternalistic system that prevailed in Brazil's small, mostly family-managed industrial organizations, in which there was very limited standardization, bureaucratization, or formalization and outdated human resources policies prevailed.

During the 1960s and 1970s, workforce problems did not pose any critical threat to the success of Brazil's mass production industry, except during short periods of skilled labor shortages. Furthermore, many workers experienced upward social mobility as they moved from rural areas into urban industrial jobs. A survey conducted by Leoncio Rodrigues (1970) in the late 1960s of workers in an auto company found very high levels of satisfaction.

A few protests were held against the military regime that was installed in 1964. During the late 1960s, for instance, demonstrations were conducted by students and some metalworkers, but this was in an area away from the region where the auto assemblers and suppliers were located.

In the late 1970s, however, massive strikes ruptured the predominant "invisible contract" between labor and management, indicating that this stable relationship had ended and a new pattern was emerging. A survey by John Humphrey (1984) disclosed high levels of dissatisfaction, particularly with the unstable employment situation, authoritarian supervision, limited promotions, and very intensive work pace. The labor movement organized demonstrations in the streets and soccer stadiums and called a series of strikes. The shift toward political liberalization in this period was crucial in opening up opportunities for organized labor to gain a voice. Skilled labor led this change process and shaped the new union strategies and actions.[3]

During the events of the late 1970s, the labor unions in the auto industry strongly resisted the government's repressive measures. Thus, it became clear that both the government and the policies of the auto companies had to be changed. Also at this time, the auto industry reached its peak with respect to both production volume and increases in real wages.[4]

A very confrontational period followed during the 1980s, and at the same time the auto industry experienced an economic crisis. Major layoffs were implemented in response to the reduced demand and the uncertainties of the national political move toward democracy. Long strikes in the ABC area were frequently followed by occupations of plants. Violent clashes between workers and the armed forces occurred every year, with greater magnitude and sophistication in "weaponry" by both parties.[5] The workers' cohesion and strength surprised the government and management.[6] Some companies agreed to establish workers councils, which were linked to the metalworkers union.[7]

---

[3]Unskilled laborers, because of their high levels of turnover, played a supportive role but were not active leaders in the process.

[4]In the late 1970s, wages paid in the automotive sector were about 25 percent higher than those in other industrial sectors.

[5]The unions implemented several different strike actions, while companies reinforced their antiunion strategies through their industrial relations departments.

[6]In 1980, a forty-day strike ended when the government intervened and arrested the labor leaders. This was one of the most important labor actions in the country's history. In 1984, union members occupied one of the GM plants and essentially kidnapped the managers and administrative employees, causing a major political setback in the public's opinion of labor unions.

[7]In most companies, the workers councils did not function as a mechanism to improve communication and relationships but rather increased the level of conflict between labor and management.

Labor's strategies and actions gradually became differentiated on a company-by-company basis. This shift was a consequence of differences in union leadership styles and ideologies and the companies' abilities to communicate directly with their employees in an effort to improve working conditions and anticipate and solve personnel problems.

After 1985, the unions began to shift the focus of their policies and strategies toward influencing political and institutional spheres and reduced their action at plant, company, and industry levels. The new Brazilian constitution of 1988 contained some elements of liberalization in the labor arena, such as the reduction of state controls. The essence of the previous framework was basically maintained, however.

During the 1980s, strikes occurred mainly for economic reasons, to pressure the government for changes in the wage policy, particularly for economic plans to control inflation through prices and wage freezes (DIEESE 1995). Some labor unions also participated in party politics, in 1981 by helping to create a new political party (Partido dos Trabalhadores, or the Workers Party) and in 1982 by influencing others by creating central union federations. Currently, there are four union federations, the most significant being the CUT, or Workers Central, and Força Sindical (Labor Power). The third such federation is the Central Labor Federation, which is more overtly political. The fourth federation, the ABC Metalworkers Union, which plays a leading political role, is of economic importance and takes strategic initiatives.

The ABC region has historically been powerful politically. The São José dos Campos Union area, where one of the GM assembly plants is located, has had aggressive and, at times, open confrontation. The Campinas Union (where the Mercedes-Benz bus assembly plant is located) has followed a similar strategy. The growth of the Fiat Motor Company has led to higher employment levels in Betim (420 miles north of São Paulo) but not an equivalent degree of power and strength.

Unionization levels have varied greatly from company to company. In the ABC area, the average level has been 78 percent. The highest has been 83 percent, at VW, and the lowest has been 35 percent, at GM–São Caetano. Fiat's plant in Betim has had only a 10 percent level (DIEESE 1995).

During the 1990s, the companies gradually started to implement new practices to reduce labor turnover, increase real wages, and stimulate skilling and training processes and to introduce participation programs, quality circles, total quality concepts, and, more recently, profit-sharing schemes. New values and assumptions about labor and the workplace were adopted, and the companies' performance was given greater importance.

Also during the 1990s, the labor unions have been involved in strategic negotiations through the Camara Setorial. This is a break from the past, in that they have been making proposals and participating in debates on the definition of a new industrial policy.

The growth in production volume has not been accompanied by an increase in employment levels, either for assemblers or suppliers, thus yielding the increase in productivity, as shown in table 14.3. Much of this increase was achieved by utilizing administrative labor more efficiently. In 1980, 75 percent of the total workforce were hourly paid workers, compared with 83 percent in 1994.

Between 1991 and 1994, there was a 20 percent wage increase within the ABC area for both assemblers and suppliers.[8] Nonetheless, a gap remained between the payment levels in the ABC area and those at Betim-Fiat, where wages, on average, were 30 percent lower (DIEESE 1995). Furthermore, in 1995, many companies in the auto sector began implementing profit-sharing schemes.

This brief history highlights the different approaches and practices auto companies and unions in Brazil have implemented. The policy differ-

Table 14.3 Employment Levels in the Brazilian Auto Industry, 1980–94

	Assemblers	Percentage of Hourly	Suppliers
1980	133,683	75	278,600
1981	103,992	75	
1982	107,137	77	
1983	101,087	77	
1984	107,447	78	
1985	122,217	79	
1986	129,232	79	291,000
1987	113,474	79	
1988	112,985	79	
1989	118,396	80	255,000
1990	117,396	80	
1991	109,428	80	
1992	105,664	81	231,000
1993	106,738	83	238,000
1994	106,207	83	234,000

Sources: ANFAVEA and DIESSE.

[8]In 1994, nominal average wages in the ABC area were approximately U.S. $1,300 per month for the assemblers and U.S. $670 for the suppliers.

ences among companies with regard to employee relations and lean production diffusion strategies reflect differences in the sources of knowledge among their multinational parents. The following case studies of General Motors and Mercedes-Benz in Brazil further illustrate those differences.

Using Multiple Sources of Learning: The Case of GMB

The case of General Motors do Brazil (GMB) demonstrates that there can be multiple sources of learning and knowledge creation with regard to production strategies and employee relations. Opel always exerted a strong influence at GMB, especially with respect to product design. Today, NUMMI is the model for GMB's organizational changes.

One of the main tools for change at GMB has been the continuous improvement process (CIP), which represents the culmination of experiments carried out at the plant since its quality of work life program was initiated in the early 1980s. CIP depends on the work of teams, which are organized on an ad hoc basis (as task forces) and involve about twenty employees from the technological function (product, process, and production engineering; quality; maintenance), some supervisors, and a few workers. This program is also applied in administrative areas.

Every manager is expected to organize one or more CIPs per month in his or her area. From February 1992 until December 1994, the number of CIP assignments in the production area totaled 1,039. Significant results were achieved in floor-area reduction, inventory reduction, productivity increases (pieces/man/hour), and throughput improvements.

Another achievement is related to the concept of "time to market." After twenty years of a very conservative product strategy, GMB set as a target the launching of two new models each year. GMB relied heavily on Opel in achieving this objective.

Based mainly on NUMMI's experience, the results achieved at the Saturn plant, and the concepts of the Toyota production system, GMB is consolidating its production. Table 14.4 provides a list of concepts implemented at GMB as part of the effort to achieve this aim.

Until early 1995, there was a significant flow of Brazilian executives to NUMMI. Twenty-four people were assigned to make two-to-four-day visits, and eighteen were involved in four-week assignments.

Organization of Work. Assembly work at GMB is distributed among teams of about ten persons, including one assigned leader. By 1994, some 856

Table 14.4 NUMMI Concepts Implemented at GMB

NUMMI Concepts	Fully Implemented	Partially Implemented
Manufacturing assembly training areas	X	
Suggestion process	X	
People assessment	X	
Andon system	X	
Operators responsible for quality checks	X	
Operators responsible for workplace	X	
Pull system		X
One-piece flow		X
Synchronous subassemblies		X
Kanban cards		X
Quick die change		X
Teamwork		X
Standardized material flow		X
Error-proofing devices		X
Standardized work (pictorial display)		X
Work cell layout		X

Source: GMB internal document.

teams had been formed; the target figure is 994. Teams are assigned a broad range of tasks and are responsible for setup times and line balancing.

Quality techniques, especially statistical process control, are utilized on the shop floor, and workers are partially responsible for their application. The number of quality inspectors has been radically reduced, and an audit function has been created. The remaining quality inspectors are ranked in the same way as direct workers. Job descriptions and professional profiles have been changed to cope with the new demands.

All assembly workers are trained to be multiskilled, in accordance with a long-term program. In the machining sections, tasks are organized in traditional ways, but teams and individuals are allowed to modify operating procedures if this is approved by their supervisors.

Human Resource Policies and Practices. Human resource policies and practices have been revised at GMB to achieve greater workforce stability and worker involvement. At the managerial level, campaigns are under way to improve relationships and change attitudes toward workers. Changes in symbols to reduce hierarchical differentiation have also been implemented. For example, all employees now use the same restaurants, whereas they were divided into three groups in the past. The current president of GMB strengthened procedures to allow employees to purchase GMB products at a discount (Ferro 1994:320).

Wage policies have been restructured around the principle of pay for knowledge, and each worker has been trained to perform a set of production activities. For each activity, four steps can be achieved, known as can assist, can do, can supervise, and can teach.

There is no bonus system at GMB in Brazil. The first negotiations and experiences involving flexible wages are currently taking place in GM's Argentinean subsidiary, in Cordoba. Brazilian plants are evaluating this experience before proceeding with more concrete plans.

Hiring and training policies are changing, and investments in labor skills are increasing. To introduce the continuous improvement program, a strong training effort was made. Quality concepts were transmitted to fifty-five hundred technical and managerial staff in thirty-hour programs. Some eighteen thousand shop-floor workers were also trained in this program. Group leaders received additional training in four day-long courses. This preparation lasted for about six months.

The GMB training program was based on one developed by NUMMI. GMB transformed eleven NUMMI courses into six core courses: (1) working in teams, (2) meetings and techniques, (3) standardized work, (4) problem analysis I (problem-solving methods) (5) problem analysis II (case studies), and (6) quality awareness.

Training materials were translated from English and adapted to local circumstances. About seventy employees acted as internal instructors. In 1995, the target for off-the-job training activities was fifty hours/employee. That was achieved and the target raised to seventy-five hours/employee in 1996. The benchmark is the Saturn plant, which allocates ninety-two hours/worker. Under these new policies and practices, labor turnover has been reduced from 7.2 percent in 1988 to 4.4 percent in 1994 and 2.2 percent in 1995.

Development of Technological Capacity. Recent changes in GMB's competitive strategy and the associated restructuring process have deeply affected the profile of its technological capabilities. Initial modifications were similar to those Robert Cole (1991) reported for NUMMI. In the GMB plants, the number of production engineers located at the shop-floor level was radically reduced, and other functions, especially those related to long-term planning, were strongly reinforced. This was achieved through the adoption of production engineering concepts and techniques by the workers as a result of the training programs.

At the same time, markets are requiring the development of other specific capacities concerning production technology. In one of the GMB plants, four models with different platforms are being assembled: Monza, Omega, Vectra, and Kadett. Thus, the production system is very complex if one takes into account that replacement parts have to be manufactured not only for current models but for those not on the line. In other countries, it may be easy to outsource replacement parts, but in Brazil outsourcing possibilities are still limited. Hence, GMB has to add to the diversity of components demanded by the current product line, which is twice as many as was previously required.

The capabilities developed by GMB to ensure the efficient performance of the new production system have received recognition worldwide. They are being transferred to other countries where the characteristics of the production processes are similar. One of the key functions is tooling. GMB's tooling function and facilities have been internationally competitive. In addition to supplying other Brazilian automobile companies, GMB exports parts to North America and Europe.

Capability in the areas of product and process design is also being upgraded, and the next new product launch will be made in Europe and in Brazil simultaneously. Brazilian engineers are working along with the GM team in Europe. This procedure is also being applied to new projects. The new Argentinean assembly plant is, to a large extent, being designed in São Paulo.

In relation to the management of the supply chain, GM has transferred its supplier assistance program (PICOS) to GMB, where it is called OTIMO (Optimization of Time, Inventory, and Labor). Under OTIMO, a GMB specialist is sent, free of charge, to the supplier firm for one week of intensive work. These services have also been provided to several firms that are potential but not current GMB suppliers (Posthuma 1995).

Overall Results. GMB's financial results have been outstanding. The declared targets, shown in charts all over the plant (codified as "1-5-30," meaning first in customer satisfaction, 5 percent reduction in costs yearly, and 30 percent market share) have been only partially achieved, however. Difficulties in forecasting future demand in the local market have damaged GMB's ability to meet its declared objectives. For example, when it introduced the Corsa line, initial estimates led the company to plan for a production capacity of fourteen cars per hour. In fact, demand was much greater and, after losing a significant market share to the Fiat Uno-Mille, GMB decided to aim for forty cars per hour.

One of the GMB plants is currently ranked in fourth place for quality achievements relative to other GM subsidiaries around the world; the other Brazilian plant is in eighth place. Another measure of overall quality is the discrepancy level per vehicle (DLPV). GMB achieved a rating of 6 for the Monza line, 7.5 for the Vectra, and 10 for the Omega lines. The benchmark is the Toyota Corolla, which has a rating of 5.5.

Conclusions. The distinctive feature of the GMB case is the firm's capacity to absorb, adapt, and apply lean production concepts and practices. This has not been a passive assimilation, since the experiments that have been conducted have generated a learning process that has enabled managers and engineers to analyze critically the potentials and limitations of the lean production model in the Brazilian environment. The access to NUMMI's and others' experiences, such as Saturn's and CAMI's, combined with the support provided by Opel has helped in this process, as has the existence of local managerial and technological capabilities.

Changes in the organization are still in the initial stages. Up to a certain point, their introduction is being facilitated by a context of growing market demand and high levels of unemployment and the relative weakness of the local union movement. Despite its successful reorganization, GMB lost second place in market share to Fiat, basically because market growth was concentrated on small cars, where the Italian company had been dominant. In 1995, GMB laid off twelve hundred people from both its plants as part of its processes of rationalizing and automating. The unions have attempted to strike but have not yet been successful.

Thus, although GMB has made considerable progress in learning from NUMMI, it still faces an uncertain future because of market and competitive developments. GMB management still believes, however, that the basic conditions needed to become a world-class car manufacturer are now in place.

Negotiated Work Restructuring at Mercedes-Benz do Brazil

Mercedes-Benz has operated in Brazil since 1956 through its subsidiary, Mercedes-Benz do Brazil (MBB). MBB has maintained its position as the major local producer of medium-sized trucks and buses, a market segment in which it was the only manufacturer for almost thirty years; VW and Ford entered this market in the mid-1980s. In the heavy trucks segment, MBB has faced fierce competition from Scania since the 1960s and from Volvo since the end of the 1970s. VW has recently become a strong competitor in the bus market.

MBB has two large plants. The first is located in São Bernardo, in the industrial belt around São Paulo. This plant is dedicated to the manufacture and assembling of chassis and trucks and employs about twelve thousand persons. MBB's other plant is in Campinas, where MBB assembles buses. This plant employs about three thousand persons. In 1994, MBB manufactured about forty thousand units, of which thirty thousand were sold in the local market. MBB's share in trucks represented 40 percent, while it held 71 percent of the bus market.

At the beginning of the 1990s, following the Sectoral Chamber agreements, MBB developed its version of production restructuring, which it called Factory 2000. The aims of this project were to increase competitive capacity, achieve international quality standards, and improve patterns related to costs and timing. In other words, the idea was to adapt lean production concepts and techniques, similar to what was happening in the parent company.

The ABC Metalworkers Union and the MBB Shop Committee made a proposal to MBB in October 1994 that sought to redefine collective bargaining issues. What became the Quality of Working Life Project included thirteen main items (from work organization to disciplinary procedures and conflict resolution) and aimed to achieve plant reorganization by upgrading working conditions and work relations.

At the beginning of 1994, the first two agreements between MBB and the union were signed. These were related to logistics and outsourcing. The union agreed to the transfer of some activities, especially services and parts manufacturing. The change in the logistics system meant that the sectors responsible for supply, production, and transport were aggregated and the thirteen professional titles linked to the former structure were reclassified in seven new functions. Training and wage increases were also part of the change process.

Manufacturing Cells Agreement. The implementation of cell systems was one of the most important issues in the negotiation process between MBB and the union. The agreement was considered in April 1994 and included the following items: three cells would be implemented as pilot projects; work in teams would be implemented after specific agreement; and salaries would be redefined according to the transformation of functional profiles.

The ABC Metalworkers Union made an assessment of the project in February 1995 and was dissatisfied with the outcomes overall. Operators from the most successful cell were interviewed. On the one hand, they commented on the improved work organization, including the more interesting and challenging tasks (resulting from tool changes and adjustments, quality inspections and control, clear documents, and so forth) and their acquisition of new knowledge and the application of different skills. Relationships with supervisors had also improved and the quality of work increased. On the other hand, operators complained about their working conditions, such as the increased noise; the workload, which required higher levels of concentration and mental effort; and the increased responsibility. Furthermore, the number of operators in each cell had been reduced from ten to four, and the total number in a cell had declined from fourteen to seven. The operators sought new job classifications and higher wages.

The other two pilot cells were not as successful as the first, and workers had even more complaints about the system. Hence, the union sought to reopen negotiations with the company.

Negotiations over the Organization of Work Teams. Discussions concerning the organization of production teams began in 1992. After initial meetings with the MBB, the ABC Metalworkers Union demanded an official visit to the MBB's head office and plants in Germany to gain firsthand knowledge regarding the formation of such teams. The first delegation of unionists and MBB managers visited Stuttgart in June 1993 and met representatives of the Mercedes-Benz National Workers Council. A second delegation made a similar visit in January 1994.

Following these visits, the union adopted the position that teamwork should be conducted in semiautonomous groups. Furthermore, the implementation of such a system should seek to preserve employment levels, increase investment, reduce working hours from forty-four to forty per week, limit the amount of overtime, revise the job structure, and improve training programs.

The "Teamwork Agreement" was signed between MBB and the union in March 1995. It is one of the most complex collective agreements concerning work restructuring signed in Brazil. Both parties accepted the definition of teamwork as work done in semiautonomous groups that would perform integrated production or service activities aimed at improving productivity, product quality, and the quality of working life.

According to the agreement, the concept of teamwork would be implemented through pilot projects in defined production areas. The expected outcome is to make feasible the performance of integrated tasks, thereby avoiding the fragmentation of work; to decentralize decision making; to eliminate dysfunctional coordination; and to enhance the skills capabilities of the workforce.

A coordination group, consisting of company representatives and members of the union and the shop committee, was created to plan and monitor the implementation of teamwork. Local monitoring groups were also established to improve communication and follow-up. They are responsible for analyzing difficulties and proposing solutions.

In the initial stage, five teams were created in different areas of the plant: one in machining, two for the assembly line, and two for the cabs assembly area. Teams are led by a foreman, and their size is negotiated by the coordination group. The union's position is that the following factors should be taken into consideration in deciding on the number of workers in each team: absences, training, meeting time, vacations, and free days. Participation in teams is voluntary.

Each team has a spokesperson, and any team member may be elected to that role. The spokesperson is the group's technical representative; he or she coordinates the group's work activities as well as interfaces with other areas. The spokesperson also conducts weekly meetings (fifteen minutes during worktime) and plans vacation schedules according to the company's rules; the spokesperson does not have the power to reward or punish and does not assume the role of the union. The spokesperson receives additional payment for taking on the spokesperson role.

Each team is expected to provide suggestions to improve products and processes. These suggestions are then sent through the foremen to higher levels of management. Each team has autonomy to change methods and practices if this does not require additional resources and improves production performance. The target is to implement teamwork in every production area over a period of three years. Two other agreements negotiated between MBB and the union concerned the introduction of kaizen activities and profit sharing.

Negotiated Approach to Change. The level of interaction that has developed between MBB and the union is rare in Brazilian industry and demonstrates both the potential and the limitations of a negotiated restructuring process. Nevertheless, this process of change will be under severe threat if

Brazil undergoes another recession. In any event, competition in the auto sector will increase in the future. Following the split of Autolatina, Ford, General Motors, and VW are all planning to invest heavily in the production of commercial vehicles.

After becoming the first auto company to distribute a bonus to its workers in 1994, MBB surprised them in 1995 by laying off fourteen hundred. MBB undertook this rationalization process without prior communication with the union, and the action was followed by a strike. As in the GMB case, the future of MBB is highly dependent on developments in the economy and in the market for cars and trucks in Brazil.

Conclusions

The Brazilian auto industry is poised for a period of growth. The new investments, estimated at U.S. $14 billion at least up to the year 2000, will enable the process of modernization to continue and provide additional capacity to reach the projected volume of 2.5 million units per year.

Many uncertainties lie ahead, however. The macroeconomic environment has improved since inflation has been brought under control, but economic pressures continue because of the negative balance of payments and the high unemployment levels. High taxes, excessive protectionism, and a delay in establishing a new Mercosur policy (a regional trade pact among South American countries) may damage efforts to stimulate market demand. The increases in production volume will not be accompanied by new job creation because the industry has to increase its levels of automation and productivity further.

Despite these uncertainties, as well as "stop-and-go policies," modernization of the industrial relations system and further dialogue and cooperation between labor and management will continue. Although the industry is in transition, since trust still is to be achieved, there are greater prospects for negotiated change. For example, Ford announced a revolutionary agreement with its workers for a flexible workweek, varying from thirty-eight to forty-four hours, depending on market conditions. Furthermore, the economic stabilization and continuing democratic regime are positive forces for the institutionalization of a new pattern of industrial relations.

The case studies in this chapter show that analysis that is focused solely on the macro level only partially captures the dynamics of diffusion of new paradigms. The company-level analysis shows how individual companies vary in their learning models. Although national cultures and institutional frameworks influence the process of diffusion, companies differ in how they apply lean production. The GMB case provides an example of learning from NUMMI, while the Mercedes case demonstrates a negotiation pattern that is influenced by the German industry and union experience.

Research conducted in other companies in Brazil has shown how a company's discretionary power influences the diffusion of new practices of production, management, and industrial relations. Examples include Volvo's advanced human resources policies (Ferro 1991), Honda's lean principles at its motorcycle plant in the Amazon area (Ferro 1989), and Ford's employee-involvement program (Silva 1991).[9]

The case studies show a contingent pattern of transfer and adoption of the new paradigms. Clearly, GMB has given high priority to the transfer of new forms of production organization. By contrast, Mercedes is concerned primarily with labor relations. These differences may be justified by the differences in union bargaining power. They also reflect differences in organizational style and the philosophy of the parent companies and the strategies pursued by their local subsidiaries. Thus, although national cultures and institutional frameworks play a significant role in shaping the process of adoption and adaptation of lean production, companies maintain a certain degree of freedom that allows them to align their competitive strategies and organizational practices with those of their parent companies.

Over the longer term, institutional constraints may introduce other, stronger restrictions on the diffusion process. In the case of Brazil, the main aspects to be considered are the educational level of the labor force and rigidities in labor legislation. These constraints have influenced the development of profit-sharing and bonus systems and may limit the ability of companies to increase their capacity to sustain competitive advantages, insofar as the development of such capacity is heavily dependent on there being cooperation among the various institutional agents (Fleury and Fleury 1995).

Auto assemblers in Brazil have overcome the initial difficulties posed by the new competitive challenge. Their success can be attributed mainly to their effective reaction to the threats they encountered in 1990. The establishment of a learning culture as the choice from among all possible social patterns that will lead to permanent improvements is not yet part of the current reality. This is the greatest challenge that Brazil will have to face in the near future.

---

[9]Elizabeth Silva compared practices in two Ford car plants (São Bernardo–Brazil and Dagenham-U.K.), showing how the different country contexts influenced their competitive dynamics and strategies (quality, flexibility, efficiency, and industrial relations).

15 Korea: Recent Developments and Policy Options

Young-bum Park and Hyo Soo Lee

Industrial relations is one of the areas that has undergone great changes during the recent rapid transformation of Korea's political, social, and economic structure. Union membership has almost doubled since 1987. Wage increases have been significant. Labor institutions, particularly labor unions, which used to be an engine for Korea's fast industrialization, have come to be regarded by some observers as a major hindrance to Korea's sustained economic development, despite their possible positive effects on productivity.

This chapter, which is based on a micro-level workplace survey of selected enterprises, analyzes changes in a set of core industrial relations and human resource management practices in the Korean automotive industry since 1987 and the effects of these practices on the efficiency or productivity of this industry. Policy options for improving efficiency are also reviewed. Our study raises the question of why lean production practices have not been diffused among Korean auto assemblers, even though Korean automakers have attempted to adopt the Japanese production system and some human resource management practices.

The growth of the Korean automotive industry has been remarkable, and it is expected to be among the top-five automakers in the world by the year 2000. It was only in the mid-1960s that Korean automakers began to assemble foreign cars with imported semi-knocked-down components. This remarkable growth has not been without problems, however. About 40 percent of Korea's industrial disputes in recent years have occurred in the automobile industry. Establishing sound industrial relations as well as rationalizing human resources are crucial to enhance competitiveness.

Recent Developments in Industrial Relations and the Labor Market in Korea

Major changes, legal reforms, and far-reaching developments have been occurring in the field of industrial relations in Korea since 1987. In 1987, there was an explosive increase in the number of labor disputes after the "Democratization Declaration." In 1987, 1988, and 1989, the number of strikes was 3,749, 1,873, and 1,616, respectively.

Before 1987, trade unions in Korea had not represented workers' interests effectively in the process of determining working conditions. Since mid-1987, however, the labor movement has expanded. For example, the number of organized establishments grew from 2,725 in July 1987 to 7,883 in December 1989, and total membership in labor unions increased from one million to almost two million during that period. Collective bargaining is now an important method used to determine the working conditions of employees. By December 1992, union membership in Korea was 1.8 million, and the rate of unionization among permanent employees was 19.8 percent. The current trend seems to be toward stabilization in the rate of unionization.

Recent developments in industrial relations are also having a significant influence on Korea's short-term as well as its long-term economic performance. Rapid wage increases have made macroeconomic management more difficult for the government. Cost-push inflationary pressures have been more severe as the increase in wages has continued at double-digit rates. Moreover, the rapid wage increases will undoubtedly mean changes in the overall comparative advantage structure of Korean products and suggests that Korea's economy may have to undergo even more rapid structural adjustments.

Since 1990, the government has been involved more closely in wage negotiations in the private sector. But even in the public sector, the government's goal of controlling wage increases has not been attained without difficulty, especially when one considers that trade unions are no longer regulated. In union settings, it seems that certain public authorities are the only institutions on which government can impose its wage restraint policy without difficulty. In 1992, the growth rate of the gross national product was 4.7 percent, which was the lowest in ten years. The unstable industrial relations as well as the rapid wage increases over the last few years were believed to have contributed to this poor performance.

Despite its troubled economy, Korea has had close to full employment since the mid-1980s. Overall employment has been stable, since the growing service sector has been absorbing additional labor. Some structural problems have intensified, however. Unemployment rates among university graduates have been far higher than the unemployment rates overall, and some sectors, such as labor-intensive small manufacturing, have been experiencing serious labor shortages. Recruiting guest workers has been proposed as a solution, although an estimated one hundred thousand undocumented foreign workers already exist in Korea.

Background on Our Study

We conducted interviews with senior and middle-level managers and with supervisors, as well as with trade union representatives in the selected firms. Eight enterprises, including three assemblers and five parts producers, were included in our sample. The assemblers were Hyundai Motor Company, Kia Motors Corporation, and Daewoo Public Motors. The parts producers were Kia Machine Tool Corporation; Daewoo Automotive Components, Ltd.; Sam Rip Industrial Company, Ltd.; Sung Rim Company, Ltd.; and Seoul Metal Company. Two of the parts producers, Kia Machine Tool and Daewoo Automotive Components, are large-scale enterprises. They produce parts under subcontracting arrangements with their owners (Kia Motors Corporation and Daewoo Public Motors). Sam Rip Industrial sells about 60 percent of its products to Hyundai, although it still supplies its parts to all three assemblers. Sung Rim (a medium-sized enterprise) and Seoul Metal (a small-scale enterprise) produce under subcontracting arrangements with Kia Machine Tool. In 1991, the proportion of Sung Rim's sales to Kia Machine Tool constituted only 2.8 percent of its total sales. By contrast, Seoul Metal was totally dependent on Sam Rip. The relationship among the companies in the survey is shown in table 15.1 and figure 15.1.

In 1992, the total revenue at Hyundai, which employs more than forty thousand workers, was more than six trillion won (U.S. $7.2 billion). Hyundai has experienced quite a few serious industrial disputes since its trade union was organized in 1987.

Kia Motors, which is the second-largest automobile manufacturer in Korea, produces a wide variety of cars. In 1991, its total sales amounted to 2.7 trillion won (U.S. $3.6 billion), and it had 22,103 employees. Kia Motors has a unique management structure in that, unlike other large enterprises in Korea, it is management-controlled. It is considered one of the few major enterprises in Korea with sound industrial relations.

Table 15.1 Characteristics of Auto Companies Surveyed in Korea

Company	Type of Activity	Nature of Ownership	Product	Number of Employees	Sales Turnover in U.S. $	Level of Industrial Disputes
Hyundai Motor Company	Auto assembly	Chaebol	Autos	40,000	7.2 billion	High
Kia Motors Corp.	Auto assembly	Chaebol/management controlled	Autos	22,000	3.6 billion	Low
Daewoo Public Motors	Auto assembly	Chaebol	Autos	2,300	355 million	Nil (no union)
Kia Machine Tool Corp.	First parts supplier to Kia Motors	Subsidiary of Kia Motors	Axles and transmissions	3,000	330 million	High
Daewoo Automotive Components, Ltd.	First parts supplier to Daewoo Public Motors	Joint venture of Daewoo Motors and GM	Various automotive components	2,000	304 million	Low
Sam Rip Industrial Co., Ltd.	First parts supplier to Hyundai, Kia Motors, and Daewoo Public Motors	Privately owned	Headlights	700	87 million	Low

| Sung Rim Co., Ltd. | First parts supplier to Hyundai and Kia Machine Tool Corp. | Privately owned | Carburetors and motorcycle components | 250 | 20 million | Low |
| Seoul Metal Co. | Second parts supplier to Kia Machine Tool Corp. | Privately owned | Transmission cases | 42 | 6 million | Nil (no union) |

Figure 15.1 Relationships among Auto Companies Surveyed in Korea

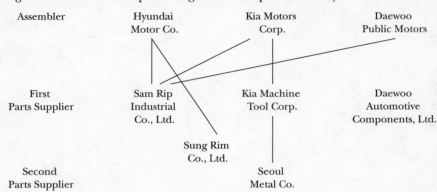

Daewoo Public Motors was established in 1991, and its total sales in 1992 were 280 billion won (U.S. $355 million). We selected the company for our survey because it has unique human resource management practices, despite its small size.

Kia Machine Tool, which is a subsidiary enterprise of Kia Motors, produces auto parts, such as axles and transmissions, for its parent company, as well as for other companies. Its sales increased significantly in 1986 with the acquisition of another large machinery company. It has experienced a chronic deficit, however, as well as severe industrial disputes since the acquisition. The number of employees at Kia Machine Tool peaked in 1989 at 2,824.

Daewoo Automotive Components, Ltd., is a joint venture between a Korean conglomerate and General Motors in the United States. It employs about two thousand workers. Its total sales amounted to 240 billion won (U.S. $304 million) in 1992. Although Daewoo Automotive Components has a militant trade union, it has had few industrial disputes.

Sam Rip Industrial, which employs about seven hundred workers, has cooperative industrial relations. It produces carburetors for automobiles as well as for two-wheel motorcycles. Its sales grew from 5.8 billion won (U.S. $7.3 million) in 1987 to 16.2 billion won (U.S. $20.5 million) in 1992.

Seoul Metal produces transmission cases almost exclusively for Kia Machine Tool. Its sales increased from 858.6 million won (U.S. $996,000) in 1986 to 4.6 billion won (U.S. $5.8 million) in 1992. The number of employees decreased from sixty-five in 1986 to forty-two in 1992, however, with the rationalization of the work design and after some work was contracted out. The union in Sung Rim is very weak, while Seoul Metal has no union.

In the larger companies, such as Hyundai and Kia Motors, the labor force at the time of our study was overwhelmingly male, whereas there were substantial numbers of female production workers in the small companies, such as Sung Rim and Seoul Metal. In 1992, for example, Kia Motors had only twenty-seven female production workers out of more than eleven thousand such workers, whereas female workers accounted for about one-third of all production workers at Sung Rim and Seoul Metal.

The educational attainment of the workers also differed depending on the size of the establishment. At Hyundai, Kia Motors, and Daewoo Public Motors, most production workers had at least a high school diploma, while only about half the workers at Sung Rim had completed high school.

At all the companies surveyed, the labor force was relatively young. In 1992, the average age of the production workers was thirty.

Product Markets

Before 1987, industrial relations was not a major strategic influence on the growth of auto companies in Korea. Since 1987, however, product competitiveness has come to depend heavily on the stability of industrial relations. The management of Hyundai, which has grown very fast, considers unstable industrial relations to be one of the major obstacles to the company's faster growth. Kia Motors benefited from its stable industrial relations when it began to produce passenger cars in 1987. A dispute in 1991 has made it difficult for the company to recover its investment for a second plant, however. The top management of the conglomerate to which Daewoo Public Motors belongs established Daewoo Public Motors even though the conglomerate already owned another car assembler. Management did this because the existing assembler had experienced several labor disputes and had had some problems with its foreign partner. Eventually, Kia Motors had to take orders away from Kia Machine Tool, even though the two companies belong to the same conglomerate, because Kia Machine Tool had several serious disputes. Only at Sam Rip and Seoul Metal has the changed labor environment since the mid-1980s not had a significant influence on the competitiveness of their products.

Labor Market

As a reflection of the fast growth of the Korean automobile industry in recent years, the largest companies experienced rapid expansion of their workforces in the 1980s. For example, the number of workers at Hyundai increased three times between 1984 and 1989. The result is that the company has a young labor force, which has substantially influenced industrial relations and human resource management. These new entrants never experienced Hyundai's difficult times in the early 1980s, and therefore their attitudes are different from those of the older workers. Many of these new workers joined the labor market in the mid-1980s as Korea was experiencing a turning point in its democratization.

In the smaller companies, the expansion of the workforce has not been as rapid as their turnover or the changes in their production capacities. Seoul Metal reduced its workforce. These companies took several labor-saving measures, including resorting to automation, renovating product processes, and contracting out.

The largest companies have not had problems recruiting workers despite the recent serious labor shortages, although the smaller companies, such as Sung Rim and Seoul Metal, whose workers number fewer than one thousand, have found this difficult. The larger companies are having more problems retaining workers. At Sam Rip, for example, the yearly separation rate is about 40 percent. The company has taken several measures to reduce labor turnover, such as altering its payment system to favor workers with longer tenure.

New Technology and/or Automation

In this study, the level of automation is classified as (1) partial automation of a unit machine, (2) full automation of a unit machine, (3) production line automation, or (4) factory automation. At Hyundai, the level of automation is between production line automation and factory automation. At Kia Motors, the level is between full automation of a unit machine and production line automation.

The major motives at Hyundai and Kia Motors to introduce new technology and automation included quality improvement and productivity enhancement. Labor savings or the improvement of the working environment were secondary considerations. At the parts suppliers, however, such as Kia Machine Tool and Seoul Metal, the levels of automation were lower than at the assemblers. The parts suppliers' motives for introducing new technology included rapid wage increases as well as improvement of the working environment, both of which the workers demanded. Since workers were being replaced, the management of Kia Machine Tool recognized that the union and the workers saw automation as a threat.

The work environments at the eight companies we studied have improved greatly since they have become more automated. Further, automation does not pose any problems to the employment stability of the existing workers since redundant workers are not dismissed easily. When workers quit, their jobs are not refilled. Before 1987, however, Hyundai, which introduced automation very early, laid off workers made redundant because of automation, reflecting the weakened union power there before our benchmark year.

Other Environmental Influences

The effects of government policies on the business and/or management strategies, human resource and/or personnel management, and industrial relations of the eight enterprises we studied have also been significant. In particular, government wage policies, such as the total wage system, influenced decisions at Hyundai, Kia Motors and Kia Machine Tool, Daewoo Public Motors, and Daewoo Automotive Components.[1]

Other government measures that affect human resource management policies at the company level include measures that promote employment of the handicapped, a recommendation to rehire workers who were laid off because of union activities, and the Vocational Training Act. Government policies concerning the payment of wages during the period of a strike and the legality of strikes over management prerogatives are also important.

The industrial relations and human resource management policies of the parts suppliers have been influenced by the policies introduced by the assemblers. As a result, wage negotiations at Sam Rip, Sung Rim, and Daewoo Automotive Components were, in turn, influenced by government measures. In addition, Korea's membership in the International Labor Organization (ILO) is expected to have some impact on the industrial relations of the country's automobile companies since the ILO has suggested that the Korean government amend some of its labor laws.

Business Strategies and Trade Unions

There are no unions at Daewoo Public Motors or at Seoul Metal. Trade unions were organized at Hyundai, Daewoo Automotive Components, and

---

[1]Following the Democratization Declaration of June 29, 1987, the government, which had been deeply involved in wage negotiations in the private sector before June 1987, maintained that wage increases should be determined mainly by autonomous bargaining between labor and management. Since the latter half of 1989, however, the government has tried to introduce measures to ensure low wage increases in response to the apparent slowdown of Korea's economy.

Sung Rim after 1987. All the unions have become much stronger since 1987, and the unions whose histories are the shortest have suffered from chronic industrial disputes. Hyundai, whose union was organized in 1987, had industrial disputes in every year except 1992. Kia Machine Tool stopped work for forty-nine days, fifty days, sixty-three days, and thirty-nine days in 1989, 1990, 1991, and 1992, respectively, even after the country's explosive strikes were subdued.

Kia Motors is considered one of the largest enterprises in Korea with sound industrial relations, in large part because no strikes of any significance occurred during 1987–88 (one lasted for only a few hours), when there were about seven thousand industrial disputes in Korea. A dispute arose in 1991, however, and as a result, the largest Kia Motors plant was closed for more than a month.

Kia Motors' trade union was organized in 1962. Its members are mostly production workers and salespeople. Nonproduction workers below management level were entitled to join the union; but only a few of them did. Before 1987, the company's labor-management relations were characterized as cooperative. The company experienced difficult times in the early 1980s, for instance, but the production workers voluntarily agreed to forgo their wages for three months. The dispute of 1991 was attributed mainly to the management style of the president who took office in 1990, as well as to the fact that more than 70 percent of the workforce was made up of young workers who did not understand the company culture.[2]

No trade unions exist at Daewoo Public Motors. Management does not appear to pursue a nonunion strategy in a concerted manner, however. Various reasons may be advanced to explain why the company is not unionized, including that its products have not sold as well as expected, the company started its operation when the overall union movement in Korea was losing strength, a "cooperative" spirit has taken root since the company sent all its workers to a training program offered by a Japanese counterpart, and there are good communications between managerial staff and production workers.

Kia Machine Tool is cited as one of the large enterprises in Korea that has unstable industrial relations. Since 1987, the operation of its plants has stopped for one to one and a half months per year because of industrial disputes. On several occasions, labor and management have become dead-

[2]The former president of Kia Motors became very well known after "saving" the company in the early 1980s. In 1990, he became the chairman. A senior vice president of the company, who had joined Kia Motors after leaving a bank a few years earlier, assumed the presidency.

locked during negotiations. There have been six union heads since 1986. Kia Machine Tool's union was one of the leading groups in the Korea Trade Union Congress. The company's very unstable industrial relations have occurred mainly because Kia Machine Tool acquired a larger company in 1986 and the unions as well as the workers from the two companies fought for union leadership. The company began to reduce its workforce in 1992 after a decline in business, and in February 1993 the union withdrew its membership from the Korea Trade Union Congress. The management style and characteristics of the company on matters of industrial relations policies are similar to those of Kia Motors.

Sam Rip Industrial is a union shop, yet its industrial relations are still considered very cooperative. First, most of the union leaders have long tenures. Second, daily communications between labor and management are relatively good. Third, a high proportion of the workers are married females (40 percent) or relatively old (53 percent are older than thirty-five), which has made the workforce more quiescent.

Sung Rim had a very militant union until 1991, but since then the union has almost been dissolved. In early 1990, the company was notified that Hyundai would not buy auto parts from Sung Rim if there was one more industrial dispute, and after that Sung Rim's management used every possible measure to weaken the union's power. Management appears to have been successful in achieving its objective. Since 1991, a labor and management council has taken on the union's role. The company still works hard to solve workers' grievances, however.

Since 1987, trade unions throughout the Korean auto industry have participated more actively with management in decision making. At Kia Motors and Kia Machine Tool, two-thirds of the members of the disciplinary committee, which consists of an equal number of representatives of labor and management, need to agree to discipline production workers. The trade unions of Hyundai and Daewoo Automotive Components have asked that their disciplinary committees be composed of equal numbers of labor and management representatives. By contrast, Kia Machine Tool's trade union has often asked for amendments in Korea's labor laws, a request that could not be met at the workplace-level bargaining table.

Even in the companies in which trade unions are not organized, employers cannot determine production workers' wages unilaterally. The labor-management councils play a somewhat unionlike role in these companies. This development indicates that at least since 1987 the managements of all eight companies, even those without unions, have come to recognize that the presence of trade unions is an important variable in their business strategies.

The managements of all the companies except Sam Rip Industrial see trade unions as potential obstacles to the achievement of their business objectives. They seldom recognize that the trade unions could contribute to the companies' growth. Even at Kia Machine Tool and Sung Rim, management blames the trade unions for forcing the companies into potentially critical situations.

Management has provided few measures to induce the trade unions to make positive contributions to the upgrading of their respective companies. The companies seem to be satisfied only with "no union" or "no strikes." This is reflected in the fact that Kia Motors underwent a serious dispute because management tried to conduct wage bargaining in an improper way. To some extent, management at all the companies has been overwhelmed by the extent to which the trade unions have become more powerful in the last ten or so years.

Core Employment Practices

Work Organization. Kia Motors has a job structure that is typical of the structure in Korea's largest enterprises. Jobs are broadly classified into nonproduction and production. Shop-floor operators in the production occupations are organized into teams of seven members (at least), which are headed by team leaders. Teams are the basic units for undertaking total quality control (TQC) activities, and team leaders are responsible for the on-the-job training of new recruits. Teams are clustered into a subsection composed of two to three teams and headed by a senior foreman. Subsections are grouped together into a section under the authority of a manager, who usually is a nonproduction employee. In practice, however, the production activities of each section are directed by a supervisor who is supposed to assist the manager and lead the senior foremen. The supervisor is classified as a production employee.[3] Above the managers in the managerial hierarchy are general managers, directors, senior directors, and so on. The top management level is classified as the senior executive director.

The job structure at the small companies is more simple. Shop-floor operators are grouped into sections, each of which is headed by a supervisor, who

[3]There are "skill masters" and "skill supermasters" above the level of supervisors. They have a status equivalent to that of managers or general managers. They do not have managerial authority, however.

is under the authority of a nonproduction manager. For example, Seoul Metal has three supervisors who are under the plant's general manager. Only the general manager has authority over the supervisors. At all eight companies, sections are also the basic unit of job structure for nonproduction employees.

In general, there are no transfers between production and nonproduction workers except at Kia Motors. In 1990, it introduced a transfer system among production, nonproduction, and sales employees to reduce conflicts among different groups.

Even though the basic unit of work organization at all eight companies is a team or section, the lines of demarcation between individual jobs are very clear. Thus, to a large extent, work is designed and organized around individuals, rather than teams or work groups, and there is no individual flexibility in working hours.

At none of the companies are shop-floor workers involved in decisions concerning the organization of production work, particularly at the design stage. Production engineers design the work organization, and shop-floor workers perform the work activities. At all eight companies except Sung Rim, there is little communication between production engineers and shop-floor workers during the initial design stage. At all the large companies, however, the shop-floor workers suggest changes that could be made in the organization of work by means of their TQC activities. Neither the trade unions nor the workers seem to be interested in becoming more involved in decision making pertaining to the organization of work.

There are no systems for measuring performance or for providing incentives for teams (or for individual production workers) at the large companies. The system of performance evaluation for production workers was abolished in 1987, when the unions started becoming stronger. The smaller companies have systems of performance evaluation for individual production workers as well as for nonproduction employees, and as a result there are differences in individual workers' wages. Tenure and performance evaluations are the core criteria for promoting both production and nonproduction workers at these companies. At all eight companies, individual nonproduction workers who perform well are rewarded with promotions, so for these workers at least, individual performance is to some extent the basis for the systems of performance evaluation and incentives.

The larger companies, including Sam Rip Industrial, operate two shifts for production workers. The day shift is from 8:30 A.M. to 5:30 P.M., while the night shift is from 6:30 P.M. to 5:50 A.M. Workers alternate shifts from week to week.

Under the Labor Standards Act, enacted in 1953, workers in Korea are entitled to paid monthly and annual leaves. In our interviews at the companies, managerial staff complained that operating the plants at peak efficiency was often difficult since some production workers did not hesitate to take advantage of the paid leaves, which, in response to management's request, they had not taken before 1987, even though they were entitled to them.

There is only one shift at Sung Rim and at Seoul Metal. In 1992, production workers at Sung Rim worked an average of 56.5 hours per week, while production workers at Seoul Metal worked an average of 55.5 hours.

In the companies with trade unions, trade unions and/or labor-management councils are the official communication channels between labor and management. At the companies where there are no unions or the unions are weak, the labor-management councils play a role similar to that of unions. With the increase in union power since 1987, the distinction between unions and labor-management councils is less clear.

At the companies with strong unions, except at Sam Rip, the official control hierarchy—shop-floor worker, group leader, foreman, supervisor, and manager—does not work very well. In the past, communication between management and shop-floor workers over grievances went through the official job-control mechanism of group leader, foreman, and supervisor. Now, union representatives play a crucial role in communication between management and shop-floor workers. At Sam Rip, where the union representatives hold supervisory jobs, the official control mechanism works very well.

By contrast, the unions are generally reluctant to promote dialogue with management. For example, at Kia Machine Tool, the union has delayed setting up a regular working-level labor-management council, which management has offered to do. This behavior is typical of militant unions in Korea, which are afraid of appearing to cooperate with management.

All the companies have implemented some production incentive schemes. Kia Motors won grand prizes in total quality control in 1991 and in total productive maintenance in 1992 at national competitions, and Kia Machine Tool won the grand prize in the TQC competition in 1987. According to managers at both these companies, their respective companies' productivity increases were less significant than was expected, however, and the results of their incentive activities were unsatisfactory because the production workers had not fully cooperated. By contrast, the management at Seoul Metal, which received the grand prize in the TQC competition for its category in 1991, regarded its TQC activities very positively.

Skill Formation among Production Workers. The larger companies we surveyed recruit production workers principally from among graduates of industrial high schools or general high schools who have completed a qualified vocational training program.[4] Establishments with 150 or more employees need to offer some vocational training courses of their own; otherwise, they need to pay a levy to the government.

Jobs are advertised in the press, but companies also rely on recommendations from current employees or local schools or from job agencies, including government employment security offices. In smaller companies, such as Sam Rip, Sung Rim, and Seoul Metal, insider contacts are the main means used to fill positions. The assemblers do not usually take into account previous experience in setting starting wages except in a few special cases. New recruits with an authorized certificate of skills, for example, are given higher starting wages.

At Hyundai, new jobs are advertised in the internal company publication. Kia Motors, which in the past heavily depended on insider contacts in selecting production workers, now hires only graduates of its own vocational training center. This change was made because of demands by the union. Through this system, management has also found that it can screen workers who might participate in industrial action.

Daewoo Public Motors has a unique selection procedure for new production workers. First, only high school graduates with no experience who have completed military service are considered eligible. Second, the training period is one year, including six months' training in Japan. Third, all trainees, except for a few poor performers, are accepted as regular workers. The principal objective of this system is not to upgrade the skills of the workers but to select workers who are trainable as well as adaptable.

Kia Machine Tool used to prefer to recruit experienced workers; however, it now plans to hire new graduates of industrial high schools since experienced workers cost too much. Sam Rip used to pay a finder's fee to

---

[4]In the largest companies, such as Hyundai, Kia Motors, Daewoo Public Motors, and Daewoo Automotive, which belong to conglomerates, the recruitment process is different for production and nonproduction workers (a common practice in Korea's conglomerates). Production workers are selected through open competition, whereas applicants for nonproduction jobs need to demonstrate their competence through a written examination or have strong recommendations from top universities. Nonproduction workers, once hired, are sent to different companies in the same conglomerate, depending on their qualifications. The company's interests are often given greater priority than workers' preferences. Even after the workers are sent to a company, the headquarters of the conglomerate still has authority to relocate them.

workers who recommended new recruits as long as the recruit stayed for at least three months. This fee has been abolished in recent years since the easing of the labor shortages.

At Sung Rim and Seoul Metal, new workers are not required to have particular skills. The management of Sung Rim claimed that it did not want experienced or skilled new recruits because they would be frustrated after a few months since the jobs required only minimal skills.

Most of the training at the companies we surveyed takes place on the job. In general, however, job rotation is implemented only within the same function or the same production unit. In the larger companies, except for Daewoo Public Motors, job rotation between functions is rarely used since the work intensity of each occupation differs. For example, workers in the press plant usually resist being transferred to a more demanding occupation. At Hyundai, job transfers within the same production unit are very frequent. This is mainly because all the members of a production unit have equal workloads. At Kia Motors, where a strong union emerged in the late 1980s, the transfer of a production worker between different functions or sectors needs to be approved by a committee that consists of management and union representatives in equal numbers as well as the head of the committee.

This limited use of job rotation prevents workers from becoming multiskilled. At Kia Machine Tool, where there has been a freeze on hiring new recruits since 1990, workers who are willing to be transferred to different functions have been offered some training. Little job rotation has been implemented, however. By contrast, at Daewoo Public Motors, job rotation is implemented relatively easily, mainly because of its method of selecting new workers.

The large companies have many training programs to upgrade workers' skills. In particular, with greater automation in the production process, many programs are in place to train workers to operate automated machines. But only Hyundai has a system at the company level for developing and coordinating training programs. It became activated in 1990. Then, in 1994, Hyundai introduced a career development program for production workers. In the other companies each department has its own skill development programs.

Managers at all the companies we surveyed emphasized the importance of using training to improve morale. For example, Kia Motors sends its production workers to a two-month on-the-job training program offered by a Japanese company with which it has a cooperative relationship. As of the end of 1992, about 12 percent of Kia Motors' production workers had finished the program. The program will continue until most of the production workers complete the training. Management expects that through this program Kia Motors employees are learning not only the skills but the work attitudes of the Japanese workers.

The small companies, including Daewoo Automotive Components, do not have systematic training programs since management believes that it takes only a few months for new recruits to acquire most of the on-the-job skills they will need. In recent years, however, since labor costs have increased substantially, these companies have come to recognize the importance of training and they now send some of their workers to foreign counterparts or parent companies.

Despite the considerable amount of automation introduced in recent years, the skill requirements have not changed much at Hyundai, Kia Motors, or Kia Machine Tool. In the context of conflictual industrial relations, management has used automation both to replace labor and to upgrade the efficiency of the enterprises. This observation implies that the higher levels of automation have been accompanied by work that to some extent has been organized in a narrower, more tightly circumscribed job-control fashion.

Compensation Schemes. The compensation schemes for production and nonproduction workers are different at all eight companies. In addition to annual wage increases, which are determined by collective bargaining (except for production workers of Hyundai and Kia Machine Tool and workers at Seoul Metal), workers can receive additional wage increases by moving up on the basic wage table. The principal determinants of a worker's wage are education and tenure. Whether he or she has special skills or skill certificates is also considered. An analysis or evaluation of skills and/or jobs is rarely conducted, however, and the proportion of the total wage that reflects such an evaluation is very small. At Kia Motors, the proportion of the total wages of sales personnel that is performance-related is greater than 50 percent; however, it has decreased since 1987 as greater emphasis has been put on achieving income stability among workers.

Hyundai tried to introduce a payment-for-skills system in 1994, but because of union resistance, the system was not implemented. Kia Motors has also considered changing its payment system, which currently applies to all workers, since the wage of a new college graduate was lower than that of a high school graduate with four years' experience.

Since 1987, the wages of individual workers at the eight companies in our study have not varied on the basis of their performance. This has been particularly true for production workers. Before 1987, a system of performance evaluations existed at Hyundai, Kia Motors, and Kia Machine Tool so that there were differences in production workers' wages. This system was abolished at the demand of the unions. At Hyundai, the results of the performance evaluation are used in making promotion decisions only. Kia Machine Tool is considering reintroducing a performance evaluation system for production workers, but currently work performance is considered only when training opportunities come available or before transferring workers to other jobs. Daewoo Public Motors has a performance evaluation system, and annual wage increases differ depending on the results.

Daewoo Automotive Components, Sung Rim, and Seoul Metal still have systems of incentives, but the extent to which they are used has diminished since 1987. Sung Rim gives larger wage increases to performers who are in the top 5 percent of the company and an additional bonus to all workers when business is good. In 1992, for example, the fixed bonus was 600 percent of the basic payment. Since the company's sales had expanded very rapidly, an additional 25 percent bonus was given to nonproduction workers and an additional 100 percent to production workers. Seoul Metal, which used to have a system of performance evaluation before 1987, still has a system of incentives under which workers who do more than their assigned tasks are given larger-than-average wage increases. Sam Rip Industrial only recently introduced a performance evaluation system for its nonproduction workers. It does not have such a system for production workers.

Since 1987, the bonus allowance has also become a fixed amount, as a result of pressure from the unions. Further, once it is increased, the bonus allowance may not be lowered. This is reflected in the practices of Kia Machine Tool, which has been operating at a loss but still pays the same bonus.

In 1992, the Korean government advised private companies to introduce what it called a total payment system, or a performance incentive, and to pay wage increases above the government guidelines when performance improved. However, in companies that introduced this system, employees were given the higher wage increases regardless of the company's performance.

The wage increases at the eight companies have been very large since 1987. For example, at Seoul Metal, wages increased by 307.4 percent from 1988 to 1992, and the wages of production workers increased more than those of nonproduction workers. As of 1992, at Kia Motors the total monthly wage of a production worker with a high school degree and four years of work experience was 100,000 won (U.S. $1,250) higher than that of a new nonproduction worker with a university diploma.

Job Mobility and Employment Security. The workforce at the eight companies has been rather unstable, reflecting the rapid expansion of the Korean automotive industry and the high labor turnover. For example, at Kia Motors only 15 percent of the production workers had been there for more than seven years in 1992 and the average tenure of production workers was 4.4 years. At the small companies, such as Sung Rim and Seoul Metal, where jobs are much more demanding, the yearly turnover rates are more than 100 percent, since most of the new entrants leave after the first few months of joining the firm.

Since 1987, workers have enjoyed the full protection of their employment.[5] At Hyundai during the periods of 1970–73 and 1980–81, a large number of workers were laid off because of business restructuring. With the union's increased power since 1987, however, workforce restructuring has not been possible. Under the collective agreement at Kia Motors and Kia Machine Tool, the disciplinary committee consists of an equal number of representatives from the union and management, and dismissal of a production worker requires the approval of at least two-thirds of the members. Except in cases when the worker is found to be guilty of committing a criminal offense or is absent from the workplace for a certain period (ten consecutive days or fifteen days in a month) without notice, all dismissals need to be approved by the committee.

Hyundai, Kia Motors, and Kia Machine Tool's only retrenchment strategy has been not to replace workers who have left their jobs. They reduced the number of job openings or contracted out work, despite 1992 sales that fell below the expected level. In fact, at the time of the survey, Kia Machine Tool, whose 1992 balance was expected to be negative, was offering a lump-sum payment in addition to the legal severance payment for workers who wanted to leave the company voluntarily under a retrenchment scheme.

At the companies where the union has been very weak and at those companies that are not unionized, the workers have no such employment protection. In general, however, since these companies, such as Sung Rim

[5]New recruits are subject to a probation period of three months under the Labor Standards Act. In practice, however, most new recruits are given permanent status if they wish to stay with the firm.

and Seoul Metal, have always experienced labor shortages and the workers were protected by the Labor Standards Act, the workers have not had to worry about employment protection. At Daewoo Public Motors, for example, management was loath to discharge workers since the initial training costs were large. By contrast, Sung Rim, which experienced serious industrial disputes in 1987 and 1988, dismissed some workers who led the industrial action, thereby weakening the union.

Only a small number of employees at the eight companies have short-term contracts to do production work. Hyundai, Kia Motors, Daewoo Public Motors, and Kia Machine Tool, despite their large workforces, have no nonregular production workers. The smaller companies, such as Sung Rim and Seoul Metal, have found it relatively easy to adjust the size of their workforces to cyclical and structural changes since their turnover rates have been very high. These companies also had a few contract workers who were paid on a piece-rate system.

Firm Governance. Compared with the period before 1987, top management at Korea's automotive companies has become much more interested in industrial relations issues. In addition, more resources have been allocated to human resource functions. For example, Kia Motors has four departments that deal with industrial relations and human resource management issues: the personnel department for nonproduction workers; the sales manpower department for salespersons; and the personnel management department and the labor-management cooperation department for production workers. Nonetheless, top management makes important industrial relations decisions more often than it did before 1987. The human resources/industrial relations personnel are still not allowed to participate in determining the overall business strategies of the company.

The trade unions do not demand to participate in strategic decisions governing the enterprise as a whole, except those concerning wages and employment security. In fact, the unions do not generally have the internal human resources necessary to participate in the decision-making process.

Most unions ask to participate on their companies' disciplinary committees, but only Kia Motors and Kia Machine Tool actually have union representatives on even this one committee. The main reason for the rather negative attitude of the trade unions toward participating in the strategic decision making of the companies seems to be that they do not want to appear to be cooperating with management.

Effects of Industrial Relations and Human Resource Practices on Productivity

Since 1987, when a union was organized at Hyundai, industrial disputes have interrupted normal operations for almost one month each year. Sales per employee continued to increase, however, from 75 million won (U.S. $87,000) in 1986 to 140 million won (U.S. $178,000) in 1992. The number of car units produced per employee decreased from 19.3 in 1986 to 17.8 in 1989, then increased to 20.4 in 1992. Net profits with respect to sales per employee decreased from 2.0 percent in 1986 to 0.7 percent in 1992. Rising labor costs were a major contributing factor since the proportion of labor costs to total manufacturing costs increased from 4.3 percent to 10.6 percent in the same period.

The labor productivity indicators for Kia Motors since the mid-1980s are also mixed. Sales per employee increased from 70.4 million won (U.S. $82,000) in 1986 to 99.6 million won (U.S. $147,000) in 1989, then to 124.3 million won (U.S. $164,000) in 1991. The number of car units produced per employee increased from 11.4 in 1986 to 17.2 in 1989, then to 19.2 in 1991. Net profits per employee decreased from 2.1 million won (U.S. $2,444) in 1986 to 0.5 million won (U.S. $740) in 1989, then to 0.2 million won (U.S. $260) in 1991. Kia Motors' rising labor costs have been a major contributing factor to the continued decrease in the company's net profits, which is reflected in the proportion of labor costs to total manufacturing costs, which increased from 8.3 percent in 1986 to 9.5 percent in 1989, then to 11.6 percent in 1991. The number of defects per hundred units of cars decreased from 7.2 in 1987 to 4.9 in 1989, then to 3.3 in 1991. The take-time, which is defined as the length of time taken to produce a car in the assembly plant, decreased from 7 minutes in 1987 to 1.75 minutes in 1989, then increased to 2.2 minutes in 1990, then decreased again to 1.92 minutes in 1991. The sharp drop in the take-time over the period from 1987 to 1989 was mainly attributed to the reorganization of the work processes.

Despite the mixed productivity results in recent years, it is doubtful that at Hyundai and Kia Motors the workforces have contributed in an efficient way to the fast expansion of the company, particularly since 1987. Promotions for production workers are basically meaningless. The company has only permanent workers with well-protected employment security. The wages of individual workers do not depend on their performance (either as part of a team or as individuals), and the bonus payment is fixed. The performance evaluation system for production workers was abolished at the demand of the union. The demarcation between production and nonproduction jobs is very clearly defined. And even in the production area, the job rotation system is hardly implemented.

Kia Motors has a long history of dealing with trade unions, yet its largest plant was closed down for more than a month because of an industrial dispute. Training programs have not been offered in a systematic way, and the official job-control hierarchy has not worked well. Neither the workers nor the union seem to be interested in productivity improvement. Most of all, management still relies on traditional ways to handle industrial relations issues instead of incorporating the expertise of personnel staff.

Management at neither Hyundai nor Kia Motors has adopted new methods to handle industrial relations and human resource management matters. At Kia Motors, the only major measure management has taken has been to change the selection method for its new production workers. To some extent, management seems to be overwhelmed by the trade union, whose strength has increased substantially within a relatively short time. Management still pursues a "no-strike" policy as its sole industrial relations strategy, although it has taken a few positive initiatives aimed at utilizing its workforce more efficiently. By contrast, management at Hyundai seems to have at least begun to examine the issues in different ways since its industrial dispute of 1993.

Except for small surpluses in 1988 and 1989, Kia Machine Tool has suffered from a chronic deficit since the acquisition of a larger machinery company in 1986.[6] From 1987 to 1992, the labor cost per production worker increased 160 percent. Nonetheless, production workers enjoy full employment security, and in 1992, even with the deficit, the company offered voluntary leavers a lump-sum payment in addition to the legally required severance payment. Because there is a freeze on the hiring of new recruits, job rotation has not been implemented. The bonus is fixed, and the performance evaluation system for production workers was abolished in 1990. Shop-floor workers have only limited involvement in decision making concerning the organization of production work.

From 1987 to 1992, industrial disputes forced the plants to stop operating for one to one and a half months each year. There have been six different leaders of the local branch of the union since 1986. Because the union, until recently, was one of the leading groups in the Korea Trade Union Congress, political issues were often the cause of deadlocked negotiations.

[6]In the case of Daewoo Public Motors, it is too early to discuss the relationship between industrial relations and productivity since the company only recently began operating.

At Kia Machine Tool, the union clearly is not contributing to the process of productivity improvement. Until 1992, rivalries among factions of the union led to work stoppages every year. Yet despite the deficits, union members' employment security was fully protected and wages continued to increase over the years, mainly because of the presence of Kia Motors, which in case of bankruptcy could have saved Kia Machine Tool. Because of the frequent work stoppages, however, in 1992 Kia Motors reduced its order of auto parts from Kia Machine Tool. Finally, in February 1993, realizing the financial difficulties the company was facing, the union for Kia Machine Tools withdrew its membership from the Korea Trade Union Congress. Since then, the local union leader and the managing director of the company have been working together to regain the orders from Kia Motors, which are fundamental to Kia Machine Tool's survival. The management of Kia Machine Tool had also approached these issues from a shortsighted perspective of "no strikes." As the union showed signs of becoming more cooperative, however, the company announced that it was planning to introduce a performance evaluation system.

Daewoo Automotive Components experienced only one dispute from 1987 to 1992, yet the company still found it difficult to adjust to the new industrial relations environment. The company has sent some workers to Japan, hoping that they would develop a more cooperative spirit from the example of the Japanese; however, the trip does not appear to have particularly affected the attitudes of the Korean workers.

Sung Rim and Seoul Metal have managed their workforces more efficiently than Hyundai, Kia Motors, or Daewoo Public Motors. Most of the production workers have enjoyed the benefits of employment security; however, management has used various measures to control the workers. Some portion of their wages depend on their individual performance and/or the company's profitability. Also, management seems to have more authority to relocate production workers than at Hyundai, Kia Motors, or Kia Machine Tool.

Economic performance at Sung Rim and Seoul Metal has been remarkable in recent years. Their sales increased more than three to five times during the period from 1987 to 1992. Furthermore, the two companies enjoyed reasonable profits. The number of workers increased at only a modest rate at Sung Rim, whereas it decreased at Seoul Metal over the same period. Our survey revealed, however, that the no-union strategy at Sung Rim was perceived to have contributed to the company's success. There is no union at Seoul Metal.

What implications can be drawn from our analysis of the effects of the new industrial relations/human resource management practices on the economic performance of the eight enterprises we surveyed? First, as Richard Freeman and James Medoff (1984) have argued, labor unions can play two different roles in affecting the efficiency of the economy of a workplace, as well as the economy at the national level. On the one hand, unions can work to raise members' wages, which may adversely affect the efficiency of the economy. On the other hand, unions can have positive effects on productivity by providing information to management on what occurs on the shop floor as well as to union members about the business performance of the company. Unions can also help in the development and retention of skills by providing a voice for workers at the workplace.

Our study shows that since 1987 unions have become one of the most powerful institutions in Korea. The unions at the companies we surveyed are interested primarily in raising the wages and improving the working conditions of their members. The unions appear to have no interest in participating in activities aimed at either productivity improvements or work redesign.

The unions have provided some protection for workers against arbitrary management decisions. Management often complains, however, that the workers cannot be disciplined, even with justifiable cause, mainly because of the presence of the unions. The leaders of the unions, according to management, are mostly interested in keeping their positions (i.e., winning the next election). This makes them afraid of appearing to cooperate with management. In the large companies, the official control mechanisms on the shop floor do not work effectively.

Who should be blamed for this? Surely, the unions are not solely responsible for the companies' poor productivity. Management at all the companies appears to be interested in maintaining industrial peace. In other words, their main objective is "no strikes." Management does not recognize the possible collective voice/institutional response face of unions. The view of management toward unions is demonstrated at Sung Rim, where the union was almost dissolved or has become nonfunctioning as a result of management's actions.

Our study did not investigate the ways in which unions might make a positive impact on productivity at the plant level. The role of the state is crucial, however. The government's wage policy has not changed. It has continued to intervene in private-sector wage determinations while preventing the emergence of strong and responsible union leaders by depriving workers of the right to choose their own representatives. By failing to democratize labor market institutions, the government has helped to prolong the interunion conflict that has limited the potential for reform of a tripartite kind. Industrial relations at the workplace are still strongly influenced by the political situation of the country. Labor and management struggle over political issues that often cannot be addressed appropriately at the workplace. This problem is more serious since the political activities of unions at the workplace are not coordinated by strong leadership at the national center.

The Korean business structure also helps to strengthen the bargaining power of unions. Even with shrinking business, production workers are hardly ever laid off, as evidenced in the case of Kia Machine Tool. The Korean business structure also makes the unions in large enterprises less sensitive to business fluctuations. Kia Motors and Kia Machine Tool belong to the same conglomerate. The bankruptcy of Kia Machine Tool would most likely lead to severe problems for Kia Motors. The bankruptcy of Kia Motors would damage the Korean economy. The government would probably then take some action to save Kia Motors. This is in part why the union at Kia Machine Tool demands high wage increases despite the troubles of the company. Ironically, this logic is also used to justify the continued intervention by the government in private-sector industrial relations.

Medium or small-scale enterprises seem to be adjusting more easily than the larger companies to the new industrial relations environment. In the medium or small companies, more initiatives tend to be undertaken to improve the use of labor. Performance evaluation systems still exist. This is not only because of the size of these enterprises. These companies are also more or less financially independent. It is assumed that other firms in the same conglomerate as Kia Motors and Kia Machine Tool or even the government will help these companies in times of financial difficulties.

Both the unions and the production workers might be persuaded to make a strong commitment to productivity improvement if they fully understood the financial difficulties their companies are facing. At Kia Machine Tool, the union became more cooperative with management when the company was forced to reduce the size of the workforce. In general, however, neither management nor the unions seem to have constructive and efficient human resource skills. Our survey found that little communication existed between management, unions, and employees at the workplace level.

Diffusion of Lean Production Practices in Korea

The slow diffusion of Japanese lean production practices in Korea is due, to a large extent, to differences in industrial relations and human resource management practices between Korea and Japan. First, in Japanese auto companies, all workers are given performance evaluations as well as skill tests, and wages as well as promotions are differentiated among individual workers. Production workers' careers also depend on their skills and contribution to the company.

Second, in Japanese companies, core industrial relations and human resource management practices, such as compensation schemes, skill formation, and staffing arrangements, are interrelated. One of the characteristics of the Japanese HR management system is that it induces workers to develop and upgrade their skills on their own. By introducing a skills-based payment system, Japanese workers increase their pay only if their skill levels meet certain requirements. Before placing a worker in a particular job, the skill level of the worker is also considered.

Third, the Japanese companies rely on temporary workers, who are laid off during difficult times. There are no such nonregular workers in the Korean companies. Thus, they have less flexibility in managing their workforces.

Fourth, and finally, the HR systems in the Japanese companies generally seem to be considered fair. Performance evaluations are based on the self-reports of the workers, although the results are open to wider scrutiny.

Conclusions

The most crucial task ahead for the Korean automotive industry is for labor and management at the workplace to establish a constructive relationship. As the results of our study indicate, however, this is not going to be easy. The scope of strategic choices for management is very limited. Management has lost a major opportunity to enhance labor productivity by not adopting appropriate compensation schemes. With the increased influence of the trade unions on wage determination in the large companies, performance-related factors have been virtually abolished from the payment scheme. In addition, opportunities for payment system reform are very limited, even at individual enterprises, because of the continued intervention of the government in wage determinations at the enterprise level. The employment security of the workers at the surveyed companies has become even stronger. Layoffs for business restructuring are very limited, and dismissals are rarely used. Because of this inflexibility in management's ability to manage the size of its workforces, management's authority over staffing arrangements has been weakened. The formal mechanisms for work control in the large enterprises do not function well. Workers tend to solve their grievances through their union representatives, rather than dealing directly with management.

Given these limitations, the only area for initiative available to management at the enterprise level seems to be to promote the skill development of its workers. Korean firms in the automotive industry have been reluctant to invest in training and education in part because Korean workers are so mobile. In recent years, however, some workers at larger enterprises (particularly male production workers with more than three years of tenure) are staying longer than in the past (Uh 1992). This can be interpreted as caused in part by the expansion of union activities, reflecting the "exit-voice effect." This finding also implies that creating a highly skilled workforce can reduce one of the main obstacles to upgrading production workers' skills.

Skills development should be pursued along with other human resource management strategies. The goal of the new human resource management system should be the maximization of workers' skills, together with the reform of the compensation scheme and staffing arrangements. A performance evaluation system could be used together with skill evaluation schemes to promote the skills of workers, and greater flexibility in the staffing arrangements could then be used to further develop skills.

The role of the state in Korea's manpower development mechanism should also be reformed. Indirect regulation by the government of vocational training is more desirable than direct involvement. More resources are required for retraining programs in the public vocational training institutes to accompany the continued upgrading of Korea's industrial structure. The role of the government in Korea's manpower development system will continue to be increasingly important since there has been market failure in the area of training.

To increase the flexibility of its workforces, management may want to further differentiate internal labor markets. The recent decrease in the number of regular workers indicates that some firms are making this strategic choice. This is not necessarily the best choice from a national perspective, however, given that more than two million people in Korea are in state-run livelihood protection programs and more than six million workers are not covered under the Labor Standards Act. The Korean government needs to undertake further efforts to increase social welfare wages for these deprived groups of workers.

Postscript

In December 1996 and January 1997, a general strike erupted in Korea that closed down the auto industry. The strike was called to protest a set of labor law amendments enacted by the government that made it easier for Korean firms to lay off workers and delayed for several years implementation of an agreed-upon set of changes in labor law that would have legalized the unions that are not part of the national Korean Federation of Trade Unions. The auto industry unions were among the largest of those affected by this delay and so this industry was one of the most directly and heavily affected by the strike. Eventually, the government was forced to modify the new legislation in response to the strikes and the protests of such international agencies as the Organization for Economic Cooperation and Development and the International Labor Organization. Thus, Korea continues to experience periods of relative quiet only to be interrupted by spikes of strike activity. All this suggests that the future of the auto industry in Korea continues to depend in large part on how the government and the employer community come to grips with the democratic labor movement.

PART **IV**

After Lean Production

16 Conclusion: After Lean Production?

Thomas A. Kochan, Russell D. Lansbury, and John Paul MacDuffie

We began this project by asking whether a new system of production and associated employment practices was diffusing across the automobile industry around the world. Our starting point was the assertion by Womack, Jones, and Roos (1990) that lean production was a universally applicable system and that those firms that did not adopt it would sooner or later be squeezed out of the market.

The data presented in the previous chapters show that there has been considerable diffusion of lean production principles to auto plants around the world in recent years. This finding reflects a continuation of a longer-term trend dating as far back as at least the mid-1980s. The case study evidence, however, suggests that the patterns that are emerging are not as singular in cause, character, or effect as Womack, Jones, and Roos (1990) predicted they would be. Moreover, what we are observing is not movement toward some new stable or steady state but what looks to be an ongoing transformation of work and employment practices to meet the demands of an evolving global marketplace. Like other experiences involving the transfer of organizational innovations, the process of adopting lean production principles has not resulted in their exact duplication or imitation. Instead, we observe interesting and important variations that reflect differences in the strategies and power of the parties involved in the transfer and learning process, as well as the effects of local institutional and cultural forces.

A key lesson that emerges from the case studies in this volume is that the decisions involved in whether or not to adopt lean production are part of a larger range of strategic choices available to firms, unions, and governments, many of which could influence the course of developments in industry. Some companies have not chosen to adopt lean production in some (or all) of their locations because its organizational and labor relations requirements are not consistent with their managerial values and traditions. Others have placed cost reduction and minimization ahead of lean production as an objective. Still others have chosen to focus on maximizing the production of popular models. Thus, the principles underlying lean production compete with other corporate concerns. Unions also have broader agendas that affect how they represent their members' interests. Whereas some have incorporated the principles of lean production into their strategies, others have not. Finally, government policies influence the environment in which the auto industry competes in a country and, through labor policy, affects union-management relations. These policies in turn influence firm and union strategies. Some of these government policies support while others reduce the likelihood that lean production will be adopted or sustained in manufacturing in general and auto manufacturing in particular.

We begin this chapter by summarizing the general conclusions we draw from the cross-national survey data and case study findings presented in the preceding chapters. We then illustrate these findings by drawing on the cases themselves. The final section outlines the implications we draw from this work for future policy and research.

Overview of the Findings

The changes in production and employment practices that are being adopted in auto manufacturing plants around the world are part of a broader transformation in employment and organizational practices that has been under way for more than a decade (Piore and Sabel 1984; Kochan, Katz, and McKersie 1992; Locke, Kochan, and Piore 1995). In response to changing international markets and technologies, firms have been seeking to increase their flexibility, lower their costs, and in some cases involve employees in efforts to improve enterprise performance. Thus, rather than viewing the diffusion of lean production as an isolated or recent phenomenon, we see it as part of the broader transformation of work, employment, and organizational practices occurring in a wide variety of industries around the world. That is why we emphasize the need to view the concept of lean production broadly, not just as a set of manufacturing practices but as an interrelated set of production, organizational, and human resource practices that when implemented together constitute a more flexible system of work and production than the traditional mass production system it seeks to replace.

MacDuffie and Pil's survey data show a general trend toward the adoption of lean production principles in auto plants around the world. Few plants that have been in operation for some time have adopted the complete bundle of lean practices, however. Rather, the process of transforming an existing physical facility and labor-management relationship is often more incremental or piecemeal in nature. This pattern gives rise to several hybrid arrangements (Boyer and Freyssenet 1995). Between 1989 and 1993 (between the time of the first and second rounds of the MIT International Motor Vehicle Program assembly plant surveys), European plants showed the largest movement in this direction, while plants in North America showed a slower pattern of diffusion. This is not surprising, since many of the American plants that implemented lean production principles had already done so by 1989.

Further, focusing on the net effects of the changes since 1989 suggests that regional and national variations have become less important and highlights differences across companies. By looking more closely both across and within regions and companies, we can achieve a better understanding of the variables that influence the adoption and diffusion of lean production principles. We believe that several variables explain the pattern of diffusion observed to date.

Exposure to International Competition. Like other industries, by far the strongest force influencing the adoption of new organizing principles in the auto industry is exposure to international competition. Those facilities that must compete on both cost and quality criteria with products from around the world experience the greatest pressure to adopt lean production principles. The reason is quite simple. Introducing an integrated bundle of flexible human resource practices and lean production techniques leads to higher levels of quality and productivity than can be achieved with traditional mass production techniques. Lean production plants also are able to manufacture a wider product mix within the same facility than more traditional plants. They also achieve higher levels of performance than plants that invest heavily in technology and automation without transforming mass production work systems and human resource practices. Thus, there are performance advantages associated with this system. It is not surprising, therefore, that the 1993 survey showed that the plants with the poorest productivity and quality performance in 1989 made the most changes in human resource and work organization practices.

Employer Choices. Not all firms responded to globalization of the industry in the same way. Some, such as GM, Volkswagen, and Fiat, initially tried a high-technology strategy that they eventually abandoned. Others have continued to view production and human resource issues as secondary, especially in plants that are producing hot-selling, high-profit products. Chrysler in the United States, for instance, has viewed continuity of production of its profitable minivans, sport utility vehicles, and light trucks as more important to its success than adopting and implementing lean principles in their manufacturing operations. Other companies, such as GM, have given top priority to lowering their costs of manufacturing by outsourcing products and components and pressuring suppliers for significant cost reductions. Other companies, such as the major Korean producers, continue to manage operations in a highly authoritarian style that is incompatible with the delegation of decision-making authority embodied in the work organization and human resource practices of lean production. In still other firms, top executives espouse support for lean principles but fail to translate them into practice.

Strong managerial support and commitment from top management are necessary conditions for any organizational change effort to succeed. The shift to lean production is no exception to this general rule. Thus, for lean production strategies to be adopted and diffused throughout a company (or specific facility), top management must be strongly commited and supportive of this process of change. For management to become committed, lean production must fit with the company's overall strategy of how it chooses to compete in the array of markets that exist in the auto industry. Management does not act alone in this industry, however. Two other actors—namely, labor unions and governments—play key roles in influencing the choice and nature of work practices.

Union Choices. The auto industry is one of the most highly unionized in the world. Except for the Japanese and German transplants in the United States, all the assembly plants surveyed as part of the MIT study are unionized. Thus, the nature of the union-management relationship and the particular vision and strategy of the unions that represent autoworkers in a facility exert major influences on the production and employment practices that are adopted. The case studies identified three different union responses to lean production concepts.

1. *Union Acceptance of Managerial Initiative.* A large number of the cases in which unions have accepted managerial initiatives to implement lean

production involve Japanese transplants or joint ventures. NUMMI in the United States, the Nissan plant in Britain, and the Honda-Rover plant in Britain are three examples. Although in each of these cases, like others, there was a significant amount of negotiation over the specific features of the production and human resource plan, the initiative and general proposal came from the employer. The unions involved generally accepted these proposals because to reject them would have meant the loss of significant numbers of job opportunities. In the case of NUMMI, the plant would have remained closed. In the case of Nissan, the new plant would not have been opened. In the case of Honda-Rover, the New Deal agreement was a last-ditch effort to stop and reverse the loss of jobs.

In some of the nonunion Japanese transplants that were opened in the United States in the 1980s, including Toyota, Nissan, and Honda, Japanese managers implemented variants of the lean production system. Thus, where managers serve as the dominant driving force in designing the production system, and especially when they are given the opportunity to design a greenfield facility and to hire a new workforce, lean principles are being widely used.

2. *Union Resistance in Adversarial Labor-Management Relationships.* Where adversarial relations exist, lean production principles diffuse slowly and partially since the full commitment and motivation and trust of the workforce cannot be achieved. This is one of the reasons we observe a relatively slow rate of diffusion of lean production principles within existing U.S. plants. Korean plants have implemented relatively few lean production principles, in part because of the long history of authoritarian management and in part because of the suppression of labor rights before 1987 and the high level of labor-management conflict that erupted after the government reduced restrictions on workers and unions in that year. As witnessed by the eruption of a general strike in Korea in late 1996 over labor law amendments, these adversarial traditions continue to dominate in this country. In such settings, managers are reluctant to decentralize authority to workers and engineers continue to attempt to build buffers and controls into the technology and manufacturing process rather than allow workers to use their discretion to eliminate variances and solve problems.

3. *Union-Management Partnership and/or Union Initiative.* Some unions have developed partnerships with employers and jointly negotiated agreements to implement some or all of the work organization and human resource management practices embodied in lean production. Moreover, some unions have developed their own vision and strategy for how to adapt

these practices so as to address their members' interests in achieving improved wages, security, and working conditions. The experiences of Saturn in the United States, the metalworkers union at Volvo and Saab in Sweden, the German metalworkers union, and the National Union of Metalworkers in South Africa serve as instructive examples of this approach. It is in these settings that we may be getting a glimpse of the employment relationships that lie beyond lean production. For this reason we will highlight some of these examples below as we review in more detail developments in various countries.

Government Policies. Macroeconomic and national labor policies play important roles in shaping the environment in which firms and unions choose their production strategies and establish their labor-management relationships. Because of the strategic importance of the auto industry to their economic development strategies, several newly industrializing countries have maintained protective barriers that limit the access of foreign competitors to their domestic markets. In some cases these barriers are erected in an effort to support the development of an internationally competitive auto industry. Korea, Brazil, and South Africa all fit this pattern. As these countries reduce their tariff barriers to conform to world trade agreements, the pressure to adapt to lean production principles increases.

In the case of Korea, for example, Alice Amsden and Jong-Yeol Kang argue that "instead of getting into a lean production mode as soon as possible, the 'Big Three (producers)' in Korea have tried to upscale step-by-step, adopting some but not all practices from advanced automobile makers, and keeping an open mind about how to improve" (1995:13). This observation is supported by evidence from the case study by Park and Lee in chapter 15 that the Korean auto industry remains strongly Tayloristic. Amsden and Kang concede that lean production may be an important goal but claim that it is not a practical proposition during the early phases of the "catch-up process" with more advanced economies. Similar views are expressed in chapter 14 with regard to the auto industry in Brazil, where the unions have sought to modify the introduction of lean production systems to fit better with the lessons learned from colleagues in the German metalworkers union. In South Africa, the government's Reconstruction Development Plan gives high priority to human resource development as part of its labor-intensive development strategy. This government policy influenced the strategies of the metalworkers union and the industry in their negotiation of agreements that voice support for lean production and work organization principles combined with an exceptionally strong commitment to skills development and training.

Organizational Learning and Implementation. Our case studies demonstrated that it is much easier to adopt the principles of lean production than it is to implement them and obtain the expected performance improvements. Analysis of the second round of survey data showed that the later adopters of some lean production practices have not achieved the same performance results as the earlier adopters. It may be that it takes time to learn how to get the most out of these practices. An alternative interpretation, which we favor but cannot prove conclusively, is that implementing the practices of lean production per se does not determine success. What is required is an organization characterized by flexibility, problem solving, and motivation, which lean practices are designed to encourage. In some plants, however, lean production practices have been accompanied by considerable downsizing and/or layoffs that served to counteract the behavioral and motivational benefits of these practices. Likewise, in some Chrysler plants, modern operating agreements were negotiated under the threat of plant closure but local managers and union leaders lacked the skills and the commitment to change their relationships in ways that would have translated the flexibility embodied in these agreements into positive results.

Lessons from the Case Studies

It is apparent from the case studies that although the lean production debate has affected all the countries involved in our project, a variety of factors have influenced the extent to which there has been diffusion or adaptation of the main principles of the system. Most European automobile firms reacted to the downturn in the market during the early 1990s and intense global competition by undertaking changes that were directly or indirectly inspired by this system. Although the result in many cases was substantial transformation of the old systems of production, as Camuffo and Micelli claim in chapter 10, the new patterns that emerged were generally idiosyncratic and nonlinear: they were nation-specific, firm-specific, and plant-specific. Accordingly, they coined the term "Mediterranean lean" to describe the new production systems that they observed in plants in Italy, France, and Spain. In their view, the Mediterranean model puts greater emphasis on the role of supervisors in leading teams of workers than is typical in lean production plants in the United States or other parts of Europe.

Since one of the primary objectives of our study has been to examine the interaction between changes in production systems and employee relations at the plant level in different countries and to observe new patterns that are emerging, it is instructive to examine the main features of our case studies that illuminate this debate.

Japan. As noted above, significant changes have affected the Japanese auto industry in recent years. Most notable was the rise in the value of the yen between 1990 and 1994, which made it increasingly difficult to sell cars produced in Japan on the international market. Fujimoto (1994) argues that the lean production model is no longer the best theoretical benchmark to use for Japan and that the industry has moved into a "post-lean" phase. Our Japanese case study, in chapter 3, which focuses on two major firms, suggests that Fujimoto's interpretation overstates the degree of change. The key features of the classic lean production system are still in place in the major plants of these firms. Ishida also argues that the key to understanding the success of the Japanese in recent years has been the degree of managerial control that operates at the shop-floor level through supervisors, although production workers also play a greater role in quality and cost-control issues than would normally be anticipated in a mass production manufacturing environment and have a high level of skills. As the reward system moves from seniority-based to ability-based wages, however, the traditional collective approach to employee relations is under challenge.

Our Japanese research team agrees with Fujimoto that Japanese companies are also facing a challenge in finding sufficiently high-skilled jobs for the number of workers whose competence is now very high. Toyota's Kyushu plant, which was opened in 1992, introduced several worker-friendly technological innovations and represents an effort to humanize auto work and thereby attract the skilled labor required. The case clearly points to new challenges facing the Japanese auto industry as it seeks to maintain its leading international role and successfully adjust to the demands by Japanese employees for more meaningful work. These challenges appear to suggest movement in the direction of a post-lean production system for the future; however, the stagnant Japanese economy, coupled with the high value of the yen, also means that much Japanese manufacturing investment will continue to gravitate to other countries where the products are to be sold or to other Asian countries where the labor costs are lower.

United States. The U.S. auto manufacturers and unions engaged in extensive experimentation and testing of work system reforms and employee-participation efforts throughout the 1980s. Although these innovations built on more modest experiments with quality of work life programs started in the 1970s, it was the dramatic increase in competition from the Japanese producers throughout the 1980s that gave urgency and momentum to this experimentation. With the arrival of Honda, Nissan, and especially NUMMI in the mid-1980s, Japanese lean production techniques demonstrated their viability and performance potential on American soil with American workers and with the American UAW at NUMMI. During this same period, GM and the UAW jointly designed the boldest new organizational form—the Saturn Corporation. At Saturn, lean production principles blend with a broad-ranging role for union representatives in the management and governance of the company.

These transplants, along with a few U.S. plants that introduced team concepts and employee participation before the Japanese transplants were created (such as GM's Shreveport plant and the Pontiac Fiero plant in Ohio), served as benchmarks for other experiments, such as the Chrysler Corporation's modern operating agreement plants. Thus, most of the U.S. plants that have implemented some or all of the lean production principles had begun to do so before publication of *The Machine That Changed the World* (Womack, Jones, and Roo 1990). As MacDuffie and Pil's survey data indicate, relatively little diffusion of these concepts occurred between 1989 and 1994. Instead, this period was dominated by efforts by GM to close a number of its plants and downsize its blue- and white-collar workforce and source components with the lowest-cost suppliers and by increasing conflicts with the UAW over these issues. Ford, meanwhile, more quietly continued to follow its incremental approach to changing production and work organization arrangements in its plants by focusing on quality improvement techniques and related human resource management practices, while Chrysler negotiated a number of modern operating agreements that embodied the full range of work organization, human resource, and manufacturing principles of lean production but moved slowly in putting them into practice. As a result, North American plants now exhibit among the widest range of practices found anywhere in the world.

Canada. Although the American and Japanese companies with plants in Canada attempt to follow essentially the same strategies as they do in the United States, opposition by the Canadian Auto Workers Union to certain aspects of lean production and team systems of work organization have produced a more mixed pattern of practices across firms. The union has chosen to guard its independence carefully and to avoid partnership arrangements with plant managers. At the same time, the union brings its own views regarding work practices, ergonomic principles, and worker voice into enterprise decision making via the collective bargaining process. The result is an incremental adjustment strategy and a pattern that mixes both traditional mass production or Fordist with lean or flexible manufacturing and labor-management practices. To date, Canadian plants that have introduced this mix of practices have performed well and, with the help of a favorable exchange rate with the U.S. dollar and the country's lower health insurance costs, have remained competitive.

Germany. The lean production "revolution" in Germany during the 1990s was a catalyst for major debate between employers and trade unions. The key elements of reform sought by employers included teamwork, continuous improvement activities, and outsourcing/subcontracting of non-core activities. IG Metall saw this move as an opportunity to introduce human-centered qualities of the lean production system and to obtain greater influence over work design through works councils, while the employers hoped to deregulate certain areas of codetermination. It was hoped that any adverse employment conditions would be offset by growth in production volume in the newly opened markets of Eastern Europe. When the recession came in 1993, however, the additional capacity built up in the East (e.g., new Opel and VW plants) only increased the pressure to reduce production in the former West Germany.

Views about the German auto industry's adaptation to lean production vary. Jürgens claims in chapter 6 that the existence of the codetermination system combined with the strength of unions in Germany's auto industry resulted in agreements that ensured that employment security would be maintained as a prerequisite for the introduction of lean production. Roth argues in chapter 7, however, that the unions' hopes for lean production were dashed during the recession when it became clear that the workforce was seen largely as a cost factor that had to be reduced. Indeed, Roth argues that the new greenfield Opel plant in Eisenach (formerly in East Germany) marks the beginning of a trend toward the introduction of concepts developed in Japanese transplants in North America. In Eisenach, according to Roth, the view is that high levels of performance are gained not from increasing employee motivation and interest in job content but from instituting narrowly prescribed, standardized, conveyor belt–dependent work. (Eisenach, as MacDuffie and Pil noted, was modeled on what GM learned from its experience at NUMMI.)

Roth also notes that the German auto industry's production strategies have been characterized by a zigzag course of changing orientations rather than by continuity. He cites success in the widespread introduction of group work among skilled workers (though not on the assembly line) and claims that there is no reason to give up hope even in the face of "Taylorized group work" in many assembly areas.

United Kingdom. The British auto industry has experienced several decades of decline, although production by U.K.-based Japanese companies has expanded rapidly since the latter half of the 1980s. The case study in chapter 8 of the joint venture between Honda and British Leyland at the Cowley plant provides an opportunity to analyze the application of lean production combined with a more cooperative approach to employee relations.

In 1992, a new assembly facility was opened at Cowley that replaced the original plant. Management was restructured, and hundreds of workers were transferred to new jobs. Both output and productivity per worker increased substantially during the following years.

Several factors contributed to the success of the Cowley plant, including improvements in logistics, greater capacity utilization, reductions in rectification costs, and greater labor flexibility. A new collective agreement was reached with the unions, known as the New Deal, under which there would be no unconstitutional industrial action and any unresolved dispute would be referred to an independent arbitrator for a binding decision. Although such an arrangement may be characterized as a new British form of lean production, Scarbrough and Terry note that the agreement was secured with the unions at a time when their bargaining power had been greatly reduced and management discretion was very high. Whether this new approach can be sustained over time and becomes the prevailing mode of auto assembly operations in Britain remains to be seen. It is worth noting that since the case study was concluded, Honda has withdrawn from the joint venture with Rover and the company is now fully owned by BMW. This means that there is no longer any wholly British-owned, high-volume automobile producer.

Italy. Fiat underwent a major restructuring at the beginning of the 1990s and introduced the concept of the integrated factory at two greenfield sites in southern Italy. The key principles include a process- rather than a functionally based organizational structure, integration of operations (direct work) and production engineering (indirect work), the introduction of relatively autonomous and self-managing manufacturing cells, and employee involvement. Underpinning Fiat's strategy is an agreement with the unions that covers such issues as work organization and cycle times, compensation systems, and mechanisms for employee consultation and involvement.

In Fiat's integrated factories, the unions do not codesign the work organization, although they are consulted during the implementation phase of new activities. The unions have cooperated with the strategy, but they are concerned about the long-term job security of their members, especially under increasingly lean forms of production. The Fiat case does not represent a "pure" lean production model, however. A strong heritage of Taylorism and unilateral managerial decision making still exist. It therefore remains to be seen what direction the Italian form of lean production will take in the future.

Sweden. The Swedish auto industry, although small by world standards, has long been regarded as a leading example of a production industry that has taken a more human-focused approach to work organization and production. Volvo became well known for its initiatives in sociotechnical work design in the early 1970s at its Kalmar plant and during the 1980s at Uddevalla. The decline in Volvo's fortunes, however, led to the closing of these two plants in the 1990s and the consolidation of production at the larger and more conventional Torslanda plant. Berggren (1995) argues that Volvo has now "normalized" its approach to production and follows a lean trajectory, thus ending an exciting period of "exceptionalism."

Nevertheless, according to Berggren, Volvo's approach has a distinctly Swedish flavor: management structures are less hierarchical; team leaders are rotated and are elected by workers rather than appointed by management; a strong sociotechnical approach to work design exists in such areas as the body shop and the door assembly and engine plant; and the role of the unions remains strong. There is now a new strategic focus on the core business, and a more active product development policy has been initiated. In chapter 11, a case study of the main Volvo car assembly plant at Torslanda, Brulin and Nilsson claim that although recent changes have embodied some elements of a lean production system, there is still a strong emphasis on group work. On the one hand, most operators report that the new system has resulted in better-structured work, more interesting job content, and fewer problems with repetitive strain injury. On the other hand, greater automation has meant that some jobs have become simplified and more arduous and the pace of work has increased.

The case study of Saab provides some valuable contrasts to Volvo. Because of financial difficulties, Saab sold 50 percent of its automobile company to General Motors in 1989 and the remaining 50 percent in 1996. A new production system was introduced in 1990 that streamlined assembly operations (making them more lean) but that also gave work groups a wider range of skills and responsibilities. The unions were more critical of Saab than of Volvo, however, claiming that there had been a reversion to the assembly line system under which work was more strictly controlled and intensified. Nevertheless, like Volvo, Saab has been able to achieve a remarkable partial turnaround while retaining and even developing its own approaches to production and employee relations. Now that Saab is wholly owned by GM, more changes are likely. This will be a case worth watching since in 1996 GM installed an executive from its Saturn Division as the head of Saab, suggesting that yet another hybrid strategy may emerge reflecting a mixture of Saturn and Saab principles.

Australia. During the past decade, the auto industry in Australia has undergone significant structural change. Tariff protection for local producers is gradually being lowered to enable a more efficient and competitive industry to develop. The number of companies operating in Australia has been reduced, so that only four companies (two Japanese- and two U.S.-owned) have plants. There are no locally owned manufacturers. In the past, most plants had low levels of automation, low output by international standards, and poor productivity. Foreign-owned companies were unwilling to undertake large capital investments and long-term future commitments, so that plants generally became outdated and inefficient. Toyota opened a major new plant in 1994, however, and Mitsubishi has expanded its production facilities with the objective of exporting vehicles to Japan and elsewhere. Ford and GM have also made new investments in plant and equipment in order to boost their export capacities.

The case studies in chapter 12 of Australia's four plants indicate that productivity and quality have improved markedly in recent years, new production concepts have been applied (especially in the Japanese transplants), training has increased substantially and skills have been upgraded, and significant improvements have occurred in employee relations as a result of enterprise-level agreements between unions and employers in the industry.

The new Toyota plant incorporates many elements of lean production, but an enterprise agreement provides the potential for the workers and their unions to exercise a strong influence in decisions at the workplace. This arrangement may create the opportunity for a form of lean production to emerge in the future that will incorporate a stronger Australian "accent."

South Africa. With its seven automobile companies producing thirty-nine models for a market of only 300,000 units annually, the South African auto industry is overtraded and inefficient by international standards. In 1992, a motor industry task group, appointed by the government to develop a long-term strategy for the industry, encouraged South Africa's auto companies to continue to produce high-volume models only, thereby recommending a drastic rationalization, accompanied by a large reduction in tariff protection.

The National Union of Metal Workers of South Africa, the main union covering workers in the auto industry, has played a significant role in developing a coherent industrywide policy on human resources and skills development. A collective agreement between NUMSA and the employers in 1991 provides for training by individual firms to be recognized across the industry so that skills will be regarded as portable and workers will be provided with career paths.

Hirschorn's case studies in chapter 13 of the Toyota and Volkswagen plants in South Africa indicate that so far only limited attempts have been made to reorganize and rationalize the industry along the lines the task force recommended. An upsurge in recent domestic sales has diverted attention from the industry's poor productivity levels and inadequate human resource development, thereby delaying recommended reforms. Pressures to introduce lean production techniques are likely to come as the industry begins to compete within the international market rather than continuing to be protected. The strength of NUMSA, however, is likely to ensure that the introduction of any new production systems will need to involve the workforce and their union representatives in decision making.

Brazil. The development and operation of the auto industry in Brazil has been subject to close government involvement, and the fortunes of the industry have reflected the cycles of boom and bust that have characterized the Brazilian economy in recent decades. During the 1990s, the government embarked on a program of economic liberalization that included reductions in tariffs from 60 percent (in 1991) to 35 percent (by

1994). Although this measure was designed to make the industry more competitive internationally, foreign auto producers questioned whether they should continue to manufacture their products in Brazil unless costs could be lowered.

The two case studies in chapter 14, of General Motors and Mercedes-Benz Brazil, provide examples of plants that have become more efficient in recent years by incorporating changes in their production systems as well as improving their employee relations. General Motors Brazil has introduced several innovations at the São Caetano plant, based on the model followed at the NUMMI plant in the United States. At São Caetano, new technical and organizational concepts have been integrated, and emphasis has been placed on continuous improvement based on the use of work teams. At the São Bernardo plant of Mercedes-Benz Trucks, management presented the workforce with a proposal entitled Factory 2000, which outlined a type of lean production system. After sending a group to visit its counterpart union in Germany, however, the metalworkers union responded with its own proposals, which argued for plant restructuring to be combined with improvements in working conditions. An agreement was concluded in 1994 that endorsed the introduction of teamwork and group technology in the context of a manufacturing cell concept. This approach has provided an example of modified lean production achieved through negotiation. Both the GMB and Mercedes cases illustrate the influence a parent company's experiences and practices can have on local operations and employment practices.

Korea. The Korean auto industry has grown very rapidly during the past decade, and Korea is forecast to be among the top-five automobile-producing countries by the turn of the century. Although strongly influenced by the Japanese, particularly during the early phase of development, the Korean industry remains strongly Tayloristic and is still in a mass production mode. Korean industrial relations have been in a process of dynamic change since the democratization of political and economic institutions began in 1987. On the one hand, although the number of strikes has declined from the highest point in the period 1987–89, rising wage costs and labor shortages continue to be a concern. On the other hand, unions complain about autocratic management practices, and strike waves continue to occur periodically, as evident by the increase in strike activity in 1996 and the general strike over labor law reforms that erupted in December 1996 and continued into early 1997.

It is apparent from the case studies in chapter 15 of three major Korean companies that management strategies vary considerably. Hence, although one auto producer continued to be plagued by industrial disputes, another was considered to be a model of progressive employment relations. On the whole, however, the industry has yet to implement major reforms in the employee relations area, which remains highly conflictual. Although Korean auto producers have experienced outstanding growth in the world market in recent years, their continued success may depend on their ability to adopt to new systems of management and employee relations in their plants in Korea and abroad. Their history does not bode well in this regard and we would thus temper predictions about the future growth of Korean firms in the global auto industry with this history in mind.

Actors and Choices That Will Shape the Future

The case study evidence broadly reinforces MacDuffie and Pil's survey results, which show a trend toward greater convergence across countries combined with divergence across and within companies. The Japanese transplants in the United States, the United Kingdom, and Australia have demonstrated that it is possible for companies to achieve high performance while making few modifications to the lean practices that they developed in their home plants. Many companies have used the Japanese producers (and Toyota in particular) as benchmarks against which to measure their performance. The failure of a number of U.S. and European firms to achieve breakthroughs by means of either high-tech strategies (as in the cases of GM, Fiat, and Volkswagen) or sociotechnical systems (as in earlier experiments by Volvo and Saab) underscores the competitive advantages of lean production. At the same time, there appears to be some convergence between companies on a regional basis, so that many European firms are seeking alliances, if not mergers, in an effort to withstand the challenge from Japan. Thus, although there is convergence around matters of principle (such as the desirability of lean production), there is a diversity of ways in which this convergence is translated into practice. As such, the auto industry may not be alone but a special case of a broader trend in employment relations that Harry Katz and Owen Darbishire are observing in other industries around the world. In a forthcoming book, they use the term *converging divergence* to capture this trend.

The tendency for divergence across and within companies is evident from much of the case study data. This tendency is seen very clearly in the United States, where GM has been very innovative at its Saturn and

NUMMI plants but has maintained traditional approaches at most of its other assembly facilities. Similarly, in Sweden, Volvo has used a wide range of approaches to assembly methods in its bus and truck plants, drawing on experiences from the highly participative systems developed at Kalmar and Uddevalla. Yet Volvo has used more conventional line operations in its large-scale assembly plants at Torslanda (Sweden) and Ghent (Belgium). Even in the case of the Japanese transplants, great variations exist between Toyota operations and the Nissan plant in the United States, and some variations can be explained by the presence of a union at NUMMI and not at Toyota's Georgetown, Kentucky, plant.

Similarly, unions in various countries have responded very differently to new forms of production and employee relations. In Germany and Sweden, for example, the metalworkers unions have developed broad strategies for dealing with employers on these matters. So too has the UAW local union at Saturn. The Canadian Auto Workers also has articulated its own strategy regarding lean production. By contrast, the national level of the UAW has had no clear national policy on work innovations, preferring to leave it to local unions to negotiate with individual employers, with mixed results.

Government policies affect the strategies of individual companies and unions by influencing how exposed or protected the domestic market is from international competition and the role the auto industry plays in the development of the domestic economy. Labor policies also influence the role of unions and management strategies toward industrial relations and therefore have an important effect on union-management relations. Thus, although the strategies adopted by companies are obviously of critical importance, to develop a full understanding of the means by which these strategies are enacted, one must account for the views and strategies of two other actors in industrial relations—unions and the government.

These conclusions are summarized in schematic form in figure 16.1. The principles of lean production are most likely to be adopted in competitive environments where the strategies of firms, unions, and governments are aligned and mutually reinforcing. We can state these conclusions more specifically in propositional form as follows:

1. Exposure to global competition and the availability of flexible technologies provide the pressures and make it technically feasible to adopt the manufacturing, organizational, and human resource practices embodied in lean production.

2. A lean production system is most likely to be adopted in settings where international competition on price and quality are high; government

policies encourage open access to domestic markets and enforce democratic and cooperative forms of labor-management relations; firms choose to compete on the basis of quality, adaptability, and productivity (costs); and firms negotiate with worker representatives to adapt lean production principles to fit with local customs and workers' expectations.

3. Multiple combinations of misaligned strategies are possible among firms, labor, and government, any of which would be expected to produce greater conflicts among these parties and to result in slower and more incremental movement toward the implementation of lean production principles and reduce the returns to the practices implemented. For example:

    a. Firm strategies that are not likely to be aligned with the adoption of lean production principles include those that have a stand-alone emphasis on high technology, cost minimization, high-volume production of popular models, authoritarian managerial cultures or styles, or adversarial labor relations strategies. Firm strategies that encourage alignment are those that seek to achieve competitiveness on the basis of cost, quality, and flexibility across models and management styles and strategies that foster participation, learning, and cooperative labor relations.

    b. Government strategies that foster alignment are those that encourage competition and access to domestic markets and that promote high labor standards and democratic and cooperative labor-management relations.

    c. Worker and union strategies that promote alignment are those that accept the principles of lean production and participation in managerial decision making and that encourage negotiating with managers to ensure that these principles are adapted to fit local customs and institutions in ways that address the interests of the workforce as well as those of the firm.

4. We in turn would expect the most innovation beyond current lean production practices to occur in settings where the strategies of firms, workers and their representatives, and government are most aligned but where labor representatives develop and have sufficient power to work with managers to implement their own vision of how to modify lean production principles to meet workers' expectations for meaningful work, improved incomes and economic security, and human capital development.

5. Implementing lean production principles into practices that pay off to the parties requires skills in adaptive learning. Such learning takes

place through negotiations among managers and workers who have benchmarked and understand the "best practices," who can then adapt these practices to fit local customs and institutions, and who over time can modify both the practices and their traditional customs and institutions in ways that address the multiple interests of the parties.

6. The most sustainable production and organizational practices will be those that address the interests and goals of the multiple stakeholders— firms, workers, and the societies—involved.

We should note that even as we predict continued movement toward the implementation of lean production principles, we do not envision a final steady state where all the participants in the global auto industry will have identical practice and performance results, any more than this was the case twenty years ago when mass production techniques dominated auto industry production. "Local," that is, national, firm, and plant, variations due to the factors outlined above and to the differential abilities of managers and worker representatives to learn from others and to implement lean production and organizational principles will continue to produce differences in results.

It is important to recognize that these predictions are meant to reflect a dynamic rather than a static state. For example, in the case of Australia a decade ago, the auto industry could be described as attempting to follow mass production manufacturing methods (albeit on a small scale), having adversarial employee relations, and being subject to considerable

Figure 16.1 Model That Emerges from Findings of International Auto Industry Study

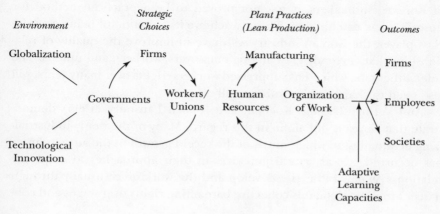

government restrictions (for example, through local content requirements). By contrast, during the past decade, the Australian auto industry has been characterized by a more cooperative approach to employment relations, gradual movement toward lean production, and a reduction in government-imposed tariff protection. Using these same dimensions, a likely future trajectory for the industry in Australia can be outlined. This emergent model, shown in figure 16.1, provides a more complex and comprehensive approach to analyzing industry trends and the underlying factors influencing these developments.

Case of the New Entrants or Newly Industrializing Nations

Taking account of the role of government policies is likely to be especially important in predicting the future of the auto industry in newly industrializing economies that are in the process of expanding auto manufacturing. According to Amsden and Kang, "Balance of payment considerations have driven the automobile industry strategies of many late-industrializing countries such as Thailand, Mexico, and Malaysia. These countries do not intend to become leading suppliers in the world automobile industry but rather have designed (if only by default) their assembly and parts operations with a view towards protecting their balance of payments" (1995:1).

The role of governments in the development of the auto industry in many of these economies, argue Amsden and Kang, is often much more interventionist than in mature economies. Korea provides a useful example in this regard. The Korean government has provided local auto producers with trade protection, subsidized credit, and export incentives. As Amsden and Kang (1995) note, although lean production is the stated goal of Korean automakers, it has not proved to be a practical method for upscaling and catching up. Thus, to achieve its ambition of being a world-class player, the Korean industry will have to improve the quality of relationships that currently exist among employers, workers, and unions. The role of the state, which has suppressed workers' rights over many years, will also need to change rather substantially.

Anil Verma, Thomas Kochan, and Russell Lansbury (1995) demonstrate that Korea is not alone in this regard. Many of the newly industrializing economies, in which much of the recent growth in the auto industry has occurred, are at critical junctures in their approaches to employee relations. As new industries develop and the workforce (usually through nascent unions) demands collective bargaining rights over wages and conditions, some employers (sometimes with the support of government) seek to suppress these developments. Others respond in more measured ways to accommodate these demands. By upgrading the skills of the workforce in order to increase value-added production, firms are sometimes able to become more profitable and therefore pay higher wages to their workers, thereby creating a "virtuous cycle" (Birdsall and Sabot 1995). Although the process is rarely this simple, the adoption of such a strategy can create comparative advantages, leading to further investment and growth, especially where private and public investments in human resource development are complementary.

Richard Doner and his colleagues (1995) argue that the most dynamic economic sectors in the countries of both Asia and Latin America are increasingly characterized by firms moving toward quicker, more efficient product and process shifts by means of close subcontracting links as well as more flexible internal patterns of production coordination. This new flexibility can have mixed outcomes for the workforce, especially in the newly emerging economies. Frederic C. Deyo (1996) found transnational auto assemblers in Thailand using low-wage casual labor while they simultaneously trained and rotated permanent workers through multiple tasks. In Brazil, studies of the auto industry have shown the emergence of constructive relationships between large and small firms, but the deregulation of employment relations has encouraged a growth in temporary and illegal labor (Abreu and Sorj 1993). If our predictions generalize to these newly industrializing countries, we are likely to see limited use of lean production principles unless government policies regulating the industry and labor relations change significantly.

Overall Conclusions

The results of our research project challenge some of the dominant views that have prevailed in recent years concerning the future direction of the international automobile industry. Companies are not simply choosing between a Fordist (or neo-Fordist) mass production approach and a Toyota-inspired lean production system. A much broader range of alternatives arise as a result of the interactions of production systems, employment relations systems, the competitive strategies, and managerial traditions of different firms and the roles played by governments and unions.

Our research shows the need for a broad political economy perspective on the international automobile industry that accounts for the interaction among production systems, the role of government, the broader socio-economic environment, and employee relations policies and practices at the enterprise, industry, and national levels. This perspective is particularly important with regard to the new entrants into the auto industry from such regions as Asia, Latin America, and Africa. Although we expect to see a general trend toward the adoption of lean production principles across the automobile industry, the actual rate of adoption and diffusion will be determined by how global competitive pressures interact and align with the strategies chosen by the firms, governments, and labor representatives involved.

References

Abo, T., et al., eds. 1994. *Hybrid Factory: The Japanese Production System in the United States.* New York: Oxford University Press.

Abreu, A., and B. Sorj. 1993. *Invisible Work: Studies in Work at Home in Brazil.* Rio de Janeiro: Rio Fundo Editora.

Adler, G. 1993. "Skills, Control, and 'Careers at Work': Possibilities for Worker Control in the South African Motor Industry." *South African Sociological Review* 5(2).

Adler, P. S. 1992. "The New 'Learning Bureaucracy': New United Motors Manufacturing, Inc." In B. Staw and L. Cummings, eds., *Research in Organizational Behavior,* vol. 10. Greenwich, Conn.: JAI Press.

———. 1993. "Time and Motion Regained." *Harvard Business Review,* Jan.–Feb.

Adler, P. S., and R. Cole. 1993. "Designed for Learning: A Tale of Two Plants." *Sloan Management Review,* Spring.

Adler, P. S., B. Goldoftas, and D. I. Levine. 1997. "Ergonomics, Employee Involvement, and the Toyota Production System: A Case Study of NUMMI's 1993 Model Introduction." *Industrial and Labor Relations Review,* April.

Ahn, C., and H. Ahn. 1991. *Study on Promotion Systems in Korean Firms.* Seoul: Korea Employers' Federation.

Amsden, A., and J. Kang. 1995. "Learning to Be Lean in an Emerging Economy: The Case of South Korea." Paper presented at the annual meeting of the IMVP, Toronto, June.

Associação Nacional dos Fabricantes de Veículos Automotores. 1990–96. *Statistical Yearbook of the Brazilian Automotive Industry.* São Paulo.

Australian Labor Party and the Australian Council of Trade Unions. 1993. "Statement of Accord by the ALP and ACTU regarding Economic Policy." Melbourne.

Australian Productivity Commission. 1996. *Automotive Case Study: Micro-reform—Study of Firms.* Canberra: Australian Government Publishing Service.

Auteri, E. 1991a. "Analysis of Leadership Style for Developing Innovative Leadership: The Fiat Experience." *Economia e Management* 4.

———. 1991b. "Fiat Structure, Organizational Excellence." *L'impresa. Rivista Italiana di management* 5.

———. 1994. "New Organizational Basis for the Firm's Excellence." *L'impresa, Rivista Italiana di Management* 1.

Automotive Industry Authority. 1994. *Report on the State of the Automotive Industry 1993.* Canberra: Australian Government Printing Service.

Babson, S. 1992. *Lean or Mean: The MIT Model and Lean Production at Mazda.* Detroit: Wayne State University Press.

Bamber, G. J., and R. D. Lansbury, eds. 1993. *International and Comparative Industrial Relations: A Study of Industrialised Market Economies.* London: Routledge.

Becchi, C. A., and S. Negrelli. 1986. *Transition in the Industry and in Industrial Relations: The Fiat Case.* Milan: F. Angeli.

Bell, T. 1990. "A Case Study of the Impact of Sanctions on the South African Motor Vehicle Industry." In C. Becker, et al., eds., *The Impact of Sanctions on South Africa.* Washington, D.C.: Investor Responsibility Research Center.

Berggren, C. 1992. *Alternatives to Lean Production: Work Organization in the Swedish Auto Industry.* Ithaca, N.Y.: ILR Press.

———. 1993. "Volvo Uddevalla—A Dead Horse or a Car Dealer's Dream?" Working paper, Royal Institute of Technology, Stockholm.

———. 1995. "A Second Comeback or a Final Farewell? The Volvo Trajectory, 1974–1994." Paper presented at the Third GERPISA International Colloquium on the New Industrial Models, Paris, June.

Besser, T. L. 1996. *Team Toyota: Transplanting the Toyota Culture to the Camry Plant in Kentucky.* Albany: State University of New York Press.

Bethlehem, L., and K. Von Holdt. 1991. "A New Deal for a New Era? The Auto Industry Settlement." *South African Labour Bulletin* 16(2).

Bird, A. 1992. "Redefining Human Resources Development within the Context of Economic and Labour Market Policies—A COSATU Perspective." Paper presented at the National Education Policy Investigation Human Resources Conference, May.

Birdsall, N., and R. Sabot. 1995. *Virtuous Circles: Human Capital, Growth and Equity in East Asia.* Washington, D.C.: World Bank.

Black, A. 1988. "Manufacturing Development and the Current Crisis: A Reversion to Primary Production?" Working paper, University of Cape Town, Economics Department.

———. 1993. *An Industrial Strategy for the Motor Vehicle Assembly and Component Sectors.* Cape Town: University of Cape Town Press.

Bolton, M. K. 1993. "Organization, Innovation and Standard Performance: When Is Necessity the Mother of Innovation?" *Organization Science* 4.

Bonazzi, G. 1993. *The Crystal Tube.* Bologna: Il Mulino.

Boyer, R., and M. Freyssenet. 1995. "The Emergence of New Industrial Models." Paper presented to the Third GERPISA International Colloquium on the New Industrial Models, Paris, June.

Bramble, T. 1993. "The Contingent Conservatism of Full-Time Trade Union Officials: A Case Study of the Vehicle Builders Employees' Federation of Australia, 1963 to 1991." Ph.D. diss., La Trobe University.

Brown, C., and M. Reich. 1989. "When Does Union-Management Cooperation Work? A Look at NUMMI and GM-Van Nuys." *California Management Review* 31(4).

———. 1995. "Employee Voice in Training and Career Development." Paper presented at the annual meetings of the Industrial Relations Research Association, Washington, D.C., January.

Brulin, G. 1995. "Sweden: Joint Councils under Strong Trade Unionism." In J. Rogers and W. Streek, eds., *Employee Participation and Work Councils.* Chicago: Chicago University Press.

Brulin, G., and T. Nilsson, T. 1991. "From Societal to Managerial Corporatism: New Forms of Work Organization as a Transformation Vehicle?" *Economic and Industrial Democracy* 12(3).

Callus, R., et al. 1991. *Industrial Relations at Work.* Canberra: Australian Government Publishing Service.

Cameron, D. 1984. "The When, Why and How of Discipline." *Personnel Journal,* July.

Campbell, D. N., R. L. Fleming, and R. C. Grote. 1985. "Discipline without Punishment at Last." *Harvard Business Review,* July–Aug.

Camuffo, A., and G. Costa. 1993. "Strategic Human Resource Management: The Italian Style." *Sloan Management Review,* Winter.

Camuffo, A., and S. Micelli. 1994. "Hierarchy Regained? Teamwork and New Models of Work Organization in the European Auto Industry." Paper presented at the Third GERPISA International Colloquium on the New Industrial Models, Paris, June.

——. 1995. "Mediterranean Lean Production? Supervisors, Teamwork, and New Forms of Work Organization in Three European Car Markets." Paper presented at the International Industrial Relations Association Tenth World Congress, Washington, D.C., May–June.

Camuffo, A., and G. Volpato. 1995. "Labor Relations Heritage and Lean Manufacturing at Fiat." *International Journal of Human Resource Management 6(4).*

Carmichael, L. 1992. *The Australian Vocational Certificate Training System: Report by the Employment and Skills Formation Council.* Canberra: National Board of Employment, Education and Training.

CAW. 1989. *CAW Statement on the Reorganization of Work.* North York, Ont.

——. 1992. *CAW-Canada/CAMI Report: Highlights of the Tentative Agreement between CAW-Canada and CAMI.* North York: Ont.

——. 1993a. *Hard Times, New Times: Fighting for Our Future: Report to the National Collective Bargaining and Political Action Convention.* North York, Ont.

——. 1993b. *Work Reorganization: Responding to Lean Production.* North York, Ont.

——. 1994. *Sectoral Overviews: Major Auto (Section I) and Independent Auto Parts (Section II).* North York, Ont.

——. 1996. *Benchmarking Auto Assembly Plants.* North York, Ont.

Cerruti, G., and V. Rieser. 1991. *Fiat: Total Quality and the Integrated Factory.* Rome: Ediesse.

——. 1992. "Fiat: An Undate on the Integrated Factory." *Quaderni di Ricerca Ires* 1.

Chandler, A. D. 1962. *Strategy and Structure.* Cambridge: MIT Press.

Clark, B., and T. Fujimoto. 1991. *Product Development Performance. Strategy, Organization and Management in the World Auto Industry.* Boston: Harvard Business School Press.

Cole, R. E. 1979. *Work, Mobility, and Participation: A Comparative Study of American and Japanese Industry.* Berkeley: University of California Press.

——. 1985. "The Macropolitics of Organizational Change." *Administrative Science Quarterly* 30.

Confederation of Australian Industry and the Australian Council of Trade Unions. 1988. *Joint Statement on Participative Practices.* Canberra: Australian Government Printing Service.

Confederation of Japanese Automobile Workers' Union. 1992. "The Japanese Automobile Industry in the Future: Toward Coexistence with the World, Consumers, and Employees." Typescript.

Cook, P. 1991. *Ministerial Statement on Industrial Relations to the Senate.* Canberra: Office of the Minister for Industrial Relations.

Cooper, D. 1991. "Locating South Africa in the Third World: Comparative Perspectives on Patterns of Industrialisation and Political Trade Unionism in South America." *Social Dynamics* 17(2).

COSATU. 1992. "COSATU's Approach to Adult Basic Education." Paper presented at the National Education Policy Investigation Human Resources Conference, May.

Cusumano, M. A. 1985. *The Japanese Automobile Industry: Technology and Management at Nissan and Toyota.* Cambridge: Harvard University Press.

——. 1994. "The Limits of 'Lean.'" *Sloan Management Review,* Summer.

Department of Industry, Science and Technology. 1995. *Report on the State of the Automotive Industry.* Canberra: Australian Government Printing Service.

——. 1996. *State of the Automotive Industry 1995.* Canberra: Australian Government Printing Service.

Dewar, S. 1990. "Total Worker Involvement at Toyota." In M. Anstey, ed., *Worker Participation: South African Options and Experiences.* Kenwyn, S.A.: Juta.

Deyo, F. C., ed. 1987. *The Political Economy of the New Asian Industrialism.* Ithaca, N.Y.: Cornell University Press.

Deyo, F. C. 1996. *Social Reconstructions of the World Automobile Industry: Competition, Power and Industrial Flexibility.* London: Macmillan.

DIEESE. 1995. "The Brazilian Metalworkers and the New Factory Challenge: Negotiated Change at Mercedes-Benz." Paper presented at the International Industrial Relations Association Tenth World Congress, Washington, D.C., May–June.

Dodson, L. 1995. "Industry Policy More Talk Than Action." *Australian Financial Review* 12.

Dohse, K., U. Jürgens, and T. Malsch. 1985. "From Fordism to Toyotism? The Social Organisation of the Labour Process in the Japanese Automobile Industry." *Politics and Society* 14(2).

Doleschal, R. 1992. "Internationalization and Reorganization of Production and Marketing in the Volkswagen Corporation." In W. Graf, ed., *The Internationalization of the German Political Economy.* New York: St. Martin's.

Doner, R., et al. 1995. "Economic Governance and Flexible Production in Latin America and East Asia: A Program of Research, Conferences and Publication Proposed by the Social Science Research Council, New York." Typescript.

Duncan, D., and B. Payne. 1992. "Just-in-Time South Africa: Japanese Production System in the South African Motor Industry." Working paper, University of the Witwatersrand.

Economist Intelligence Unit. 1993. "Inside SEAT's Martorell Plant." *European Motor Business,* 2nd quarter.

Edwardes, M. 1983. *Back from the Brink.* London: Pan.

Ferro, J. R. 1989. "Strategy Alternatives for the Brazilian Motor Vehicle Industry." Paper presented to the Third IMVP Forum, Acapulco, May.

——. 1991. "Deciphering Organizational Cultures." Ph.D. diss., Fundação Getulio Vargas de São Paulo.

——. 1992. "Lean Production in Brazil." In J. Womack, D. T. Jones., and D. Roos, eds., *The Machine That Changed the World.* Rio de Janeiro: Campus Press.

——. 1994. "*Collision in Brazil.*" In M. Keller, ed., *Collision.* Rio de Janeiro: Campus Press.

Fleury, A., and M. T. Fleury. 1995. *Innovation and Organizational Learning: The Japanese, Korean, and Brazilian Experiences.* São Paulo: Atlas Press.

Follis, M., P. Pessa, and M. Silveri. 1991. "Summary of the Auto Industry." Working paper, Force Project, European Commission.

Freeman, R., and J. Medoff. 1984. *What Do Unions Do?* New York: Basic Books.

Freyssenet, M. 1993. "The Renault Trajectory." Paper presented at the Third GERPISA International Colloquium on the New Industrial Models, Paris, June.

Fucini, J., and S. Fucini. 1990. *Working for the Japanese: Inside Mazda's American Auto Plant.* New York: Free Press.

Fujimoto, T. 1994. "The Limits of Lean Production in the Future of the Japanese Automotive Industry." *International Political Gesselschaft* 1.

Fujimoto, T., and T. Matsuo. 1995. "An Evolutionary Process of Toyota's Final Assembly Operations: The Role of Ex-Post Dynamic Capabilities." Paper presented at Third International Workshop on Assembly Automation, University of Venice.

Fujita, E., et al. 1995. "The New Workshop Organization under the Changing Environment: Tahara No. 4 Assembly Plant of Toyota." *Journal of Social Sciences* 34.

Galbraith, J. R. 1977. *Organization Design.* New York: Addison-Wesley.

Garrahan, P., et al. 1992. *The Nissan Enigma: Flexibility at Work in a Local Economy.* London: Mansell.

Gerst, D., et al. 1994. "Plant Experiments with Group Working." *Angewandte Arbeitswissenschaft* 1.

Gindin, S. 1995. *The Canadian Auto Workers: The Birth and Transformation of a Union.* Toronto: Lorimer.

Graham, L. 1995. *On the Line at Subaru-Isuzu.* Ithaca, N.Y.: ILR Press.

Grassi, F. 1993. "Important Agreement for Melfi and Pratola Serra." *Personale e Lavoro* 371.

Hackman, J. R., and Oldham, G. R. 1980. *Work Redesign.* Reading, Mass.: Addison-Wesley.

Hammarström, O. 1994. "Local and Global: Trade Unions in the Future." In J. R. Niland, R. D. Lansbury, and C. Verevis, eds., *The Future of Industrial Relations.* London: Sage.

Hancke, R. 1993. "Technological Change and Its Industrial Constraints: The Politics of Production at Volvo Uddevalla." Working paper no. 93-05, Science, Technology, and Public Policy Program, Kennedy School of Government, Harvard University.

Harbour. 1995. *The Harbour Report 1995.* Troy, Mich.: Harbour and Associates.

Hartz, P. 1994. *Every Job Has a History: The VW Case.* Frankfurt: Campus Verlag.

Holmes, J. 1992. "The Continental Integration of the North American Auto Industry: From the Auto Pact to the FTA and Beyond." *Environment and Planning* 24.

——. 1996. "Restructuring in a Continental Production System." In J.N. H. Britton, ed., *Canada and the Global Economy.* Kingston: McGill-Queen's University Press.

Holusha, J. 1989. "No Utopia, but to Workers It's a Job." *New York Times,* Jan. 29.

Hudson, H. 1988. "Ford's Drive to Remodel Its Awards." *Workplace Change* 2.

Humphrey, J. 1984. *Capitalist Control and Labor in the Brazilian Auto Industry.* São Paulo: Cebrap.

Huxley, C., J. Rinehart, and D. Robertson. 1995. "Challenging Lean Production: Workers and Union at a GM-Suzuki Transplant." Paper presented at the International Industrial Relations Association Tenth World Congress, Washington, D.C., May–June.

Income Data Services. 1995. *IDS Report no. 680.* London.

Industrial Strategy Project. 1994. "Industrial Strategy for South Africa: The Recommendations of the ISP." *South African Labour Bulletin* 18(1).

Industry Canada. 1991. *Industrial Competitiveness: A Sectoral Perspective.* Ottawa: Supply and Services Canada.

——. 1992. *Canadian Automotive Industry: Issues and Solutions. Report of the Automotive Advisory Committee.* Ottawa.

Ishida, M. 1990. *Social Foundation of Wages.* Tokyo: Chuokeizai-sha.

Itoh, I. 1992. "Cooperation in Hierarchical Organizations: An Incentive Perspective." *Journal of Law, Economics and Organization* 8.

Ittner, C. D., and J. P. MacDuffie. 1994. "Exploring the Sources of International Differences in Manufacturing Overhead." Paper presented at IMVP research briefing meeting, June.

Jenkins, R. 1985. "Internationalization of Capital and the Semi-Industrialized Countries: The Case of the Motor Industry." *Review of Radical Political Economics* 17(1/2).

Jürgens, U. 1992. "Lean Production in Japan: Myth and Reality." In Institute of Work and Technology, ed., *Lean Production? A New Production Concept for a More Humanized Work?* Dusseldorf: Hans Boeckler Foundation.

———. 1995. "Volkswagen at the Turning Point: Success and Crisis of a German Production Concept." Working paper, GERPISA, Evry, France.

Jürgens, U., T. Malsch, and K. Dohse. 1993. *Breaking from Taylorism: Changing Forms of Work in the Automobile Industry.* Cambridge, U.K.: Cambridge University Press.

Kaplinsky, R. 1995. "Technique and System: The Spread of Japanese Management Techniques to Developing Countries." *World Development* 23(1).

Katz, H. C. 1997. *Telecommunications.* Ithaca, N.Y.: Cornell University Press.

Katz, H. C., and O. Darbishire. 1997. "Converging Divergences: Worldwide Changes in Employment Relations." Working paper, School of Industrial and Labor Relations, Cornell University.

Katz, H. C., and T. A. Kochan. 1992. *An Introduction to Collective Bargaining and Industrial Relations.* New York: McGraw-Hill.

Katz, H. C., and N. Meltz. 1989. "Changing Work Practices and Productivity in the Auto Industry: A U.S.–Canada Comparison." In M. Grant, ed., *Proceedings of the Twenty-Sixth Conference of the Canadian Industrial Relations Association.* Quebec City: Canadian Industrial Relations Association.

Katzenbach, J. R. and D. K. Smith. 1993. "The Discipline of Teams." *Harvard Business Review,* March–April.

Keller, M. 1989. *Rude Awakening: The Rise, Fall and Struggle for Recovery of General Motors.* New York: Harper Perennial.

Kenney, M., and R. Florida. 1993. *Beyond Mass Production: The Japanese System and Its Transfer to the U.S.* New York: Oxford University Press.

Kern, H., and C. F. Sabel. 1994. "Fading Virtues: The Crisis of the German Production Model." *Soziale Welt,* special issue 9.

Kochan, T. A. 1980. *Collective Bargaining and Industrial Relations.* Homewood, Ill.: Irwin.

Kochan, T. A., H. C. Katz, and R. McKersie. 1992. *The Transformation of American Industrial Relations.* New York: Basic Books, 1986. Reprint, Ithaca, N.Y.: ILR Press.

Kochan, T. A., R. M. Locke, and C. H. Heye. 1992. "Industrial Restructuring and Industrial Relations in the U.S. and Italian Automobile Industries." In D. Lessard and C. Antonelli, eds., *Managing the Globalization of Business.* Naples: Editoriale Scientifica.

Kogut, B., and U. Zander. 1992. "Knowledge of the Firm, Combinative Capabilities, and the Replication of Technology." *Organization Science* 3(3).

Kraak, A. 1992. "Human Resource Development and Organised Labour." In G. Moss. and I. Obery, eds., *South African Review 6.* Johannesburg: Ravan Press.

Kumar, P., and N. Meltz. 1992. "Industrial Relations in the Canadian Automobile Industry." In R. P. Chaykowski and A. Verma, eds., *Industrial Relations in Canadian Industry.* Toronto: Dryden.

Kyoya, E. 1993. *What Is Flexibility?* Tokyo: Mado-Sha.

Lansbury, R. D., and G. J. Bamber. 1995. "Changing Employment Relations and Production Systems in the Australian Automotive Industry." Paper presented to the International Industrial Relations Association Tenth World Congress, Washington, D.C., May.

Lansbury, R. D., and E. M. Davis. 1990. *Employee Involvement and Workers' Participation in Management: The Australian Experience. Advances in Industrial and Labor Relations,* vol. 5. Greenwich, Conn.: JAI Press.

Lansbury, R. D., and D. Macdonald. 1992. "Automakers." In R. D. Lansbury and D. Macdonald, eds., *Workplace Industrial Relations: Australian Case Studies.* Melbourne: Oxford University Press.

Lansbury, R. D., and M. Marchington. 1993. "Joint Consultation and Industrial Relations: Experience in Australia and Overseas." *Asia Pacific Journal of Human Resources* 31(3).

Lansbury, R. D., and J. R. Niland. 1994. "Trends in Industrial Relations and Human Resource Policies and Practices: Australian Experiences." *International Journal of Human Resource Management* 5(3).

Lave, J. 1988. *Cognition in Practice.* Cambridge, U.K.: Cambridge University Press.

Lawler, E. E., III. 1988. "Substitutes for Hierarchy." *Organizational Dynamics,* Summer.

Lawler, E. E., III, and S. A. Mohrman. 1995. "Quality Circles after the Fad." *Harvard Business Review* 85.

Lawrence, P. R., and J. W. Loersch. 1967. *Organization and Environment: Managing Differentiation and Integration.* Cambridge: Harvard University Press.

"Lean Production—and Rover's 'New Deal.'" 1992. *IRS Employment Trends* 514.

Lee, H. S. 1991. "Employment Relations in Korea, Japan, and the United States." *Korean Social Science Journal* 17.

———. 1996. "The Interaction of Production, Distribution, and Rule-Making Systems in Industrial Relations." *Relations Industrielles/Industrial Relations* 51.

Lever-Tracy, C. 1987. "The Supervisor and the Militant Shop Steward: Evidence from the Australian Motor Industry." *Journal of Industrial Relations* 29(3).

———. 1990. "Fordism Transformed? Employee Involvement and Workplace Industrial Relations at Ford." *Journal of Industrial Relations* 32(2).

Lewchuk, W. 1988. *American Technology and the British Car Industry.* Cambridge, U.K.: Cambridge University Press.

Locke, R. M. 1992. "The Demise of the National Union in Italy: Lessons for Comparative Industrial Relations Theory." *Industrial and Labor Relations Review* 2.

———. 1995. *Remaking the Italian Economy.* Ithaca, N.Y.: Cornell University Press.

Locke, R. M., T. A. Kochan, and M. Piore, eds. 1995. *Employment Relations in a Changing World Economy.* Cambridge: MIT Press.

Locke, R. M., and S. Negrelli. 1989. " The Fiat Case." In M. Regini and C. Sabel, eds., *Strategies for Industrial Adjustment.* Bologna: Il Molino.

Lovell, M., et al. 1991. *Report on the Chrysler UAW Modern Operating Agreement (MOA) Experiment.* Washington, D.C.: Department of Labor.

MacDuffie, J. P. 1991. "Beyond Mass Production: Flexible Production Systems and Manufacturing Performance in the World Auto Industry." Ph.D. diss., Sloan School of Management, MIT.

———. 1995. "Human Resource Bundles and Manufacturing Performance: Organizational Logic and Flexible Production Systems in the World Auto Industry." *Industrial and Labor Relations Review* 48.

———. 1996. "International Trends in Work Organization in the Auto Industry: National-Level vs. Company-Level Perspectives." In L. Turner and K. Wever, eds., *The Comparative Political Economy of Industrial Relations*. Madison, Wisc.: Industrial Relations Research Association.

———. 1997. "The Road to 'Root Cause': Shop-Floor Problem Solving at Three Auto Assembly Plants." *Management Science* 43(4).

MacDuffie, J. P., L. W. Hunter, and L. Doucet. 1995. "What Does Transformation Mean to Workers? The Effects of the New Industrial Relations on Union Employees' Attitudes." Paper presented at the Academy of Management meetings, Vancouver, August.

MacDuffie, J. P., and T. A. Kochan. 1995. "Do U.S. Firms Invest Less in Human Resources? Training in the World Auto Industry." *Industrial Relations* 34(2).

MacDuffie, J. P., and J. Krafcik. 1992. "Integrating Technology and Human Resources for High-Performance Manufacturing: Evidence from the International Auto Industry." In T. A. Kochan and M. Useem, eds., *Transforming Organizations*. New York; Oxford University Press.

MacDuffie, J. P., and F. K. Pil. 1995. "The International Assembly Plant Study: Philosophical and Methodological Issues." In S. Babson, ed., *Lean Production and Labor: Critical and Comparative Perspectives*. Detroit: Wayne State University Press.

———. 1996. "From Fixed to Flexible: Automation and Work Organization Trends from the International Assembly Plant Survey." In U. Jürgens and T. Fujimoto, eds., *Transforming Auto Assembly: International Experiences with Automation and Work Organization*. Frankfurt: Springer Verlag.

MacDuffie, J. P., K. Sethuraman, and M. L. Fisher. 1996. "Product Variety and Manufacturing Performance: Evidence from the International Automotive Assembly Plant Study." *Management Science* 42(3).

Macken, J. 1989. *Award Restructuring*. Sydney: Federation Press.

Magnabosco, M. 1993. "The Intellectual Productivity of Blue-Collar Workers." *Personale e Lavoro,* September.

———. 1994. "The Integrated Factory: Birth and Features." *Personale e Lavoro,* January.

Maller, J. 1992. *Conflict and Co-operation: Case Studies in Worker Participation*. Johannesburg: Ravan Press.

———. 1994. "Worker Participation and Trade Unionism: Case Studies of Workplace Democracy in South Africa." *Economic and Industrial Democracy* 15.

Maller, J., and B. Dwolatsky. 1993. "What Is Fordism? Restructuring Work in the South African Metal Industry." *Transformation* 22.

Mathews, J. 1992. "Ford Australia Plastics Plant: Transition to Teamwork through Quality Enhancement." Studies in Organisational Analysis and Innovation Report no. 3, Industrial Relations Research Unit, University of New South Wales.

McCallum, R., G. McCarry, and P. Ronfield, eds. 1994. *Employment Security*. Sydney: Federation Press.

Mealor, T. 1996. "From Confrontation to Collaboration at ICI Botony." In E. M. Davis and R. D. Lansbury, eds., *Managing Together.* Melbourne: Addison Wesley Longman.

Middlebrook, K. 1991. "The Politics of Industrial Restructuring: Transnational Firms' Search for Flexible Production in the Mexican Automobile Industry." *Comparative Politics* 23(3).

Milkovich, G. T., and A. K. Wigdor, eds. 1991. *Pay for Performance: Evaluating Performance Appraisal and Merit Pay*. Washington, D.C.: National Academy Press.

Mintzberg, H. 1979. *The Structuring of Organizations*. Englewood Cliffs, N.J.: Prentice Hall.

Monden, Y. 1983. *Toyota Production System*. Norcross, Ga.: Institute of Industrial Engineers.

Mueller, F. 1994. "Teams between Hierarchy and Commitment: Change Strategies and the Internal Environment." *Journal of Management Studies* 31.

Müller-Jentsch, W. 1995. "From Collective Voice to Co-Management." In J. Rogers and W. Streeck, eds., *Works Councils: Consultation, Representation, and Cooperation in Industrial Relations.* Chicago: University of Chicago Press.

Murakami, T. 1995. "Teamwork and Participation in the German Car Industry." Paper presented at the International Industrial Research Association Tenth World Congress, Washington, D.C., May–June.

Muster, M., and U. Richter. 1990. *Full Throttle into the Traffic Jam: Automobile Production, Company Strategies, and the Prospects of an Ecological Traffic System.* Hamburg: VSA-Verlag.

Nattrass, N. 1991. "No Cooperation at Toyota." *South African Labour Bulletin* 16(2).

Nohria, N., and C. Garcia-Pont. 1991. "Global Strategic Linkages and Industry Structure." *Strategic Management Journal* 12.

Nomura, M. 1992. "Farewell to Toyotaism? Recent Trends of a Japanese Automobile Company." Discussion paper, GERPISA, Evry, France.

Norris, K., and M. Wooden. 1995. "The Changing Australian Labour Market." Economic Planning Commission paper no. 11, Canberra.

Oberhauser, A. 1993. "Semiperipheral Industrialization in the Global Economy: Transition in the South African Automobile Industry." *Geoforum* 24(2).

O'Brien, P., and Y. Karmokolias. 1994. "Radical Reform in the Automotive Industry: Policies in Emerging Markets." International Finance Corporation discussion paper no. 21, World Bank, Washington, D.C.

Oliver, N., and B. Wilkinson. 1992. *The Japanization of British Industry.* 2d ed. Oxford: Blackwell.

One Hundred Year Almanac and Automotive News Market Data Book. 1996. Detroit: Crain Communications.

Park, D., and K. Park. 1990. *Korea's Trade Unions II.* Seoul: Korea Labor Institute.

Park, Y. B. 1994. *Labor Institutions and Economic Development in Asia: Exploratory Micro-Level Research on Labor Institutions and Productivity in the Korean Automotive and Garment Industries.* Geneva: International Institute for Labour Studies.

Pessa, P., and L. Sartirano. 1993. "Fiat Auto: Research on Organizational Innovation." Typescript.

Pil, F. K. 1996. "Understanding the International and Temporal Diffusion of High-Involvement Work Practices." Ph.D. diss., Wharton School, University of Pennsylvania.

Pil, F. K., and J. P. MacDuffie. 1996a. "The Adoption of High-Involvement Work Practices." *Industrial Relations* 35(3).

———. 1996b. "Japanese and Local Influences on the Transfer of Work Practices at Japanese Transplants." In P. Voos, ed., *Proceedings of the Forty-eighth Annual Meeting of the Industrial Relations Research Association.* Madison, Wisc.: Industrial Relations Research Association.

Piore, M., and C. Sabel. 1984. *The Second Industrial Divide.* New York: Basic Books.

Poole, M. 1988. *Industrial Relations: Origins and Patterns of National Diversity.* London: Routledge.

Rehder, R. 1994. "Saturn, Uddevalla and the Japanese Lean System: Paradoxical Prototypes for the Twenty-first Century." *International Journal for Human Resource Management* 5(1).

Rieser, V. 1993. "Fiat and the New Rationalization Phase." *Quaderni di Sociologia* 1.

Rimmer, M. 1992. "Motor Engine Company." In *Workplace Reform and Award Restructuring: Progress at the Workplace.* Canberra: Australian Government Printing Service.

Rinehart, J., C. Huxley, and D. Robertson. 1997. *Just Another Car Factory? Lean Production and Its Discontents.* N.Y.: ILR/Cornell University Press.

Robertson, D., et al. 1993a. *The CAMI Report: Lean Production in a Unionized Auto Plant.* North York, Ont.: CAW.

——. 1993b. "Team Concept and Kaizen: Japanese Production Management in a Unionized Canadian Auto Plant." *Studies in Political Economy,* Autumn.

Rodrigues, L. 1970. *Industrialization and Workers' Attitudes.* São Paulo: Difel Press.

Roth, S. 1992. *Japanization, or Going Our Own Way?: New Lean Production Concepts in the German Autombile Industry.* Dusseldorf: Hans Boeckler Foundation.

——.1995. "Rediscovering Its Own Strength? Lean Production in the German Automobile Industry." Paper presented at the International Industrial Relations Association Tenth World Congress, Washington, D.C., May–June.

——. 1996. "Production Concepts in Japan and Germany." In K. Zwickel, ed., *Model Japan.* Frankfurt: Otto Brenner Foundation.

Roth, S., and H. Kohl. 1988. *Prospects of Group Work.* Cologne: Bund-Verlag.

"Rover's 'New Deal.'" 1992. *European Industrial Relations Review* 223.

Sandberg, Å., ed. 1995. *Enriching Production: Perspectives on Volvo's Uddevalla Plant as an Alternative to Lean Production.* Avebury, U.K.: Aldershot.

Schumann, M., et al. 1994. *Trends in Industrial and Work Organization.* Berlin: Sigma.

Shadur, M. A., and G. Bamber. 1994. "Towards Lean Production? The Transferability of Japanese Management Strategies to Australia." *International Executive* 36.

Shadur, M. A., et al. 1994. "Quality Management and High Performance: Inferences from the Australian Automotive Sector." *International Journal of Human Resource Management* 5(3).

Shimada, H., and J. P. MacDuffie. 1987. "Industrial Relations and Humanware: Japanese Investments in Automobile Manufacturing in the United States." Working paper, Sloan School of Management, MIT.

Shimizu, K. 1995. "Humanization of Work at Toyota Motor Co." *Okayama Economic Review* 27(1).

Silva, E. 1991. *Remaking the Fordist Factory.* São Paulo: Hucitec Press.

Simmons, D., and R. D. Lansbury. 1996. "Work Reform and Worker Involvement at the Ford Motor Company Australia." In E. M. Davis and R. D. Lansbury, eds., *Managing Together? Consultation and Participation in the Workplace.* Melbourne: Longman.

Smith, B. 1990. "Volkswagen's Holistic Approach to Worker Participation." In M. Anstey, ed., *Worker Participation: South African Options and Experiences.* Kenwyn, S.A.: Juta.

Smith, D. 1988. "The Japanese Example in South West Birmingham." *Industrial Relations Journal* 19.

Snape, E. J., T. Redman , and G. Bamber. 1994. *Managing Managers.* Oxford: Blackwell.

Society of Motor Manufacturers and Traders. 1996. *Monthly Statistical Review.* London.

Southhall, R. 1985. "Monopoly Capital and Industrial Unionism in the South African Motor Industry." *Labour, Capital and Society* 18(2).

Springer, R. 1993. "New Forms of Work Organization." *Angewandte Arbeitswissenschaft* 137.

Standard & Poor's. 1996. *Industry Profile: Automotive Australia.* Melbourne.

Staw, B. 1976. "Knee-Deep in the Big Muddy: A Study of Escalating Commitment to a Chosen Course of Action." *Organizational Behavior and Human Performance* 16.

Swedish Metalworkers Union. 1989. "Solidaristic Work Policy for Rewarding Jobs." Conference report, Stockholm.

Taylor, R. 1994. *The Future of the Trade Unions.* London: Andre Deutsch.

"TGWU's Response to Lean Production at Rover." 1993. *IRS Employment Trends.* April.

Thompson, J. D. 1967. *Organizations in Action.* New York: McGraw-Hill.

Toyota Shop Stewards Council. 1992. "Toyota South Africa: The Workers' Voice." *South African Labour Bulletin* 16(5).

Tropitzsch, H. 1994. "Efficiency Improvement through Greater Participation: Mercedes-Benz's New Labour Policy Bears Fruit." *Angewandte Arbeitswissenschaft* 142.

Turner, L. 1991. *Democracy at Work: Changing World Markets and the Future of Labour Unions.* Ithaca, N.Y.: Cornell University Press.

Uh, S.B. 1992. *Korea's Labor Mobility.* Seoul: Korea Labor Institute.

Verma, A., T. A. Kochan, and R. D. Lansbury, eds. 1995. *Employment Relations in the Growing Asian Economies.* London: Routledge.

Vernon, J. 1994. *BMW Tomorrow: The New Deal at Longbridge.* Oxford: Ruskin College.

Volpato, G. 1978. " The Great Crisis and Scientific Unemployment in Italian Industry." In G. Toniolo, ed., *Industry and Banks in the Great Crisis, 1929–1934.* Milan: Etas Libri.

———. 1983. *The International Auto Industry.* Padua: Cedam.

Walton, R. E., J. Cutcher-Gershenfeld, and R. McKersie. 1994 *Strategic Negotiations.* Boston: Harvard Business School Press.

Ward's Automotive Yearbook 1994. 1994. Southfield, Mich.: Ward's Communications.

Ward's Automotive Yearbook 1995. 1995. Southfield, Mich.: Ward's Communications.

Warnecke, H.-J. 1992. *The Fractal Factory: A Revolution of Company Culture.* Berlin: Springer Verlag.

Williams, K., J. Williams, and C. Haslam. 1987. *The Breakdown of Austin Rover.* Leamington Spa: Berg.

Williams, K., et al. 1994. *Cars: Analysis, History, Cases.* Providence. R.I.: Berghahn Books.

Womack, J. P., and D. T. Jones. 1994. "From Lean Production to the Lean Enterprise." *Harvard Business Review,* March–April.

Womack, J. P., D. T. Jones, and D. Roos. 1990. *The Machine That Changed the World.* New York: Rawson Associates.

Young, M. 1992. "A Framework for Successful Adoption and Performance of Japanese Manufacturing in the United States." *Academy of Management Review* 17.

Contributors

Paul S. Adler is an associate professor in the Department of Management and Organization in the School of Business Administration at the University of Southern California (USC). A past chair of the Technology and Innovation Management Division of the Academy of Management, he has published widely in academic and management journals in the United States and overseas and is the editor of two volumes, *Technology and the Future of Work,* and *Usability: Turning Technologies into Tools.*

Greg J. Bamber is a professor and the director of the Graduate School of Management at Griffith University in Brisbane, Australia. He was formerly director of the Centre in Strategic Management at Queensland University of Technology and is a past president of the Australian and New Zealand Academy of Management. He has coauthored several books, including *Managing Managers, International and Comparative Industrial Relations, Organisational Change Strategies: Case Studies of Human Resource and Industrial Relations Issues, and New Technology: International Perspectives on Human Resources and Industrial Relations.*

Göran Brulin is an associate professor in the School of Business at Stockholm University and a senior research associate at the Swedish National Institute of Working Life. His research areas include work organization, development work, and industrial relations. He is the author of a wide range of publications in Swedish, French, and English.

Arnaldo Camuffo is an associate professor of human resource management in the Department of Business Economics and Management at

Ca'Foscari University in Venice, Italy. He is also a research affiliate with MIT's International Motor Vehicle Program. He has been published in many international management journals, including *Sloan Management Review, Industrial and Corporate Change,* and the *International Journal of Human Resource Management.*

José Roberto Ferro teaches in the School of Business Administration at Fundação Getulio Vargas in São Paulo, Brazil. He is the Brazil coordinator for MIT's International Motor Vehicle Program.

Afonso Fleury is a professor in and the head of the Production Engineering Department at the University of São Paulo. His main research focus is technology and work. Since 1992, he has been involved in the activities of GERPISA, "the Permanent Group for the Study of the Automobile Industry and Its Employees," as an analyst of the Brazilian auto industry. He has also conducted research for several institutions, including the International Labour Organisation.

Maria Tereza Fleury is a professor at the School of Economics and Business Management at the University of São Paulo. She has been a visiting research fellow at the Institute of Development Studies at the University of Sussex and at the Institute of Developing Economies in Tokyo and a visiting professor at the Ecole Superieure des Sciences Economies et Commerciales in Paris. Her research focuses on human resource management, organizational culture, and organizational learning.

Philip Hirschsohn is a senior lecturer in the Department of Management at the University of the Western Cape in Cape Town, South Africa, and a doctoral student in the Industrial Relations Section at the Sloan School at MIT. His research addresses the changing nature of trade union strategy and the process of developing industrial relations institutions. Other research interests include trade unions as social movements and management approaches to worker participation.

John Holmes is a professor and head of geography and a faculty associate in the School of Industrial Relations at Queen's University in Kingston, Ontario. His teaching and research interests center on the geographical aspects of contemporary economic change in North America. He is the author of numerous journal articles and chapters on the restructuring of the automobile industry and, more recently, has also written on the pulp and paper industry.

Mitsuo Ishida is a professor in the Department of Sociology at Doshisha University in Kyoto, Japan. Among his recent publications are *Contemporary British Industrial Relations* and *The Social Foundation of Wages*.

Ulrich Jürgens is a privatdozent (external professor) at Berlin Free University and a senior researcher at the Social Science Research Center Berlin (WZB). He has directed international projects on such topics as company strategies, industrial relations, and work organization, with a focus on the automobile industry. He is the coauthor of several major publications, including *Breaking away from Taylorism: Changing Forms of Work in the Automobile Industry* and *Explaining the Japanese Productivity Success: Labor Relations and Performance Regulation in Two Japanese Auto Companies*.

Thomas A. Kochan is a professor of management at MIT's Sloan School of Management and codirector of the Industrial Relations Section. He is the author of numerous books, including *The Transformation of American Industrial Relations, An Introduction to Collective Bargaining and Industrial Relations, Transforming Organizations, The Mutual Gains Enterprise,* and *Employment Relations in a Changing World Economy*.

Pradeep Kumar is a professor in the School of Industrial Relations at Queen's University in Kingston, Ontario. He and John Holmes are studying the impact of restructuring on industrial relations/human resource policies and practices at the Big Three auto plants in Canada. Kumar is the author of several books on unions and collective bargaining, including *From Uniformity to Divergence: Industrial Relations in Canada and the United States* and *Unions and Workplace Change in Canada*.

Russell D. Lansbury is a professor in and head of the Department of Industrial Relations at the University of Sydney. He has taught at several universities in Europe, North America, and Asia and has been a senior Fulbright Scholar at both MIT and Harvard University and a consultant to industry, government, and trade unions. Lansbury's publications cover a wide range of subjects, including organizational change, work design, comparative industrial relations, and human resource management.

Hyo Soo Lee is a professor of economics and industrial relations at Yeungnam University in Korea. He has been active in the Korean Labor Economics Association and the Korean Industrial Relations Association and served as a member of the National Committee for Employment as well as on the Committee for Industrial Relations in Kyongbuk Province. His most recent book is *A Labor Market Structure: Theoretical and Empirical Investigations into the Korean Labor Market.*

John Paul MacDuffie is an assistant professor in the Department of Management at the Wharton School of Business at the University of Pennsylvania. His research explores technology, production systems, and human resource policies in manufacturing settings, focusing on the world automotive industry. Using data he has collected for MIT's International Assembly Plant Study, he is investigating the factors underlying changes in manufacturing performance over time, the diffusion of lean production systems worldwide, and the consequences for managers, workers, and unions.

Stefano Micelli is an assistant professor of business strategy at the University of Udine in Italy. He is currently involved in GERPISA at the Université d'Evry Val d'Essonne in France. He has participated in and given presentations at many international conferences and is the author of many publications in Italy, the United Kingdom, and France.

Tommy Nilsson is an associate professor at the Swedish National Institute of Working Life in Stockholm. His research areas include work organization for blue- and white-collar workers, industrial relations, and wage formation systems. He is the author of several publications in Swedish, French, and English.

Young-bum Park is a professor of economics at Hansung University in Korea. His primary research interests are industrial relations and human resource management practices in selected Korean industries, including the public sector, and international migration.

Frits K. Pil is an assistant professor at the Katz School of Business and a research scientist at the Learning Research Development Center at the University of Pittsburgh. His research and publications have focused on organizational learning and change, with an emphasis on work practices and production systems. With financial sponsorship from MIT's International Motor Vehicle Program, Pil and John Paul MacDuffie administered the largest survey ever undertaken of automobile assembly plants around the world.

Siegfried Roth is on the headquarters staff of IG Metall's head office. He directs a joint comparative study being conducted by the German and Japanese metalworkers unions of production systems. He has reported on the results in *Model Japan?; Group Work as a New Perspective; Information without Limits; Japanization, or Going Our Own Way?;* and *New Ways of Thinking Instead of Changing Concepts.*

Saul Rubinstein is an assistant professor at the Rutgers University School of Management and Labor Relations. Through MIT's International Motor Vehicle Program and a grant from the National Science Foundation, he has studied the impact of new forms of firm governance and comanagement that have resulted from joint labor-management efforts to transform industrial relations and manufacturing systems at General Motors' Saturn Corporation.

Harry Scarbrough is a senior lecturer and member of the Industrial Relations Research Unit at the Warwick Business School at the University of Warwick in the United Kingdom. His research has focused on the social implications of new technology in industry. He is currently engaged in a study for the Institute of Personnel and Development in the United Kingdom of the people management implications of lean organizations.

Michael Terry is a reader in industrial relations in the Industrial Relations Research Unit at the Warwick Business School at the University of Warwick in the United Kingdom. He has written extensively on aspects of British and wider European industrial relations, particularly patterns of shop-floor industrial relations and union organization. He is currently involved, with Harry Scarbrough, in examining the labor relations implications of lean production across a range of U.K. industries and companies.

Giuseppe Volpato is a professor of management and the director of the Department of Business Economics and Management at the Ca'Foscari University in Venice, Italy. He is currently involved in the International Care Distribution Program and GERPISA at the Université d'Evry Val d'Essonne. His research focuses on the supply chain of the international automobile industry. He has participated in and given presentations at several international conferences and has published books, essays in books, and articles in Italy, the United Kingdom, and France.

Index

Thomas A. Kochan is the George Maverick Bunker
Professor of Management at the Sloan School of Management,
Massachusetts Institute of Technology.

Russell D. Lansbury is Professor of Industrial Relations
and head of the department at the University of Sydney.

John Paul MacDuffie is Associate Professor
at the Wharton School, University of Pennsylvania.